NYIF INVESTOR'S DESK REFERENCE

Victor L. Harper

New York Institute of Finance

Library of Congress Cataloging-in-Publication Data

Harper, Victor L.
    NYIF investor's desk reference.

    Includes index.
    1. Investments--Handbooks, manuals, etc.
2. Investments--United States--Handbooks, manuals, etc.
I. New York Institute of Finance.   II. Title.
HG4527.H33   1988   332.6'78   88-9872
ISBN 0-13-504747-1

This publication is designed to provide accurate and authoritative information in regard to the subject matter covered. It is sold with the understanding that the publisher is not engaged in rendering legal, accounting, or other professional service. If legal advice or other expert assistance is required, the services of a competent professional person should be sought.

*From a Declaration of Principles Jointly Adopted by
a Committee of the American Bar Association and a
Committee of Publishers and Associations*

©1988 by NYIF Corp.
A Division of Simon & Schuster, Inc.
70 Pine Street, New York, NY 10270-0003

This book is adapted from the *Handbook of Investment Products and Services,* 2nd edition.

Printed in the United States of America

10 9 8 7 6 5 4 3 2 1

New York Institute of Finance
(NYIF Corp.)
70 Pine Street
New York, New York 10270-0003

To my blue chips. . .

Anne,

Kathryn,

Landon,

Francis

Contents

Bonds and Other Fixed-Income Securities: An Introduction, 68

Corporate Bonds, 94

Municipal Bonds, 106

United States Government Securities, 124

Mutual Funds, 153

Closed-End Funds, 182

Systematic Investing: The Small Investor, 192

Annuities, 205

Options, 220

Futures, 237

Index, 375

Preface

At one time, investing was limited almost exclusively to buying and holding stock. Saving money meant depositing it in a bank account. To be insured against death or catastrophic illness, you purchased a life insurance policy. And the pension fund and Social Security were intended to be the mainstays of a quiet retirement.

Today, however, determining what to do with your money entails much more complicated decision making. Brokerage firms offer "cash management accounts," the equivalent of savings and checking accounts, and they will even sell insurance-related investment products, such as annuities. Banks offer discount brokerage services, and they are lobbying to enter into full-service brokerage activities and investment banking. Insurance companies offer more than policies, branching into the investment arena. And there are all kinds of pension and profit-sharing plans, as well as a number of "deferred compensation" plans for individuals.

Given the complex array of investment instruments now available, reliable information is needed by: Active investors.* Those who simply wish to do more with their money than deposit it in a savings account.

The aim of this book is to provide such information on every investment vehicle from A to Z—from annuities to zero coupon bonds. Each section deals with a specific type of product, such as stocks, bonds, savings accounts, pension plans, and the like. Within each section, you will learn:

*Individuals requiring a better understanding of their pension, profit-sharing, or insurance programs.

- The product itself.
- Its risks and rewards.
- The type of investor it best suits.
- Where and how it is available.

This is a book that explains the choices available to investors, such as:

- Where do T-bills fit into an investment portfolio, and when are they appropriate?
- Should you trade options and/or futures?
- What is an IRA, and how does it differ from a Keogh plan?
- How does a certificate of deposit differ from a "savings account"?
- What type of benefits does your pension plan really offer?

These and many other investment-related questions are answered for you, all in clear, concise language that is readily understandable by anyone, in the *NYIF Investor's Desk Reference*.

Savings Vehicles Offered by Commercial Banks and Savings & Loan Associations

Background

Commercial banks and savings and loan associations offer a wide variety of savings and investment vehicles to individuals. Generally, a bank or thrift institution receives deposits depending on the convenience and service it offers. Savers maintain accounts at these depository institutions, despite a relatively small return, because the accounts are convenient, practical, and risk-free. The types of accounts offered range from highly liquid passbook savings accounts to certificates of deposit with maturities as long as eight years. Retirement accounts continue to be available.

Until the mid-1970's, banks and savings and loan associations were the primary providers of short-term investments. All banks paid the same interest and offered the same type of checking and savings accounts. Savings and loan institutions also offered the same types of accounts, but were able to pay a little higher rate of interest, usually ¼% higher than that paid by other institutions.

As inflation rates climbed, as savers became more sophisticated, and as interest rates increased, the outcry for the demise of the 5% savings account became louder and louder. Fixed-rate savings accounts no longer provided an acceptable return, and deposits were being lost. In an attempt to keep savings deposits in depository institutions, banks and savings and loans have sought to make savings accounts and certificates more available and attractive to investors by deregulating fixed rates and minimum balances.

In 1980, the Depository Institutional Deregulation Committee was appointed to oversee the gradual burial of Regulation Q (the federal regulation that controls interest rates) and the end of the ceiling rates that banks and savings and loans were allowed to pay. As has been witnessed in the last few years, new types of savings accounts will continue to mushroom. Investors will have to spend more time investigating alternatives and penalties involved in various savings programs. For example, a primary reason savers turn to depository institutions is the insurance. Yet, many banks and savings and loans offer commercial paper, which is not insured as are certificates of deposit.

The following sections discuss several types of savings plans provided by banks and savings and loans. Again, investors need to be cautioned that the type of plans offered by both banks and savings and loans may be drastically changed as time goes by. Inasmuch as certificates of deposit are no longer regulated, banks are now free to make their own terms and conditions.

Fixed-Rate Time Deposits (Certificates of Deposit)

Prior to July 1, 1979, federal regulations required a $1,000 minimum deposit on most fixed-rate time deposits (certificates of deposit) with maturities of four years or more. This requirement no longer exists and banks usually set their own minimum deposits, usually $100 to $500. This enables many savers to obtain interest rates greater than the passbook savings rates for fixed periods of time. Typical maturities and maximum rates are shown in the following figure.

Maturity		*Maximum Percentage*
30 days	or more but less than 90 days	5¼
90 days	or more but less than 1 year	5¼
1 year	or more but less than 30 months	6
30 months	or more but less than 4 years	6½
4 years	or more but less than 6 years	7½
6 years	or more but less than 8 years	7½
8 years	or more	7¾

Savings and loans have similar maximum allowable interest rates but in the past usually were allowed to pay a one-quarter-of-one-percent higher rate.

Before investing funds in any of these certificates, investors should know they are nonnegotiable and subject to substantial penalties for early withdrawal. The penalty for withdrawal of any money before maturity for deposits with an original maturity of one year or less, is usually set at three months' worth of simple nominal interest.

Example: A depositor buys a one-year 10% certificate of deposit for $10,000. At the end of six months, the depositor withdraws all of the money. He or she would be subject to a penalty of $250 (10% × $10,000 = $1,000 ÷ 4 = $250).

For deposits with a maturity of one year or longer, the penalty is set at an amount equal to six-months simple, nominal interest. One implication of the penalties is that an investor can forfeit part of the principal if the withdrawal is made during the early months of the deposit.

Some banks have even stricter penalties. Because of the severity of penalties, depositors should always check the penalty provisions and their own circumstances as to when the money deposited may be needed. There are many instances where people purchased certificates of deposit and later found out they needed the money. For some strange reason, the penalty was a surprise.

As many savers painfully learned in the early 1980s, interest rates rise and fall. While these savers enjoyed high double-digit yields when the certificates were first purchased, they were shocked upon maturity when the certificates had only single-digit yields.

Small Saver Certificates (SSCs)

To further accommodate the depositor of moderate means, the Small Saver Certificate (SSC) was created. This certificate has undergone several changes in recent years and will probably continue to change as new regulations are made and Regulation Q is phased out. The certificate has no minimum deposit, but banks have established minimums that are usually $100 to $500.

The SSC, as it was called, was amended to a 2½-year maturity. The ceiling rate *floated* at ¾% below the 2½-year U.S. Treasury bond yield. The rate was further established between 9.25% and 11.75%. The ceiling interest rate was determined every two weeks by the U.S. Treasury. Although the ceiling rate floated, the rate on individual certificates once issued did not change until maturity.

The SSC also was subject to the six-month simple, nominal interest penalty for early withdrawal. If savers wished to withdraw their funds for any reason other than an emergency, they had to determine exactly the terms on which he or she must reinvest in order to justify the early withdrawal.

The following figure illustrates these terms when the rate is 9.25%, the maximum allowable interest rate that the Federal Reserve member banks could pay when the average yield on a 2½-year U.S. Treasury bond is below 9½%.

Cost of Terminating a Small Saver Certificate (with a Deposit of $500).

Two-and-One-Half-Year Notes, at 9¼% Compounded Daily

End of Month	Balance on Account	Penalty for Withdrawal	Rate Needed to Break Even
3	$512	$23.125	12.72% (2.25 years)
6	524	23.125	13.15% (2 years)
12	549	23.125	14.09% (1.5 years)
15	562	23.125	14.85% (1.25 years)
18	575	23.125	15.93% (1 year)
24	603	23.125	20.67% (0.5 year)
30	632	23.125	20.67% (0.5 year)

Six-Month Money Market Certificates (MMCs)

For investors with $10,000 or more, commercial banks and savings and loans offer a six-month money market certificate. This very simple certificate provides the investor with a relatively risk-free and convenient way to earn the higher yields available in the short-term money market.

The Federal Reserve Board and the Federal Home Loan Bank Board set the minimum allowable interest rate at ¼% above the yield on the six-month Treasury bill rate. As with the SSC, the rate floats, but once the certificate is issued, the rate is fixed for the entire six-month period. Interest paid on MMCs is not compounded, but can usually be paid monthly and deposited into another type of savings account to obtain some compounding.

Yankee Certificates and Bonds

Yankee CDs are nonnegotiable certificates of deposit issued and payable in U.S. dollars to a borrower (owner). Yankee CDs and bonds, sometimes referred to as *foreign-domestic paper*, are usually issued by the U.S. branches of major foreign banks.

The foreign issuers of Yankee paper are usually well-known international banks headquartered primarily in Western Europe, England and Japan. The market for Yankee CDs is primarily a short-term market. Most newly issued instruments have maturities of three months or less.

The U.S. branches of foreign banks at first placed most of their Yankee CDs directly with established loan customers who, through experience, were familiar with the reputations and financial statements of the issuers. Because they were not generally well known, as time went on the issuers relied heavily on dealers for placement. The popularity of Yankee paper has grown to such a point that there is an active retail market and the Yankee paper now trades frequently in secondary markets.

Yankee bonds are bonds issued by foreign corporations, usually to U.S. buyers and with dollars as a denomination. On the other hand, foreign bonds are issued by corporations and other issuers domiciled outside the United States and are issued in their local currencies.

Euro-dollars

Euro-dollars are deposits of banks located outside the United States that are denominated in U.S. dollars. Euro-dollar deposits may be owned by individuals, corporations, or governments from anywhere in the world.

The term *euro-dollar* dates from an earlier period when the market was located primarily in Europe. Although the bulk of euro-dollar deposits is still held in Europe, dollar-denominated deposits are held in such places as the Bahamas, Bahrain, Canada, the Cayman Islands, Hong Kong, Japan, Panama, and Singapore as well as Europe.

Banks in the euro-dollar market compete with United States banks to attract dollar-denominated funds worldwide. Because the euro-dollar market is relatively free of regulation, banks in the euro-dollar market can operate on a narrower margin (spread) than can banks in the United States. This allows euro-dollar deposits to compete effectively with U.S. banks for the investor's money. In fact, arbitrage keeps interest rates closely aligned between euro-dollars and those of U.S. banks.

Euro-Dollar Instruments

The majority of money in the euro-dollar market is held in *fixed rate time deposits (TDs).* The maturities of the euro-dollars (TDs) range from overnight to several years, with most held in one-week to six-month maturities. These TDs are different from those held in the United States only in that they are liabilities (deposits) of financial institutions located outside the United States. They pay rates of return that are competitively derived, but fixed for the term of the deposit.

Euro-dollar negotiable certificates of deposit have been issued since 1966. Most are three-month certificates issued by banks to "tap" the market and are therefore called *tap CDs.* These tap CDs are usually issued in denominations of $250,000 to $5 million. Larger euro-dollar CD issues are marketed in several portions in order to satisfy investors with preferences for smaller investments. These are known as *tranche CDs.* Tranche CDs are issued in aggregate amounts of $10 million to $30 million and are offered to individual investors in $10,000 certificates with each certificate having the same interest rate, issue date, interest payment dates and maturity.

In recent years, *euro-dollar floating rate CDs (FRCDs)* and *euro-dollar floating rate notes (FRNs)* have come into use as a means to protect both borrower and lender against interest rate risk. These "floaters" shift the burden of risk from the principal value of the paper to its coupon. Euro-dollar FRCDs and FRNs are both negotiable borrower paper. The coupon or interest rate is reset periodically, typically every three or six months, at a small spread above the corresponding LIBOR euro-dollar FRCDs yield. (London Inter Bank Offer Rate (LIBOR) is the rate at which major international banks are willing to offer term euro-dollar deposits to one another.) Depending upon maturity, this spread is between ⅛ and ¼ percent over the six-month LIBOR. They are an attractive alternative to placing six-month time deposits at the LIBOR. Euro-dollar FRNs usually have margins of ⅛ to ¼ percent over either the three- or six-month LIBOR.

Euro-dollar FRCDs have been issued with maturities from 1½ to 5 years. Also, euro-dollar FRNs have been issued in maturities of 4 to 20 years, with the majority in the 5 to 7 year range.

A secondary market exists in euro-dollar FRCDs and FRNs although dealer spreads are quite large.

Common Stock

What Is Common Stock?

Let's assume that an entrepreneur, Mr. Smith, has discovered a new gasoline additive that increases gas mileage by 50%. Though the potential earning power of such a product is thought to be enormous, Mr. Smith does not have the capital to acquire manufacturing facilities, distribution networks, and so on. One alternative is to borrow money from banks or other sources, thereby making the lenders creditors of his enterprise. Instead, Mr. Smith decides to approach several friends to raise *capital* in return for partial ownership.

Mr. Smith and his friends are advised that a business may be one of various legal entities.

1. a *proprietorship* (single owner),

2. a *partnership* or *joint venture* (many owners), or

3. either a *corporation* or *Subchapter S corporation* (multiple ownership, limited liability).

After some negotiation, they decide to incorporate the business and sell stock as a method of raising money. They estimate they will need $50,000 to start the operation. The newly formed company, Mileage Reduction, Inc., authorizes the issue of 100,000 shares at $1 per share. Mr. Smith is given 25,000 shares at no cost for his efforts in discovering the new product and organizing the company; 20 of his friends buy 50,000 shares at $1 per share thereby raising the necessary $50,000. Mr. Smith owns 25% of the *authorized shares,* but he owns 33⅓% of the company's *issued-and-outstanding stock* (75,000 outstanding). (*Authorized stock* is the number of shares the directors authorize. Once the stock is issued, it is referred to as *issued-and-outstanding,* or outstanding. When a corporation purchases its own stock in the open market, it is called *treasury stock.*)

One friend who bought 1,000 shares owns 1% of the authorized stock for a contribution of $1,000; another owns 10,000 shares or 10% by contributing $10,000. Note that even though 100,000 shares have been authorized, only 75,000 are issued and outstanding—Mr. Smith's 25,000 and the 50,000 sold at $1 each. Each stockholder is issued a stock certificate as evidence of his ownership in the corporation.

After the first full year of operation the business is very successful. Mileage Reduction, Inc., reports earnings of $11,250 on the 75,000 outstanding shares or 15¢ per share. But additional capital is needed for expansion because the company could sell more additive than it presently produces. Therefore the Board of Directors pays each shareholder only 5¢ per share in dividends from the 15¢ per share earnings: The holder of 1,000 shares receives $50, the owner of 10,000 shares receives $500. Ten cents per share is retained to finance the expansion program. Federal and state income tax must be paid on the earnings *before* dividends are paid.

More money is needed, however, so the company decides to sell the additional 25,000 shares initially authorized but unissued. The question arises as to what the stock in Mileage Reduction, Inc. is now worth. The answer is determined by supply and demand—or simply what buyers are willing to pay for it. The stock is obviously worth whatever a buyer will pay. With the tremendous progress of Mileage Reduction, Inc., it is felt that the new shares can now be sold at $1.50 per share for a sum of $37,500. The increase in price of the stock does not alter each holder's proportionate ownership, only the value of each common share certificate to its holder.

Many of Mr. Smith's friends who did not get in on the original offering are now extremely interested. However, it is deemed unfair to dilute the holdings of the initial stockholders. So a *right* is attached to each of the original 75,000 shares issued; this right gives the shareholder the preemptive privilege to participate in new capitalization. By exercising his or her privilege, the shareholder can maintain a proportionate share of ownership. The Mileage Reduction Directors decide that for each 3 shares held, one new share can be purchased at $1.50 per share. The shares not taken by the original holders are to be sold to new investors at $1.50, increasing the shares outstanding to 100,000.

For future expansion Mileage Reduction may either borrow money (that is, issue *debt instruments*), or create new shares, selling them to the same and/or new investors. Newly issued additional shares, however, obviously decrease the available earnings per share for each of the original shareholders and theoretically reduce the amount available for dividends. This is referred to as *dilution*. If Mileage Reduction, Inc., is able to borrow money via a bond issue, and earn more on the borrowed money than it is paying in interest (*debt service*), the earnings per share and, in theory, the dividends can be increased. Also, the price of the stock generally goes up in such cases.

Several years after incorporation, Mr. Smith has built a company from a simple idea to a multimillion-dollar manufacturing complex. He has retained his original 25% interest in the corporation. However, he now wants to diversify his holdings and obtain additional cash. He could sell a part of his interest in Mileage Reduction, Inc., and the sale of stock would not affect the earnings or dividends per share of the company because no new stock is issued. An organizer of a company who gains wealth in the stock market by owning stock with a high market value is said to have created *paper money*.

But suppose Mileage Reduction, Inc., failed after five years because it turns out the additive gradually causes metal to rust. The company declares bankruptcy, and all the shareholders lose is the amount paid for the stock—their liability is limited to the dollar amount of their investment.

If, on the other hand, only a small profit is earned and the potential is not as large as originally thought, perhaps new investors would be willing to pay only 50¢ per share for the stock, thus creating a loss for the original shareholders.

Why Buy Common Stock?

Common stocks represent ownership in a corporation. As an owner, the holder of common stock has:

1. the right to *dividends*, which are portions of the corporation's after-tax earnings that are declared by the Board of Directors;

2. the right to *vote* on essential matters such as mergers, reorganization, recapitalizations, as well as the election of directors at the annual meeting—shareholders elect directors, directors elect officers; and

3. *limited liability,* that is, the shareholder's loss is limited to the amount paid for the common stock.

While dividends represent one form of return on this type of investment, most common stockholders also seek appreciation in the value of the investment, that is, capital gain. How much gain shareholders seek and how fast they expect it depends on whether they are investing or speculating.

1. An *investor* is usually defined as an individual willing to assume moderate risks for a moderate return on his or her investment. The individual seeking moderate dividend returns, as well as growth on money in excess of what could be earned in fixed-dollar instruments (savings accounts, for example), buys common stock in a conservative company with a record of earnings increases, a long-term record of dividend payouts, and periodic increased payouts.

2. The *speculator,* by comparison, is usually an individual who assumes greater risks for a larger potential profit. The speculator is more interested in developments producing substantial future earnings increases, thereby causing significant, perhaps rapid, increases in the price of the common stock.

Dividends

As explained in the Mileage Reduction, Inc. example, common stockholders receive dividends, a portion of the after-tax earnings as declared by the Board of Directors. A conservative investor should research the background of a company, its dividend policy, and its history of earnings. Such information may be obtained from many of the investment services such as Standard and Poor's, Moody's, Value Line, and so on. The *current yield* on a common stock is determined by dividing the current dividend by the current price.

Example: A stock paying $1 per share, with the current market price of $20 is yielding 5% ($1 ÷ $20 = .05).

To many investors, continually increasing dividends are just as important as current yield (dividend). Increasing dividends help investors keep pace with inflation. A review of the dividend history of many well-known companies indicates that even though many stock prices traded within a very narrow range during the 1970s, dividend increases often kept pace with inflation.

The Dividend Cycle. Investors need to understand key dates that apply to dividend payments.

Example: Picture an investor who knows his or her dividends on a stock arrive about August 3 or August 4. The investor buys 100 additional shares, but gets no extra dividend. When calling the broker for an explanation, the investor learns that the stock should have been owned on July 1st to get the August dividend.

Then there is the investor who sells 100 shares of the same stock on June 24th, and still expects to receive the dividend. The investor is surprised when no dividend arrives because he or she owned the stock when the dividend was declared.

These situations, or variations of them, are not as unusual as one may think. Not only are many investors confused about dividend dates, but many of the explanations are just as confusing.

In the purchase or sale of any security, there are two dates: the trade date and settlement date.

1. The *trade date* is the day on which the trade is executed.

2. The *settlement date* is the day on which money is due the broker on a purchase, or the certificate is due the broker on a sale.

Most purchases or sales settle *regular way*. This means the settlement date is five business days after the trade date.

Example: An investor buys or sells on June 20th (trade date), the settlement date is June 27th—five business days after the trade date.

JUNE						
SUN	MON	TUES	WED	THUR	FRI	SAT
16	17	18	19	20	21	22
23	24	25	26	27	28	29
30						

JULY						
SUN	MON	TUES	WED	THUR	FRI	SAT
	1	2	3	4	5	6
7	8	9	10	11	12	13
14	15	16	17	18	19	20

Example: A trade executed on July lst would have a settlement date of July 9th. (July 4th was a holiday; therefore it is not counted as a business day.) When determining settlement after a purchase or sale, investors need to skip any holidays or banking holidays.

It is important for investors to realize that the purchaser becomes the owner and the seller ceases to own the security on the trade date! Trade and settlement dates *must* appear on all confirmations. However, it is possible that a security can be traded on a *next day settlement,* which means payment and delivery of the certificate is due the following day. A *cash trade* settles the same day as the trade.

A brief review of the important dividend dates are:

- *Declaration date:* The day a corporation's board of directors meets, decides upon the amount of the dividend and makes the public announcement.

- *Exdividend date:* The day a security begins trading with a purchaser *not* entitled to the dividend. Because most securities trade regular way (five business days' settlement), the exdividend date is usually the fourth business day before the record date.

- *Record date:* The day the corporation closes (tallies) its transfer books to determine which holders receive the dividend. The record date is set by the directors when the dividend is declared.

- *Payment date:* The day the corporation makes payment of the dividend to holders of record on the record date.

An example of the dividend dates and how they apply is:

Example: Universal Leaf Tobacco Company's board of directors met on June 2nd (declaration date), and declared a dividend of 47 cents per share to be paid August lst (payment date), to holders of record July 1st (record date). The exdividend date on this example is June 27th (the fourth business day before the record date).
A purchaser who bought 100 shares on June 24th would receive the dividend because he or she would be listed in the transfer books on July 1st (settlement and record date). A buyer on June 27th would not receive the dividend because he or she would not be listed in the transfer books until July 5th (settlement date).

A good rule to remember is: If the settlement date is any day up to and including the record date, the buyer is entitled to the dividend. If settlement date falls after the record date, the dividend belongs to the seller.

Often the registration of a stock cannot be removed from a corporation's records before the record date. If the buyer is entitled to a dividend, but the certificate is not transferred by the record date, the brokerage house executing the sell order is responsible for claiming the dividend from the seller and ensuring payment to the buyer. When this occurs, a seller receives a dividend claim *from the broker.*

Any open buy or sell stop orders are automatically reduced by the exact value of the forthcoming dividend distribution on exdate unless the order is marked *do not reduce (DNR).* Ordinarily, if a cash dividend is for 12½ cents per share the order will be reduced by ⅛ of a point, or if the dividend is 25 cents per share the order will be reduced by 25 cents per share. If the distribution is not precisely divisible by ⅛ and so on, the price for the appropriate orders must be reduced by the next higher ⅛. Therefore, a 26-cent distribution requires a price reduction of ⅜; a 51-cent dividend, ⅝; a $1.20 dividend is reduced by 1¼, and so forth.

Some corporations pay *stock dividends* rather than cash dividends. The price of open orders is adjusted as explained previously for the approximate amount of the value of the stock dividend on the date of distribution.

Stock Splits. Like dividends, it is necessary for investors to understand the mechanics of stock splits. Confusion arises when investors buy and/or sell during, right after, stock splits. To fully understand stock splits, it is necessary to understand the mechanics. When a stock splits, for example 2-for-1, this does not mean the value of an investor's holdings of a company doubles. It only means the number of shares owned doubles.

Example: In early 1981 Chevron sold for about $85 per share, at which time the company declared a 2-for-1 stock split. The record date of the split was February 6th, and the payment date was March 10th. This meant that the holders of 100 shares as of the record date February 6th, were entitled to receive an additional 100 shares. The new certificate was mailed on March 10th to owners of record on February 6th.

After March 10th, the *WI* (When Issued) stocks started selling for about 42½, which is about one-half the presplit price. To obtain the information on the split, one had to only look at the stock tables in the newspapers. When issued trades are basically open-ended as to settlement date; this means that a buyer will not get the certificate until it is issued, and a seller cannot make delivery of a certificate until after the stock is issued.

Stocks usually trade when issued for the convenience of those who want to sell split shares before the additional shares are received.

Confusion reigns when a large number of companies split their stock and the prices of the underlying shares become more volatile. The question of who is entitled to the split or additional shares when a sale takes place between the record and payment dates is very important. This period is called the *due bill period* because the seller must surrender the split shares to the buyer when they are received. The reason is obvious. In the previous example, the buyer invests about $8,500 in the company's common stock when buying 100 shares. After the split, his or her 100 shares are only worth about $4,250. The additional certificate brings the value up to the original investment.

What is dubbed the *due bill period* runs from the record date to five days following the payment date. This means that anyone buying shares with the settlement date between the record date and five days after the payment date is entitled to the split shares, and anyone selling with settlement dates during the due bill period must surrender his or her shares.

As in cash or stock dividends, the brokerage house representing the buyer is responsible for obtaining the additional shares from the seller. The seller will receive a *due bill notice.*

A 2-for-1 split is simple to understand. A 3-for-2, 6-for-5, or 4-for-3 split can become a little more confusing but the math is exactly the same.

	"Old" Shares	Additional Shares Received On Split	New Number of Total Shares Owned After Split
3 for 2 split	600	300	900
6 for 5 split	600	120	720
4 for 3 split	600	200	800

Advantages of Stock Splits. By splitting the stock, a company increases the number of shares outstanding, but not the total market value of the company. By increasing the number of shares, in theory, a broader market exists for the stock, meaning that more investors might be inclined to buy.

Splitting a company's stock reduces the stock's price to a more favorable trading range. Reducing the price often increases investor appeal, particularly for investors with small amounts of money. Generally, if the number of buyers of a stock increases more than the number of sellers, the stock price usually continues to increase.

In reviewing several stock splits, one can see a correlation between stock splits, stock prices, and relative stock values.

Examples: Tandy had 4 splits in 15 years and the price increased from 2 to over 65 during the time span. IBM had 5 splits in 15 years with the price ranging from 20 to over 115. Hospital Corporation of America had 3 splits in 6 years with the price increasing from 4 to 50.

Usually companies with a record of splitting their stocks are those that have increased tremendously in value, and the split is a mechanism to reduce the price level to encourage continued investor support.

Dividend Reinvestment Plans. Dividend reinvestment plans are an important part of the savings plans of many investors. Some investors need the income to pay current bills. Their dividends are a vital part of their livelihood. Many investors have as an objective to accumulate additional assets to provide future income. They want, or should want, to reinvest their dividends so their net worth increases each year to a larger and larger extent.

Many corporations provide a convenient way for stockholders to use their dividends to buy additional shares. These companies utilize the reinvestment of dividends as a means of raising additional capital.

The basic dividend reinvestment plan is simple. Shareholders sign and send an authorization form to the company. Instead of sending a check when the next dividend is paid, the company buys the shareholder more shares. The number of shares acquired is usually calculated to three decimal places. Shortly after the transaction, the shareholder receives a statement showing the details and the number of shares held by the transfer agent. (The investment shares are usually held in unissued form by the transfer agent.)

Even though the basic plan is simple, there are many variations. Some companies pay all of the reinvestment costs including brokerage fees. Many companies with reinvestment plans absorb all brokerage costs and other fees. Some companies issue new stock, which is a means of raising additional capital, while others go into the market and buy existing shares. This practice is thought by many to support a stock's price. A few companies even allow shareholders to reinvest dividends at a discount (it is usually 5%).

Another variation of the dividend reinvestment plan is to allow shareholders to buy additional shares for cash. The limit is usually $25 to $3,000 per quarter.

The major disadvantage of the dividend reinvestment plan is taxes. As explained later, all dividends reinvested must be included as taxable income in the year reinvested even though the investor never receives cash. If the dividends are reinvested at a discount, the discount is usually considered taxable income.

An investor utilizing the dividend reinvestment plan must keep records so a cost basis for all reinvested dividends, as well as the cost of the original stock, can be maintained. The records determine the amount of gain or loss when and if the shares are sold. The amount of the dividends reinvested are added to the original cost basis of the stock in determining cost when calculating gains or loss upon a sale. To redeem reinvested dividends, a letter must be written to the reinvestment agent (usually a bank) whose name appears on the transaction (confirmation) statement.

Clearly the biggest advantage of dividend reinvestment plans for investors is convenience. It is a simple way of investing money, particularly small amounts of money. Dividend reinvestment plans are another means of forced savings. Most people spend the dividends they receive; they do not save them.

Most plans allow investors to write the transfer agent and have certificates issued for whole shares but not for fractions of a share. The fraction will be sold and cash sent to the investor. Many plans allow stockholders of preferred shares to have the preferred dividends reinvested into common shares.

Capital Appreciation

Capital appreciation, perhaps the more prevalent reason for buying common stock, is the increase of the shares' market value. If, because of certain corporate developments, there are more investors wanting to buy Mileage common stock than there are those willing to sell at a given price, the demand increases over the supply, and the price goes up. The price will continue to rise until it reaches a level where the number of sellers equals the number of buyers. Conversely, if a corporate development encourages selling, rather than buying, the supply of available stock increases over demand, and the price falls until buyers equal sellers.

The value of common stock is what someone is willing to pay for it. Stated another way, investors purchase common stock for future potential. That is, purchases are based on what they think the company will do in the future—which is usually reflected by expected earnings increases, new-product development, and so on.

Increased research expenditures frequently precede substantial increases in future earnings. Examples are the introduction of the computer by IBM, instant photography by Polaroid, copying machines by Xerox, or the sale of personal computers and electronics by Tandy. Each of these events opened up an entirely new area of investment growth. More importantly, these companies' stockholders made a great deal of money.

The common stock of a company with (1) a high dividend payout relative to earnings and (2) consistent but small dividend increases, such as a utility, is generally considered a conservative investment. Such a stock is usually called an *income* stock, because more of the company's income is distributed to the shareholder than is retained by the company for future expansion.

Example: Exxon, which in later 1983 had a current price of approximately $39, was earning about $5.00 per share and paying dividends of $3.20 per share. Paying out 64% of its earnings with a yield of 8.2% (retaining $2.80), Exxon is generally considered an income stock with limited appreciation potential.

On the other hand, many companies pay out very little of their earnings in the form of dividends. Instead, they plow back substantial amounts of earnings for expansion to create future increases in earnings per share, offering the investor more potential profit. This type of stock is generally referred to as a *growth* stock.

Example: Because IBM's earnings have increased much faster than those of Exxon, investors generally are willing to pay a higher price for IBM's earning power than for Exxon's. Since IBM's price is almost 16 times as great as its earnings ($132 ÷ $9.00), and its yield is only 2.9%, IBM stockholders must feel the shares will increase in value much more rapidly than Exxon because Exxon is selling at eight times its earnings ($39 ÷ $5.00), yielding 8.2%.

Analyzing and predicting stock behavior, which is not dealt with in this book, is a highly technical and widely debated topic. Investment analysis forms part of the services most full-service brokerage firms provide their clients. In addition, hundreds of investment advisory services are available to the investor on a subscription basis.

The investor is best served by first establishing his or her own investing philosophy, preferably in writing, and then seeking investment counsel, brokerage services, and a registered representative consonant with that philosophy.

How to Read the Quotations

Anyone investing in stocks should be able to read the quotations in the newspaper. To assist in reading, understanding, and interpreting the information in the newspaper, the following chart explains how to interpret the figures.

How to Read Newspaper Stock Listings.

Listed

39⅜	27⅛	Exxon	3.20	8.2	7	8618	39⅜	38¾	39	+⅛
(1)	(2)	(3)	(4)	(5)	(6)	(7)	(8)	(9)	(10)	(11)

(1),(2) is the 52-week high/low. These figures indicate the highest and the lowest prices at which the stock traded (this takes into account prices on all exchanges—composite transactions).

(3) is the name of the company, the Exxon Corporation.

(4) indicates the dividend for the next 12 months, $3.20 per share.

(5) is the yield in percent, 8.2%.

(6) is the price/earnings ratio, the current price is 7 times the last 12 months'earnings.

(7) is the number of shares traded, in hundreds. On this day, 861,800 shares of Exxon traded.

(8) is the highest price the stock traded on the day.

(9) is the lowest price the stock traded on the day.

(10) is the closing price on the day.

(11) is the net change from the prior trading day's closing price.

Other symbols and codes that investors should be familiar with are:

---

s this letter behind a stock indicates that the stock has split or had a stock dividend of 25% or more in the past 52 weeks. The high/low prices are adjusted for any such stock split or stock dividend.

n indicates that it is a new issue in the past 52 weeks. The high/low range begins with the start of trading and may not cover the entire 52-week period.

x indicates the stock was exdividend or exrights.

wd means the stock will not be delivered until it is distributed.

wi means the stock will be delivered when issued.

ww indicates the stock is trading with warrants.

xw indicates the stock is trading without warrants.

Over the Counter

MCI Communi	3470	36⅝	36¾	−⅛
(1)	(2)	(3)	(4)	(5)

(1) is the name of the company.

(2) is the number of shares traded in hundreds. This would be 347,000 shares traded.

(3) is the closing bid price.

(4) is the closing ask price.

(5) is the change in the bid price from the previous day.

Where Common Stocks Are Traded

Common stocks, such as those of the fictitious Mileage Reduction, are bought and sold either on stock *exchanges* (the New York Stock Exchange or American Stock Exchange, to name two) or in the *over-the-counter market.*

One major reason for investing in common stocks as opposed to alternative investments is *liquidity,* the ease of converting to cash. Because of today's modern trading facilities, an investor can usually quickly convert his or her ownership of American industry as represented by stock certificates to cash or into another sector of American industry.

If, for example, you decide you no longer want to own a chemical company and want to become part owner (share the profits or losses) of a major technology company, the transactions can be accomplished in a matter of minutes or possibly seconds. The trading facilities are in place.

The Mileage Reduction example illustrates how an idea can be developed into a business. The business becomes more successful and attracts outside investors. Early transactions are usually privately negotiated between persons who know each other or have been introduced by mutual acquaintances.

Once a company has become large enough or well known enough to attract investors unknown to the owners, a brokerage firm enters the scene. The *underwriter,* as the broker is called, forms a *syndicate,* or group of brokers, to sell the stock to investors. The motivation behind the syndicate selling stock to the public is that it is often easier to raise $1,000,000 from 1,000 people contributing $1,000 each rather than $1,000,000 from one individual. The brokers get paid (fees) for their services.

After a public offering, stocks usually trade in the over-the-counter market. One or several brokers, referred to as *dealers,* will maintain positions in the stock. This means the dealers will continually offer to buy and sell shares.

The Over-the-Counter Market (OTC)

The *over-the-counter market* is a network of dealers dealing with each other by telephone and transacting orders for individual investors. The dealers buy and sell from their own accounts. OTC transactions can occur anywhere, usually by phone, most often with the buyer and seller represented by dealers registered with National Association of Securities Dealers (NASD). Thus, the OTC market is referred to as a *negotiated market* because the dealers negotiate among themselves in establishing price. Prices are quoted as *bid* and *ask.* The *bid price* is what the dealer (or market-maker) is willing to pay for the stock when buying from another dealer. The *ask price* is the price at which the dealer will sell to other dealers. The difference between the bid and ask prices is the *spread*.

Example: Blue Chip Investments, a dealer in Mileage Reduction, buys 1,000 shares at 10 ($10 per share) anticipating to sell at a higher price. However, shortly after the purchase, Mileage Reduction announces lower than expected earnings, followed by a decline in the price to 9. He now sells the stock for $9 a share and takes the $1,000 loss.

On the other hand, Blue Chip may sell 1,000 shares of Mileage Reduction that it does not own at 10½, the ask price, anticipating to repurchase the stock shortly at 10, the bid price. However, if the price increases to 12, and the stock is purchased (covered) at 12, the result is a loss of $1.50 per share, or $1,500. Ideally, the dealer effects a nearly simultaneous transaction buying 1,000 shares from one individual and almost immediately reselling it to another individual, making a profit from the spread.

The specialist performs the duty of *auctioneer* in transactions between floor brokers in his or her assigned stocks. As an auctioneer the specialist calls bids and ask prices in an attempt to encourage trades between the bid and ask. When trading is in a dramatic imbalance, more buyers than sellers (or vice versa), the specialist is charged with the responsibility of requesting a trading halt.

As a *catalyst,* the specialist brings buyers and sellers together. The specialist becomes a vital information base or a conduit of information to ensure that all buyers and sellers are as equally informed as possible on the floor of the New York Stock Exchange.

Specialists are rated on their performance by means of a quarterly survey submitted by floor brokers. They do not go unchecked as many would believe. In fact, the majority of exchange trades are done with no involvement of the specialists.

When transacting with the individual investor, the dealer marks the bid price down to add a commission to the sale; and when selling to an individual investor, marks the ask price up to include the commission. Investors buying on a net basis should realize that the commission is generally added into or subtracted from the price. The dealer may buy or sell on the bid or ask. If this is done, a commission is added to buys, and subtracted from sales.

The OTC market is actually a nationwide, computerized system that collects, stores, and disseminates up-to-the-second quotations from all dealers making a market in stocks anywhere in th nation. The National Association of Securities Dealers Automated Quotations (NASDAQ as the system is called) has over 2,400 stocks quoted in the system. Because market-makers are required to trade at least 100 shares per transaction on their bid or ask price, the more dealers in a stock generally the more marketable the stock.

Through its NASDAQ stock information system, NASD provides bid and asked prices to newspaper and computer quotation equipment located in many brokerage and investment offices. For example, the quote could be 20¼ bid and 20¾ ask.

Many brokerage houses do not make markets in stocks, but rather buy or sell on an *agency basis:* That is, the brokerage house will find the dealer offering the best ask price, purchase the stock from him or her, and usually add a commission to that price. On the sell side, the brokerage house seeks out the best bid, sells the stock to that brokerage house, and subtracts a commission to the customer.

The Exchanges

The exchanges provide a centralized place for member firms to buy and sell stock for their customers. They provide what is called an *auction market,* because all dealings in a given stock occur at a specific location at the exchange (called a *post*), with representatives of all interested buyers and sellers physically present at the time a transaction is made. All announce their bids and offers in open outcry. Membership in an exchange is usually referred to as *owning a seat.* Currently there are seven major stock exchanges. They are: New York Stock Exchange, American Stock Exchange, Boston Stock Exchange, Mid-West Stock Exchange, Pacific Stock Exchange, Philadelphia Stock Exchange, and the Cincinnati Exchange.

The exchanges also have *specialists,* individuals designated to assist in the trading of each stock on that exchange and to provide a fair and orderly market in that stock. Obviously, a specialist must have substantial wealth and experience to be able to maintain a fair and orderly market, often buying and selling stock for his or her own account. There are many misconceptions about the role of a specialist. He or she acts as an agent, dealer, auctioneer, and market catalyst.

As an *agent,* the specialist holds limit orders for floor brokers. A *floor broker* is a member of the exchange who represents broker dealers around the country in buying and selling for their clients' account. The agency service relieves the clients' broker from remaining at the trading post until the specified limit price is reached. For this service, the specialist usually receives a small portion of the brokerage commission. It is not an additional charge to the customer.

As a *dealer,* the specialist buys and sells assigned stock for his or her own account in order to improve or maintain an orderly market. Stocks are usually bought or sold against a prevailing trend. A dealer usually buys for his or her own account when others are buying. These trades are known as *stabilizing* transactions.

Designated Order Turnaround (DOT). The New York Stock Exchange has an order routing system called Designated Order Turnaround system, or DOT. It is a routing mechanism for market orders and round-lot day-limit orders of 100 to approximately 10,000 shares to bypass the floor brokers and be electronically communicated directly to the specialist. The DOT system also automatically and electronically gives a report of the trade to the broker. The upside limit is continually being increased as technology and efficiency improve.

The DOT system is not an automatic pricing mechanism, but a *routing* mechanism. One specialist on the floor of the New York Stock Exchange said, "The DOT system brings the orders to the specialist more quickly, therefore providing increased efficiency and better order flow to the New York Stock Exchange." The specialist must execute or stop a market DOT order at or within the quotation in effect at the time he or she physically receives the order. Thus, the specialist has become the backbone of the auction market system.

Example: A stock is quoted 57½ bid and 57¾ offered, and the specialist receives a market order to buy 100 shares. First, the specialist must offer the market order to all traders around the post at 57⅝ to see if anyone will execute lower than the quotation. This is one of the benefits of an auction market: all orders are exposed to the crowd, everyone at the post, not just one dealer or firm. If there are no takers, the specialist then executes the order and sells to the buyer 100 shares at 57¾.

Stopping an order is when the specialist guarantees the price, for example, 57¾, while attempting to obtain a better price.

Automatic Pricing and Reporting System (APARES). The New York Stock Exchange also has a system to assist investors in the buying or selling of *odd lots* (less than 100 shares) to obtain quick and efficient executions. The system is called Automatic Pricing and Reporting System, or APARES.

An order to purchase or sell an odd lot is entered by a brokerage firm by one of several methods. The odd lot orders are entered into the Common Message Switch where they are validated for conformity with the exchange standard order format. Once the order is entered into the system, the automatic pricing function is carried out by the odd lot computer service. The system then matches the round lot sales data to the pending execution file. Market orders, those entered to be bought or sold at the best prevailing price, are priced automatically by using the next round lot sale received after receipt of the order by the system. Each odd lot dealer (specialist) has the option of charging or not charging a differential, usually ⅛ of a point (12½ cents per share). In practice, except for odd lot orders entered before the market opening, the ⅛ of a point is almost always charged.

Many of the organized exchanges now participate in what is called the Inter Market Trading System (ITS). This system has quotation equipment at the specialist's booth for stocks in the system. The quotation is given for each of the other exchanges such as the bid and ask on the Pacific or the Midwest Stock Exchanges.

If the floor broker or specialist realizes there is a better price on another exchange than offered on the New York Stock Exchange, the order can be automatically entered into the ITS system for execution. The ITS system is obviously a forerunner to a mandated national system. It enables the stocks in the system to be traded on any exchange.

Over the last few years, the exchanges have started to develop automated trading and an interexchange ability so that orders can be traded on the various exchanges. For example if

Exxon is trading on the Pacific Exchange at a better price than in New York, a New York broker can trade on the Pacific.

American Depository Receipts

Many larger foreign companies have their shares traded either on a major U.S. securities exchange or on the U.S. OTC market. British Petroleum and Sony Corporation, for example, trade on the New York Stock Exchange while Honda Motors trades OTC.

An investor purchasing these shares will usually purchase an *American depository receipt* (ADR). ADRs look much like standard stock certificates, but actually represent shares of a foreign company being held by an American bank issuing the ADR. In essence, the foreign shares have been "Americanized" by the use of the ADR. ADRs are then issued by the banks when the foreign company perceives there is sufficient investor interest in the stock to warrant the effort and expense.

The use of ADRs gives foreign shares good marketability, especially if they are traded on a major U.S. securities exchange. However, there are relatively few ADRs outstanding, and those usually represent the larger foreign firms. The investor still must evaluate the investment merits of the firm whose ADRs are being considered.

Investing in ADRs requires some expertise because there are many accounting variations from country to country, especially in the area of reserves. The role of the foreign government in its economy may be quite different from the role of the U.S. government in overseeing corporations and securities. Also, income tax structures can vary greatly among countries.

Many commonly accepted financial ratios may have little use when applied to a foreign company. Capital structures may be quite different and inflation may be more or less of an important consideration in foreign investing, especially if a foreign film has heavy export sales.

Ways of Trading Common Stock

The basic ways of trading in common stocks are

1. *Buying*—establishing a long position, and

2. *Selling*—closing a long position or establishing a short position.

Example: To buy, Joe Smith, who wants to participate in the ownership of AT&T, simply *buys* whatever number of shares he can afford. If Joe buys 100 shares at $70 per share, his $7,000 investment (plus commissions) entitles him to dividends declared ($5.40 per share in early 1983). Further, Joe has only his $7,000 at risk—that is all he can lose. Upon buying, Joe receives a certificate representing ownership of 100 shares.

   To *sell,* Joe simply enters an order with his broker to sell (types of orders are discussed later). If he sells at $75, he grosses $7,500 (less commissions and fees), and his profit is $500, or 5 points per share. (A point is $1; ⅛ of a point is 12½ cents; ¼ is 25 cents; ⅜ is 37½ cents; ½ is 50 cents; ⅝ is 62½ cents; ¾ is 75 cents; and ⅞ is 87½ cents.) In the event that AT&T declines to $62, and if Joe feels because of corporate developments or the stock market in general that the price decline will continue, or if he feels his $6,200 (the value of his 100 shares at that time) could produce better results in other securities, he will sell. Joe's loss would be 8 points ($800 plus commissions and fees). After selling, Joe must surrender the certificate representing 100 shares to the broker, who will send it through proper channels, and another certificate representing that 100 shares will be issued to the new buyer.

   When an investor sells short, he or she is selling stock not owned with the expectation of purchasing it later at a lower price. The difference between the original sale and the subsequent purchase (at a lower price) represents the investor's profit. On an exchange, a short sale may be executed only on an *uptick* or a *zero-plus tick.* An uptick occurs when a stock trades at least ⅛ higher than the previous trade.

Example: Given a change from 27 to 27⅛ the second trade is an uptick. A *zero-plus tick* occurs when a stock trades at the same price as the previous trade that was at least ⅛ point higher than the previous different price. (For example, given 16¼ to 16⅜ to 16⅜, the second trade is an uptick, the third trade is a zero-plus tick.)

   The reason for this rule is that short selling could precipitate more selling, thereby forcing the stock to decline unnecessarily or out of proportion to normal supply-demand relationships. A large number of short sellers could precipitate an enormous decline.

Example: Mary Brown feels that IBM is overvalued at its current price of 97⅛ and the price will soon fall to $87. She sells short at 97⅛, selling 100 shares of IBM she does not own for $9,712.50 (less commissions.).

A certificate representing the 100 shares must be delivered to the buyer on the opposite side of Ms. Brown's sell. Most brokerage houses can arrange the borrowing of the stock for delivery. At some time in the future, however, Ms. Brown must purchase 100 shares of IBM and return a 100 share certificate to the investor who loaned it. (Short sales are always considered potential buying demand because the stock must be repurchased (*covered*), whereas a buyer may buy and hold forever.)

Later, IBM falls to 87⅛ and Mary buys 100 shares, realizing a profit of 10 points ($1,000) less commissions. The certificate representing the purchase is delivered to the investor from whom Mary's broker borrowed the stock. Thus the short sale is closed (covered).

If after selling short, IBM's price rises to 107⅛, and Ms. Brown buys at that price to close her short sale, her loss would be 10 points or $1,000 (plus commissions). The person selling short must deliver to the individual or institution loans the stock the cash representing any dividends declared.

Another type short sale is *short-against-the-box*. This transaction is usually used when the owner of a stock wants to postpone the tax liability on a gain from one year to the next.

Example: Ms. Brown owns 100 shares of IBM which she purchased years ago. Her cost basis is $1 a share or $100. If she sells the stock at $98 she will realize a $9,700 long term capital gain. She is satisfied with her profit, but wishes to postpone her tax liability to the following year.

She believes IBM's stock prices are about to decline so she sells short-against-the-box, thus locking in her profit. She places her 100 shares with her broker who borrows 100 shares from someone else as in the previous transaction. Her 100 shares are collateral against the transaction. In the following year, she will instruct her broker to *flatten* or *cover* the position by using her long position to replace the borrowed stock. In the year the position is covered, her gain will be subject to tax.

In this transaction, Ms. Brown has several alternatives. If the stock price declines, she can purchase 100 shares of IBM and deliver the purchased shares against the borrowed stock. If the price of IBM increases, Ms. Brown can deliver her 100 shares and cover the loan thereby locking in the $98 sale price. On a price increase, she could also buy another 100 shares to deliver and establish a long-term loss.

In a short position, or when short-against-the-box, investors should be aware of *mark-to-the-market.* Short sales must take place in a margin account. If the price *increases* from the price at which the stock was sold, the brokerage firm will charge interest on the increase. The interest is, in essence, a charge based on the increased collateral placed with the individual or firm from whom the stock is borrowed.

In buying a stock, an investor only risks the money invested. Conversely, in selling short, the risk is unlimited. The price of the stock could continue to rise for an indefinite period of time. Selling short is speculative and should only be entered into by investors willing to assume the risk. Short sales also represent future buying demand because the stock must eventually be bought to close the transaction.

Types of Order

In buying or selling stock, investors utilize certain types of orders. Basically, there are only three types of orders:

1. market orders,

2. limit orders, and

3. stop orders.

Many times investors want to modify the order with special instructions, but the basic type remains unchanged. Further, only certain types of orders are allowed on some exchanges and in the over-the-counter market. At times the exchanges will suspend the use of certain types of orders.

An investor should always inquire as to the types of orders permissible, and be sure that he or she and the broker have the same understanding of the meaning of any order that is entered.

1. A *market order* is placed when the investor wants a trade executed immediately at the best prevailing price. A market order to buy requires purchase at the current offering (asked) price. A market order to sell requires a sale at the current bid price.

2. By entering a *limit order*, the customer sets the maximum price he or she is willing to pay if buying, or the minimum price he or she is willing to accept if selling. While the words "or better" may not be given with the order, it is understood that the broker should take a better price if it is available.

The danger in using limit orders is that the order may miss being executed by a fraction, and the investor will fail to buy or sell.

Example: Jane Jones has been watching the trading pattern of Eastern Airlines for years. She feels that if the stock can be bought at $5 a share, she will have an opportunity to sell at $14 within a year or so.

While the stock is trading around $6, she places a limit order to buy at 5. She will not buy the stock unless it trades at 5 or below.

After buying the stock she tries to pick a selling price and places a limit order to sell at that price. For example, she picks the price of $14 a share.

Another use of limit orders is buying in a weak market or selling in a strong market.

Example: If the general direction of the market is weak (stock prices are falling), and you want to buy a certain stock, you would place a limit order. Perhaps placing a buy order ¼ to ½ a point under the market would result in saving a few dollars. Conversely, if you are going to sell stock in a strong market (stock prices generally increasing), perhaps a limit order placed a fraction above the current market would result in a little additional profit.

An investor may hear *stock ahead* from his or her broker as an explanation for *not* buying (or selling) stock at a limit, even though one or more trades may have been executed at the limit price. These executions were done for other investors with similar orders previously entered.

3. A *stop order* is a memorandum to buy or sell as soon as trading reaches a certain price level. Once the stock trades at the stop price, the order becomes a market order and is executed at the best prevailing price (unless a limit is also placed on it).

Example: Jane Jones places a *buy-stop* order on AT&T at 55 when it is trading at 53. If AT&T trades at 55 or higher, her order becomes a market order and is executed at the next best possible price, which may be any price after the first trade at 55, depending on subsequent transactions.

A *sell-stop* order is entered below the prevailing market price and is usually used to:

1. curtail a loss,

2. preserve a profit, and

3. enter into a short sale.

Example: A sell-stop entered on IBM at 90 when the stock is selling at 100 becomes a market order if the stock hits 90 or lower.

Limit and stop orders may usually be placed as *good-until-canceled,* or for a definite duration such as a week, a month, and so on.

Margin

Most investors pay for their stocks in full. Jake Diamond, for instance, has a *cash account* with Blue Chip Investment Brokers. When he buys 100 shares of IBM at $125 per share, he pays his broker $12,500 plus commission. However, some investors transact orders in a *margin account:* that is, they borrow part of the purchase price from the brokerage house. For example, if Jake has a margin account and he buys 100 shares of IBM at $125 per share, he pays Blue Chip $6,250 and borrows the additional $6,250 from Blue Chip. Buying stock on margin is a kind of leverage (that is, the use of borrowed money to make money).

The brokerage house holds the certificate as collateral against the loan and often pledges the stock to borrow the money to be loaned to investors. The rate of interest charged is generally a little higher than prevailing short-term (*call money*) rates.

When establishing a margin account, an investor must sign a *margin agreement,* which authorizes the brokerage house:

1. to charge interest on the *debit balance (amount borrowed);*

2. to pledge the securities as loan collateral (brokerage houses are limited as to the amount that can be pledged); and

3. to sell the securities if certain relationships between equity and debit balances are not maintained.

The Federal Reserve Board, under *Regulation T,* establishes margin regulations; one fundamental rule is that short sales must be transacted in margin accounts. Exchanges also have margin requirements that their members must maintain. In addition, most brokerage houses have their own requirements. Therefore, investors wishing to transact business in margin accounts should investigate completely the requirements and risks involved.

To understand the risk and corresponding potential of margin, or leverage transactions, refer to Jake Blake's purchase of 100 shares of IBM on margin.

Example: Jake Blake purchased 100 shares of IBM at $50 a share, or $5,000, putting up $2,500 in cash and borrowing the balance from Blue Chip. IBM declined to $40 a share and Jake elects to sell. He now has to repay Blue Chip the loan of $2,500 plus commission and interest. Therefore the sales proceeds of $4,000 (100 shares @ $40 a share), after payment of commissions and the repayment of the $2,500 loan plus interest, results in less than $1,500 cash to Jake. He invested $2,500 and lost more than 40% of his original invested capital as IBM declined 10 points ($50 to $40), or 20%.

Had he transacted in a cash account, he only could have purchased 50 shares ($2,500 divided by the price per share of $50 equals 50 shares), and his loss would have been $500 (10 points on 50 shares), that is, 20% of his original capital investment. On margin, he would have lost 40% on a 20% decline in the price of IBM shares.

In a margin account, if IBM goes to $60 a share and Jake sells, his profit is $1,000 ($6,000 sales proceeds for $5,000 in cost). After the debit balance of $2,500 plus interest is repaid, Jake has approximately $3,500 cash—a 40% profit with a 20% increase in price.

Nonpurpose Loans. The primary use of margin accounts is to leverage stock purchases. Other uses are what are generally referred to as *nonpurpose loans.* Many people use margin accounts to secure loans for business purposes, to buy automobiles, children's education, vacations, and so forth.

Example: Mr. and Mrs. Jones have a substantial stock portfolio. Most of the stocks were given to them by their parents and grandparents, therefore their cost basis is very low relative to the current market value. The stocks are of good quality with good potential. Mr. and Mrs. Jones do not want to pay capital gains tax. They establish a brokerage account with Blue Chip and when it comes time to pay their children's school tuitions, buy a car, or take a vacation, they take a loan from Blue Chip. They allow the dividends to reduce the loan. In addition, they make periodic payments to the account in order to reduce the debit balance.

Note: In order to deduct the interest on a margin account, the interest must be paid by payments to the account. Such credits could be dividends, interest payments, sale proceeds, or actual cash payments.

Many brokerage firms have different rules and regulations (called *house rules*) on margin accounts and nonpurpose loans. When considering using margin accounts it is always advisable to discuss the *house rules* and learn as much as possible about the margin requirements.

Installment Stock Purchases

The concept of buying by installment plan (paying monthly) is not new to American consumers. For years, buying houses, cars, and appliances as installment purchases has become a fact of life. Americans do not want to wait; they want to own things now. (One of the more popular forms of installment purchasing described in the chaper "Mutual Funds," is referred to as *dollar-cost averaging.*)

In June 1980, Virginia Electric & Power Company, now known as Dominion Resources, instituted a program to allow its customers the right to become part owners of the company by buying its common stock on an installment basis. In its first year of operation,the program was immensely successful. The company raised about $550,000 a month, almost $6.5 million, which represented about 10% of the company's annual capital requirements.

Under the plan, participants made monthly payments of $10 or more to a bank that was agent for the plan. The participants were given a coupon book looking like that for any other installment obligation. After a year, the deposits, plus 8% interest that VEPCO paid to use the money, were used to buy shares in the company.

The amount of stock each participant received was based on the average of the high and low prices for VEPCO common stock on the New York Stock Exchange composite tape on the 20th day of each month during the 12-month period. Participants did not receive dividends on the stock until it was issued at the completion of the plan.

Any participant whose monthly payment was 40 days in arrears would be discontinued from participation. In that event, all installment payments made would be returned to the participant, and the accrued interest would be forfeited.

A survey conducted by the company showed that 49% of participants in the plan did not own any common stock before entering the plan. A total of 76% of the participants did not own VEPCO's stock. Surprisingly, 40% of the participants bought the stock for long-term growth, and 30% for total return (price appreciation plus dividends). These figures are surprising since a utility is considered a conservative income investment.

Sources of Information: Corporate Statements

Investment decisions concerning common stock should be made only after careful study and consideration of a wide range of available information such as world events, domestic news, industry reports, and corporate announcements. Perhaps the most important documents to understand are the company's financial statements, the statements of the company's financial situation. A basic understanding of financial statement analysis, therefore, is essential.

Any corporation with $1 million in total assets and at least 500 stockholders must register its securities with the Securities and Exchange Commission (SEC). Exempted from this requirement are banks and insurance companies regulated by state or federal authorities whose regulations parallel the SEC's authority; many charitable religious and educational organizations are also exempt.

Even though registered firms must report significant events and changes periodically, the information released is generally not accompanied by an explanation or analysis as to how it may affect the future of the company. The stockholder must draw his or her own conclusions. The analysis required is often difficult, but a basic understanding of the principles of accounting and financial statement analysis is a great help.

The two basic financial statements included in all corporate reports are:

1. the balance sheet, and

2. the income statement.

In order to explain financial statements, the following information is taken from the January 1983 annual report of Best Products Co., Inc. Best was the creator of catalog showroom retailing and has enjoyed extremely good growth after going public in 1970.

The Balance Sheet

The balance sheet is a statement listing all of a corporation's (1) assets, (2) liabilities, and (3) shareholders' equity on a specific date in the year. That date may be the end of the company's fiscal year or the end of any month or quarter. (Incidentally, the fiscal year need not be the same as the calendar year; it may begin and end at any point decided on by the company.)

The balance sheet gets its name from the arrangement of the information it contains—roughly, a T-shape with assets on the left side and liability and shareholders' equity on the right.

Assets must equal liabilities plus shareholders' equity.

The total value of the assets on the left always equals the total value of the liabilities plus shareholders' equity:

Total Assets = Total Liabilities + Shareholders' Equity

The above formula, restated in terms of shareholders' equity or in terms of total liabilities, is a useful device for balance sheet analysis:

Total Assets − Total Liabilities = Shareholders' Equity

Total Assets − Shareholders' Equity = Total Liabilities

A more detailed sample balance sheet is shown on page 38.

Assets. Assets may be:

1. current,

2. fixed,

3. miscellaneous, and

4. intangible.

1. *Current assets* can easily be converted into cash, generally within one year at most.

Inventory, usually considered a current asset, should be discussed in more detail because of its effect on earnings and the many changes in valuation. Inventory generally consists of raw materials, work in progress, and finished merchandise awaiting sale. The most popular methods of inventory accounting are (1) first-in/first-out (FIFO), and (2) last-in/first-out (LIFO).

Let's look at the effects of a corporation's inventory assets and earning adjustments.

Illustrative Balance Sheet

Consolidated Balance Sheet
Best Products Co., Inc.
(In thousands)
(January 29, 1983)

Assets
Current assets:

Cash	$ 15,444
Accounts receivable	42,003
Merchandise inventories	547,668
Deposits and prepaid expenses	6,990
Total current assets	612,105
Property and equipment, net	252,156
Investment in property under capital leases, net	180,395
Other assets	13,940
Total assets	$1,058,596

Liabilities and stockholders' equity
Current liabilities:

Note payable	
Accounts payable, trade	$ 306,975
Accrued expenses and other	67,533
Income taxes payable	21,993
Current maturities on long-term debt	5,437
Current portion of capital lease obligations	6,533
Total current liabilities	408,471
Long-term debt	133,093
Capital lease obligations	173,174
Deferred credits	12,113
Stockholders' equity	331,745
Total liabilities and stockholders' equity	$1,058,596

Example: A firm manufactured four items of the same product in a fiscal year at total costs per unit as follows:

Unit 1	$100
Unit 2	110
Unit 3	120
Unit 4	130
Total cost of inventory	$460

In the beginning of the next fiscal year the company disposes of one unit for $140. If it uses FIFO, the unit sold is the first manufactured with a cost of $100. Thus this transaction yields a profit of $40, which appears on the income statement. Under the LIFO method, the same transaction would yield a profit of only $10, because the $140 sale is applied against the last unit manufactured at a cost of $130.

Inventory valuation methods, therefore, have significant effects on the income statement. During periods of inflation, FIFO results in larger profit margins and higher inventory figures on the balance sheet, because the inventory remaining has a higher cost basis. In a recession LIFO may cause earnings losses sooner than FIFO, because the profit margins are smaller. It may also produce lower inventory valuations on the balance sheet, because the remaining inventory was manufactured at less cost.

2. *Fixed assets* are physical assets that can be expected to require more than one year to convert to cash at prices equal to its estimated worth.

3. *Miscellaneous assets* are assets held for an indefinite period of time, generally including unimproved land, deferred charges,* and securities of affiliated and subsidiary companies. Most sundry assets are carried on the balance sheet at cost. When land is eventually improved, it is generally reclassified as a fixed asset.

4. *Intangible assets* are those whose true worth is difficult to determine and includes such items as goodwill, reputation, patents, copyrights, franchises, leasehold improvements, and trademarks.

Liabilities. Liabilities represent the amount a company owes; and, as in assets, liabilities are subdivided as:

1. current liabilities,

Deferred charges, expenses to promote or improve the long-term outlook of business, may be charged against earnings over a period of years instead of in the one year in which the money is spent. Capitalizing expenses is a management decision acceptable under most accounting standards and practices.

2. fixed liabilities, and

3. miscellaneous liabilities.

   1. *Current liabilities* are obligations that are scheduled for payment within one year, such as accounts payable, accrued expenses, accrued and withheld taxes, unearned revenues (deposits), dividends declared but unpaid, and, often, current maturities of long-term debt.

   2. *Fixed liabilities,* which include promissory notes, bank notes, and bank loans not payable within one year, represent debts of a corporation.
The face value, interest rate, maturity date, and other pertinent information regarding long-term bonds should be presented separately for each issue. Bonds are frequently arranged in ascending order of interest rates.

   3. *Miscellaneous liabilities* are difficult to classify as current or fixed, but are obvious debts of a corporation.

   Shareholders' Equity. Shareholders' equity represents the value of the corporation belonging to the owners. If total liabilities and total shareholders' equity are added up, the sum always equals total assets. Stated another way, shareholders' equity equals the difference between total assets and total liabilities.
The shareholders' equity appearing at the bottom right of the balance sheet fully describes the circumstances regarding:

1. *capital stock* (the number of shares authorized, issued, outstanding, and held in treasury) as well as par or assigned values, and conversion or liquidation rights;

2. *paid-in capital* (the excess of the stocks' market value when sold over par value); and

3. *retained earnings* (the portion of profits not distributed to stockholders).

   The dollar figures in the *capital stock* account under shareholders' equity result from multiplying the *par,* or stated, value of the stock by the number of shares outstanding. Unissued shares are not calculated.

Example: Besides its common stock, Best Products Co., Inc., has outstanding, 6% preferred stock* with a $10 par value; 40,000 shares are authorized but only 36,800 are outstanding. The resultant shareholders' equity section of the balance sheet reflects a value of $368,000 ($10 par × 36,800 shares). The shareholders' equity in the balance sheet appears as follows:

Shareholders' Equity

Preferred stock ($10 par value)—	
6% cumulative: 40,000 shares authorized: 36,800 issued	
and outstanding	$ 368,000
Common stock ($1 par value): 20,000,000 shares authorized;	
9,703,000 shares issued and outstanding	9,703,000
Additional paid-in capital	40,134,000
Retained earnings	$162,952,000
Total	$213,157,000

These figures, however, can be misleading: Discrepancies result from the bookkeeping procedure of recording common stock at par value per share. Very often, common shares are issued at higher prices than their par, or stated, value. The difference between the entry and the proceeds realized from the offering is carried in a common-stock account identified as *paid-in capital.* For example, if stock with $1 par was originally offered at $5 per share, the $4 difference per share on 16,500,000 shares outstanding would be reflected as $66,000,000 in the paid-in capital account.

    Further, the shareholders' equity portion of the balance sheet must reflect an additional category referred to as *retained earnings.* This account represents profits earned by the corporation over a period of time and not distributed to the shareholders. An increase in undistributed profits causes the value of retained earnings to rise, whereas cash dividend payouts obviously reduce the account.

    If a corporation declares a *stock dividend,* the market value

*Chapter 3 explains how preferred stock differs from common. For this example, the distinctions are not important.

of the newly issued shares as of the date of issue must be deducted from the retained earnings account. The par value of the newly issued shares is added to the authorized and issued account and the difference between par and market values added to paid-in capital.

A stock split must be reflected by splitting the par value. Stock splits create an offsetting transaction (debit) to authorized capital.

Stock dividends and stock splits do not affect the shareholders' percentage of ownership, only the number of shares he or she owns, because each shareholder benefits in proportion to his or her original percentage of ownership.

Example: If Best Products stock is selling at 36½ (November, 1983) and the company declares a 10% stock dividend, the owner of 1,000 shares receives 100 additional shares. The owner retains his or her percentage of ownership because the number of shares owned has increased in proportion to the total number of issued shares. Initially, the stock's market price might decline 10%, or approximately 2 points to reflect the additional shares.

If a stock splits 2-for-1, every shareholder receives an additional share for every one he or she has in possession.

Treasury stocks are shares that are reacquired through purchase in the open market by a corporation. When reacquired, treasury stock loses some basic privileges and gains a unique accounting characteristic. Obviously, these shares do not receive dividend distributions or voting privileges. Therefore they are not considered issued and outstanding in a calculation of earnings per share, and the earnings per share of issued and outstanding stock consequently goes up.

Treasury stock may be utilized by the management of a corporation to:

1. exchange for shares of another corporation with whom they would like to merge;

2. fulfill commitments they have made with respect to pension plans, profit-sharing plans, employment contracts with key personnel; or

3. reoffer for sale in the marketplace at a later date—hopefully at a profit (ordinarily, the profit on such a transaction is not taxable to the corporation).

The balance sheet allows analysis of the relative worth of a corporation. Because a balance sheet reflects a company's status at a particular point in time, comparing successive statements, if possible, should reveal whether the company is progressing at a respectable rate—or progressing at all. The net tangible asset value per common share outstanding is the *book value*. This calculation is not a company's liquidation value as is often believed. Instead, the book value per share can:

1. determine the company's profitability by computing the net income available for common shareholders, known as return on common equity (net profits per share are divided by the book value); or

2. evaluate the market price of a company by dividing the market price of the stock by its book value.

Income Statement

Sometimes referred to as the profit and loss (P&L) statement, the income statement documents revenues and expenses over a period of time. This statement may reflect income and expenses for a period of one fiscal year, six months, three months, or even less. Obviously, a fiscal year is a more accurate basis for judgement than a shorter period of time.

An income statement is a simple report of success or failure. As its title implies, the statement details the monies received by the corporation. First, *gross sales* are totaled up for the year. Then from that figure are deducted monies paid out because of returned goods, discounts on sales, refunds, or other allowances, to arrive at net sales. Many large corporations omit the gross sales and deductions and merely report net sales; such is the case for Best Products.

Many deductions, however, must still be made from the net sales or net revenue before the shareholder may share in any profits. The cost of sales and operating expenses plus overhead must be accounted for, such as:

1. cost of goods sold (new materials, processing or manufacturing);

2. operating expenses, which include:

An Income Statement

Consolidated Statements of Earnings
Best Products Co., Inc.
(In thousands, except per common share data)

	Fiscal Year Ended January 29, 1983	Seven Months Ended January 30, 1982	Fiscal Year Ended June 27, 1981
Net sales	$1,581,650	$772,727	$1,002,037
Cost of goods sold	1,192,314	582,550	755,033
Gross margin	389,336	190,177	247,004
Other costs and expenses:			
Selling, general and administrative	268,519	123,393	162,966
Depreciation, amortization and operating rentals	39,607	16,595	23,821
Interest, net	25,134	13,375	16,462
Total other costs and expenses	333,260	153,363	203,249
Earnings before provision for income taxes	56,076	36,814	43,755
Provision for income taxes	27,256	17,303	19,594
Net earnings	$28,820	$19,511	$24,161
Net earnings per common share	2.45	2.01	2.49
Cash dividends declared per common share	0.32	0.14	0.24
Average common shares outstanding	11,773	9,075	9,690

a. selling expenses (advertising, salespeople's commissions, salaries);

b. administrative expenses (executives' salaries, office payroll, and so forth); and

c. depreciation, an allowable noncash charge against income to reflect the gradual deterioration or obsolescence of many fixed assets, such as buildings, machinery, office equipment, and so on. (The cash reserved is supposed to be used to replace those assets when they are no longer of use; however, a corporation is not required to use the depreciation to replace the depreciated assets); or depletion, a noncash charge referring to the "wasting value" of natural resources as they are used up.

After all these deductions are taken out, *the net operating income* remains. Out of this income, the corporation pays interest on all debts, bonds and notes, then taxes, and finally all dividends on common and preferred stock.

When all payments except dividends are made, the *income before taxes* remains. Subtract federal and state taxes and the *net income* is left—income the corporation may use in any way it sees fit.

From the information in an income statement, a company's operating efficiency may be determined and compared with previous results or with the efficiency of other companies in the same industry. This simple analysis is referred to as *margin of profit,* which is the net operating income divided by net sales. In the Best Products statement, the margin of profit is about 1.8% (28,820 ÷ 1,581,650). Other financial information, important to the stockholder, may be derived from both the balance sheet and the income statement.

Perhaps *earnings per share* and the *growth of earnings per share* are the two most important indicators for the shareholder, because expectations of the future earnings per share greatly affect the market price of a company's stock. To determine the earnings per share:

1. obtain the *net income* from the income statement and the number of outstanding shares from the balance sheet; then,

2. subtract any preferred and/or common stock dividends paid to arrive at net earnings; then,

3. divide the net earnings by the total number of shares outstanding.

The price/earnings (P/E) ratio, the price of the common stock divided by the earnings per share, can also be very important. Comparing one company's P/E ratio with others' in the same industry gives the stockholder an idea of a firm's intrinsic value, also thus providing a relative market value of the stock.

Best Products

$$\frac{\$28,820,000 \text{ Net earnings}}{\$11,773,000 \text{ Average shares outstanding}} = \$2.45 \text{ EPS}$$

P/E (Price/earnings ratio)

$$\frac{\$36.50}{\$2.45} = 14.9 \text{ P/E (November 1983)}$$

Finally, *cash flow,* the net income plus annual depreciation, represents the total available cash for use by a corporation and is a good indicator of its business volume.

Best: (000) $28,820 + $39,607 = $68,427 (000)

The ownership of common stocks over a period of years has made many investors wealthy while they participated in the growth of companies and the expansion of the American economy. In a *bull market,* when stock prices are generally increasing, profits are made more easily than in *bear markets,* when stock prices are generally declining. However, common stock investment should be viewed over a longer term—through sometimes deceptive business cycles, the bull and bear markets.

The best approach, therefore, to investing in equities is an understanding of the companys' products and services, as well as careful analysis of where corporate money is invested. No investment is without risk, but the risk can be minimized with study, understanding, and making the best possible use of available information. Investment in common stocks can be extremely profitable, if carefully approached and managed over a number of years.

Methods of Stock Analysis

Security analysts are professionals who estimate the future value of stocks and make recommendations for rational investment decisions. Analysts study stocks in order to determine when they are over- or undervalued. If the stocks' estimated value is above the market price, the analyst usually recommends that the stock be bought. If the estimated value of the stock is less than the market price, the analyst usually recommends that the stock be sold.

There are two basic types of security analysts that are classified by their forecasting techniques.

1. *Fundamental* analysts study companies' earnings, managements, economic forecasts, competition, market conditions, and many other factors.

2. *Technical* analysts study the market price fluctuations in particular stocks and use charts to make forecasts of future prices.

Fundamental Analysis

Fundamental analysis is a complicated process by which the analyst estimates the *intrinsic* value of a given stock. Basically, the fundamental analyst determines the value of future dividends to be paid. The security analyst gets the earnings per share from the corporation's accountants and then multiplies it by an earnings multiplier to determine the value of dividends to be distributed in the future. The determination of the earnings multiplier is the difficult task facing the analyst. Much of his or her work centers on determining the appropriate multiplier or capitalization rate to apply to future earnings. Four major factors are usually considered:

1. the risk of the security,

2. the growth rate of the dividend stream,

3. the duration of expected growth, and

4. the dividend payout ratio.

Multiples (a company's P/E ratio) are also affected by changes in economic conditions such as interest rates and inflation. The complex mathematical techniques for evaluation of the four major factors are omitted due to the scope of this book. However, there are subjective considerations in the determination of a stock's intrinsic value.

Any growth in earnings also must take into account the industry and development of new products and technology. Although it is impossible to quantify information of this kind, experienced analysts use their skills and recognize significant factors in determining the value of the multiplier.

In forecasting the risk and earnings of a corporation, fundamental analysts also evaluate management. They include the depth and experience of management; its age, education, and health. The existence of any potential conflicts that may adversely affect the operation of the corporation is a warning sign. In addition to how well managed the corporation is, analysts assess the company's potential growth areas and how risky it is. These factors also affect the multiples.

In an effort to forecast earnings, dividends, and their multiples, financial statements must be considered.

Financial Statement Analysis. In order to gain a better understanding of financial analysis and corporate financial statements, this section is devoted to the understanding of financial statements. The ratios here are by no means complete and exhaustive. They are merely included to give investors an idea of how the fundamental analyst determines the value of a stock and what information is conveyed in an annual report.

Often, the information presented in financial statements is not enough to determine the financial condition and performance of a corporation. However, certain yardsticks, such as financial ratios, make the information more usable.

Ratios. Analysts use ratios to relate two or more items in the firm's financial statements in order to better understand its financial condition and performance. Ratios are useful because they can be compared both *internally* and *externally* with those of other financial statements. The analyst can compare present ratios *internally* with those of the same corporation for previous years or time periods. He or she can study the composition of change and determine whether there has been an improvement or a deterioration in the company's financial condition and performance over time. Financial ratios can be projected for comparison with present and past ratios.

Another method of comparison involves comparing the ratios of one firm with those of similar firms or an industry average at the same point in time. Such a comparison gives insight into the relative financial condition and performance of the firm. Financial ratios for various industries are published by Robert Morris Associates, Dun & Bradstreet, Prentice-Hall (*Almanac of Business and Industrial Financial Ratios*), the Federal Trade Commission, and the Securities and Exchange Commission.

Indiscriminate "rules-of-thumb" should be avoided. It is important to realize that a financial ratio in and of itself conveys very little information. The ratio must be compared to some other ratio or average in the same industry in order to evaluate the *relative* financial condition and performance of the firm. For example, the 2-to-1 current ratio (rule-of-thumb) may be accurate for a corporation involved in the manufacture of household appliances but the current ratio for a utility may be far smaller.

For our purposes, financial ratios can be divided into four types: liquidity, debt, profitability, and coverage ratios. The first two types are computed from the balance sheet; the last two are computed from the income statements and, sometimes, from both the income statement and balance sheet. No one ratio provides sufficient information to judge the financial condition and performance of a corporation; a group of ratios may be analyzed to make a reasonable judgement.

Basically, only a few ratios are actually necessary to make an evaluation of a company. Needless computations of many superfluous ratios only may add to the complexity and confusion.

In order to illustrate the ratios presented in this chapter, we use the Best Products Co., Inc. balance sheet and income statement.

Liquidity Ratios. Liquidity ratios are used to judge a company's ability to meet short-term obligations. Such ratios give insight into the present cash solvency of a company and its ability to remain solvent in an adverse economic climate.

1. The most general and frequently used of these ratios is the *current ratio:*

$$\frac{\text{Current assets}}{\text{Current liabilities}} = \text{Current ratio}$$

For Best Products, the ratio for January 29, 1983 is:

$$\frac{\$612,105,000}{\$408,471,000} = 1.50$$

2. To determine a corporation's ability to meet a temporary financial crisis, the liquidity ratio (sometimes referred to as the *quick asset ratio* or *acid test ratio*) is determined by the following formula:

$$\frac{\text{Current assets} - \text{Inventories}}{\text{Current liabilities}} = \text{Liquidity ratio}$$

For Best Products, the ratio for the 1981 year-end is:

$$\frac{\$64,437,000}{\$408,471,000} = .158$$

In addition to the liquidity ratio, it is often helpful to determine the actual amount of *working capital*—the money available to carry on normal everyday operations and to meet unforeseen emergencies.

Current assets − Current Liabilities = Working Capital

For Best Products, the amount of working capital available at the 1983 year-end is:

$612,105,000 − $408,471,000 = $203,634,000

Supposedly, the higher the liquidity ratios, the greater the firm's ability to pay its current bills. However, these ratios must be regarded as crude because they do not take into account the liquidity of individual components of current assets. The quick ratio does tend to determine the liquidity of a company with large amounts of inventory. But financial analysts often use ratios that measure the turnover of accounts receivable and inventories in order to develop a true picture of the corporation's liquidity.

Debt Ratios. Whereas liquidity ratios are used to determine the ability of the corporation to meet its short-term obligations, *debt ratios* are used to measure its ability to meet long-term obligations. Debt ratios are also used to determine the amount of debt encompassed in the capital structure.

Corporations use debt in order to leverage their earnings, or earn greater amounts on the capital invested in the corporation. However, too much debt in the capital structure brings great risk when earnings decline.

1. The *debt ratio* measures the amount of debt relative to the net worth of the corporation.

$$\frac{\text{Total debt}}{\text{Net worth}} = \text{Debt ratio}$$

For Best Products, the ratio for January 29, 1983 is:

$$\frac{\$328,430,000}{321,695,000} = 1.02$$

A comparison of the debt ratio for a corporation with the ratios of others in the same industry gives the analyst a general indication of the credit-worthiness and financial risk of the firm.

2. In addition to the debt ratio, the analyst may wish to compute the *long-term debt* ratio, which deals with only the long-term capitalization of the firm:

$$\frac{\text{Long-term debt}}{\text{Total capitalization}} = \text{Long-term debt ratio}$$

For Best Products, this ratio for the 1981 year-end is:

$$\frac{\$133,093,000}{\$650,125,000} = .205$$

This measure tells the analyst the relative importance of long-term debt in the capital structure of the corporation.

Profitability Ratios. There are two types of profitability ratios, those that show profitability relative to sales or relative to investment. The margin of profit ratio explained earlier shows profitability relative to sales and indicates the efficiency of corporate operations. There are several methods of determining profitability relative to investment.

The rate of return on common stockholders' equity ratio indicates to the analyst the earning power on the shareholder's book investment. It is frequently used in comparing two or more firms in an industry.

$$\frac{\text{Net profits after taxes less preferred dividends}}{\text{Net worth less par value of preferred stock}}$$

For Best Products, the ratio for January 29, 1983 is:

$$\frac{\$28,820,000 - 22,080}{\$321,695,000 - 368,000} = 8.96\%$$

Analysts also use ratios to measure the turnover of sales to assets and net profits to assets.

Coverage Ratios. Coverage ratios relate the financial charges of a corporation to its ability to service its debt. There are many complicated ratios to measure a corporation's ability to meet its fixed expenses of interest on outstanding debt. The most widely accepted coverage ratio relates the earnings of the corporation to the total amount of interest payments encountered. The *cumulative coverage* ratio is:

$$\frac{\text{Total net income}}{\text{Interest expense}} = \text{Cumulative coverage ratio}$$

For Best Products, the ratio for the 1983 year-end is:

$$\frac{\$28,820,000}{\$25,134,000} = 1.15 \text{ times}$$

In other words, Best Products' earnings after taxes are 1.15 times its fixed interest expenses. Coverage ratios are used extensively by Moody's Investors Service and Standard and Poor's in order to determine the relative risk of specific bond issues. The higher the coverage ratios, the less the risk that the corporation will not be able to meet its interest payment obligations.

Technical Analysis

Technical analysis is based on the premise that stock prices are determined by supply and demand. Therefore, the technical analyst studies historical price changes of stocks with the use of charts and models.

The basic assumptions of technical analysis are:

1. Market value is determined solely by supply and demand.

2. Supply and demand are governed by numerous factors, both rational and irrational.

3. Disregarding minor fluctuations in the market, stock prices tend to move in trends that persist for an appreciable length of time.

4. Change in trends are caused by shifts in supply and demand.

5. Shifts in demand can be detected sooner or later in charts of market action.

6. Some chart patterns tend to repeat themselves.

Whereas the fundamental analyst estimates the intrinsic value of the stock, the technical analyst seeks to estimate future stock prices. They try to forecast short-run shifts in supply and demand that will affect the market price of one or more securities. Most technical analysts do not accuse fundamental analysts of being illogical or conceptually in error. They merely assert that technical analysis is easier, faster, and can be simultaneously applied to more stocks at once than fundamental analysis.

The Dow Theory. The Dow Theory is one of the oldest, and most famous technical tools. It was originated by Charles Dow, founder of the Dow Jones Company, and editor of the *Wall Street Journal* around 1900. Dow died in 1902 and the *Wall Street Journal* staff developed his theory and named it after him. Today, many versions of the theory are used and it is the basis for many other techniques used by technical analysts.

The Dow Theory is used to indicate reversals and trends in the market as a whole or in individual securities. The theory asserts that there are three types of movement in the prices of the market represented graphically.

1. Daily fluctuations—the narrow movement from day to day.

2. Secondary movements—the short swing running from two weeks to a month or more.

3. Primary trends—the main movement covering at least 4 years in duration.

Dow Theory asserts that daily fluctuations are meaningless, but must be charted day by day in order to outline the primary and secondary trends. Secondary trends last only a few months. The primary trends are often called bear or bull markets.

Charts. Technical analysts use three basic types of charts: (1) line charts, (2) bar charts, and (3) point and figure charts.

This chart merely follows the daily price of the stock on a graph, with the vertical axis as price and the horizontal axis as time. Bar charts differ in that, rather than one continuous line denoting price, a vertical line is drawn denoting the high and low price traded each day; a small tick on each bar denotes its closing price. All charts usually have a bar graph along the bottoms to show the volume of shares traded in each time period. (Trading volume is secondary in importance only to price.)

Example: Consider a pattern called the head and shoulders formation. (Chartists find this formation in all three types of charts.) A *head and shoulder top* (HST) is a formation that signals that the stock's price has reached a top, and will decline in the future. As the name indicates, the HST has a left shoulder, a head, and a right shoulder. The market action can be explained in four phases:

1. *Left Shoulder.* A period of heavy buying followed by a lull in trading pushes the price up to a new peak before the price begins to slide down.

2. *Head.* A spurt of heavy buying raises prices to a new high and then allows the price to fall back below the top of left shoulder.

A Daily Bar Chart.

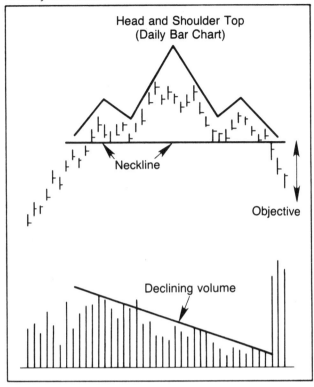

Head and Shoulder Top
(Daily Bar Chart)

Neckline

Objective

Declining volume

A Line Chart.

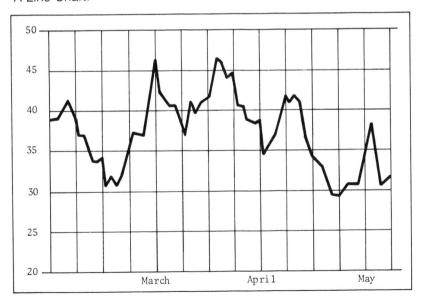

A Head and Shoulders Top.

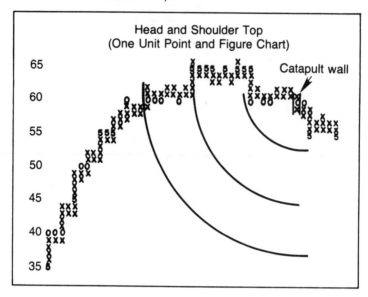

3. *Right Shoulder.* A moderate rally lifts the price somewhat but fails to push prices high as the top of the head before a decline begins.

4. *Confirmation or Breakout.* Prices fall below the neckline, that is, the line drawn tangent to the left and right shoulders. This breakout is supposed to precede a price drop and signal to sell.

Many other formations are used to forecast future stock prices as well.

Preferred Stock

What Is Preferred Stock?

Preferred stock is equity in a corporation issued to an investor in return for the use of his or her money. Generally, preferred stockholders have no voice in the management of the company, but are entitled to certain other privileges that are discussed in this chapter.

When issuing preferred stock, a corporation assigns a *par value* to each share, usually $100. The par value of some preferred stocks have been established at $25 and $50 in recent years. Usually, the company also sets a *fixed dividend,* which is determined by the general interest rates at the time of issue: higher dividends prevail at times when general interest rates are high; dividends are low when rates are low. The reason, of course, is that the preferred stock must compete for the investor's money with bonds and other interest-bearing investment vehicles.

Preferred stock is therefore similar to bonds in that a fixed amount is paid to the investor for the use of his or her money. However, there are differences. For one thing, preferred stock has no maturity date. Also, in the event of liquidation, although preferred stockholders are always paid before common stockholders, bondholders are paid before *any* stockholders. The reason is that bondholders are creditors, and shareholders are owners.

Why Buy Preferred Stock?

There are other important features regarding (1) marketability, (2) stability, (3) yield, and (4) favorable income tax treatment for corporate investors, which make preferred stock more desirable than bonds for many investors with limited money to invest seeking high income.

Marketability

Any preferred stocks are traded on exchanges in units of 10 shares *(a round lot)*. Even at $100 a share, a round lot costs only $1,000. Though inconvenient, odd-lot transactions in preferred stock are far easier and cheaper to accomplish than most odd-lot bond transactions. A round lot in bonds is usually 10 bonds with a $10,000 face value. Buying or selling two, four, or five bonds (odd lots) involves such additional premiums—if you can find a bond dealer who will sell them—that the yield is less attractive. An 8% bond may have a market price of $1,000, but to purchase two bonds, the investor may have to pay 104 ($1,040) for a yield of 7.69% ($80 [annual income] ÷ $1,040 [cost of bond] equals 7.69% yield). The same lack of marketability applies to odd-lot bond sales. The 8% bondholder may be able to realize only 96 ($960), if a buyer can be found at all.

Stability

Like corporate bonds, preferred stock is ultimately backed by the earning power of the issuing corporation. The relative investment merit and stability of a particular issue may be gauged by the number of times the corporation is able to cover the preferred dividends. This figure may be quickly determined by dividing the total preferred dividends into the corporation's after-tax income, resulting in the number of times the earnings cover the preferred dividends.

This figure lends weight to the corporate earning power in light of the following: Interest on bonds is paid before taxes and is a tax-deductible expense. If we assume that a corporation pays 50% of its net earnings in taxes, it only takes $1 of earnings to pay $1 of interest on a bond. However, dividends on common and preferred stock are paid from after-tax dollars. Assuming a 50% tax rate, the corporation must therefore earn $2 to pay $1 of preferred or common dividends at a 50% tax rate.

Yield

Most potential preferred stock investors are interested in *yield* the dividends paid on an issue expressed as a percentage of the current price. For example, if a preferred stock, with a par value of $100, has a current *market price* of $100 and pays a dividend of $8, the yield is 8%. Should the market price increase to $112 ($12 over par), the payout of $8 remains constant; the yield is therefore reduced to 7.14% ($8 ÷ $112). Conversely, if the market price declines to $90 ($10 under par), the yield increases to 8.89% ($8 ÷ $90).

With a constant payout, therefore, the only way yield can change on a preferred issue is if the market price changes. One factor influencing market price, as previously mentioned, is general interest rates: As rates on interest-bearing investments decline, the higher dividends on many preferred issues become more attractive. As they become more in demand, of course, their market price goes up. Anyone who can anticipate such a decline in rates has an excellent profit opportunity in preferreds.

Example: If interest rates are 8.5% and an $8.50 preferred has a market value of $100 per share, a 2% drop in general rates to 6.5% would theoretically increase the preferred's market price to $130.75 ($8.50 ÷ $130.75 equals 6.5%), a 30.75% increase, although the actual rise may be limited by the call feature, which will be discussed shortly.

The investor should appreciate that "Wall Streeters" usually refer to a *common* stock by its title—when they say "General Motors" they are speaking of General Motors *common stock*. All corporations have a common stock outstanding, but only *some* issue preferred stock. When a corporation does have preferred stock outstanding, it is fairly usual to have many different types of preferred! One preferred issue can be distinguished from another by their dividend rates. A preferred for a given company might be known as the $8 preferred—or a $10 preferred. The former issue would pay an annual dividend of $8 ($2 each quarter), while the latter would pay $2.50 each quarter for a total of $10 in a given year.

Example: Some companies express the preferred stock annual dividend rate as a percentage rather than as a specific dollar figure. This percentage, when utilized, refers to par value.

Example: An 8 percent preferred, on a $100 par preferred stock, would indicate an annual rate of $8. If that preferred stock had a par value of $10, then the annual rate would be only $.80.

While the par value of a common stock is merely a bookkeeping item and not of interest to the average investor, one must be particularly careful to note the par value on any preferred stock.

The Corporate Preferred Stock Investor

Corporations receive corporate dividends 80% tax-free. This means that a corporation receiving $100 in dividends from ownership of other domestic corporate stock pays federal income tax on only $20.

Otherwise, preferred stocks are usually purchased for high yield. Therefore, investors in lower tax brackets and tax-exempt institutions (pension and profit-sharing plans) are also possible investors. Many other investors are simply interested in total yield on an investment portfolio. For them, some preferred stocks can offer both yield and relative stability.

Capital gain dividends (distributions) from a regulated investment company (mutual fund) or real estate investment trust, and distributions reported as "return of capital," such as those paid by many utilities, do not qualify for the 85% dividend exclusion.

The Deficit Reduction Act of 1984 included several provisions intended to curb what were perceived as abuses of the 80% dividend exclusion advantage. They are:

1. The Act requires a corporation to hold a stock for 46 days to be entitled to the exclusion. Under previous law, only 16 days were required.

2. Selling a stock shortly after a dividend payment usually resulted in a short-term loss because the price of the stock normally declined in price by the amount of the dividends. The act stipulates that a corporation that receives dividends and sells

the stock before holding it for less than one year must reduce the basis in the stock by the amount of dividend excluded from income.

3. The Act eliminated the benefit of a corporation borrowing money, and then deducting the interest, to finance a stock portfolio in order to receive the 80% dividend exclusion. Now, the amount of the dividend that may be excluded from income is reduced by the interest on the loan to finance the portfolio. There are specific rules as to how the calculations are made.

Types of Preferred Stock

Preferred stock offers a high rate of return on invested capital and relative stability. However, because bonds usually carry an equal yield and a creditor status, many preferred stocks include special privileges to make them more attractive.

Cumulative Preferred

Cumulative preferred allows an investor to claim any dividends omitted in previous years. The deferred dividend accumulates, and the amount of arrears must be paid in full before any distributions may be made to the common stockholders. Unless the corporation gets into financial difficulty, in which case a partial payment settlement may be negotiated, the investor eventually receives the stated dividends. If a preferred stock is *noncumulative,* any omitted dividends are no longer a contingent liability of the issuer.

Participating Preferred

Participating preferred allows the investor to receive extra dividends if declared by the corporation. After the common stockholders receive dividends equal to the preferred dividends, additional distributions are shared equally by common and preferred stockholders. Unless a corporation is in dire need of capital, it is reluctant to include the participating privilege, which is an unusual feature in a preferred.

Convertible Preferred

Convertible preferred stock permits the stockholder to exchange his or her shares for a predetermined number of common shares at any time. To understand the relationships between common- and preferred-stock prices, several terms must be defined. *Parity* exists when the price of the convertible issue is exactly equivalent, on an exchange basis, to the current price of the common stock.

Example: If a preferred with a market price of $100 may be converted to 5 common shares, parity exists when the common is selling for $20 a share (5 common × $20 = 1 preferred @ $100).

If the preferred is selling above parity, it is said to be selling at a *premium;* below parity, at a *discount.* (*Parity,* incidentally should not be confused with *par.*)

The price of a convertible preferred issue is usually influenced more by price fluctuations of the underlying common stock than by its own payout. Convertible preferred usually sells at a premium over conversion parity because investors are willing to pay that premium for the higher yield and a more limited risk provided by the preferred stock. However, as the price of the common increases, the premium above parity decreases; and, conversely, as the common price goes down, the premium goes up.

Example: Ethyl Corporation had a $2.40 preferred that was convertible into 1.3 shares of common. In one year, the highest price of the common was $32; the lower, $23. In the same year, the convertible preferred high was $47.50; and the low, $36.75. The premium over parity at the high point was 14.2%; at the low point, 22.9%.

	High Point	Low Point
1. Common price	$32	$23
Conversion ratio	× 1.3	× 1.3
Exchange value of Convertible preferred	$41.60	$29.90
2. Preferred market price	$47.50	$36.75
Percentage premium	14.2%	22.9%

From *Moody's Industrial Manual.*

Ethyl Corp. $2.40 Cum. Cv. Second Pfd. Ser. A

AUTHORIZED—All Series, 10,000,000 Shares; outstanding, series A, Dec. 31, 1970, 1,728,011 shares; in treasury, 232,000 shares; reserves for options, 13,744 shares; par $10.

PREFERENCES—Has preference over com. and after 1st pfd. for assets and divs.

DIVIDEND RIGHTS—Entitled to cum. cash divs. of $2.40 a sh. annually, payable quarterly, Jan. 1, etc.

DIVIDEND RECORD—Initial dividend of $0.56⅔ per share paid Oct. 2, 1967; regular quarterly dividends paid thereafter.

LIQUIDATION RIGHTS—In any liquidation, entitled to the greater of (1) $42 a sh. plus divs. or (2) book value of com. stock into which pfd. is convertible.

VOTING RIGHTS—Has one vote per sh. if divs. are in arrears for 6 quarterly payments, then pfd., voting as a class, is entitled to elect 2 additional directors. Consent of 66⅔% of 2nd pfd. necessary to (1) authorize or increase authorized amount of any prior stock; (2) change terms adversely; 3) authorize 2nd pfd; 4) authorize or increase authorized amount of any parity stock, except may authorize shares of equal rank at twice the number of $2.40 preferred shares and issue these on basis of ½ the number of cum. first preferred.

CALLABLE—As a whole or in part after Aug. 1, 1972, on at least 30 days' notice at $75 a share, plus accrued dividends.

CONVERTIBLE—Into com. at any time (if called on or before redemption date) at rate of 1.3 com. shs. for each Ser. A sh. No adjustment for interest or divs. Cash paid in lieu of fractional shs. Conversion privilege protected against dilution.

LISTED—On New York Stock Exchange.

TRANSFER AGENTS—First & Merchants National Bank, Richmond, Virginia; Chase Manhattan Bank (N.A.), NYC.

REGISTRARS—Bank of Virginia, Richmond, Va; Morgan Guaranty Trust Co., NYC.

PURPOSE—(1,914,201 shares) issued Aug. 1, 1967 in connection with merger of Oxford Paper Co.

PRICE RANGE	1970	1969	1968	1967
High	39	53¼	57½	68¾
Low	28½	34¾	45¾	46⅞

From *Moody's Public Utility Manual.*

Virginia Electric & Power Co. $8.84 Cum. Pfd.

AUTH. All Series, 4,500,000 Shs; (increased from 2,500,000 shares to 4,500,000 shares Apr. 21, 1972): outstg., this series, 350,000 shs.; par $100

PREFERENCES—Has equal preference with other series outstg. as to assets and divs.

DIVIDEND RIGHTS—Entitled to cum. cash divs. of $8.84 per sh. annually, payable quarterl, Mar. 20, etc.

LIQUIDATION RIGHTS—In liquidation, entitled to $100 a sh. plus divs., if involuntary; if voluntary, redemption price.

VOTING RIGHTS—Same as $5 cum. pfd.

CALLABLE—As a whole or in part, on at least 30 days' notice to each Aug. 31, incl. as follows (per Sh. plus divs.): 1977, $109; 1982, $107; 1985, $104; thereafter at $101.
Not callable, however, prior to Aug. 31, 1977 thru refunding at an interest cost or dividend rate less than 8.95%.

PREEMPTIVE RIGHTS—None.

PURPOSE—Proceeds to retire short-term debt.

OFFERED—(350,000 shs.) at $100 a sh. (proceeds to Co., $98.77 a sh.) on Sept. 10, 1970 thru Merrill Lynch, Pierce, Fenner & Smith and associates.

LISTED—on NYSE (Symbol: VEL Pr G).

The convertible feature therefore enables the holder to participate in the growth of the corporation, at the same time allowing the issuer to pay a lower dividend than otherwise required. Also, while allowing participation on the upside with the common, the conversion capability does not prevent an investor from limiting his or her downside risk, on a yield basis, by the fixed payout.

Callable Preferred

Callable preferred is preferred stock with a call feature. The *call feature* permits the issuing corporation to retire the preferred shares at its option by paying the shareholders a predetermined amount for their shares. The call price may be at par, but is usually greater than par value, because most corporations are willing to pay a small premium for the shareholders' inconvenience.

Generally, an issuer calls, or redeems, an issue when money market conditions warrant replacing an older issue by preferred stock at a lower cost (perhaps because of a drop in interest rates). Sometimes a call is exercised to force conversion. Some preferred issues are called by provisions of a sinking fund (money set aside regularly by the corporation to redeem its bonds, debentures, or preferred stock).

Example: Should a preferred that is convertible into two shares of common stock, each with a market value of $75, be called at $102 per share, the converted common shares would have a value of $150. Therefore, the issue should be converted rather than redeemed on the call. In the event of a call, the holder of convertible preferred stock should review the terms of that particular issue in the services published by Moody's or Standard and Poor's. The call feature of Virginia Electric and Power Co. $8.34 preferred, for instance, is shown in the sheet on page 64.

A call feature can limit the upside potential of a preferred. If an $8 preferred is selling at $100 and is callable at $150, a drop in interest rates effects less of a price increase than if the stock were not callable. Investors would hesitate to pay much over $105, since the issue could be called at that price. This applies only to "straight" (nonconvertible) preferred issues.

Prior Preferred

Prior preferred, sometimes known as *preference stock,* generally has seniority over other preferred issues in the right to receive dividends and in the claim upon the corporate assets in the event of liquidation. To determine the extent of preference, check the original offering prospectus or corporate information published by Moody's or Standard and Poor's.

Adjustable Rate Preferred Stock (ARP)

During economic periods of rising inflation, or volatile movements in interest rates, many issuers find it virtually impossible to raise capital through offerings of preferred stock. After all, preferred stock, as a limited form of equity, is entitled only to fixed-dollar dividends and has little if any voting privilege. Why should someone buy that security when for the same money he or she could buy a similar rated *debt* security of the same issuer, receive the same dollar payments in the form of interest, and have a higher repayment status as a creditor in the event of bankruptcy?

The answer is obvious but, remarkably, preferred stock with these basic characteristics still has some appeal for a particular type of investor—a corporation! Corporate investors in preferred stocks receive special tax benefits from dividends paid on such holdings. As much as 80% of dividends received by corporate investors in equity securities can be excluded from their federal income tax liability. Thus, only 20% would be subject to taxation—and that, at worst, at the maximum corporate bracket of 34%.

The principal objection voiced by these investors is the fact that prevailing economic conditions assuredly make these investments worth less money in secondary trading markets. Even corporations become reluctant to buy preferred stock when they realize that a fixed dividend cannot always compete for investor dollars with higher rates of interest paid by issuers of debt securities. Market values of existing preferred stocks must fall to price levels where the fixed dividend offers attractive percentage yields in comparison to similar debt instruments. No one likes to invest in any security and see its value decline!

To address these problems and preserve the integrity of preferred stock financings, investment bankers have developed a new equity product. It is officially titled *adjustable rate preferred* stock, or ARP. Some investors call this instrument a "variable rate preferred" or even "floating rate preferred" stock. All descriptions refer to an equity security whose changeable dividend payment is keyed to an interest rate index of specific debt instruments. The dividend requirement is calculated, adjusted, and paid on a quarterly basis.

Typically, those debt instruments are U.S. Treasury securities and the appropriate rate is the highest yield prevailing on the dividend calculation date among 90-day bills, 10-year notes, and 20-year bonds. With some of these preferred issues, the dividend rate is stated as a percentage of premium above the highest Treasury yield. Virtually all ARPs also carry a cap and a collar. That is, despite the quarterly formula calculation there is, nevertheless, a stated maximum and minimum rate paid by the issuer. For example, in mid-1984 the typical cap for an ARP was 15½% and the collar was 7½%, both determined as an annual percentage payment.

The result of these determinations is a preferred stock paying a dollar rate of return continuously in accord with current money market conditions. Consequently, this preferred stock can compete successfully with comparable corporate debt securities and, more important, gives its secondary market price stability. To enhance stability of principal, some issuers of these "floaters" also include conversion, exchange or some other interesting feature to attract public and institutional investment dollars.

Bonds and Other
Fixed-Income Securities:
An Introduction

What Are Bonds?

A *bond* is simply a long-term promissory note of an issuer. The issuer can be a corporation, the U.S. government, or a state or local municipality. Bondholders are creditors of the issuer— they loan money to the issuer. The *face value* is the amount on the face of the security indicating the amount loaned that must be paid back to the lender at the *maturity* (expiration date) of the debt issue. The most common denomination (face value) is $1,000, or multiples thereof. Later examples of bond market price quotes will be based upon the $1,000 denomination. Some older bonds were issued in $550 and other denominations (*baby bonds*).

Periodic *interest payments* (usually every six months) are made up to the maturity date of the bond. The stated interest rate is fixed (thus the term, *fixed-income*) throughout the life of the bond. A bondholder's evidence of his or her creditor position consists of a certificate noting face value, stated interest rate, and maturity.

In earlier days, bonds had a series of interest coupons actually attached to the certificate. It was the bondholder's responsibility to clip coupons, and present them to the payment agent in order to receive his or her interest payments. The stated interest rate came to be known as the *coupon rate,* a term still in widespread use today.

Coupon or Registered Form

Bonds are issued in either coupon or registered form:

- *Coupon bonds* (also known as *bearer bonds* because interest and principal are payable to the bearer) are transferable simply by delivery; therefore, whoever has possession of the bonds is the owner (the bearer).

- *Registered bonds* are registered on the books of the issuer, and title can only be passed by proper endorsement, with signature guarantees. An advantage of registered bonds is that if they are lost or stolen, the owner is better protected against loss because legal title to the bonds is registered on the books of the issuer. Coupon bonds are usually more marketable due to the ease of transfer.

No coupon bonds have been issued since July 1, 1983; as a result of legislation included in the Tax Reform Act of 1982. Apparently, the IRS felt many individuals were not properly reporting their ownership of such bonds or the interest on them.

When considering buying or selling bonds, one should always inquire as to whether the bonds are coupon or registered. Sometimes a registered bond will have a slightly lower sales price because it is more difficult to pass title. Al bonds are now issued in registered form. The broker has an obligation to indicate on all bond orders whether they are coupon or registered bonds.

Coupon bonds have coupons that represent interest due. Investors must detach (clip) the coupons from the bonds to receive their interest payments. Interest payments on registered bonds, however, are mailed directly to the registered owner on each interest payment date, because these bonds are registered on the books of the issuer.

Sometimes coupon bonds are registered as to principal only, or as to principal and interest.

- If registered as to *principal only,* the coupons remain attached and must be presented on interest dates for payment; however, at maturity, the registered owner is the only person who can present the bond for collection of principal.

- If registered as to *principal and interest,* the coupon bond in effect becomes a registered bond and interest checks are mailed directly to the registered owner.

At maturity, whoever holds coupon bonds presents them to the issuer's agent bank or a brokerage firm to collect the principal (face value or par). Registered bonds must also be presented at maturity for payment, but they must be properly endorsed, with a signature guarantee.

Sinking Funds

A *sinking fund* requires the issuer to set aside money periodically for the retirement of the bond issue. Not all bonds have sinking funds. The bonds that do have sinking funds provide additional security to the bondholder. Many investors are surprised to learn that the sinking fund for their issue does not provide for 100% retirement of principal. The issuer either plans to cover the remaining principal balance with internally generated money, or plans to sell new debt to use to repay the older, maturing debt. This process is called *refunding* when long-term debt is matured and is repaid with a new long-term bond, or a *rollover* if short-term debt is sold to repay maturing short-term debt.

The two main methods of retiring bonds with a sinking fund are:

1. Use of a lottery system to call in a portion of the bonds each year. Usually a bondholder receives a small premium over par value when the bond is called by a sinking fund.

2. Purchase of the bonds in the open market. When the bonds are selling below face value (*par*), it is to the company's advantage to buy in the open market rather than calling the bonds at a premium.

There are numerous other procedures for retiring debt. The investor should always check into the procedures for sinking fund payments, if any.

Call Provision

Recently, many debt issues have included *call provisions* allowing the issuer to require holders to redeem prior to maturity. This method of retirement allows the issuer to retire bonds before maturity if a favorable market exists. These markets would include periods when interest rates are declining since the time of original issue or when the corporation has surplus funds. Usually the issue includes a clause providing that, if called before maturity, the bonds will be redeemed somewhat above par. The bond services include information on the exact terms of any issue's call provisions.

Interest payments on a bond cease after it is called, making it imperative that an owner tender (send the bond certificate to transfer agent for payment) as soon as possible after receiving a call notice. In addition, a call provision usually limits the upside potential on a bond, even if interest rates are declining. Understandably, an investor would hesitate to pay much over the call price.

When soliciting a bond order, the broker is required to inform the buyer of any call provisions. The call provision is a *corporate* strategy, allowing corporate financial managers additional flexibility in managing debt issues. The investor can do nothing but respond to the call by sending his or her bonds for redemption, and usually receive a small premium, the *call price*, as payment for the inconvenience. The call premium can be as much as one year's "extra" interest if the bond is called within the first few years. After that period, the call premium declines.

The Indenture

All the terms and related contractual obligations of the issuer are completely spelled out in the indenture. The complete indenture can take over a hundred pages to list all the terms and agreements. Details found in the indenture may include:

1. The basic terms, including face amount of the issue, interest rate, maturity, and interest payment schedules.

2. A full description of any property or other assets to be used as security.

3. Provisions for redemption and calling procedures.

4. Financial restrictions on management, known as the *covenants,* specifying:

   —limitations on dividends,

—limitations on further debt,

—sinking fund procedures,

—minimum current liquidity measures, and

—controls on use of property pledged as security.

The Trustee

Most investors are not likely to read the indentures of bonds they are considering for purchase. The *trustee* for the bond is responsible for monitoring the issuer's compliance with the terms of the indenture. The trustee can be an individual, but usually the duties are handled by a large commercial bank.

Example: The VEPCO 8⅝ mortgage bonds of March 1, 2007 have Chase Manhattan Bank as the trustee.

The trustee is responsible for protecting the interest of the bondholders, acting under the provisions of the Trust Indenture Act of 1939. If the issuer is not complying with terms of the indenture, the trustee must take prompt legal action to protect the interests of the bondholders.

The Transfer Agent

The transfer agent, usually a commercial bank, is responsible for keeping records of who owns the bonds of a particular issue. When a bond is transferred by sale, gift, or for other reasons, the transfer agent receives the older bond and issues a replacement.

The transfer agent requires signature of the registered owner and guarantee of signature. Usually, an officer of a commercial bank or an officer or member of a securities exchange firm can guarantee signatures.

New Bond Offerings

New bonds and debentures are sold to the public by way of an important financial intermediary known as the *investment banker.* This traditional name for the firms involved is often misleading to the layperson, for investment bankers neither invest nor bank. The function of investment bankers is to assist issuers in selling new securities to the investing public. The services they provide are many and essential.

Underwriting

Underwriting new issues is one way investment bankers take a risk in the process of bringing new securities to market. When an investment banker *underwrites* a security issue, an entire block of securities is bought from the issue corporation or municipality. (The U.S. Treasury does not use investment bankers as underwriters.) In nearly all cases, a group of investment bankers collectively buys an issue, thus spreading the risk among several firms. A best efforts underwriting is where the investment banker makes no guarantee to take the whole issue.

Selling the New Issue

Often, the managing group of investment bankers underwriting a new issue will arrange a *selling group* of securities firms to take portions of the issue and sell them nationwide. The underwriters and sellers earn a fee for their services, the fee being paid by the corporation issuing the new security.

The spreads charged for underwriting and selling can range as high as 10 + % on common stock issues, and as low as ½% on high-quality bond issues. Investors should be aware that, although the prices of new issues appear to be commission-less, a "commission" *has* been paid by the issuer. Remember, there is no free lunch. Usually the broker will make more money by selling new issues than by trading in already existing securities.

Advice on Price and Market

In successful new bond issues, the investment banking firm has advised the issuer as to the proper level of interest rates, market timing, and many related issues. The entire issue will be placed in a matter of a few days, sometimes in only a few hours.

Selecting the Investment Banking Firm

Selecting an investment banker to handle the underwriting and selling group for a security can be accomplished by a competitive bidding process or by a negotiated transaction.

- *Competitive bids,* as implied, occur when many investment banking firms are invited to bid on a new issue: required on many municipal issues, normally optional on corporate issues.

- In *negotiated offerings,* the corporation usually selects a high-quality firm with which it has done business over time, negotiates the prices or interest rates to be offered, and settles on a fee. If negotiations break down, a different investment banking firm may be offered the opportunity of negotiating for the business.

Investors often ask why they should buy a new issue instead of buying an existing bond in the secondary market. New issues usually carry a little better yield than comparable issues offered in the secondary market because the objective is to get the new bonds sold.

How Bond Quality Is Rated

In earlier discussions of investor risks, the business risk was mentioned as the risk that the issuer would go bankrupt. If the company has declared bankruptcy, it will obviously default on the interest and principal payments of its bonds. Therefore, in bond trading circles, the business risk is referred to as the *default risk.* Bonds with a very low probability of default are said to be of high *investment quality.*

There are bond quality rating services that assign most debt issues letter ratings denoting the investment quality of issue. Ratings are not absolute measures of quality; rather, they are general appraisals of a bond's investment grade, taking into account such information as:

1. the issuer's past earnings record and future earnings expectations;

2. the issuer's financial condition, such as working capital, coverage of interest payments, ability to meet all debt and financial obligations, and the value of tangible assets;

3. nature of the issuer's business and comparisons to other concerns in the same business;

4. backing for the particular issue, such as sinking fund, call protection, liens, real estate, and so forth; and

5. appraisal of the management of the issuer.

Ratings should be used as a guide to the suitability of a particular issue for a specific investment purpose and for the type of account into which it is to be placed. The three major services and letter symbols used to designate relative quality of specific bond issues in descending order of quality are as follows:

	Fitch	*Moody's*	*Standard & Poor's*
Top quality	AAA AA A	Aaa Aa A	AAA AA A
Medium quality to speculative	BBB BB B	Baa Ba B	BBB BB B
Poor quality	CCC CC C	Caa Ca C	CCC CC C
Value is questionable	DDD DD D		DDD DD D

Because the letter ratings are, to a certain extent, subjective appraisals of investment quality, it sometimes happens that an issue will carry a *split rating,* perhaps "A" by one service and "AA" by another. In these situations, the buyer must evaluate the issue to make his or her own subjective decision as to whether the issue meets the investment objectives.

U.S. government bonds are not rated because they are backed by the full faith, credit, and taxing power of the U.S. government; thus, they are considered the safest securities an investor can purchase. However, they usually carry a lower yield than other bond issues. (Government bonds are discussed in a later section.)

Ratings affect the price of an issue. Generally, the investor is willing to accept lower interest for high quality; conversely, the lower the quality, the higher the interest. In addition, if one or more services lower the rating of an issuer, all existing bonds of that issuer will generally decline in value, reflecting the investor's consideration of a higher yield justified by the lower quality. If the services raise the rating, all existing issues usually increase in value because higher quality usually results in lower yield.

Before an issuer sells a bond, it will usually pay the rating services a fee to review the details and place a rating on the issue. After the initial rating, the services continuously survey the issue and the issuer to determine if the rating should remain the same or be lowered or raised. The ratings of issues in a portfolio of bonds should be reviewed periodically to see if any ratings have changed or can be expected to change.

The ratings may be used as guides in selecting bonds. Most banks, especially those that have no bond research department and rely on the ratings, will usually buy for their own account and trust portfolios issues rated A or better, and perhaps the conservative individual investor may want to employ these same ground rules.

How to Read Bond Quotations

The price of bonds fluctuate in the marketplace just as stock prices do. Yet unlike stock quotations, bond quotations must contain specific details regarding not only the issuer, but also the rate of interest, maturity, and price:

Example: A quote like "Am Mot 6s '88 at 87" contains all the necessary details in concise form:

1. *Issuer:* "Am Mot" is American Motors.

2. *Interest Rate:* "6s" is the notation for 6% interest. In other

words, this bond pays 6% annual interest per bond. In dollars, this rate comes to $60 ($1,000 par × 0.06).

3. *Maturity:* "'88" signifies that the bond matures in 1988. At this time, the par value is returned to whoever then holds the bond.

4. *Price:* "at 87" indicates that this bond is trading at a price of 87, which translates into $870. If the bond were trading at *par,* the price would be "100" ($1,000). This Am Mot bond is said to be trading *at a discount* because its price is below par. If it were trading above 100, it would be trading at *a premium.*

As another example, the "AT&T 8.7s '02 at 107¼" signifies the 8.7% American Telephone & Telegraph bonds that pay $87 annual interest per bond, that mature in 2002, and that have a market price per bond of $1,072.50

Bond prices can be quoted a number of ways: as a percentage of yield or as a percentage of the par or face value. We shall start with the percentage of face value.

As a Percentage of Par

This is probably the simplest form of quote. To get the dollar value, simply add zero to the quoted price for each $1,000 of face value.

Example:
.97 becomes $970.
.83 becomes $830.
.107 becomes $1,070.
.110 becomes $1,100. And so on.

Percentages are also used to convert other par values to dollar figures. Corporate, municipals, and U.S. notes are priced at a percentage of face value.

Example: A quote of, say, "75" means "75%" of any par value. To get the dollar figure, simply multiply the decimal form of the percentage by the face amount. In this case, since "75" would mean "75%," or as a decimal, 0.75. You see that it reflects a price of $750 when multiplied by a par of $1,000. Obviously, as long as the par is $1,000, you can skip the decimal step. If it were the price of a $10,000 bond, it would be $10,000 × .75 or $7,500. A $40,000 bond, $40,000 × .75 or $30,000.

Other examples are:

Quote	Percentage	Dollars
75	75%	$ 750
102	102%	$1,020
104½	104½%	$1,045

On order tickets, trade reports, and other memoranda, the $1,000 par value is often abbreviated by the Roman numeral "M." So an order for one bond is written as "1M," five bonds as "5M," and so forth.

Fractions

The use of fractions presents only a minor difficulty in converting quotes to dollar values. You simply follow the same steps as for whole numbers or percentages, but you use the decimal forms of the fractions. (Note that, although "eighths" represent portions of $1 in stock quotes, they represent portions of $10 in bond prices.)

Example: A quote of "91⅛" must be translated into decimal form before the standard conversion can be carried out:

Percent	Decimal	Dollars
91⅛	.91125	$911.25
83½	.8350	$835.00

To make these conversions quickly in your head, you should *memorize* the following table:

⅛ = 0.125 or $1.25 per bond

¼ = 0.250 or $2.50 per bond

¾ = 0.375 or $3.75 per bond

½ = 0.500 or $5.00 per bond

⅝ = 0.625 or $6.25 per bond

¾ = 0.750 or $7.50 per bond

⅞ = 0.875 or $8.75 per bond

Some bonds, particularly U.S. government securities, have such good marketability in a keenly competitive market that they trade in thirty-seconds or even sixty-fourths rather than eighths. To obtain the dollar values, you follow the same steps, but you convert the fractions into decimals. (The following table assumes par to be $1,000.)

32nds	64ths	Per $1,000	32nds	64ths	Per $1,000
+	1	.15625	16+	33	5.15625
1	2	.31250	17	34	5.31250
1+	3	.46875	17+	35	5.46875
2	4	.62500	18	36	5.62500
2+	5	.78125	18+	37	5.78125
3	6	.93750	19	38	5.93750
3+	7	1.09375	19+	39	6.09375
4	8	1.25000	20	40	6.25000
4+	9	1.40625	20+	41	6.40625
5	10	1.56250	21	42	6.56250
5+	11	1.71875	21+	43	6.71875
6	12	1.87500	22	44	6.87500
6+	13	2.03125	22+	45	7.03125
7	14	2.18750	23	46	7.18750
7+	15	2.34375	23+	47	7.34375
8	16	2.50000	24	48	7.50000
8+	17	2.65625	24+	49	7.65625
9	18	2.81250	25	50	7.81250
9+	19	2.96875	25+	51	7.96875
10	20	3.12500	26	52	8.12500

32nds	64ths	Per $1,000	32nds	64ths	Per $1,000
10 +	21	3.28125	26 +	53	8.28125
11	22	3.43750	27	54	8.43750
11 +	23	3.59375	27 +	55	8.59375
12	24	3.75000	28	56	8.75000
12 +	25	3.90625	28 +	57	8.90625
13	26	4.06250	29	58	9.06250
13 +	27	4.21875	29 +	59	9.21875
14	28	4.37500	30	60	9.37500
14 +	29	4.53125	30 +	61	9.53125
15	30	4.68750	31	62	9.68750
15 +	31	4.84375	31 +	63	9.84375
16	32	5.00000	32 +	64	10.00000

In this table, each thirty-second or sixty-fourth is accompanied by the appropriate dollar value—again some portion of $10. The plus signs in the "32nds" columns have a special significance: If a 32nd has a plus sign after it, then it is the equivalent of the next highest 64th.

Example: A $^{10}/_{32}$ + is the same value as $^{21}/_{64}$ ($^{10}/_{32}$ + $^{1}/_{64}$ = $^{20}/_{64}$ + $^{1}/_{64}$).

Government bond quotes look like this:

Example: (a) 96.6; (b) 98.8 +

The numbers to the right of the decimals represent 32nds. Price (a) is therefore 96$^{6}/_{32}$, which translates to 96$^{3}/_{16}$ or $961.875. Price (b) is 98$^{8}/_{32}$ plus $^{1}/_{64}$, which comes to 98$^{17}/_{64}$ or $982.65625. You will also see 96.06 or 98.08 +; it means the same thing.

Points and Basis Points

The term "point" means different things in stocks and bonds. A point in stock quotations is the same as $1. *In bond quotations, a point is $10.*

Example: If a bond's price changed from, say, 80 to 81, it is said to have changed by 1 point; that is, from $800 to $810 dollars.

A point should not be confused with a *basis point, which in bonds quotes is one-hundreth of a percentage point.* (.01%).

Example: If a Treasury bill's price drops from, say, "7.17 basis" to "7.10 basis," it is said to have declined seven basis points.

Interest Rates

In a technical sense, *interest* is the amount paid in order to borrow money. There is not one interest rate, but a whole variety of rates.

The common interest rate known to most people is the *prime rate*. The prime rate is the amount that America's most credit-worthy corporations pay to borrow money. Many other individuals and corporations pay a rate of interest based on the prime rate.

Example: An individual may pay 2% over prime and a corporation may pay 1% over prime.

The level of interest rates usually varies, with short-term interest rates normally being lower than longer term rates.

Example: In mid-1985, six-month Treasury bills were yielding approximately 7½% and 29-year government bonds were yielding a little over 10¾%.

Another way of explaining an interest rate is that it is the price of borrowing money so that a consumer or business can make use of goods or services now rather than saving and making purchases in the future. Interest rates could be considered a premium that must be paid in exchange for a current benefit.

A good explanation of interest exists in the housing market. Very few home buyers save enough money over a period of years to pay cash for their homes. They usually make a down payment and borrow 75 to 80% of the balance from a bank, savings and loan, or insurance company. Each monthly payment includes a portion of repayment of the original amount borrowed and interest on the balance. The interest is the additional cost of the house so that your family can enjoy its benefits while it is being paid for. Obviously an increase in interest rates means that the cost of consuming goods today rises as interest rates increase and conversely declines as interest rates drop.

It is generally believed that two components make up interest rates.

1. The *real rate of interest* is the portion of interest rate expected in return for future rather than current use of money. It is always positive because people have a time preference for money; they would always have it now rather than later. In addition, there are many productive uses that money can be put to. People expect to be compensated for not putting money to productive use at the present time.

2. The *nominal rate of interest* includes the real rate, but adds a premium for inflation. When the prices of goods are rising, people expect to receive a larger premium so that their purchasing power is not diminished by inflation. There are few investors willing to accept a 5% return when the inflation rate is above 10%. The inflation premium is based on expected inflation, not the current levels. Therefore the nominal interest rate equals the real rate of interest and the expectation of inflation over the contract period.

Bond Prices

What makes bond prices change? If bonds represent loans with fixed interest rates and other terms, how can the relative worths change in the marketplace? Supply and demand, call features, sinking fund features, the issuer's ability to pay, and for some corporate bonds, convertible features (which are treated later)—all exert pressures on the value of bonds. Perhaps the strongest influence, however, comes from prevailing interest rates.

Bond prices depend on a number of factors, such as the ability of the issuer to make interest and principal payments and how the bond is collateralized.

An across-the-board factor that affects bond prices is the level of prevailing interest rates. For example, an 8% bond yields different rates depending on whether it is sold at a premium or discount. But *why* should the bond sell for more or less than its face value? The reason has to do with interest rates.

Example: Assume the 8% bond was issued 5 years ago, when prevailing interest rates (on other investment vehicles) were about 8%. Further assume that current prevailing interest rates are about 9%. Why should investors buy a five-year-old bond yielding 8% when they can buy a newly issued 9% bond? The only way an 8% bond holder can find a buyer is to sell the bond at a discount, so that its yield to maturity is the same as the coupon rate on new issues.

Interest rates increase from 8% to 10%. With 15 years to maturity, an 8% bond has to be priced so that the discount, when amortized over 15 years, has a yield to maturity of 10%. That discount is a little under $200:

$$YTM = \frac{\text{Coupon rate + Prorated discount}}{(\text{Face value + Purchase price}) \div 2}$$

$$= \frac{\$80 + (\$200/15 \text{ years})}{(\$1,000 + \$800) \div 2}$$

$$= \frac{\$93.33}{\$900}$$

$$= 10.4\%$$

The 8% bond with 15 years to maturity must sell at a little over $800 to compete with 10% issues.

The possibility that interest rates will cause outstanding bond issues to lose value is called "interest rate risk."

Yet there is an upside to this risk. If interest rates decline during the five years that the 8% bond is outstanding, the holder could sell it for enough of a premium to make its YTM rate equal to the lower yields of recent issues.

For instance, should interest rates decline to 7%, the price of the 8% bond with 15 years to maturity will increase by about $100.

$$YTM = \frac{\text{Coupon − Prorated premium \%}}{(\text{Face value + Purchase price}) \div 2}$$

$$= \frac{\$80 - (\$100/15 \%)}{\$1,000 + \$1,100) \div 2}$$

$$= \frac{\$73.33}{\$1,050}$$

$$= 7.0\%$$

All other influences set aside, the general principle is that bond prices tend to increase when interest rates fall, and they decline when interest rate are rising.

Essentially, when you buy a bond, you become a lender. As a lender, you naturally want to be paid the highest interest rate possible for your loan. So, disregarding all other factors, a bond that pays, say, 8% is worth more to you than one that pays 6%. In principle, the effect of interest rates on bond prices is as simple as that.

In practice, however, things are a little more complicated. For one thing, why do interest rates change at all? Why should a municipal bond issued this year have a higher or lower rate than a bond issued last year? The rates change for a number of economic, monetary, and fiscal reasons as well as the influence of the Federal Reserve. As new issues appear on the market with higher interest rates, those with lower rates become less attractive. The prices for those older issues must therefore be adjusted downward—that is, discounted—so that their *yield* is the same as that of the new issues. Let's take a highly simplified case:

Example: The county has an outstanding 5% bond with a 1990 maturity date. It now issues another for 8% with a maturity date of 2000. The face value for both is $1,000 per bond. If the price of both is $1,000, then you'd be foolish to purchase the 5% bond. The price of the 5% bond must be lowered to compete with the later issue.

But how much should the price come down? The answer to that question has to do with the various types of yields that bonds offer:

1. nominal yield (coupon rate),

2. current yield, or

3. yield-to-maturity.

Nominal Yield. This is the annual interest rate stated in the indenture, the dollars actually paid to bondholders.

Example: The nominal yields of our county are 5% and 8%. In dollars,

$1,000 × 0.05 = $50
$1,000 × 0.08 = $80

Nominal yield is synonymous with *coupon rate.*

Current Yield. This figure represents how much of a return the bondholder gets in terms of today's market price—not necessarily for the face amount. So that all bonds may be directly compared, everyone uses this formula:

$$\text{Current yield} \ = \ \frac{\text{Coupon rate}}{\text{Current price}}$$

By common agreement current yield is always measured as a percent, and it is always annualized—that is, it is presumed that the owner will hold the bond for one year. In this way, bonds of the same type will tend to have approximately competitive yields.

Example: If the 8% county bond is a competitive yield for municipal bonds, we would expect the bond to sell at or near par.

$$\frac{\$80}{\$1,000} = 8\%$$

The 5% bond, in order to be competitive in yield will be discounted in the marketplace so that its yield is competitive. Thus, if it were to sell at $640, its current yield would be:

$$\frac{\$50}{\$640} = 7.71\%$$

Current yield is a measurement of simple interest—that is, annual interest that will be spent on consumer items or used to supplement income. Simple interest—that is, current yield—is important to the investor who wants additional income and in this respect current yield can be compared to the current yield on stocks.

There is, however, one artificial element in current yield: we presumed that we would hold it one year. In practice, investors hold bonds much longer—many till maturity—and they do not spend the annual interest payments. They reinvest such payments in order to compound their interest. Thus, in practice, bonds—while often compared by simple interest—are priced in terms of yield to maturity.

Yield-to-Maturity. In this calculation, you factor in the value of the discount or premium, a gain or loss, which is considered to be distributed—that is, prorated over the remaining time to maturity. To obtain the yield-to-maturity, simply add the prorated discount or subtract the prorated premium from the annual nominal yield. A simplified formula is called the *Rule of Thumb*.

$$\text{Yield-to-maturity} = \frac{\begin{array}{c}(+\text{Prorated discount or}\\ \text{Coupon rate} - \text{Prorated premium})\end{array}}{(\text{Purchase price} + \text{Par}) \div 2}$$

Example: An investor buys a $1,000 par bond at $920, for an $80 discount. The bond has 10 years to maturity, and it pays 5% annually. The discount adds a prorated (annual) value to the bond of $8 ($80 divided by 10 years). So the dollar "return" is $58 ($50 + $8). What is the yield-to-maturity? You can use the Rule of Thumb formula:

$$\begin{aligned}\text{Yield-to-maturity} &= \frac{\$50 + 8}{(\$920 + \$1,000) \div 2}\\ &= \frac{\$58}{\$960}\\ &= 6.04\%\end{aligned}$$

You can see that the discount makes the bond more attractive the shorter the time to maturity. If the bond had, say, 5 years remaining, the prorated discount would be $16 annually, and the yield-to-maturity, 6.88%. Conversely, a longer time to maturity reduces the yield-to-maturity: 20 years remaining would mean a prorated discount of $4 annually and a yield-to-maturity of 5.63%.

The following table summarizes the effects of a discount and premium on yields for an 8%, $1,000-par bond with 10 years remaining to maturity:

		Discounted Bond ($900)	*Premium Bond ($1,100)*
Nominal (Coupon) Yield		Remains same 8% ($80)	Remains same 8% ($80)
Current Yield	=	Higher than nominal	Lower than nominal
$\dfrac{\text{Coupon Yield}}{\text{Price (\$)}}$		8.89%	7.27%
Yield-to-Maturity	=	Higher than nominal; higher than current	Lower than nominal; lower than current
$\dfrac{\text{Nominal Yield} + \dfrac{\text{— Prorated Premium } or}{\text{Prorated Discount}}}{(\text{Price} + \text{Face amount}) \div 2}$		9.47%	6.67%

Bond Tables. In practice, computations of yield-to-maturity can become rather complicated. So calculations for the most common coupons, maturities, and yields-to-maturity are published in the *Expanded Bond Basis Book,* put out by the Financial Publishing Company (Table 2.4).

This table lists yields-to-maturity down the left hand column. Yields-to-maturity are also called "basis" prices. Quoting a bond as trading at "7.80 basis" is the same as saying it has a yield-to-maturity of 7.8%. The other columns represent the dollar values of the bond prices at various periods to maturity, in 6-month increments:

Bond Table, 6.50% Coupon Rate, 10 Years, 6 Months to 14 Years to Maturity.

Yield-to-Maturity	Years and Months Prior to Maturity							
	10-6	*11-0*	*11-6*	*12-0*	*12-6*	*13-0*	*13-6*	*14-0*
4.00	121.26	122.07	122.87	123.64	124.40	125.15	125.88	126.60
4.20	119.37	120.10	120.81	121.51	122.19	122.86	123.52	124.16
4.40	117.51	118.16	118.79	119.42	120.03	120.62	121.21	121.78
4.60	115.68	116.26	116.82	117.37	117.91	118.44	118.95	119.45
4.80	113.89	114.40	114.89	115.37	115.84	116.30	116.75	117.19
5.00	112.14	112.57	113.00	113.41	113.82	114.21	114.60	114.97
5.20	110.42	110.79	111.15	111.50	111.84	112.17	112.50	112.82
5.40	108.73	109.03	109.33	109.62	109.91	110.18	110.45	110.71
5.60	107.07	107.32	107.56	107.79	108.01	108.23	108.45	108.65
5.80	105.45	105.63	105.82	105.99	106.16	106.33	106.49	106.65

Yield Curves

The combined effects of changes in (1) inflationary expectations, (2) changing money supply, and (3) credit demand cause the level of bond and other fixed-income yields to vary widely over time. However, the term structure of interest rates (called *yield curves*) also varies because of economic conditions and market psychology.

Bonds and other fixed-income investments have differing maturity dates (the date upon which bond owners are repaid their money). For example, the U.S. Treasury, corporations, and municipalities have outstanding issues with maturities ranging from three months to thirty years. Any given issuer usually has different yields on its various fixed-income securities.

The following figures show graphs of normal and inverted yield curves. Of course, many factors control interest rates other than maturity. Because of these factors, it is not possible for economists and academicians to come up with a unified theory

Yield Curves.

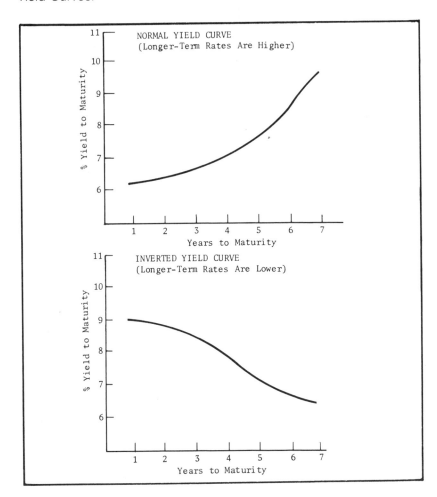

on the behavior of yield curves. However, there are several theories of determining factors that are easily explainable:

1. The *liquidity premium theory* asserts that long-term yields should average higher than short-term yields. This theory asserts that investors pay a premium price resulting in lower yields on

short maturities in order to avoid the risk of principal more prevalent in long-term maturities. Therefore, the upward sloping curve is called *normal*.

2. The *expectations theory* asserts that long-term yields are the average of the short-term yields prevailing. This implies that if investors expect rates to rise, the yield will slope upward, and remain unchanged. It will be horizontal or fall (slope downward) if investors expect rates to fall.

3. The *segmentation theory* assets that the yield curve is composed of a series of independent maturity segments. For example, conventional banks demanding short-term maturities, savings and loans demanding intermediate maturities, and life insurance companies demanding long-term maturities. Yields are determined by the prevailing supply and demand conditions in each segment.

Fiscal Policy. Fiscal policy primarily involves the use of powers of the federal government to spend and tax so as to influence the demand for money and, ultimately, interest rates. If expenditures are increased without an equivalent increase in taxes, the funds to pay for the excess spending must be obtained in some other way. The government may raise the money needed either by borrowing, thus increasing the amount of its debt, or by creating additional money.

Conversely, when tax revenues are greater than expenditures (which has been unusual in recent years), the excess revenues can be used to retire existing debt or reduce the money supply. There is little doubt among economists that deficit spending financed by the creation of new money on a short-term basis promotes economic growth. However, when the deficits are financed through debt, the usual result is higher interest rates. If there is a deficit, nominal and real interest rates usually rise because of the need to sell more government securities to finance the debt, meaning more competition for investors' money.

To attract more investors, the government would have to raise interest rates. The increase in the U.S. Treasury Bond sales also has a *crowding out* effect. The sale of additional U.S. Treasury debt is believed to take money away from private borrowers.

Monetary Policy. There are three principal methods by which the Federal Reserve Board can control the money supply that affects the level of interest rates through its monetary policy. They are:

1. open market operations,

2. changes in the discount rate, and

3. changes in the reserve requirements of member banks.

1. *Open market operations.* Open market operations usually are considered the most important tool of the Federal Reserve in controlling monetary policy. It is the purchase and sale of securities (usually U.S. government securities) by the Federal Reserve in the open market through a series of dealers.

The open market policy is established by the Federal Reserve Open Market Committee and is carried out through its manager of the open market account. Transactions are conducted at the trading desk of the Federal Reserve Bank of New York under the direction of the Federal Reserve Open Market Committee.

If the Federal Reserve wishes to expand the money supply, it will generally purchase securities that will put additional money into the system very rapidly. The purchase of securities by the Federal Reserve expands the volume of bank reserves. The newly created reserves of member banks can be loaned in order to create more money. Conversely, if the Federal Reserve wishes to curtail the growth in the money supply, it merely enters the market and sells securities. This takes money out of the system.

The advantage of open market operations is that they are flexible and can be changed quickly. This tool is suitable for fine tuning market conditions and can be implemented for any number of reasons. The primary disadvantage usually is believed to be that the Federal Reserve Open Market Committee is unable to effect massive changes in the short term through open market operations. There are also negative psychological effects in the marketplace when the Federal Reserve is rumored to be selling securities.

2. *Discount rate.* The Federal Reserve controls the money supply through changes in the *discount rate.* The discount rate is the interest rate charged by the Federal Reserve to member

commercial banks when those banks borrow from the Treasury. The borrowing is usually short term, fifteen days or less. The Board of Governors of the Federal Reserve determines the rate.

When the Federal Reserve wishes to expand the money supply more rapidly, they lower the discount rate. This move encourages member banks to increase their borrowings in order to expand reserves. When loans are made on the increased reserves, more money is created in the system. When the Federal Reserve wishes to curtail monetary growth, it can raise the discount rate and discourage member banks from borrowing. This means fewer loans and smaller monetary growth.

It is generally believed that changes in the discount rate will ultimately be reflected in the rates banks charge their customers, and to some extent will affect the rates that banks and savings and loans pay on deposits.

3. *Reserve requirements.* Reserve requirements are seldom adjusted as a means of monetary control but changes in the requirements are very powerful tools. Every member bank of the Federal Reserve system is required to maintain a specific percentage of its deposits in the form of reserves either as cash in the vault or as deposits with a Federal Reserve bank. Changes in the specific percentage have substantial impact on the lending ability of individual banks and, indeed on the total credit-creating power (lending ability) of the entire banking system.

The Federal Reserve could increase the reserve requirements on time or demand deposits if it desired to reduce the availability of credit in the banking system. Conversely, the central bank could decrease the reserve requirements in order to increase the availability of the banking system to expand its lending. The decrease of the reserve requirement would in theory expand monetary growth, but only if banks chose to use the newly created excess reserves for new loans.

Margin Requirements

Margin requirements refer to the percentage of market value of stocks and bonds purchased and pledged as collateral that the customer must pay for at the time of purchase. The remaining portion may be borrowed from the broker or bank.

The Federal Reserve has control over the margin requirement and may curtail monetary growth by raising the margin requirement to reduce borrowing. Conversely, the Federal Reserve can decrease the margin requirement in an attempt to encourage new loans for the purchase of investments. Even though the Federal Reserve establishes margin requirements under Regulations T and U, banks and brokerage houses can establish more stringent regulations if they wish.

In addition to initial margin requirements, banks and brokers usually require that after certain levels of decline in stock and/or additional collateral. This is referred to as a *maintenance call*.

Corporate Bonds

Types of Corporate Bonds

Corporate bonds are usually classified by type of issuer:

1. industrial,

2. utility,

3. finance, and

4. railroad.

Industrial Bonds

Industrial bonds are issued by corporations engaged in manufacturing, retailing, wholesaling, and so on. They are usually issued in order to increase working capital, to finance expansion (such as a building program), or to refund a previous issue. Another reason for an industrial corporation to issue debt is to increase the return on the shareholders' equity, thereby increasing the earnings per share, which, hopefully, will result in an increase in the market price of the issuer's common stock.

Utility Bonds

Regulated companies that provide electric, gas, and telephone service to the public issue *utility bonds*. The rate of return that can be earned on utilities' invested capital is regulated by state and federal authorities. Usually, the regulatory agencies allow rate increases so that the return on capital is regulated by state and federal authorities. Usually, the regulatory agencies allow rate increases so that the return on capital is sufficient for new financing and an ample return to the equity investors. Partially because of the steadily increasing demand on utilities to expand, an increasing supply of these bonds has come to market, causing higher interest rates.

Finance Bonds

Finance issuers include such corporations as banks, finance or loan companies, REITs, and insurance companies. These companies borrow money at one rate and then relend that money at higher rates, earning their profits on the spreads between the interest rates. Money is their primary asset. For example, insurance companies must invest their cash reserves in order to meet their potential policy obligations.

Railroad Bonds

Railroads generally issue two kinds of bonds:

1. *industrial bonds*, like those discussed earlier, to finance expansion (buildings, track, and so forth); and

2. a special type called the *railroad equipment trust,* to finance the purchase of cars and locomotives. The rolling stock is collateralized and the bond is usually issued serially. As the bonds are paid off, the remaining bonds become more valuable because of the increased equity in the rolling stock.

The railroad equipment trust is issued in either of two ways:

- The *Philadelphia plan*, in which the title remains with a trust (usually a bank) until the bonds are retired.

- The *conditional sale*, in which the title to the rolling stock remains with the railroad.

Debentures

Investors frequently do not distinguish between bonds and debentures. Bonds have a specific asset pledged as security for the debt issue. Debentures are backed only by the general earning power of the issuer. Bondholders, then, are *secured creditors,* while debenture holders are *general creditors.* In the event of a bankruptcy, the secured creditors have first claim on the assets named in the bond indenture.

Mortgage Bonds

A *mortgage bond* is a classic example of a debt issue with security, the security being real property. The mortgage has a lien against specified real property. As in home mortgages, there can be more than one lien on the same property. The first mortgage has the *senior lien,* and the other mortgages have *junior liens,* in respective order. The junior liens are said to have claims *subordinated* to the senior lien.

Terms. The following important legal terms about the mortgage should be understood. A *closed-end mortgage* does not allow any additional equal liens on the named real property.

Example: If a $4 million plant has been mortgaged in the amount of $2 million with a closed-end first mortgage, there can be no further first mortgage debt sold against the plant and land. A second mortgage, with *junior lien,* could still be sold.

If there is no mention of a closed-end clause, the mortgage bond is considered to be *open-end,* and additional debt can be sold with the same property used as security. In the previous example, had the mortgage been open-end, then additional debt might have been sold with an equal lien against the property.

A *limited open-end mortgage* is more common. In this arrangement, the indenture in the first issue sold states a maximum limit of debt that can be sold against the value of the property.

Example: A typical arrangement in electric utility first mortgage bonds to finance plant construction is to allow 60% of the value of the property to be encumbered with equal, first mortgage claims. There may be several first mortgage bonds sold against the same property, until the total claims equal 60% of the total value.

The previous examples have illustrated *specific liens* against specific property. A *blanket lien* has claim against all real property of the company. An effective way of providing debt management flexibility to the issuing corporation is to add an *after-acquired* clause to an open, or limited open-end mortgage. The after-acquired clause provides that any new real property acquired in the future shall also go under the lien. A growing company will have a growing asset base to use for mortgage financing. The after-acquired clause protects the bondholders by putting new properties under the same indenture and lien, and allows the company some "open-endedness" in being able to sell more debt against the growing value of properties.

Security of a Debenture vs. a Bond

The implied security of bonds developed in the previous discussion should be put into proper perspective. The investor should not forget that the most important security for the corporate debt holder is the issuer's ability to generate a profit. The discussion so far has been emphasizing security-in-event-of-default. The earning power of the corporation is what will keep the bond in existence and fulfilling its contractual obligations.

Investors should not be lulled into a false sense of security by thinking that the mortgage bonds of a weaker company are more secure than the debentures of a strong company. Some companies are so strong that they do not find it necessary to pledge assets in order to sell debt. AT&T, for example, has primarily used debentures for billions of dollars of debt financing since World War II. AT&T debentures carry the highest quality ratings (AAA) while the first mortgage bonds of many large electric utilities are rated single-A.

At the other extreme, a company may have mortgaged every piece of qualifying property it owns, and only have the debenture option left as a means of long-term debt financing. You can learn this type of information from studying analysts' reports and bond quality ratings as well as Moody's and Standard and Poor's reports.

Subordinated Debentures. In the descriptions of mortgage bonds, the second mortgage was mentioned as an example of the junior lien. Any debentures structured to have a lower claim on income and assets than other senior debt are thus *subordi-*

nated debentures. Like the second mortgage, they have willingly subordinated their claim to some senior issue.

The default risk in subordinated debentures is, by design, higher than the risk in the senior debt securities. Investors expect additional return for the additional risk, so subordinated debt should provide a higher rate of return than the senior debt.

Convertible Debt

Some corporate debt allows the investor to convert from a creditor position to an ownership position by converting bonds or debentures into common stock.

The *conversion ratio* specifies how many shares of common stock are received in exchange when a debt issue is surrendered.

Example: If a convertible debenture with par (face) value of $1,000 has a conversion ratio of 20, then the *conversion price* is

$$\$1,000 \div 20 \text{ sh} = \$50$$

When any bond or debenture (convertible or not) is selling at a discount well below par, it is known as a *deep discount* bond.

The owner of a convertible debenture may convert to common stock any time he or she chooses, but common sense dictates that the owner will only convert to obtain a profit.

Example: The convertible (abbreviated in the trade as a "CV") is selling at par, convertible into 20 shares, the conversion price being $50. If the common stock rose to $65 per share, the investor would have,

$$\$65 \times 20 = \$1,300$$

conversion value in the issue. (The CV value is also called the *stock value.*)

Conversion ratios need not be fixed over the life of the issue. The ratio can have a *sliding scale,* structured to encourage early conversion.

Example: The conversion ratio of 20 shares per one debenture could "slide" downward every year, and convert to 18.75 shares during the second year after issue, 17.50 shares the third year and every year thereafter.

The alert investor may have already raised the question of stock splits. If the common stock were to split, then all CV indentures will provide for a proportional increase in the conversion ratio.

Example: A two-for-one stock split in our example would raise the ratio from 20 to 40 shares.

Calls to Force Conversion

If the issue does not contain a call provision, the investor could choose to "ride along" and watch the value of the convertible increase in proportion to the conversion value. Stated another way, the bond price would follow the conversion value. No modern issuer would sell a convertible without inserting a call provision on the issue, however. With a call provision inserted, the issuer can *force* conversion. The logic is simple.

Example: Suppose you owned the convertible we have been discussing, with the stock price now at $65, and a call provision is in existence. All the issuer has to do is send out proper notice of the call, and you have the following choices:

- you can accept the call price, which would be stated in the indenture, at $1,040 (a typical call price).

- you can convert, and receive $1,300 worth of common stock. (Remember, $65 × 20 shares.)

Obviously, the rational investor will convert to common shares, in order to get the higher investment return.

Benefits/Risks of Owning Convertibles

The convertible is unusual in that it usually serves three objectives: (1) security, (2) income, and (3) growth. Very few securities offer that combination. In the heyday of convertibles, the 60s, the selling phrase was that convertibles offered..."the best of two worlds—growth and security." Security was also phrased as "downside protection." Growth was to be achieved by an increase in common stock price, followed by conversion. Downside protection was provided by the creditor position of the debenture, and the contractual interest payments provided by the debenture.

The Convertible Issuer's Advantages

The issuer's advantages in a convertible are numerous. First, the issuer was selling *cheap debt*—the coupon interest rate in convertibles is substantially lower than regular debt (also called *straight debt*).

The second major advantage to the convertible issuer is that the issue allows the corporation to sell its common stock at an above-market price. The conversion value of the stock is usually priced about 15 to 20% above current market price of the common stock.

A third interesting advantage for issuers is that the bond really should not mature, if it was priced well in a receptive market. The game plan is for the stock price to rise to the point that the investor will find it prudent to convert, especially in the face of a pending call of the convertible issue.

The final issuer advantage is a corporate financial management advantage in that the issuer can, stock price permitting, control the timing of the conversion. When corporate financial managers decide that the time is right to adjust the firm's debt-to-equity balance, they can force the conversion of debt to equity by exercising the convertible call provision. Again, market conditions have to be conducive to the timing of the call.

The Cost of the Conversion Privilege

Let's compare the investor's position to the issuing corporation's stance. The "best of both worlds" begins to sound hollow against the formidable position of the convertible issuer. The "best of both worlds" does not come free, either. Investors pay for the conversion privilege up front. They "pay" by accepting a lower coupon rate on the issue.

Example: GTE has a convertible maturing in 1996 that pays 6¼% coupon rate, and a straight debt issue maturing in 1995 with a 9¾% coupon rate. Simple calculations demonstrate that the annual income lost by accepting the lower coupon rate is $35 per bond. The price of the conversion privilege for ten bonds is $350.

This analysis is not intended to paint a cynical view of the convertible—it tells both sides of the story, giving the true price of having growth and downside protection, too. There have been many investor situations in the past in which convertibles provided an excellent match between certain investors and market securities available. The future may present similar opportunities as well. The markets of the late 60s and much of the 70s, for example, provided a hostile environment for convertibles; much of these periods were characterized by rapidly rising interest rates and depressed stock prices. Rising interest rates cause bond values to be discounted in the market and low stock prices prevent conversion opportunities.

Convertibles are a long way from being a "dead" security, however. Whenever stable or downturning interest rates combine with rising stock prices, convertible debentures provide a suitable market medium for issuers and investors alike.

Floating Rate Notes (FRNs)

As already explained, as interest rates increase, bond prices decline. After bonds are sold, issuers are usually locked into paying a fixed amount (interest rate) until maturity or call date. At maturity, bond owners are paid the face value. In 1979, to allow investors to hedge against losses in periods of rising interest rates, to make their debt more marketable, and to prevent issuers from being locked into high interest payments, many bank holding companies began issuing *floating rate notes*. The notes (and bonds) got their names because the rate of interest, which is tied to some benchmark, will change each six months. The rate paid was usually set at ½% to 1% more than the benchmark, normally the six-month Treasury bill rate.

Example: In late 1979, Chase Manhattan Corporation, the parent company of Chase Manhattan Bank, issued a debenture maturing May 1, 2009. The initial rate of interest was set at 10¾% but was only set for six months. At the end of the original payment, a new rate was to be established at 0.6 percent more than the six-month yield on Treasury bills. The semiannual payments from May 1, 1984 through April 30, 1989 will be 0.55% more than the Treasury bill rate. Thereafter the yield will be 0.5% more than the benchmark.

The Chase floating rate note included several kickers. The kickers were included in the issue to increase their marketability. The notes will not pay less than 6.5%, and at the option of the owner they can be converted into 8.5% debentures maturing May 1, 2009. Should the six-month Treasury bill rate decline to a point where,with the additional kicker, the yield would be less than 8½%, the holder can convert and have an immediate capital gain.

Example: Also in April of 1979, Chemical New York Corporation, the parent company for Chemical Bank, issued a floating rate note maturing May 1, 2004. The rate paid by this issue was pegged at 1% more than the six-month Treasury bill rate until May 1, 1989, and 0.75% more than the benchmark until maturity.

The Chemical notes will have a minimum rate (7.5% to May 30, 1984, 7% to May 30, 1989, and 6½% to maturity), but are not convertible into long-term bonds. Because they are not convertible, they pay a higher amount over the benchmark than the comparable quality Chase Manhattan notes.

One bond expert noted that the floating rate notes, even though listed on the major exchanges, are neither fish nor fowl. They are not short-term obligations or long-term debt. The expert's advice to bond buyers was, "If you want short-term obligations, buy money market certificates, Treasury bills, or money market funds. If you want long-term bonds, you don't have to settle for a less than market rate."

Accrued Interest

When bonds trade, the buyer must usually pay the seller "accrued interest"—in addition to the purchase or sale price. *Accrued interest* is the interest that the buyer must pay the seller in compensation for the time the seller owned the bond since the last interest payment date.

Example: Consider a regular way trade of 10 XYZ, Inc. FA-10% of '99 bonds at 96⅜ on April 5. The total proceeds that the buyer has to pay the seller is equal to the trade price *plus* the accrued interest. The purchase price is equal to 96⅜ or $963.75 per bond. Since the trade is for 10 bonds, the trade price is $9,637.50.

You must calculate the accrued interest, which takes two steps. The first step is to determine the number of days that the seller has owned the bond from the last payment date. Interest accrues to the seller until *the day before* the trade settles (*regardless* of which settlement option is used). For corporate bonds, the convention is to assume that each whole month has *30 days* regardless of the actual number of days in the month. Since each month is assumed to have 30 days, then each year must contain 360 days (12 months X 30 days per month).

Example: Thus, if the trade was made on April 5 with a regular way settlement, it settles on April 12, five *business* days after the trade date. The number of days of accrued interest in April would therefore be 11 days—*up to and including the day before the settlement date.*

April*

S	M	T	W	T	F	S
					1	2
3	**4**	**5**	6	7	8	9
10	**11**	12	13	14	15	16
17	18	19	20	21	22	23
24	25	26	27	28	29	30

*Boldface days are accrued days.

Since the bond last paid interest on February 1, the seller is also entitled to receive interest for the entire month of February and the entire month of March (30 days for each month by convention), in addition to 11 days accrued in April, for a total of 71 days accrued.

The second step is to solve this equation:

$$\text{Accrued interest} = \text{Principal} \times \text{Rate} \times \text{Time}$$

The *principal* is $10,000 because the trade is for 10 bonds.

(Note that the purchase price makes no difference.) The *rate* is the bond's coupon yield expressed as a decimal. The *time* is equal to the number of days accrued divided by 360.

The formula for accrued interest for this bond therefore becomes:

$$\text{Accrued interest} = \$10{,}000 \times 0.10 \times (71/360) = \$197.22$$

So the total number of dollars due to the seller from the buyer for this trade is:

Purchase Price	$9,637.50
Accrued interest	$ 197.22
	$9,834.72

Let's now look at a more unusual example.

Example: Consider a next-day settlement trade of 20 XYZ, Inc. MS-15 8% bonds at a price of 61⅛ with a July 3 trade date. The purchase price is equal to 20 times $611.25 or $12,225. The formula for calculating the accrued is:

$$\text{Accrued interest} = \text{Principal} \times \text{Rate} \times \text{Time}$$
$$= \$20{,}000 \times 0.08 \times T$$

The value of T is equal to the number of days over which interest accrued divided by 360.

On the following calendar, the trade settles on July 7. The day after the trade, July 4, is a legal holiday, and the fifth and sixth are weekend days. So the next business day is the seventh, and the trade settles on that day. Therefore, in July there will be 6 days accrued.

			July			
S	*M*	*T*	*W*	*T*	*F*	*S*
		1	2	3	4	5
6	7	8	9	10	11	12
13	14	15	16	17	18	19
20	21	22	23	24	25	26
27	28	29	30	31		

Since the last interest payment is on March 15, we now have to compute the number of days from March 15 to July 6.

Month of March (starting on March 15)	15 days
Month of April	30 days
Month of May	30 days
Month of June	30 days
Month of July	6 days
	111 days

So the accrued interest calculation becomes:

$$\text{Accrued interest} = \$20,000 \times 0.08 \times (111/360) = \$493.33$$

and the total dollars due the seller on settlement day become: $\$12,225.00 + \$493.33 = \$12,718.33$.

While almost all bonds trade with accrued interest, bonds that are in default or income bonds that are not currently paying interest will trade *flat,* that is, without accrued interest. If a bond is trading flat, the seller must disclose that fact to the buyer before the trade is consummated.

Municipal Bonds

What Are Municipal Bonds?

Municipal bonds are debt obligations issued by states, territories, or possessions of the United States or their subdivisions (such as counties; cities; school districts; sewer, water, or fire protection districts; or public agencies or authorities of those governmental units).

The special feature of municipal bonds is that the interest on such debt obligations is exempt from current federal income taxes. Since the inception of the Federal Income Tax Law in 1913, interest on "...obligations of a State, a Territory or a possession of the United States, or any political subdivision of any of the foregoing, of the District of Columbia" is specifically excluded from gross income in calculating taxable income, thereby exempting such interest from federal income tax.

By reason of *reciprocal immunity,* the federal government will not tax interest paid on municipal obligations, and local governments will not tax interest paid on federal obligations. No specific statement of reciprocal tax immunity appears in the Constitution, but the Supreme Court has consistently recognized this doctrine over the years. (The best known Supreme Court cases upholding the doctrine of reciprocal immunity are *Collector v. Day,* 1971; *Pollock v. Farmers Loan and Trust Company,* 1895; and *National Life Insurance Company v. United States,* 1926.)

In addition, states and their subdivisions seldom tax interest on municipal bond obligations that are issued to residents in their domain, *which means that the interest on such obligations is usually totally tax-free for residents of the issuer's state.*

The tax-exempt status of municipals is controversial, with advocates and critics in great number. This discussion attempts only to answer questions investors may have about municipal bonds in terms of their own investment objectives.

Tax-exempt bond funds, investment companies organized to assemble portfolios of municipal bonds, represent an alternative to ownership of individual municipal issues. This type of fund is discussed in a separate chapter.

Types of Municipal Bonds

There are four general types of municipal bonds:

1. general obligations,

2. special tax,

3. revenue, and,

4. new housing authority.

General Obligation Bonds

General obligation bonds are secured by the issuer's pledge of its full faith, credit, and taxing power for the payment of interest and repayment of principal at maturity. If the issuer's taxing power is limited to a maximum tax rate, the bond will remain a general obligation but is usually called a *limited tax bond*. Investors should be informed of such limitations on the taxing authority of an issuer.

Special Tax Bonds

Special tax bonds are payable from the proceeds of a special tax, such as a highway bond issue that is payable only from a gasoline tax. A special tax bond may become a general obligation bond when, in addition to being secured by the special tax, it is also secured by the full faith, credit, and taxing power of the issuer. A type of special tax bond is the *special assessment bond,* which is payable only from assessments against those who benefit from the facilities constructed with the proceeds from the sale of the bonds. Special assessment bonds may also be a general obligation if secured by a pledge of the full faith, credit, and taxing power of the issuer. Special assessment bonds are usually issued in connection with construction of street, sidewalks, and, at times, water and sewer works.

Revenue Bonds

Revenue bonds are payable only from revenue derived from toll charges or rents paid by those who use the facilities constructed with the proceeds from the bonds. For example, construction funded by revenue bonds includes toll roads, ports, bridges, and water and sewer projects.

Revenue bonds may also be general obligation bonds if they are secured by a pledge of the full faith, credit, and taxing power of the municipality.

Industrial revenue bonds are a type of revenue bond whereby an industrial revenue or developmental authority created by a municipality issues bonds to construct a facility to be leased to a private corporation. This type of obligation is utilized to encourage business to locate in certain areas. It affords the corporate lessee a smaller interest payment. The bond issue is therefore secured not by the local government's taxing power, but by a lease to the private corporation. Industrial revenue bond issues—other than pollution control issues— are usually limited to $10 million.

Pollution control industrial revenue bonds are also issued by an industrial revenue or developmental authority, which uses the proceeds of the issue to add pollution control or environmental devices to facilities. These special bonds are exempt specifically because pollution control is beneficial to an entire community.

Housing Authority Bonds

Housing authority bonds are issued by a municipality's public housing authority and secured by the net rental revenues of that authority and by the Public Housing Administration of the United States (a part of HUD). Net rentals should cover interest payments and retirement of the issue at maturity. A contractual agreement between the municipal public housing authority and the Public Housing Administration includes the federal government's pledge of its faith and credit to pay some of the revenues, but the issues are not direct obligations of the federal government.

The proceeds of public housing authority bonds are used to provide low- and moderate-income housing and urban redevelopment programs. State housing development authority bonds are issued to purchase mortgages on certain properties that provide housing to low- and moderate-income families. The mortgages are usually guaranteed by FHA or VA, which are the only federal backing for most state housing development authority issues.

In general terms, it can be said that public housing authority bonds provide funds to build the project, and state housing development authority bonds provide funds to purchase mortgages on low- and moderate-income housing. Interest on both types is exempt from federal income taxes.

Prerefunded Bonds

A *prerefunded bond* is an issue—it can be any of the four types described—that is "called" before its call date by issuing a new bond at a lower rate of interest than the original issue. Prerefunding usually occurs because a decline in interest rates or a rise in the issuer's credit rating lowers the net interest cost of a new issue. The proceeds of the new issue are generally deposited with a trustee, who invests the funds in United States government securities so that payment will be available to redeem the called bonds. If the proceeds are invested in government securities, the rating services usually change the rating of the called issue to AAA because it is then backed by United States government securities, which imply the full faith, credit, and taxing power of the United States government.

Tax codes prevent municipalities from issuing *arbitrage bonds*—that is, from using the proceeds of a tax-exempt issue to purchase taxable bonds, which pay higher interest. The proceeds of a bond issue used to pre-refund an existing issue must be invested so that the income produces only enough to cover the interest payable on the prerefunded issue: The investment must show no profit. An exception: The proceeds of an issue intended to fund a new facility may be invested for three to five years while construction proceeds. A nonarbitrage certificate must be delivered to the buyer of such an issue.

The Municipal Bond Offering

Before a bond offering, the issue is submitted to a bond attorney, who prepares the papers and renders an opinion on its validity. This assessment determines whether the issuer has the right to issue the bond and has met all legal requirements. The bond attorney's formal opinion also states that the issue meets requirements necessary for its interest to be exempt from federal income taxes. The legal opinion does not assess an issue's value, only its legality; however, it must be given to a buyer to consummate a sale. In recent years, the legal opinion has been printed on the reverse side of the bond certificate.

Generally, *underwriters* are institutions that purchase new issues at competitive bidding and resell them to the investing public. *Competitive bidding* is the procedure by which an investment banking firm or a group of investment banking firms submit bids to an issuer for the purchase of the entire issue. An offering is *negotiated* when an investment banking firm, or group of firms, reaches an agreement directly with an issuer concerning interest to be paid on the issue, maturities, and so on. The issuer sells the issue to the group of investment bankers offering them at the lowest net cost, and the investment bankers reoffer those bonds to the investing public.

Municipal bonds are issued to obtain funds to construct, repair, and/or improve public facilities such as schools, bridges, streets, highways, and so on. Bonds are generally issued to finance major capital improvements that will be used over a number of years so that, in effect, taxpayers may enjoy the improvements on a "pay-as-you-go" basis.

Maturities

Maturities of tax-exempt bonds are usually referred to as:

1. serial,

2. term, or

3. dollar bonds.

A *serial bond* is a multiple issue with varying maturities.

Example: A 25-year, $25 million issue may mature at a rate of $1 million each year, thereby retiring 1/25 of the issue every year.

A *term bond* is an issue with a single maturity.

Example: A 25-year, $25 million bond issued January 1, 1974, and maturing January 1, 1999.

A bond issued can be serial for part of the issue, with a *balloon term* at the final maturity.

The figure on page 112 is a copy of the front of the prospectus for Virginia Housing Development Authority Mortgage Purchase Bonds, 1985 Series A. Notice that the issue consists of both current interest-paying bonds and capital appreciation bonds, with maturities ranging from 1985 to 2005.

Maturities are usually arranged to the advantage of the issuer and to afford the best marketability for sale to investors. An issuer generally does not want all outstanding bonds maturing in one year.

Because a large number of term bonds are available with the same interest and maturity, they are generally more marketable and better suited for the individual investor. The investor who intends to hold bonds to maturity may find an odd lot of a serial bond attractively priced because of its potential marketability problem. Large investors, who are usually interested in owning issues in size, are generally not interested in purchasing ten, fifteen, or twenty serial bonds because they may have difficulty finding additional bonds with the same coupon and maturity to accumulate desired size.

Dollar bonds are municipal issues that are quoted and traded on a dollar price, such as 101½ bid, 103 asked. Most revenue bonds trade as dollar bonds, whereas others trade on a yield basis requiring a yield calculation to determine price. Usually, *concessions* (commissions) must be added to or subtracted from the price on dollar bonds to determine the price to the investor. When bonds are quoted on a yield basis, the price usually includes an eighth- or quarter-point concession. When obtaining quotes, always ask if the quote includes the concession.

In the opinion of Bond Counsel, under existing statutes and court decisions, interest on the Series A Bonds is exempt from federal income taxes, except that no opinion is expressed as to the exemption from such taxes of interest on any Series A Bond for any period during which such Bond is held by a person who, within the meaning of Section 103(b) of the Internal Revenue Code of 1954, as amended, is a "substantial user" of the facilities with respect to which the proceeds of the Series A Bonds were used or a "related person". See "Tax Exemption" herein.

The Act provides that the bonds of the Authority and the income therefrom, including any profit made on the sale thereof, shall at all times be free from taxation of every kind by the Commonwealth of Virginia and by the municipalities and all other political subdivisions of the Commonwealth.

NEW ISSUE

$30,277,495.25
VIRGINIA HOUSING DEVELOPMENT AUTHORITY
Multi-Family Housing Bonds, 1985 Series A

Dated: April 1, 1985 for the Current Interest Paying Bonds   **Due:** November 1 and May 1
May 7, 1985 for the Capital Appreciation Bonds   as shown below

The Capital Appreciation Bonds and principal on the Current Interest Paying Bonds are payable at the principal office of Bank of Virginia Trust Company, Richmond, Virginia, Trustee, at maturity or redemption. Semi-annual interest on the Current Interest Paying Bonds is payable November 1 and May 1, commencing November 1, 1985 by check or draft of the Trustee mailed to the registered owner of each bond. The Series A Bonds are issuable as fully registered bonds in $5,000 denominations for the Current Interest Paying Bonds and in $5,000 maturity amounts for the Capital Appreciation Bonds, and in integral multiples thereof.

The Series A Bonds are subject to redemption prior to maturity as set forth herein.

SUMMARY OF MATURITY SCHEDULE
Current Interest Paying Bonds

$7,040,000 Serial Bonds with November 1 maturities from November 1, 1985 to November 1, 1989
$9,025,000 Serial Bonds with May 1 and November 1 maturities from May 1, 1990 to November 1, 1993
$7,340,000 Serial Bonds with November 1 maturities from November 1, 1994 to November 1, 1998

Capital Appreciation Bonds

$2,644,314.65 Serial Bonds with May 1 maturities from May 1, 1994 to May 1, 1998
$4,228,180.60 Serial Bonds with May 1 and November 1 maturities from May 1, 1999 to November 1, 2005

A detailed maturity schedule is set forth on the inside front cover

The Series A Bonds are secured by Mortgage Loans, Revenues and other funds and assets of the Authority pledged thereto, and are general obligations of the Authority, subject to agreements heretofore or hereafter made with holders of notes and bonds, other than the Series A Bonds, all as more fully described herein.

The Authority has no taxing power. The Series A Bonds do not constitute a debt or grant or loan of credit of the Commonwealth of Virginia, and the Commonwealth shall not be liable thereon, nor shall the Series A Bonds be payable out of any funds other than those of the Authority.

The Series A Bonds are offered when, as and if issued and received by the Underwriters, subject to prior sale, or withdrawal or modification of the offer without notice, and to the approval of legality by Hawkins, Delafield & Wood, New York, N.Y., Bond Counsel to the Authority. Certain legal matters will be passed upon for the Authority by its Counsel, Christian, Barton, Epps, Brent & Chappell, Richmond, Virginia and for the Underwriters by their Counsel, Haynes & Miller, Washington, D.C. It is expected that the Bonds in definitive form will be available for delivery in New York, N.Y. on or about May 7, 1985 at the principal office of Kidder, Peabody & Co. Incorporated or through the facilities of the Depository Trust Company.

Kidder, Peabody & Co.
Incorporated

Salomon Brothers Inc   **E.F. Hutton & Company Inc.**

PaineWebber   **Dean Witter Reynolds, Inc.**
Incorporated

Craigie Incorporated   **Wheat, First Securities, Inc.**

April 16, 1985

The Secondary Market

After the original offering is distributed, the bonds trade in the secondary market. The market for muni bonds is primarily over-the-counter, and most trades are made by dealers.

Unit of Trading

There is no specific unit of trading for municipal bonds. However, larger purchases tend to have a "better price" than smaller purchases. Occasionally secondary market trades are quoted all-or-none (AON); in this case, the quote is firm only for the number of bonds given.

Quotations

Serial bonds are usually quoted on a yield-to-maturity basis with a dollar price added as a convenience. *Term bonds* are often quoted only as a percentage of face value.

Example: The quotation of 92 1/8 is a percentage. Hence it would mean a dollar value of $921.25 for a $1,000-par bond but $4,606.25 for a $5,000-par bond.

Spread

In the secondary market, the *spread* is not the difference between the underwriter's purchase and sale prices; it is the difference between the quoted bid and asked prices.

As such, the spread is based on issuer quality, time to maturity, supply and demand, and other market factors. In practice, the spread on municipal bonds ranges from 1 to 3 points; on municipal notes, from 1/8 to 1/2 point.

The spread is also called the dealer's markup or markdown. In the OTC market, when a dealer buys a security from a market-maker and sells it to a customer at a higher price, the difference is a *markdown.* Either way, the markup or markdown determines the spread. Neither need be itemized on the customer's trade confirmation in principal transactions. We should add that there are some who act as "broker's brokers"—that is, as agents in municipal bond transactions. They charge a fee for their service. Agents are used if the buyer/seller want to preserve confidentiality.

Firm Quotes

Since almost all trading in munis is over-the-counter, dealers must be able to communicate quickly and accurately with one another, almost always by phone. Thus, a dealer who gives another a "firm" quote must be ready to transact all that quote, even though the dealer who receives the quote is not obliged to do business.

How does the second dealer know whether the quote—firm or not—is the best available? Generally, a dealer giving a quote allows the inquiring dealer up to one hour to make a transaction. If during that hour, a third dealer wishes to take advantage of the quote, the original inquirer has usually 5 minutes to make a sale or forego the quote.

The most common sources of municipal bond information are:

1. *the Blue List of Current Municipal Offerings,*

2. *the Daily Bond Buyer,* and

3. *Munifacts.*

The Blue List

Bonds available for resale in the *secondary* market are listed by state, along with such information as the number of bonds offered, issuer, maturity date, coupon rate, price, and dealer making the offering. Ratings are *not* included. But there are sections on settlement dates of recent new offerings, pre-refunded bonds, and miscellaneous offerings (some U.S. government and agency obligations, railroad equipment trust certificates, corporate bonds, and even preferred stocks). The dollar value of listing, referred to as the *floating supply,* gives an indication of the size and liquidity of the secondary municipal market.

The Blue List
of Current Municipal Offerings
(A Division of Standard & Poor's Corporation)

Published every weekday except Saturdays and Holidays by
The Blue List Publishing Company, 25 Broadway, New York, N. Y. 10004
Telephone 212 208-8200
Reg U S Patent Office • Printed in U S A

The bonds set forth in this list were offered at the close of business on the day before the date of this issue by the houses mentioned, subject to prior sale and change in price. Every effort is made by The Blue List Publishing Company and the houses whose offerings are shown in The Blue List to avoid mistakes and inaccuracies, but due to the fact that many offerings come in by wire and that the list is published after the offering houses have closed for the day, occasional errors are unavoidable. Neither The Blue List Publishing Company nor the offering houses take responsibility for the accuracy of the offerings listed herein.

ANNUAL SUBSCRIPTION RATE (approximately 250 issues): Hand Delivery (Wall Street Area) $440.00; First Class Mail $570.00

* Items so marked did not appear in the previous issue of The Blue List.
+ Items so marked are changed from previous issue.
c Prices so marked are changed from previous issue.
c Items so marked are reported to have call or option features. Consult offering house for full details.

AMT. M	SECURITY	PURPOSE	RATE	MATURITY	YIELD OR OFFERED PRICE	BY
	ALABAMA					
45	ALABAMA		10.70	9/1/92	7.65	FIRSTEMUB
325	ALABAMA		7.70	9/1/93	7.40	CITIBANK
+ 100	ALABAMA		7.90	9/1/94	7.50	C.S.T
900	ALABAMA		11.10	9/1/94	7.45	NEWMAN
	(P/R 3/1/92 @ 103)					
1000	ALABAMA		8	3/1/95	7.65	CITIBANK
+ 500	ALABAMA		8.375	9/1/95	7.65	CITIBANK
75	ALABAMA HIGHWAY AUTH.		3.60	11/1/01	8.40	FICANY
150	ALABAMA HIGHWAY AUTH.ETM		6.70	11/1/86	5.50	HYANBECK
					5.00	BANKBOST
3000	ALABAMA HIGHWAY AJTM.		9	9/1/89	6.80	SHEARNTS
920	ALABAMA HIGHWAY AJTM. ETM		7.25	8/1/90	6.50	CHASEMAN
75	ALABAMA HIGHWAY AJTM.		10	9/1/95	8.35	PORTER
190	ALA.HSG.FIN.AU.		7.65	11/1/07	9.50	ROTHCHLD
70	ALA.HSG.FIN.AU.	SNGL.FAM	8.50	10/1/90	7.60	CENTRKBM
	ALABAMA—CONTINUED					
100	ALA.HSG.FIN.AU.		8.75	10/1/91	103	PORTER
75	ALA.HSG.FIN.AU.		13.875	12/1/11	12.00	CHEMICBK
100	ALA.Pug.SCH.&COL.AU.	CA @ 105	9.75	12/1/88 C85 *	8.20	TRUSICOG
285	ALA.PUB.SCH.&COL.AU.		6.75	12/1/89	8.40	CENTRKBM
+ 100	ALA. ST.DOCK DEPT.HV		5.40	3/1/93	5.75	STEGLITZ
300	ANISTON MED.CTR.BD.		7.10	7/1/95	8.35	DUNCANWM
50	ARAB MTR.MKS.BD.		7.40	6/1/00 C92 *	7.35	SMUCHET
	(P/R @ 107/40)					
55	BIRMINGHAM INU.MTR.BD ETM		4.90	7/1/90	7.10	FIRSEMOB
+ 990	BIRM.JEFF.CVC.CTR.AU ETM		5.80	9/1/93	7.50	FIRSTCHI
30	COOSA RVR.MTR.SWRKFIRE AU.		9	11/15/95	25 7/8	STERLING
50	COURTLAND I.D.R.	(CHAMP.INTL	5.75	11/1/97	77	BAKRBRUS
50	COURTLAND I.D.R.	SER.67	5.75	11/1/97	76	BEARSTER
	(CHAMPION INTL.)					

THE BLUE LIST
OF CURRENT MUNICIPAL OFFERINGS

Volume 199 Number 33

May 16 1985 Thursday

FLORIDA--CONTINUED

Amt	Issuer	Coupon	Maturity		Yield	Dealer
10	PINELLAS PARK I.D.R.	12.50	10/ 1/96		100	BUCHANAN
20	PINELLAS PARK I.D.R.	13.25	10/ 1/08		100	BUCHANAN
20	PINELLAS PARK W/S RV.OID MBIA	8.000	10/ 1/07		6.90	HOUGHMMB
25	PLANTATION MOR.IZN	9.75	3/ 1/86		9.00	MORIZON
25	POLK CO.M.F.A. SNGL. FAM.	7.50	3/ 1/86		5.00	KIDUHNTA
50	POLK CO.MLTH.FAC.AUTH (ROYAL REGENCY)	15.25	10/ 1/12		48F	MABONIDB
10	POLK CO.I.D.A. (1ST.MTGE.ROYAL REGENCY)	13.50	1/ 1/88		36 1/2F	TOWNESCO
10	POLK CO.I.D.A. (BIO-CHEM)	13	1/ 1/94		20F	MABONIDB
10	POLK CO.I.D.A. (SPRG.HAVEN)	12.25	10/ 1/12		46	GLICKEN
100	POLK CO.I.D.A. (SPRINGHAVEN)	12.25	10/ 1/12		46	TENNCAPC
75	POLK CO.I.D.A. (ROYAL REGENCY)	15.25	10/ 1/12		42	AMERMUNS
10	POLK CO.I.D.A. (ROYAL REGENCY)	15.25	10/ 1/12		39	HENDATL
20	POMPANO BEACH	5.50	1/ 1/92		8.00	STOEVERG
20	PUNT E EVERGLADES AU.RV	5.50	10/ 1/07		9.20	HOUGHMMO
100	PUNTA GORDA MLTH.FAC.AU.	7.80	10/ 1/89		6.50	CHASEMAN
100	PUNTA GORDA MLTH.FAC.AU. AMBAC (ADVENTIST)IADN)ICA @ 100)	9.75	10/ 1/04 C95		9.00	JURANHOF
50	RIVIERA BCH.HSG.CORP.ETM	6.875	12/20/87		5.75	ADVESTFL
10	ST.JOHNS CO UTIL.REV.	4.40	1/ 1/91		9.00	HOUGHMMG
10	ST.JOHNS CO.	7	1/ 1/93		9.75	GAHHILLE
40	ST.LEO HSG.CORP.REV.	6.15	1/ 1/07		9.75	SEMUNISP
10	ST.LUCIE CO.P.C.R.	5.20	1/ 1/00		7.30	GRUNTAL
10	ST.PETERSBURG PUB.UTIL.RV. ETM	5.50	8/ 1/94		8.20	GRUNTAL
10	SARASOTA	5.80	10/ 1/88		7.15	FMS
10	SARASOTA CO.SPL.UTIL.DIST. #1					
10	SEBASTIAN GOLF COURSE REV.	7.00	3/ 1/86		7.00	SEMUNISP
170	SEBRING UTIL.COMM.	11.25	10/ 1/99 C		100	GLICKEN
5	SEBRING UTIL.COMM.	11.25	10/ 1/08		100	MALLIOUH
140	SEBRING UTIL.COMM. ETM	6.875	12/ 1/08 C		9.35	SMITHH
35	SEBRING UTIL.COMM.	9.75	10/ 1/11		11.00	GLICKEN
15	SEBRING UTIL.COMM.	9.75	10/ 1/11		11.00	MALLIEUR
5	S.W.FLORIDA M.D.C. FMA	10	2/ 1/22		11.00	STERLING
20	STUART UTIL. REV. W/S	5.40	10/ 1/99		102	GRUNTAL
	(RICHMOND HEALTH)	13.25	7/ 1/87		9.50	MOORESCH
					8.75	SWINKATL
25	TALLAHASSEE ELEC.RV. S/O	4.60	10/ 1/85		4.75	GLICKF1F
55	TALLAHASSEE MLTH.FAC.AU. MIBI	5.60	10/ 1/92		8.00	HOUGHMMC
10	TALLAHASSEE MLTH.FAC.AU. S/O	3.90	10/ 1/86		9.00	HOUGHMMC
10	TAMPA ETM MBIA	2.30	1/ 1/87		6.10	THOMSON
160	TAMPA GTD.ENTIT.RV.	7	1/ 1/98		6.50	HOUGHMME
525	TAMPA HSG.DEV.CORP. HME.MTG.	0.000	10/ 1/87		10.85	OPCONY
1175	TAMPA HSG.DEV.CORP. ORIG.10.875	0.000	10/ 1/14		10.75	DREXNYEX
10	TAMPA HOME MTGE.REV.					
	TAMPA SPTS.AU.SPL.REF.RV.ETM (ZEROX INS.)	5.50	7/ 1/05		8.80	HOUGHMMB
					9.00	HOUGHMMC
35	TAMPA WTR & SWR RV. AMBAC	10	10/ 1/04		8.15	MERRILNY
500	TAMPA WTR.REV. ETM	6.25	10/ 1/97		103	TENNCAPC
65	TARPON SPGS.1ST MTG.NRSG.HOME RV (GOLDEN MLTH.) (FHA)	14.50	12/ 1/12			
30	TAYLOR CO.I.D.A. (PROCTER&GAMBLE)	5.40	10/ 1/03		8.75	HOUGHMMC
					8.50	HOUGHMME
35	(TREASURE ISLAND C5MY.RV. AMBAC	8.90	5/ 1/96			

GEORGIA--CONTINUED

Amt	Issuer	Coupon	Maturity		Yield	Dealer
300	GA.MUN.ELEC.AU.PHR.RV	9.75	1/ 1/94		8.80	TRUSTCOG
100	GA.MUN.ELEC.AU.PHR.RV	8.80	1/ 1/95		100	AUVESINY
250	GA.MUN.ELEC.AU.PHR.RV	8.80	1/ 1/95		100	MBANKNOU
250	GA.MUN.ELEC.AU.PHR.RV	8.80	1/ 1/95		100	CENTBKBH
100	GA.MUN.ELEC.AU.PHR.RV	8.80	1/ 1/95		100	COLUMCG
100	GA.MUN.ELEC.AU.PHR.RV	8.80	1/ 1/95		100	CRAIGIE
250	GA.MUN.ELEC.AU.PHR.RV	8.80	1/ 1/95		9.00	CBT
50	GA.MUN.ELEC.AU.PHR.RV	8.80	1/ 1/95		100	BURALL
150	GA.MUN.ELEC.AU.PHR.RV	8.80	1/ 1/95		100	DUFTCO
200	GA.MUN.ELEC.AU.PHR.RV	8.80	1/ 1/95		100	FIRSTALB
500	GA.MUN.ELEC.AU.PHR.RV	8.80	1/ 1/95		100	FDC
250	GA.MUN.ELEC.AU.PHR.RV	8.80	1/ 1/95		100	FIKSTCHI
100	GA.MUN.ELEC.AU.PHR.RV	8.80	1/ 1/95		100	LEMISMG
100	GA.MUN.ELEC.AU.PHR.RV	8.80	1/ 1/95		100	JACK
500	GA.MUN.ELEC.AU.PHR.RV	8.80	1/ 1/95		100	AMERMUFL
140	GA.MUN.ELEC.AU.PHR.RV+HEG*	8.80	1/ 1/97		100	SALUMUN
100	GA.MUN.ELEC.AU.PHR.RV	8.80	1/ 1/95		100	SIMUNIM
250	GA.MUN.ELEC.AU.PHR.RV	8.80	1/ 1/95		100	SMISSAM
125	GA.MUN.ELEC.AU.PHR.RV	8.80	1/ 1/95		100	THOMSUN
500	GA.MUN.ELEC.AU.PHR.RV	8.80	1/ 1/95		100	TOLLBEAN
1000	GA.MUN.ELEC.AU.PHR.RV	12	1/ 1/97 C92		100	TRIPPCO
60	GA.MUN.ELEC.AU.PHR.RV	6.70	1/ 1/98		100	FICANY
2265	GA.MUN.ELEC.AU.PHR.RV	9.80	1/ 1/98		8.40	WEISSEHM
1000	GA.MUN.ELEC.AU.PHR.RV	10.20	1/ 1/99		100	SHATKLEE
2770	GA.MUN.ELEC.AU.PHR.RV	10	1/ 1/01		8.90	SUCKLMAN
233	GA.MUN.ELEC.AU.PHR.RV	6.625	1/ 1/02		8.40	STERNREG
215	GA.MUN.ELEC.AU.PHR.RV	9.75	1/ 1/05		9.10	BEANSTEH
200	GA.MUN.ELEC.AU.PHR.RV	7.50	1/ 1/07		9.20	BEANSTEH
135	GA.MUN.ELEC.AU.PHR.RV	6.20	1/ 1/11		9.25	SMITHB
25	GA.MUN.ELEC.AU.PHR.RV	7	1/ 1/14		9.40	BLANSTEH
30	GA.MUN.ELEC.AU.PHR.RV	9.80	1/ 1/15 C86		9.25	HOUGHMMB
250	GA.MUN.ELEC.AU.PHR.RV	10.25	1/ 1/20		9.85	SALUMON
500	GA.MUN.ELEC.AU.PHR.RV	10.25	1/ 1/20		9.25	HOUGHMMB
15	GA.1ST.HOSP.AU.REV.	10.25	12/ 1/20		9.40	TAYLORGY
100	GA.1ST.HOSP.AU.REV.	4.10	10/ 1/87		9.25	SMITHB
100	GA.ST.HOSP.AU.REV.	5	12/ 1/86		100 1/2	SALOMON
25	GEORGIA ST.HWY.AU.	3.30	7/ 1/86		9.02	BEANSTEH
425	GEORGIA ST.HWY.AU.	5.20	12/ 1/87		8.00	CENTBANM
25	GEORGIA ST.HWY.AU.	4.75	12/ 1/87		8.00	PHESCUTN
20	GEORGIA ST.HWY.AU.	5	12/ 1/87		100	ESSEXCO
100	GA.HES.FIN.AU.	5	12/ 1/85		5.00	MERRILNY
					5.02	TRUSTCOG
100	GA.HES.FIN.AU.	5	12/ 1/86		5.75	CITIZATL
500	GA.HES.FIN.AU.	5.40	12/ 1/88		100	TRUSTCOG
10	GA.HES.FIN.AU. SNGL.FAM.	7.50	12/ 1/94		5.50	TRUSTCOG
					5.50	BEANSTEH
25	ALBANY DOUGH.PAYROLL DEV.AU.	5.40	12/ 1/95		5.40	BEANSTEH
25	ALBANY DOUGH.PAYROLL DEV.AU. (FIRESTONE)	5.25	11/ 1/92		8.00	STOEVERG
					8.30	TRUSTCOG
					80	BARRBKUS
					65	TUCKEHNY

PRE-REFUNDED BONDS-CONTINUED

100 ALBUQ.HOME MTG.RV.4M SNGL.FAM.	7.125	3/ 1/10	8.90	ROTHCHLD
30 HOUSTON ARPT.REV,TX	6	7/ 1/10	8.70	HOUGHMMC
225 MET.GOVT,NASH-DAV.CO5,MAE.IN ETM	6.10	7/ 1/10	8.65	BRADTENN
(VANDERBILT)				
25 N.J.HWY.AUTH.REV.	6.50	1/ 1/11	.75	SMITHB
400 MANATEE CO.SWR.REV,FL ETM	5.90	9/ 1/11	8.60	SMITHB
45 HOUSTON ARPT.REV,TX	6.25	7/ 1/12	8.70	HOUGHMMC
320 JACKSONVILLE EL.RV,FL ETM	4.80	7/ 1/12	9.00	KIDDERTA
300 JACKSON H/S RV.3/D.TN ETM	7.20	7/ 1/13	8.70	UNIONPLA
100 N.J.TPKE.AUTH.REV.	5.70	5/ 1/13	.74	OLLNHEAD
250 N.J.TPKE.AUTH.REV, ETM	5.70	5/ 1/13	73 1/2	MABONNET
25 N.J.TPKE.AUTH.REV,	5.70	5/ 1/13	71	SMITHB
125 N.J.TPKE.AUTH.REV, ETM	6	1/ 1/14	75	SMITHB
500 ST.LOUIS CO.MO	8.000	8/ 1/14	8.30	VININGSP
750 GAINESVILLE UTIL.RV,FL ETM	8.125	10/ 1/14	8.35	BEARSTER
650 GAINESVILLE UTIL.RV,FL ETM	8.125	10/ 1/14	8.45	MERRILNY
500 GAINESVILLE UTIL.RV,FL ETM	8.125	10/ 1/14	8.75	SMITHBTA
45 N.M.SUB.MUN.JT.ACTION MTR.RV,IL	4.50	1/ 1/15	8.75	HOUGHMMC
20 HEARTLAND CONS.PWR.DST.3D ETM	8.375	1/ 1/16	8.75	BEARSTER
115 HEARTLAND CONS.PWR.DST.SD	8.375	1/ 1/16	8.65	HOUGHMMC
100 DUPAGE CO.CUSD,IL	6.90	12/ 1/18	12.88	SHEARNYA
25 OHIO WATER DEVEL.REV. ETM	8	12/ 1/18	97 1/2	PRUBACIN
100 OHIO WATER DEVEL.REV. ETM		5/ 1/23	96 1/2	BARRBROS
20 U.N.DEV.COMP.REV,NY	5.90			

CORPORATE BONDS AND DEBENTURES

10 ALABAMA POWER CO.	9.875	11/ 1/98	11.40	KUHLESNY
100 ALABAMA POWER CO.	7	11/ 1/98	11.70	PRESCOTN
98 ALABAMA POWER CO.	12.625	3/ 1/10	12.50	KUHLESNY
150 ALABAMA POWER CO.	15.25	9/ 1/10	110	KUHLESNY
400 ALABAMA POWER CORP	17.375	4/ 1/11	110 1/2	KUHLESNY
70 ALLSTATE FINANCE CORP	7.875	9/15/87	10.15	FREEMAN
500 AMAC,INC	0.000	9/15/92	9.50	PRESCOTN
500 AMERICAN BRANDS	9.75	1/ 1/93	11.25	PRESCOTN
30 AMERICAN CAN CO.	13.25		10.20	PRESCOTN
55 AMER.EXPRESS CREDIT	12.875	1/15/91 C88		
500 AMER.HOSP.SUPPLY COMP.	13.125	9/ 1/92 C90	10.75	PRESCOTN
55 AMERICAN ILL.TEL	5.125	9/ 1/01	11.40	KUHLESNY
250 APPALACHIAN PWR.CO.	7.625	7/ 1/13	12.00	GOLDMACB
55 ARIZONA PUBLIC SVC.	12.75	7/ 1/13	12.90	KUHLESNY
10 ARKANSAS PWR.&LT. CO.	4.625	9/ 1/95	13.00	ABROWNCB
2 ARKANSAS PWR.&LT. CO.	4.625	9/ 1/95	13.00	KUHLESNY
50 ARKANSAS PWR.&LT. CO.	5.875	9/ 1/97	13.10	KUHLESNY
70 ARKANSAS PWR.&LT. CO.	8	7/ 1/02	13.00	KUHLESNY
	14.125	12/ 1/14	101 3/4	KUHLESNY
400 ASSOCIATES CORP,N.A.	11.85	2/ 1/89	10.90	PRESCOTN
473 ASSOCIATES CORP,N.A.	14.375	2/ 1/90	10.35	MABONCB
55 ASSOCIATES FIN.CO.	7.375	12/ 1/98	11.00	MABONCB
100 ATCH-TOP.SANTA FE	4	1/ 1/95	11.00	FREEMAN
51 ATLANTIC CITY ELEC.	4.75	7/ 1/90	10.75	PRESCOTN
10 ATLANTIC CITY ELEC.	4.375	3/ 1/93	10.90	ROALESNY
100 AVCO FINANCIAL	7.75	8/ 1/03	11.25	PRESCOTN
	12.50	10/15/93	11.25	KUHLESNY
	4.375	3/ 1/93	10.80	FREEMAN
5 BALTIMORE GAS & ELEC.	4.50	7/15/94	11.50	ABROWNCB
25 BALTIMORE GAS & ELEC.	5.125	4/15/96	11.50	ABROWNCB
25 BALTIMORE GAS & ELEC.	7.125	1/ 1/02	12.00	ABROWNCB
250 BANK OF CALIFORNIA	4.55	12/15/88	11.15	KUHLESNY
300 BELL TEL.CANADA	9		10.40	KUHLESNY
75 BELL TEL. OF PA.	3.25	5/ 1/96	11.70	KUHLESNY
19 BELL TEL. OF PA.	6.75	5/ 1/08	11.55	KUHLESNY
150 BELL TEL. OF PA.	8.625	7/15/14	11.65	MABONCB
30 BENEFICIAL CORP.	7.50	5/15/98	11.80	ABROWNCB
10 BENEFICIAL CORP.	7.50	5/15/02	11.85	ABROWNCB
10 BENEFICIAL FINANCE CU	4.75	5/15/93	10.75	KUHLESNY
5 BOSTON EDISON	6.875	11/ 1/98	10.75	KUHLESNY
100 BOSTON DISKS			11.05	FREEMAN
135 BRITISH COLUMBIA HYDRO	14.50	4/15/91	110 1/4	DOMINION
109 BRITISH COLUMBIA MYDRO	9.625	8/ 1/05	11.95	DOMINION
20 BURLINGTON INDS.INC.	7	12/14/85	11.55	DOMINION
			8.80	FREEMAN
			11.00	MCLEODYU
50 CANADA (GOVT.)	8.20	10/ 1/85	9V 3/4	MCLEODYU
50 CANADA (GOVT.)	8.625	4/ 1/98	11.30	MCLEODYU
272 CANADIAN NATL.RY.CU.	14.25	1/15/86	114 1/2	DOMINION
305 CANADIAN NATL.RY.CU.	10.25	3/ 1/07	125 1/2	DOMINION
100 CAROLINA PWR.&LT.	4.375	4/ 1/94 C89	11.50	KUHLESNY

The Daily Bond Buyer

In addition to important news, this periodical contains news of pending offerings, official notices of sale, and such statistical information as:

1. *20-Bond Index*—a sampling of medium-quality (Baa) to high-quality (Aaa) bonds with 20-year maturities, indicating a hypothetical composite "bid" by a dealer. If the index were at 6.25%, it would give an indication of the rate at which *new* issues rated A+ (the average rating of the 20 bonds) would have to be offered in order to compete with *outstanding* issues.

2. *11-Bond Index*—contains only Aa-rated issues and thus has a higher rating and a lower yield than the 20-bond index.

3. *Placement Ratio (Acceptance Ratio)*—the percentage of bonds sold from those offered for sale as new issues during the previous week. A high placement ration (90% or more) indicates the public's ready acceptance of the new offerings and gives an insight into the underwriter's risk.

4. *30-Day Visible Supply*—new offerings announced for sale within the next 30 days. This gives an idea of the supply "overhanging" the market at a given time. The visible supply does not include short-term offerings.

Munifacts

The *Bond Buyer* also provides a subscription wire service geared to the municipal bond trade called *Munifacts*. This service is similar to the Dow Jones or Reuter News services, but it is aimed at the municipal securities professional.

How Municipals Are Rated

Municipal bonds are rated by the three rating services, just as are corporate bonds. Ratings are a general appraisal of a bond's investment grade, not an absolute measure of quality. See the complete discussion of bond ratings on page 74–76.

How Munis Are Taxed

The most important tax advantage in the ownership of municipal bonds, as mentioned previously, is that the interest is exempt from current federal income taxes. Neither a broker nor an individual investor should *ever* attempt to be a tax expert, but both should be aware of tax treatment and its relationship to the suitability of certain issues to overall investment requirements.

A municipal bond purchased in the secondary market at a price below its par value (a discount bond) results in a capital gain for individuals or corporations other than banks when redeemed at maturity. (Banks must include the discount on matured municipal bonds purchased below par as ordinary income.)

However, a municipal bond purchased at a price higher than its par value (a *premium* bond) does not afford the investor a capital loss when the issue is redeemed at maturity, and for tax purposes the premium should be amortized over the holding period of the bond.

Example: If a 10-year bond is purchased at 110, the 10-point premium is amortized at one point per year. If the bond is sold in five years, the investor's cost basis by then has become 105 for tax purposes. The premium is amortized to prevent the investor from claiming a loss when the bond is held to maturity, as, by maturity, the investor's cost has been amortized down to par.

Interest paid on a debt incurred to purchase or carry tax-exempt bonds or other nontaxable obligations is not deductible. Similarly, other expenses of owning wholly tax-exempt interest are not deductible by an investor. Thus, an investor who incurs a significant amount of interest expense may find that tax-exempt interest yield investments are not particularly attractive.

Example: John Smith borrowed $100,000 under his line of credit to purchase tax-free bonds. He is paying 12% interest on the money and if the interest were tax deductible Mr. Smith, who is in a 28% tax bracket, would have a net interest cost of only 8.6%. Because he is able to earn 10% free of federal taxation, he is pocketing 1.4%.

Example: Mr. Jones has an investment account worth $200,000.

He uses an investment advisor and pays a fee of 2% for the account to be managed. The portion of the fee that is attributable to the municipal bond income is not deductible.

If you are considering borrowing money or using borrowed money to purchase or to continue to own municipal bonds, you should obtain tax or legal advice, else you may hamper your tax planning.

The 1969 Tax Reform Act also requires that the difference between the purchase and redemption prices of discount bonds, when bought and redeemed by commercial banks, is now taxed as ordinary income; whereas before, the discount, if the bond was held for longer than 6 months, was taxed as a long-term capital gain at the corporate capital tax bracket of 30%. This means that banks are no longer actively in the "deep discount" bond market, and the yields on these bonds are more attractive to individuals. This is a strong point for the individual investor considering discount bonds. Corporations that might purchase tax-exempt income with their excess cash reserves are subject to a 30% capital-gain rate when discount bonds mature.

The discount bond is attractive to the investor who can benefit from current tax-exempt income and wishes to postpone a part of the return to some future maturity date. Discount bonds are usually priced below equivalent full coupon bonds on a yield basis. A 4% bond selling at 90 with maturity in five years offers a 4.44% current yield and a ten-point, or 2% per year, capital gain 6.44% yield-to-maturity. The 10-point capital gain is subject to capital-gain tax but could be offset by other capital losses. An equivalent par bond, for instance, may carry a 6.25% or less coupon.

Tax-Equivalent Yields

With ever-increasing taxes, the tax-exempt income provided by municipal bonds has become increasingly important to investors concerned with maximizing their retained spendable income. Compare taxable income with tax-exempt income: The higher the individual investor's tax-bracket, the more advantageous tax-exempt income becomes.

The *tax-equivalent yield* is the percentage of taxable income from an investment to be equivalent to a tax-exempt yield in your tax brackets. The tax bracket refers to taxable income, that is, gross income less all deductions.

Example: For a person in a 38.5% tax bracket, an 8% tax-exempt yield would be equivalent to a 13% return on taxable income—not including any possible state and local tax exemptions, which would be an additional advantage.

Anyone considering tax-exempt bonds should have a tax-equivalent table and calculator available. The mathematics of tax exemption will be startling to many investors, and will open other avenues of consideration.

A simple formula works almost as well as a tax-equivalent table. The computation shows the percentage of taxable income required to be equivalent to a nontaxable yield.

An investor can subtract his or her marginal tax bracket (maximum percent applied to taxable income) from 1. This is the reciprocal of the investor's tax bracket.

By dividing the reciprocal into the yield available on a municipal bond, an investor can determine whether it is advantageous to own bonds paying taxable income or tax-free income.

Example: An investor in a 30% tax bracket is considering the purchase of a municipal bond paying 7%. The bond is selling at par ($1,000).

Subtract 30% from 1, which determines the reciprocal (.7). The .7 is divided into the municipal bond yield of .07. The answer is 10%, which is the taxable yield required to equal a 7% tax-free yield.

Starting Number	1.00
Less: tax bracket (30%)	−.30
Reciprocal of tax bracket	.70
Municipal bond yield (7%)	.07
Divided by reciprocal	÷ .70
Taxable income to equal 7% tax-free income	10%

This calculation tells investors that, if a taxable yield of more than 10% can be obtained, the taxable income puts more after-tax dollars into their pocket than the tax-free income. This is not the whole story.

Remember: An investor does not pay state income tax on

income paid by municipal bonds issued in his or her state of residence. For example, Virginia residents do not pay Virginia income tax on municipal bonds issued within the State of Virginia. But if they buy a bond issued in another state, they would pay Virginia income tax on the income. Also, keep in mind that state and local income tax is deductible from federal income tax.

Who Buys Municipal Bonds?

Who should consider investing in municipal bonds? Years ago only institutions such as banks, insurance companies, and savings and loans bought tax-free bonds.

Times have changed! Because of our progressive tax rates and inflation, more and more individuals find themselves in higher and higher tax brackets. These investors are turning (and they should) to municipals to shelter some of their income from taxes. Many municipal bond experts say that individuals are now the largest buyers of tax-free bonds.

The investor considering municipal bonds should be aware of their main advantages:

1. *Tax exemption of interest income.* This, of course, is the most important feature of municipal bonds; the income is exempt from current federal income taxation, which affords the upper-income investor a much larger spendable income than could otherwise be obtained. An investor should compute his or her tax equivalent yield (page 120). A relatively low-yielding municipal bond might very well give an investor dramatically more after-tax dollars than a corporate or government bond with a similar maturity and coupon rate.

2. *Safety.* Municipal bonds offer the highest degree of safety next to U.S. government securities. During the Depression, 98% of the outstanding municipal bonds remained in good standing. Obviously, some loss of interest and principal did occur, but an extremely high percentage did retain their credit-worthiness.

3. *Collateral.* The Federal Reserve Board establishes regulations to the extent that securities may be used as collateral. No restrictions are placed on the collateral value of municipal bonds; therefore, investors are usually able to borrow a very

higher percentage of the bonds' value. It should be pointed out that interest expense to carry investments in tax-exempt securities is not tax deductible.

4. *Capital Appreciation.* Discount bonds offer an investor the opportunity for guaranteed capital gains when the bonds are redeemed at par or maturity.

5. *Diversification.* The investor has the opportunity to purchase a variety of municipal issues, which can reflect geographical considerations, desirable interest rates, and maturities.

6. *Marketability.* Municipal bonds enjoy a broad over-the-counter market, which tends to give investors an opportunity to sell their bonds with relative ease whenever desired.

7. *Municipal Bond Swaps.* As in the management of any bond portfolio, bond swaps have become more important. The necessity of bond swaps has grown because of large swings in interest rates, changing markets, and the increasing sophistication of investors. Bond swaps are discussed in more detail in the next chapter.

United States Government Securities

What Are Government Securities?

You may choose to become a creditor of the U.S. government by buying its debt securities, which are sold and managed by the U.S. Treasury Department. In terms of safety, an investor cannot purchase higher-quality debt instruments than U.S. government obligations. These *direct* obligations are backed by the full taxing power of the federal government to fulfill payments of interest and principal at maturity. The only risk in their ownership is with the rise and fall of general interest rates (the interest rate risk). Almost of equal credit standing are the obligations of federal agencies, which are *indirect* obligations of the United States. The authority of federal agencies to issue debt securities was created by Congress, thereby implying the federal government's guarantee. Agency obligations are so respected that national banks can invest in them without limit. The Federal Reserve accepts them as security for advances to its members. They are sometimes referred to as *agency paper*.

The U.S. Treasury Department is responsible for issuing, and paying interest and principal on, all *direct* U.S. government obligations. As for *indirect* obligations, each federal agency issues its own, paying interest and principal. Both the Treasury Department and federal agencies use Federal Reserve banks as fiscal agents, to perform all duties associated with the issuance, collection, redemption, transfer, and handling of their issues. To get answers to your questions about government or agency issues, call any of the Federal Reserve banks or their branches. When calling, ask for the Fiscal Agency Department, which will be able to answer most questions. The names of government securities dealers in any given area may also be obtained from this department.

Addresses and Phone Numbers
of Federal Reserve Banks and Treasury.

Federal Reserve Bank of	*Address* (*Mark envelope "Attention: Fiscal Agency Department."*)
BOSTON	600 Atlantic Avenue, Boston, Massachusetts 02106—(617) 973-3800
NEW YORK	33 Liberty Street (Federal Reserve P.O. Station), New York, NY 10045 (212) 791-5823 (Telephone 24 hours a day, including Saturday & Sunday)
Buffalo Branch	160 Delaware Avenue (P.O. Box 961), Buffalo, New York 14240—(716) 849-5046
PHILADELPHIA	100 North Sixth Street (P.O. Box 90) Philadelphia, Pennsylvania 19105—(215) 574-6580
CLEVELAND	1455 East Sixth Street (P.O. Box 6387), Cleveland, Ohio 44101—(216) 579-2490
Cincinnati Branch	150 East Fourth Street (P.O. Box 999), Cincinnati, Ohio 45201—(513) 721-4787 ext. 332
Pittsburgh Branch	717 Grant Street (P.O. Box 867) Pittsburgh, Pennsylvania 15230—(412) 261-7864
RICHMOND	701 East Byrd Street (P.O. Box 27622), Richmond, Virginia 23261—(804) 643-1250
Baltimore Branch	114-120 East Lexington Street (P.O. Box 1378), Baltimore, Maryland 21203—(301) 576-3300
Charlotte Branch	401 South Tyron Street (P.O. Box 30248), Charlotte, North Carolina 28230—(704)373-0200
ATLANTA	104 Marietta Street, N.W. (P.O Box 1731), Atlanta, Georgia 30301—(404) 586-8657
Birmingham Branch	1801 Fifth Avenue, North (P.O. Box 10447), Birmingham, Alabama 35202—(205) 252-3141 ext. 215
Jacksonville Branch	515 Julia Street, Jacksonville, Florida 32231—(904) 352-8211 ext. 211
Miami Branch	3770 S.W. 8th Street, Coral Gables, Florida 33134 (P.O. Box 847), Miami, Florida 33152—(305) 591-2065
Nashville Branch	301 Eighth Avenue, North, Nashville, Tennessee 37203—(615) 259-4006
New Orleans Branch	525 St. Charles Avenue (P.O. Box 61630), New Orleans, Louisiana 70161—(504) 586-1505 ext. 230, 240, 242

Federal Reserve Bank of	*Address (Mark envelope "Attention: Fiscal Agency Dept.")*
CHICAGO	230 South LaSalle Street (P.O. Box 834), Chicago, Illinois 60690—(312) 786-1110 (Telephone 24 hours a day, including Saturday & Sunday)
Detroit Branch	160 Fort Street, West (P.O. Box 1059), Detroit, Michigan 48231—(313) 961-6880 ext. 372, 373
ST. LOUIS	411 Locust Street (P.O. Box 442), St. Louis, Missouri 63166—(314) 444-8444
Little Rock Branch	325 West Capital Avenue (P.O. Box 1261), Little Rock, Arkansas 72203—(501) 372-5451 ext. 270
Louisville Branch	410 South Fifth Street (P.O. Box 899), Louisville, Kentucky 40201—(502) 587-7351 ext. 237, 301
Memphis Branch	200 North Main Street (P.O. Box 407), Memphis, Tennessee 38101—(901) 523-7171
MINNEAPOLIS	250 Marquette Avenue, Minneapolis, Minnesota 55480—(612) 340-2051
Helena Branch	400 North Park Avenue, Helena, Montana 59601—(406) 442-3860
KANSAS CITY	925 Grand Avenue (Federal Reserve Station), Kansas City, Missouri 64198—(816) 881-2783
Denver Branch	1060 16th Street (P.O. Box 5228, Terminal Annex), Denver, Colorado 80217—(303) 292-4020
Oklahoma City Branch	226 Northwest Third Street (P.O. Box 25129), Oklahoma City, Oklahoma 73125—(405) 235-1721 ext. 182
Omaha Branch	102 South Seventeenth Street, Omaha, Nebraska 68102—(402) 341-3610 ext. 242
DALLAS	400 South Akard Street (Station K), Dallas, Texas 75222—(214) 651-6177
El Paso Branch	301 East Main Street (P.O. Box 100), El Paso, Texas 79999—(915) 544-4730 ext. 57
Houston Branch	1701 San Jacinto Street (P.O. Box 2578), Houston, Texas 77001—(713) 659-4433 ext. 19, 74, 75, 76
San Antonio Branch	126 East Nueva Street (P.O. Box 1471) San Antonio, Texas 78295—(512) 224-2141 ext. 61,66
SAN FRANCISCO	400 Sansome Street (P.O. Box 7702), San Francisco, California 94120—(415) 392-6639
Los Angeles Branch	409 West Olympic Boulevard (P.O. Box 2077, Terminal Annex), Los Angeles, California 90051—(213) 683-8563
Portland Branch	915 S.W. Stark Street (P.O. Box 3436), Portland, Oregon 97208—(503) 228-7584

SAN FRANCISCO (*Continued*)

Salt Lake City Branch	120 South State Street (P.O. Box 30780), Salt Lake City, Utah 84127—(801) 355-3131, ext. 251, 270
Seattle Branch	1015 Second Avenue (P.O. Box 3567), Seattle, Washington 98124—(206) 442-1650
TREASURY	*General information and application for new Bills*
	Bureau of the Public Debt, Securities Transactions Branch, Main Treasury Building, Room 2134, Washington, D.C. 20226—(202) 566-2604
	Specific account information and transaction requests Bureau of the Public Debt, Book-Entry Washington, D.C. 20226—(202) 634-5487

A booklet entitled *Buying Treasury Securities of Federal Reserve Banks* may be obtained free of charge by writing to: Federal Reserve Bank of Richmond, Public Services Department, P.O. Box 27622, Richmond, VA 23261.

Types of Government Debt

U.S. government debt is divided into three categories:

Direct:

- nonmarketable securities,
- marketable securities, and

Indirect:

- obligations of government agencies or government-sponsored corporations.

Nonmarketable Securities

Nonmarketable securities issued by the U.S. government include Series EE and Series HH Savings Bonds. These bonds are issued only in registered form, are payable only to the registered owner, and may not be used as collateral for loans. These nonmarketable securities can be purchased by making application to a commercial bank or directly with the Federal Reserve Banks or their branch offices.

Series EE Bonds

These savings bonds are appreciation-type bonds issued on a discount basis at 50% of their face value in denominations of $50, $75, $100, $200, $500, $1,000, $5,000, and $10,000. (Before July, 1981, the Treasury issued Series E bonds which were appreciation-type debt.) Interest on these bonds is the difference between the price paid and redemption value.

Interest on Series EE bonds compounds semiannually and is computed on a graduated scale to maturity. A smaller effective rate is paid if the bonds are redeemed before maturity. The rate of interest is adjusted periodically to keep it at 85% of the yield on five-year Treasury issues.

When the Treasury increases the interest rate on new issues, the rate is also increased on all outstanding bonds. Therefore, the amount paid at maturity will be more than the face value if the interest rate increases during the holding period. The Treasury publishes redemption tables for Series EE bonds that give the redemption values for specific purchase dates. Most commercial banks and Federal Reserve offices have copies of the tables. A copy of the tables can be obtained from the U.S. Government Printing Office for a small fee.

No tax is due on Series EE bonds until redemption; then the difference between the amount paid and the redemption value is included as ordinary income. The accrued interest may be included in gross income each year if the holder chooses to do so.

Prior to May 1981, the Treasury had always extended the maturity on Series E bonds, and, whenever the rate of interest earned on new issues was increased, the rate on all outstanding issues was increased. Series E bonds issued between May 1941 and April 1952 will not have their maturities extended, and the bonds must be submitted for redemption or conversion to new HH bonds (discussed later).

Following is the Series E extended maturity schedule. Owners should be careful to take action at maturity so as not to lose any interest:

Date of Issue	*Date of Maturity (including new extension)*	*Term of Bond*
May 1941-April 1952	May 1981-April 1992	40 years
May 1952-Jan. 1957	Jan. 1992-Sept. 1996	39 years, 8 months
Feb. 1957-May 1959	Jan. 1996-April 1998	38 years, 11 months

June 1959-Nov. 1965	Mar. 1997-Aug. 2003	37 years, 9 months
Dec. 1965-May 1969	Dec. 1992-May 1996	27 years
June 1969-Nov. 1973	April 1995-Sept. 1999	25 years, 10 months
Dec. 1973-Dec. 1979	Dec. 1998-Dec. 2004	25 years
Jan. 1980-June 1980	Jan. 2005-June 2005	25 years (payroll issues only)

A single registered owner is limited to purchasing $15,000 issue amount ($30,000 face value) in Series EE bonds in any year.

Series HH Bonds

These savings bonds are 10-year, current-income bonds issued in exchange for Series E and EE bonds and savings notes at par in denominations of $500, $1,000, $5,000, and $10,000. They are issued and redeemed at par but may not be redeemed until six months after the issue date.

The interest is computed at a set percentage (7½% in 1985) over the life of the bond. Interest is paid in equal payments over the 10-year life of the bond, which is subject to extension at maturity. Interest checks are mailed to the registered owner semiannually.

As with Series EE bonds, the Treasury has always been willing to extend the maturity and probably will continue to in the future. When interest is increased on new Series HH bonds, payments on outstanding issues are also increased.

An investor may elect to exchange Series E or EE bonds for Series HH bonds (there is no limitation on amount) and have no income tax liability on the accrued interest from the Series EE bonds until the Series HH bonds are redeemed or finally mature. Interest on converted EE bonds never goes totally untaxed. Whenever the bonds (or HH bonds) are surrendered for redemption, the owner is liable for tax on all accumulated income (both EE and HH). As in all direct obligations of the federal government, income on Series E, EE, H, or HH bonds is subject to federal income tax, but not state or local income tax.

Retirement Plan Bonds

From January 1, 1963 to April 30, 1982, Retirement Plan Bonds were issued only under Bond Purchase Plans pursuant to the Self-Employed Individuals' Tax Retirement Act of 1962. *Retirement plan bonds* were only issued in single ownership and beneficiary form and cannot be redeemed except on the owner's death, disability, or attainment of age 59½.

Retirement bonds were issued in denominations of $50, $100, $500, and $1,000. A maximum of $10,000 could be purchased each year. Interest on these bonds was compounded semiannually and, with principal, payable only upon redemption. However, interest ceased five years after the death of the registered owner.

Upon redemption, the interest and principal, which was used as a tax deduction under provision of the Self-Employed Individual's Tax Retirement Act of 1962, is taxable as current income. An owner does not have to redeem all his or her retirement bonds at one time. He or she can redeem them periodically when cash is needed.

Marketable Securities

Certain U.S. government obligations are termed *marketable securities* because, after original issue, they are freely traded in secondary markets. (The original sale is made through a Federal Reserve bank.)

Treasury Bills

Treasury bills are short-term debt obligations of the federal government that carry maturities of up to one year and are issued on a discount basis; the face amount is payable upon maturity.

T-bills are issued in *book entry form* only, that is, certificates are not issued for them. An investor buying bills receives a receipt for the purchase that indicates that the bills are held on the books of the Treasury Department. This is referred to as *book entry.*

There is no certificate to be pledged against a loan. However, if an investor wishes to borrow money using the bill as collateral, he or she may sign the appropriate papers and have ownership transferred to the lending institution (bank). The bank holds the bill for the investor's account.

How T-Bills Are Quoted

Treasury bills are quoted and sold in the secondary market on a discount basis.

Example: The investor pays $9,000 for a 1-year Treasury bill with a face amount of $10,000. Upon maturity 12 months later, he or she receives a check for the face amount.

The difference between the purchase price and the redemption proceeds at maturity is the interest received on this investment. It is taxable as ordinary income, whether purchased on original subscription or in the secondary market.

Treasury bills are the only government securities always quoted and traded on a discount basis; therefore, their bids and offerings distinguish them from other government obligations. A typical quotation for a six-month bill is:

Example:

Bid	*Asked*
8.77	8.69

Note that the bid yield is higher than the asked yield. This reflects the price in terms of the discount from par (face value), the larger discount is really a lower dollar price. The difference in dollar amount between the bid and asked price is the *spread*— the profit of the market maker. A Treasury bill bought at the asked price and redeemed at maturity would yield a 9.21% return on the original investment.

Treasury bills are quoted daily in most financial journals. The following figure shows the *Wall Street Journal's* "Treasury Bill Quotes."

U.S. Treas. Bills Mat. date	Bid	Asked	Yield Discount	Mat. date	Bid	Asked	Yield Discount
1985-				-1985-			
5- 9	7.94	7.82	0.00	9-12	7.76	7.72	8.04
5-16	7.70	7.64	7.76	9-19	7.80	7.74	8.08
5-23	7.64	7.56	7.69	9-26	7.70	7.64	7.98
5-30	7.28	7.22	7.35	10- 3	7.84	7.80	8.17
6- 6	7.30	7.26	7.40	10-10	7.89	7.85	8.24
6-13	7.48	7.42	7.58	10-17	7.90	7.86	8.26
6-20	7.39	7.35	7.52	10-24	7.90	7.86	8.27
6-27	7.42	7.38	7.56	10-31	7.90	7.86	8.29
7- 5	7.60	7.56	7.76	11-29	7.96	7.92	8.37
7-11	7.68	7.64	7.85	12-26	7.95	7.91	8.38
7-18	7.70	7.66	7.88	-1986-			
7-25	7.69	7.65	7.89	1-23	8.06	8.02	8.52
8- 1	7.75	7.71	7.96	2-20	8.09	8.05	8.59
8- 8	7.76	7.74	8.00	3-20	8.09	8.05	8.62
8-15	7.76	7.72	8.00	4-17	8.08	8.04	8.65
8-22	7.76	7.72	8.01	Source— Federal Reserve			
8-29	7.76	7.72	8.02	Bank.			
9- 5	7.78	7.74	8.05				

Where to Buy T-Bills

Bills can be either purchased from government dealers or subscribed to on the original issue from the Federal Reserve. Bids are entered weekly for 91- and 182-day bills and monthly for 1-year bills. Figure 4-8 shows an offering circular and its accompanying tender of Treasury bills form. The offering announces on Tuesday that the auction for the bills will be the following Monday and that the bills must be paid for on the Thursday after the auction.

Tenders may be made through the Federal Reserve or any of its branches, most commercial banks, and some brokerage houses. If an individual submits a tender or a nonbank tenders for an individual, a cashier's or certified check for the face value must be submitted with the tender form. Upon acceptance of such a tender, the investor receives a check for the difference between face value and purchase price. At maturity the investor receives a check for the face amount or can use the bill to pay for the tender of another issue.

The *tax anticipation series* is a type of Treasury bill offered by the Treasury at competitive bidding to provide an investment medium for money set aside specifically to pay income taxes. The maturities vary and are arranged to mature a few days after one of the major corporate income tax payment dates—April 15, June 15, September 15, or December 15. If a corporation actually uses these bills in order to pay income taxes, it receives a few days' extra interest as a bonus.

Who Buys T-Bills

Treasury bills are not suitable for many small investors, because denominations range upward from a minimum purchase of $10,000 in multiples of $5,000.

Treasury bills are a good short-term investment because of the liquidity provided by a good secondary market. The risk is minimal because the bill is short-term, the trading volume is large, and the dealers in the secondary market are of good quality. If an investor wants to redeem a Treasury bill, it is easy to sell that bill to a government dealer at the bid price. If an investor wants to sell a bill, he or she will usually receive a part of the original discount, which represents interest for the time the bill was owned.

"52-WEEK BILLS"

FORM PD 4632-1
Dept. of the Treasury
Bur. of the Public Debt
(Rev. Jan. 1980)

INSTRUCTIONS FOR COMPLETING FORM PD 4632-1
"TENDER FOR TREASURY BILLS IN BOOK-ENTRY FORM
AT THE DEPARTMENT OF THE TREASURY
52-WEEK BILLS ONLY"

USE OF TENDER FORM

This form should be used only to submit a bid for the purchase of 52-week Treasury bills in book-entry form if the Department of the Treasury is to establish and maintain the book-entry account for the securities. If bills are to be held in book-entry form by a financial institution or a dealer in securities, the institution or dealer will supply the form to be used.

TENDERS MUST BE SUBMITTED IN ACCORDANCE WITH THE INSTRUCTIONS IN THE CURRENT PUBLIC ANNOUNCE-MENT. REGULATIONS GOVERNING BOOK-ENTRY TREASURY BILLS ARE CONTAINED IN DEPARTMENT CIRCULAR, PUBLIC DEBT SERIES NO. 26-76.

The following instructions are keyed to the headings on the form:

FOR OFFICIAL USE ONLY
Do not write in these spaces.

MAIL TO
This tender may be submitted either to the Bureau of the Public Debt, Securities Transactions Branch, Room 2134, Main Treasury, Washington, D.C. 20226, or to the Federal Reserve Bank of your district. If the latter, indicate the name of the Bank or Branch. Tenders must be timely submitted, as provided under "Type of Bid".

TYPE OF BID
NONCOMPETITIVE
Check this block if the tender is being submitted on a noncompetitive basis. To be considered timely, a noncompetitive bid must be received by the Treasury or a Federal Reserve Bank or Branch no later than 1:30 p.m., Eastern time, on the auction date, or, in the case of direct submission by mail to the Treasury, postmarked no later than midnight the prior day. Do not enter a price.

COMPETITIVE
Check this block if the tender is being submitted on a competitive basis. If this block is checked, enter the price offered, which must be expressed on the basis of 100, with three decimals, e.g., 99.920. Fractions may not be used. To be considered timely, a competitive bid must be received by the Bureau of the Public Debt or a Federal Reserve Bank or Branch no later than 1:30 p.m., Eastern time, on the auction date.

IF NEITHER BLOCK IS CHECKED OR IF NO PRICE IS ENTERED THE TENDER WILL BE CONSIDERED NONCOMPETITIVE

AMOUNT OF TENDER
Enter the total par amount of bills being requested. Amount must be a minimum of $10,000 or a multiple of $5,000 over the minimum amount.

ACCOUNT IDENTIFICATION
a. Print the name or title of the Depositor for whom the account is to be maintained on the books of the Bureau of the Public Debt. Accounts will be established in the name or names of individuals, executors, trustees, partners, officers of corporations or unincorporated associations, natural or voluntary guardians, etc. Accounts for individuals must be shown in one of two forms: (i) single name or (ii) two names joined by the connective "or". No other form of recordation in the names of individuals is permitted. Accounts for corporations, associations, fiduciaries, partnerships, etc., must show the name of the entity. In order to facilitate transactions which may be necessary prior to maturity, the name of a corporation or association should be followed by the name of one individual authorized to request transactions. By identifying an authorized individual as part of the recordation, the Treasury Department will recognize the request by that individual to dispose of the account without requiring any other supporting evidence such as resolutions, powers of attorney, etc. Paragraphs 2.a. and b. on the back of this instruction sheet provide examples of the forms in which accounts will be maintained.

b. Enter the Depositor's home address or the address to which the Bureau of the Public Debt is to mail notices and payments.

c. Enter the Depositor's taxpayer identifying number. If recordation in the names of two individuals is requested, enter the appropriate number for each Depositor. Treasury bills will not be recorded on the books of the Bureau of the Public Debt unless the appropriate number(s) is furnished. Paragraph 2.c. on the back of this instruction sheet provides information regarding the number to be used.

DISPOSITION OF PROCEEDS
Reinvestment (roll-over) may be authorized by checking this block. After issue, reinvestment may be cancelled by completing Form PD 4633 "Request for Transactions in Book-Entry Treasury Bills Maintained by the Bureau of the Public Debt." Reinvestment may also be authorized after issue by completing Form PD 4633-1 which is mailed with the statement of account.

METHOD OF PAYMENT
PAYMENT IN FULL MUST ACCOMPANY ANY TENDER SUBMITTED DIRECTLY TO THE BUREAU OF THE PUBLIC DEBT OR A FEDERAL RESERVE BANK OR BRANCH. The amount of the payment should be shown on the form. If payment is made by check, the check must be issued by a commercial bank, savings or thrift institution, savings and loan association, or credit union; or the check must be certified. Checks must be drawn to the order of (a) the Bureau of the Public Debt if this tender is submitted to the Bureau of the Public Debt, or (b) a Federal Reserve Bank or Branch if the tender is submitted to one of them. If matured or maturing Treasury securities are submitted for redemption and the proceeds are to be applied to the purchase price of Treasury bills, enter the par amount of securities presented. Describe the securities by title in the space above the words "Maturing Treasury Securities", e.g., Treasury Bills Due 6-2-77.

DEPOSITOR'S AUTHORIZATION
Sign and date the tender. A telephone number, including area code, is requested so that you may be contacted in the event questions arise concerning the account.

(SEE REVERSE SIDE)

GENERAL INFORMATION REGARDING
TREASURY BILL BOOK-ENTRY ACCOUNTS
MAINTAINED AT TREASURY

1. SCOPE OF TREASURY BOOK-ENTRY SYSTEM -- The book-entry system maintained by the Bureau of the Public Debt, Department of the Treasury, is designed to serve those who invest in Treasury bills with the intention of holding them to maturity. The Treasury WILL NOT.

    a.   Arrange for, conduct or handle cash transfers incident to transactions after original issue;

    b.   Recognize the pledge of book-entry Treasury bills deposited with it; or

    c.   Transfer bills between accounts it maintains, except in the case of lawful succession.

2. RECORDATION — The Bureau of the Public Debt will maintain book-entry accounts in the forms prescribed in Sections 350.7 and 350.14 of Department Circular, Public Debt Series No. 26-76.

    a.   Individuals. Accounts for book-entry Treasury bills may be held in the names of individuals in either of two forms: single name, i.e., "John A. Doe (123-45-6789)"; or two names, i.e., "John A. Doe (123-45-6789) or Mary B. Doe (987-65-4321)".

    b.   Others. Accounts for book-entry Treasury bills may be held in the names of fiduciaries and other entities in the forms indicated by the following examples:

    John Smith and First National Bank, ex uw of James Smith (456-78-9123)

    John Smith, Tr u/a Sara E. Coe dtd 5-27-76 (12-3456789)

    Smith Manufacturing Co., Inc., James Brown, Treas (98-7654321)

    Grey and White (21-3456789), John Grey, Gen Partner

    John Doe, Secy-Treas of Local 100, Brotld of Locomotive Engineers, uninc assn (89-1234567)

    John R. Greene, as natural gdn of Maxine Greene (321-45-6789)

    John A. Jones, as voluntary gdn of Henry M. Jones (789-12-3456)

    c.   Taxpayer Identifying Numbers The appropriate taxpayer identifying number (the number required on tax returns and other documents submitted to the Internal Revenue Service) must be furnished for each account established at the Bureau of the Public Debt. In the case of an individual, it is the social security number of the Depositor, i.e., "123-45-6789". In the case of a partnership, company, organization, or trust, it is the employer identification number, i.e., "12-3456789". In the case of a guardian, it is the social security number of the beneficial depositor, i.e., "987-65-4321". In the case of a deceased person, it is the social security number of the decedent, i.e., "231-45-6789", or the employer identification number of the estate, i.e., "89-1234567".

3. TRANSFERS FROM THE BUREAU OF THE PUBLIC DEBT — The Bureau of the Public Debt will transfer book-entry securities under the following conditions:

    a.   A book-entry account will be transferred through the Federal Reserve Bank communications system to a book-entry account established and maintained by (i) a member bank of the Federal Reserve System, or (ii) an entity providing securities safe-keeping services for customers (e.g., a nonmember bank, thrift institution, securities dealer, etc.) which has a related book-entry account at a member bank. The transfer will be made only in the name or names of the Depositor(s) as recorded on the books of the Bureau of the Public Debt.

    b.   To obtain a transfer, a request certified by an officer authorized generally to certify assignments of registered Treasury securities under Department Circular No. 300, current revision, must be submitted by or on behalf of the Depositor. (Form PD 4633 should be used for this purpose.) CERTIFICATIONS BY NOTARIES PUBLIC ARE NOT ACCEPTABLE FOR TRANSFERS. Each request must (i) identify the account by name(s), address and taxpayer identifying number(s); (ii) specify the amount, maturity date and CUSIP number of the bills to be transferred; and (iii) specify the name of the member bank to or through which the transfer is to be made, the type of account at the member bank, the name of the commercial bank's branch, to whose attention the transfer should be sent and, when appropriate, the entity which is to maintain the book-entry account.

    c.   Transfers of bills from accounts maintained by the Bureau will not be made earlier than twenty (20) business days after the issue date or the date the bills were transferred to the Bureau, nor later than twenty (20) business days before maturity.

    d.   All transfers must be in the minimum amount of $10,000 or a multiple of $5,000 above that amount. Withdrawals may be made in whole or in part, provided that partial withdrawals do not reduce the balance in the account below $10,000.

4. OTHER TRANSACTIONS — To insure the proper delivery of checks, all requests for change of address, change of name, recognition of fiduciaries or persons entitled, etc., must be received no later than twenty (20) business days before maturity. (Form PD 4633 should be used to provide such notices.) The signature to such requests must be certified by an authorized certifying officer. A notary public is considered an authorized certifying officer in these cases.

5. CONFIRMATION OF TRANSACTION — The Bureau of the Public Debt will issue to each Depositor a statement of account confirming the establishment of a book-entry account or any transaction or change affecting such an account.

6. CORRESPONDENCE — All inquiries regarding book-entry accounts or requests for transactions after original issue should be addressed to Bureau of the Public Debt, Book Entry, Washington, D.C. 20226.

FORM PD 4632-1
Dept. of the Treasury
Bur. of the Public Debt

TENDER FOR TREASURY BILLS
IN BOOK ENTRY FORM AT THE
DEPARTMENT OF THE TREASURY
52 WEEK BILLS ONLY

MAIL TO:
☐ Bureau of the Public Debt, Securities Transactions Branch
Washington, D.C. 20226
☐ Federal Reserve Bank or Branch
of your District at _____

FOR OFFICIAL USE ONLY

F.R.B. Request No. _____

Issue Date _____

Due Date _____

Cusip No. 912793

**BEFORE COMPLETING THIS FORM READ THE
ACCOMPANYING INSTRUCTIONS CAREFULLY**

Pursuant to the provisions of Department of the Treasury Circular, Public Debt Series No. 27-76, the public announcement issued by the Department of the Treasury, and the regulations set forth in Department Circular, Public Debt Series No. 26-76, I hereby submit this tender, in accordance with the terms as marked, for currently offered U.S. Treasury bills for my account. (Competitive tenders must be expressed on the basis of 100, with three decimals. Fractions may not be used.) I understand that noncompetitive tenders will be accepted in full at the average price of accepted competitive bids and that a noncompetitive tender by any one bidder may not exceed $500,000.

TYPE OF BID
NONCOMPETITIVE ☐ or COMPETITIVE ☐ at Price _____

AMOUNT OF TENDER $ _____
(Minimum of $10,000. Over $10,000 must be in multiples of $5,000.)

ACCOUNT IDENTIFICATION: (Please type or print clearly using a **ball-point pen** because this information will be used as a mailing label.)

Depositor(s) _____
_____
_____

Address _____
_____
_____
_____

PRIVACY ACT NOTICE
The individually identifiable information required on this form is necessary to permit the tender to be processed and the bills to be issued, in accordance with the general regulations governing United States book-entry Treasury bills (Department Circular PD Series No. 26-76). The transaction will not be completed unless all required data is furnished.

**DEPOSITOR(S)
IDENTIFICATION
NUMBER**

SOCIAL SECURITY NUMBER   EMPLOYER IDENTIFICATION NO.

FIRST
NAMED ☐☐☐ – ☐☐ – ☐☐☐☐ OR ☐☐ – ☐☐☐☐☐☐☐

SOCIAL SECURITY NUMBER

SECOND
NAMED ☐☐☐ – ☐☐ – ☐☐☐☐

DISPOSITION OF PROCEEDS
The par amount of the account will be paid at maturity unless you elect to have Treasury reinvest (roll-over) the proceeds of the maturing bills. (See below)

☐ I hereby request noncompetitive reinvestment of the proceeds in book-entry Treasury bills.

METHOD OF PAYMENT
TOTAL
SUBMITTED$ _____ Cash $ _____ Check $ _____

Maturing
Treasury
Securities $ _____

DEPOSITOR'S AUTHORIZATION

Signature _____ Date _____

Telephone Number
During Business Hours _____

FOR OFFICIAL USE ONLY

Received by _____ Date _____

STATEMENT OF ACCOUNT		Issue Discount Price $		Amount of Discount $	
Date	Transaction	Par Amount Transacted		Account Balance	Authority Reference	Validation
		Decrease	Increase			
		$	$	$		

A: Department of the Treasury Copy

Example: An investor purchased a $10,000, 91-day bill at a 6% discount. His or her discount would have been $150. If the investor wants to liquidate that bill in 60 days, the proceeds received in the secondary market theoretically will be $100 higher than the purchase price, representing two-thirds of the discount.

Only a change in general interest rates will have an effect on the amount of discount received. An increase in rates will lower the portion earned, and a decline in rates will increase the portion earned. But because bills are short-term, changes in general rates have a minimal effect on price.

In considering the purchase of Treasury bills, the "coupon equivalent rate" is very important. *Coupon equivalent* is a computation to help investors compare the yields on Treasury bills with those of other investments not sold at a discount.

Example: If an investor buys a 10%, $10,000, one-year certificate of deposit from a depository institution, at the end of one year he or she will have $11,000. If the investor buys a one-year Treasury bill at a 10% rate, the purchase price will be $9,000 and the proceeds of maturity will be $10,000. The yield is 11.1%. Therefore when considering a 10% add-on interest rate as compared to a 10% discount rate, the interest equivalent yield is 11.1%.

The coupon equivalent yield is even more complicated because when Treasury bills are bought at a discount, a check for the amount of the discount, $1,000 in this example, is mailed to the investor. If the investor invests the discount and earns interest, the additional interest adds to the yield.

How T-Bills Are Taxed

For tax purposes the income on a Treasury bill is not earned until maturity.

Example: An investor has a Treasury bill maturing on January 2, 1984. Even though the bill was purchased in 1983, it does not yield taxable income until 1984. In addition, no state or local income tax is due on Treasury bill income.

Sources of Information

Information on Treasury bills can be obtained through a broker's bond department or the closest Federal Reserve Fiscal Agency Department of a bank.

Treasury Notes

Treasury notes are debt obligations of the federal government issued in registered form in denominations of $1,000 and up, with maturities of more than 1 year, up to 10 years. They carry a fixed rate of interest (coupon) and are issued, quoted, and traded as a percentage of their face value. The owner of a Treasury note in registered form will receive an interest check semiannually. At maturity, the holder surrenders the note, properly endorsed, to a brokerage office, bank, or a Federal Reserve office for payment of face value.

Treasury notes are quoted in most financial publications daily and a market is usually available from most government bond dealers.

Treasury Notes and Bonds

Treasury Bonds and Notes

Rate	Mat. Date		Bid	Asked	Bid Chg.	Yld.
3 1/4s,	1985	May	99.15	100.15	− .2	0.00
4 1/4s,	1975-85	May	99.16	100.16	− .1	0.00
9 7/8s,	1985	May n	100.3	100.7	....	5.98
10 3/8s,	1985	May n	100.1	100.5	....	0.00
14 1/8s,	1985	May n	100.3	100.7	− .1	0.00
14 3/8s,	1985	May n	100.3	100.7	− .1	1.10
14s,	1985	Jun n	100.26	100.30	− .1	7.06
10s,	1985	Jun n	100.7	100.11	− .1	7.32
10 5/8s,	1985	Jul n	100.17	100.21	− .1	7.50
8 1/4s,	1985	Aug n	100	100.4	....	7.63
9 5/8s,	1985	Aug n	100.12	100.16	....	7.57
10 5/8s,	1985	Aug n	100.21	100.25	....	7.88
13 1/8s,	1985	Aug n	101.10	101.14	....	7.48
10 7/8s,	1985	Sep n	100.30	101.2	− .1	8.16
15 7/8s,	1985	Sep n	103.1	103.5	− .1	7.49
10 1/2s,	1985	Oct n	100.31	101.3	....	7.92
9 3/4s,	1985	Nov n	100.21	100.25	+ .1	8.18
10 1/2s,	1985	Nov n	101	101.4	....	8.41
11 3/4s,	1985	Nov n	101.20	101.24	....	8.22
10 7/8s,	1985	Dec n	101.12	101.16	....	8.44

Treasury Bonds

Treasury bonds are direct United States debt obligations issued in registered form with maturities ranging from 10 to 35 years. Treasury bonds carry a fixed interest rate (coupon) and are issued, quoted, and traded as a percentage of their face value. They are offered in denominations of $500 and up, although these bonds are usually quoted and sold in $1,000 denominations.

Some Treasury bonds include a call feature in the indenture, which permits the government to redeem them prior to maturity. The yield-to-maturity on Treasury bonds is calculated only to the call date, but it is rare that the Treasury Department exercises its call privilege. The Treasury bond that includes a call feature, often referred to as a *term bond,* can be easily identified in financial publications and offering circulars by the description of the bond itself.

Example: 4⅛ of 1989-94 May. The maturity date of the foregoing issue is May 1, 1994. However, at any time between May 1, 1989, and May 1, 1994, the Treasury Department reserves the right to redeem this bond at face value plus accrued interest.

Should the Treasury call a callable bond, it must give the holder four months' notice.

How T-Bonds Are Traded and Quoted

Most government bonds are so marketable that they trade in variations of thirty-seconds or sixty-fourths rather than eighths or quarters. In a written quote, the fraction is separated from the whole number by a decimal point and the denominator is dropped. The price represents a percentage of the par value (usually $1,000), and the fraction represents thirty-seconds.

Example: $98.6 = 98\frac{6}{32}\% = \$981.875$

If the fraction is followed by a plus sign (+), it signifies that $\frac{1}{64}$ should be added.

$$81.15+ \ = \ 81\tfrac{15}{32} + \tfrac{1}{64} \ = \ 81\tfrac{31}{64} \ = \ \$814.84375$$

The following table shows the value equivalents of thirty-seconds and sixty-fourths. Refer to this table to translate the fractional quote quickly into the actual dollar amount.

Value Equivalents of Thirty-Seconds and Sixty-Fourths per $1,000

32nds	64ths	Per $1,000	32nds	64ths	Per $1,000
+	1	.15625	16+	33	5.15625
1	2	.31250	17	34	5.31250
1+	3	.46875	17+	35	5.46875
2	4	.62500	18	36	5.62500
2+	5	.78125	18+	37	5.78125
3	6	.93750	19	38	5.93750
3+	7	1.09375	19+	39	6.09375
4	8	1.25000	20	40	6.25000
4+	9	1.40625	20+	41	6.40625
5	10	1.56250	21	42	6.56250
5+	11	1.71875	21+	43	6.71875
6	12	1.87500	22+	44	6.87500
6+	13	2.03125	22+	45	7.03125
7	14	2.18750	23	46	7.18750
7+	15	2.34375	23+	47	7.34375
8	16	2.50000	24	48	7.50000
8+	17	2.65625	24+	49	7.65625
9	18	2.81250	25	50	7.81250
9+	19	2.96875	25+	51	7.96875
10	20	3.12500	26	52	8.12500
10+	21	3.28125	26+	53	8.28125
11	22	3.43750	27	54	8.43750
11+	23	3.59375	27+	55	8.59375
12	24	3.75000	28	56	8.75000
12+	25	3.90625	28+	57	8.90625
13	26	4.06250	29	58	9.06250
13+	27	4.21875	29+	59	9.21875
14	28	4.37500	30	60	9.37500
14+	29	4.53125	30+	61	9.53125
15	30	4.68750	31	62	9.68750
15+	31	4.84375	31+	63	9.84375
16	32	5.00000	32	64	10.00000

Flower Bonds

Flower bonds are government bonds with special provisions that, when owned by a decedent at the time of his or her death, permit redemption at face value plus accrued interest in payment of federal estate taxes. This valuation applies even if they have a current market value substantially below face value at the time. These flower bonds have often sold at 25% discounts from face value. The special provisions of these bonds make them attractive to individuals with sizable estates; therefore, they carry a smaller yield than would otherwise be required in the marketplace.

There have been no new issues of flower bonds since April 1971. The following table lists eligible Treasury bonds that include this estate-tax payment feature.

Series	Dated	Due
3's 1995	Feb. 15, 1955	Feb. 15, 1995
3½'s 1990	Feb. 14, 1958	Feb. 15, 1990
3½'s 1998	Oct. 3, 1960	Nov. 15, 1998
4¼'s 1987-92	Aug. 15, 1962	Aug. 15, 1992
4's 1988-93	Jan. 17, 1963	Feb. 15, 1993
4⅛'s 1989-94	April 18, 1963	May 15, 1994

Who Buys Flower Bonds

For the privilege of acquiring an instrument that can show a substantial profit if used to pay estate taxes, investors usually receive a lower yield.

Example: In mid-1980 a 4% Treasury bond maturing February 15, 1993 was selling at 75. The bond had a current yield of 5.3% and a yield-to-maturity of 6.9%. A comparable issue, the 7.875% of February 15, 1993 sold for approximately 76¼. The current yield was 10.3% and the yield-to-maturity was 11.3%. It is obvious that the owner of the "flower bond" was giving up approximately 5% current yield and about 4½% yield-to-maturity in order to obtain the potential profit at death.

Another potential problem is that the current income is substantially less than on comparable issues. Most people do not want to buy flower bonds until death is in the foreseeable future (if that is possible). Often, an agent acting for an ill or injured person will immediately buy flower bonds.

The Bureau of Public Debt may refuse to redeem the bonds

if they were bought by an agent on behalf of a comatose individual (a person who cannot act for him- or herself). The question is cloudy as to whether the decedent actually bought the bonds before his or her death or knew of the purchase.

In the mid-1970s, an individual purchased $200,000 face value of flower bonds to pay federal estate tax while his father was deathly ill in the hospital. The Internal Revenue Service ruled that the individual had no authority to buy the bonds and the comatose individual did not know of the purchase. The use of the ballooning feature (some $50,000) to pay estate taxes was disallowed. Experts advise anyone acting as an attorney-in-fact, or using a power of attorney to buy flower bonds for an incapacitated individual, to consult legal counsel. Several questions need to be asked: Does the power of attorney contain specific provisions authorizing the purchase of flower bonds? Are the flower bonds actually owned by the decedent before his or her death? If a loan was made to buy the bonds, how was the loan arranged? The answers to these questions obviously need to come from a competent legal source.

The remaining U.S. Treasury bonds carrying the "flower provisions," if properly handled, can be very profitable in the settlement of an estate.

"Stripped" Treasury Securities

Initially, to help foreign domiciled investors avoid withholding taxes on interest received from U.S. Treasury securities, the brokerage industry began separating the interest coupons from the principal amount of certain government securities. Proceeds from sales of the parts were greater than the market value of the issue sold intact. The affected securities were identified as *stripped treasuries*. It made this market very complicated because it introduced so many additional varieties; that is, the same specific issue selling with or without the interest payments for the life of the security, and at vastly different prices.

TIGRs and CATS. Two large government securities dealers, almost simultaneously, then created and marketed a new product designed to satisfy investor preferences as well as to resolve Federal Reserve Board objections. It was an instant success and its concept was soon adopted by other dealers who often offered it under their own copyrighted titles.

The product, developed by Merrill Lynch Government Securities, Inc., is called Treasury Investment Growth Receipts (TIGR, pronounced Tiger). The same version created by Salomon Brothers, Inc., is called Certificates of Accrual on Treasury Securities (CATS). In both cases these firms assemble a sizable package of U.S. Treasury notes and/or bonds and place them in custody with a selected commercial bank. The bank is appointed as administrator for the portfolio.

Merrill Lynch or Salomon Brothers, as the cases may be, concurrently sell participations in this unique portfolio with maturity dates corresponding to the maturity dates of the underlying government securities. Subscribers to this package are not entitled to and do not receive interest or principal monies prior to maturity. Each purchase represents a right to a single payment, but only at maturity! Consequently, TIGRs and CATS are offered during their lifetime at significant discounts from face value. The actual offering price is negotiable and influenced by several factors, including (a) the period of time until redemption, (b) prevailing yields for government issues with the same maturation year, and (c) market force relationships of supply and demand.

Who Buys Stripped Securities. Investors considering purchases of TIGRs and CATS should bear in mind that securities underlying these investments are U.S. Treasury issues whose interest and principal payments are guaranteed by the U.S. government. Accordingly, the government's willingness and ability to repay its debt is unquestioned and these issues carry the highest credit ratings.

Nevertheless, prospective investors subject to U.S. income tax may find these instruments unsuitable. The Internal Revenue Code requires the purchase discount be amortized over the life of the issue and the annual accretion be treated as interest subject to tax liability for the holder each year. Consequently, the principal purchasers of TIGRs and CATS in the U.S. appear to be retirement plans such as pension trusts, IRAs, and Keogh Plans that have no current tax liabilities.

Zero Coupon Bonds

In 1981, Wall Street created a new form of bond in the image of the popular Treasury bills and savings bonds. The bond is sold at a steep discount, pays no interest, and matures at par (usually $1,000). The new bonds are called *zero coupon bonds* or, simply, *zeros.*

Generally, when an investor buys a bond, two things are obtained. The first is the right to receive the face at maturity, and the second is semiannual interest payments. Investors buying zeros give up semiannual interest in return for a known compound rate of return.

Example: If an investor purchases a seven-year zero coupon bond for $365 in 1984 that matures in 1991, the issuer will pay $1,000 at maturity. This is an average annual compound rate of return of about 14.75%.

There are no semiannual interest payments (spendable income), nor does the buyer of zeros need to be concerned about the reinvestment of income.

Who Buys Zeros. The advantages to the issuer are its ability to issue a security that does not pay any interest until maturity (retained cash flow). The issuer gets an annual tax deduction on the interest not paid, and the net cost of financing is more attractive than if coupons were sold and interest were paid on a semiannual basis.

The zeros are attractive to investors who don't have any tax liability until assets are distributed, such as retirement plans (IRAs, Keogh plans, pension and profit sharing plans, or small endowments). For a taxable individual, that is, anyone who has a tax liability, the potential tax consequences of owning zero coupon bonds are rather severe. An annual income tax liability exists to the extent of the original issue discount.

Example: An investor buys a ten-year zero bond for $300 that matures for $1,000. The 70-point discount must be amortized over the ten years. Therefore 7 points ($70 per $1,000 face value) must be included each year in taxable income.

To make a long story short, taxpayers who own zero coupon bonds would have an annual income tax liability but no cash to pay the taxes. It is suggested that zero coupon bonds are ideal for custodian accounts when children pay little or no income tax. It is a means of planning, so an investor will know the exact dollars that will be available at a predetermined date.

Obviously, the new IRA regulations passed by Congress in 1981 acted as a mentor to zero coupon bonds. With a $2,000 annual limitation it is difficult to find an investment that can lock up high interest rates over a long time and provide for compounding. In addition, many investments that can be placed in an IRA will present problems of reinvesting smaller amounts such as $25 or $50. Zero coupon bonds overcome many of these difficulties.

How Direct Treasury Obligations Are Taxed

Interest or any increase in value on savings bonds or Treasury bills, whether held to maturity or redeemed before maturity, is considered ordinary *income* for tax purposes. Also, income from direct U.S. government obligations (Series E, EE, H and HH bonds, as well as Treasury bills, notes, and bonds) is subject to federal income tax. These securities are also subject to capital gains, estate, inheritance, gift, or other excise taxes imposed by the federal, state, or local governments. However, interest on direct Treasury obligations is *exempt* from all income or property taxes by all states, possessions of the United States, or any local taxing authority. Many investors are not awared that these obligations are exempt from state and local income and property taxes, and they erroneously include such interest on their state and local returns.

U.S. Government-Sponsored Corporations and Agencies

Securities in this category are usually not direct obligations of the U.S. government but are moral obligations and carry an implied guarantee. The acts of Congress that created the agencies also authorized their securities, which are issued and payable through the facilities of Federal Reserve Banks. Government-sponsored corporation and agency obligations usually offer a slightly higher return than direct obligations of the Treasury. Their extreme high quality and marketability are reflected in the large number of issues and their ready acceptance by investors.

Who Buys These Obligations?

These issues are generally suitable for institutional investors. As a rule, individuals would be advised to invest in direct Treasury obligations. However, a brief discussion of some agency securities may be helpful. Because of size, number of issues, and marketability, some agencies are not included.

Banks for Cooperatives (Co-op)

Under the supervision of the Farm Credit Administration, Co-op issues debt obligations to arrange for the financing of loans to eligible farmers' cooperative associations. The capital stock is owned by the cooperative associations, which are, in turn, owned and controlled by farmers.

Even though Banks for Cooperatives are operated under federal charter and are government supervised, the government assumes no direct or indirect liability for their debentures other than its moral obligation.

The bonds are not subject to call for redemption prior to maturity. The banks issue bonds each month with original maturities of six months, and occasionally they issue bonds of intermediate-term maturity.

The debentures are issued only in book entry form, in denominations of $5,000, $10,000, $50,000 and $100,000.

Interest on these obligations is subject to federal income tax, but is exempt from state and local income and property taxes.

Federal Home Loan Banks (FHLB)

Wholly owned by the members, these banks operate as a credit reserve system for savings and loan associations, homestead associations, savings banks, and insurance companies that apply for membership and qualify. Federal Home Loan Banks issue debentures to finance the home-building industry by means of mortgage loans.

The debentures are issued in bearer form in denominations of $10,000, $50,000, $100,000 and $1,000,000. They are not direct or indirect obligations of the United States; however, they are obligations of the banks operating under federal charter with government supervision.

Interest on these obligations is subject to federal income taxes but is exempt from state and local income and property taxes.

Bonds issued with maturities of one year or less are designated *notes.* Gains from the sale or other disposition and transfer by inheritance of the obligations are subject to federal and state taxation. Interest on notes is paid at maturity and bonds are issued in book entry form only.

Beginning in 1974, the FHLB initiated the issuance of a new security, *consolidated discount notes,* in denominations of $100,000 and $1,000,000. These notes are offered in maturities of 30 to 270 days at the discretion of the buyer. They are identical to other FHLB obligations as to legality, acceptability as security, and tax status. These notes are distributed by four major dealers chosen by the FHLB.

Federal Intermediate Credit Banks (FICB)

These banks operate under supervision of the Farm Credit Administration and make loans to agricultural credit corporations and productive associations by issuing debt securities. FICB obligations are neither direct nor indirect obligations of the federal government, even though they operate under federal charter with government supervision.

The FICB issues monthly obligations, in bearer form only, in denominations of $5,000, $10,000, $50,000, $100,000, and $500,000. Most issues mature in nine months; interest and principal are payable at maturity. The bonds are not subject to call for redemption prior to maturity.

Interest is subject to federal income taxes but exempt from state and local income and property taxes. Gain from sale or other distribution of the bonds, and transfer by inheritance and gift are subject to federal and state taxation.

Federal Land Banks (FLB)

The Federal Land Banks, a government-owned corporation, arranges loans secured by first mortgages on farm properties for general agricultural purposes.

These obligations too are neither direct nor indirect obligations of the federal government but operate under federal charter with government supervision.

The debentures are issued in bearer form in denominations of $1,000, $5,000, $10,000, $50,000 and $100,000.

The interest is subject to federal income taxes but is exempt from state and local income and property taxes.

Federal National Mortgage Association (FNMA)

The Federal National Mortgage Association is a government-sponsored, publicly owned corporation that was established to provide liquidity for mortgage investments. The corporation purchases and sells mortgages by making purchases when mortgage funds are in short supply, and sales when mortgage funds are plentiful.

FNMA sources of income are the interest it receives on mortgages it owns and commitment fees.

To finance its operations, FNMA (called "Fannie Mae") issues debentures and bonds, in bearer form only, in denominations of $10,000 and $5,000 multiples. It will also issue short-term discount notes, similar to commercial paper, with maturities ranging from 30 to 270 days. The minimum size for the discount short-term paper is $50,000.

Interest on FNMA obligations is subject to all federal and local taxes.

FNMA common stock is traded on the New York Stock Exchange.

Government National Mortgage Association (GNMA)

A wholly owned government corporation operated by the Department of Housing and Urban Development (HUD), Government National Mortgage Association provides liquidity in home and federal agency mortgage financing for the *primary market* (the loan market in which the lender deals directly with the borrower). GNMA securities, nicknamed "Ginnie Maes," offer investors an opportunity to participate in pools of qualified mortgages on private enterprises that are fully guaranteed by the federal government.

The registered owner of the mortgage pools receives interest and principal payments on the fifteenth of each month for the life of the mortgage pool. A monthly statement is also submitted to each registered holder, showing the amount of principal and interest represented by that payment and the outstanding principal balance after crediting current payments. Monthly payments may be adjusted by prepayments or other early recoveries of principal on the pooled mortgages.

GNMA has three major functions:

1. it aids in the financing of residential housing through commitments to mortgage lenders when existing funding is inadequate:

2. it manages the portfolio of federally owned mortgages originated by FNMA (in 1983 the portfolio's value was in excess of $3.2 billion);

3. it administers the government mortgage-backed securities program.

Through the issuance of the Guaranteed Mortgage-Backed Security, the GNMA pass-through program seeks to facilitate the flow of new funds into first mortgage loans both from traditional and non-traditional mortgage investors and to increase the liquidity of the secondary mortgage market.

Guaranteed Mortgage-Backed Securities (Pass-Throughs). The GNMA Guaranteed Mortgage-Backed Security is a fixed-income investment that evidences the registered owner's right to receive interest and principal payments made with respect to a pool of mortgages. Although technically issued by a mortgage banker or other FHA-approved mortgagee, the timely payment of principal and interest is guaranteed by GNMA. Each of the individual mortgages in a pool is required to be insured by the Federal Housing Administration (FHA) or guaranteed by the Veterans Administration (VA).

The Department of Justice has rendered an opinion that the GNMA guarantee constitutes a general obligation of the United States Government backed by its full faith and credit, and the Secretary of Treasury has ruled that GNMA may properly borrow without limitations from the Treasury. The GNMA is doubly secured because the mortgages underlying the pass-through pools are initially insured or guaranteed by either FHA or VA.

The GNMA pass-through represents a participation in a pool of single or multiple-family FHA or VA mortgages and offers investors:

1. government guarantee,

2. attractive yield,

3. monthly cash flow,

4. secondary market liquidity, and

5. negotiated settlement dates.

Because the GNMA pass-through represents a mortgage pool, each month GNMA pays interest and principal to the pass-through owner. While the minimum cash flow received by the owner is constant, monthly payments are subject to potential increase due to voluntary prepayments by the mortgagors of the pool or payments on foreclosures made by FHA or VA. The additional cash flow is passed through to the certificate holder on a pro-rata basis as the events occur.

Even though the pass-throughs are issued on a 30-year basis, it is impossible to predict with certainty if or when payments will be made on a specific mortgage pool. The average life of the multiple family mortgages has been approximately 12 years.

The form on page 151 is a copy of the pass-through statement received from HUD (Form 1714) on approximately the 15th of every month together with a check. This form describes, in detail, principal amortization, interest payments, principal prepayments, if any, and the outstanding balance on the holder's investment as of the end of the month.

The interest received on the mortgage pass-through is taxable income for federal income tax purposes. It is exempt from state and local taxes. Any amounts received as prepayment are considered return of capital and are therefore non-taxable.

Although settlement dates may be arranged for any day of the month, the general rule is that most trades will settle between the 15th and the 20th of any specific month. The record date for interest and principal payment is the last business day of the month.

The minimum investment in GNMA pass-throughs is $25,000 and multiples of $5,000 thereafter. The yields on GNMA pass-throughs are generally higher than those of comparable U.S. Treasuries. GNMA experts say that the yield should be compared to ten-year treasuries because of the potential repayments. Because interest is paid monthly rather than the conventional semiannual payment from bonds, the additional compounding under monthly payments makes the effective yield on GNMA pass-throughs higher than the effective yield on traditional bonds. The following table indicates the amount added to obtain an equivalent bond yield:

| Net Taxable Income | | 1987 Tax Bracket | To equal a tax-free yield of* | | | |
Single	Joint		6.5%	7% a taxable investment	7.5% must earn	8%
$16,800 to 26,999	$28,000 to 44,999	28%	9.03%	9.72%	10.42%	11.11%
27,000 to 53,999	45,000 to 89,999	35	10.00	10.77	11.54	12.31
54,000 +	90,000 +	38.5	10.57	11.38	12.20	13.00

Pass-through statement.

U.S. Department of Housing and Urban Development Government National Mortgage Association MORTGAGE BACKED SECURITIES PROGRAM ISSUER'S MONTHLY REMITTANCE ADVICE	I S S. N O. 72400

TO THE FOLLOWING SECURITY HOLDER:

GNMA POOL NUMBER	DATE
.4881CD	JUN. 15, 1981

CERTIFICATE NUMBER	REPORTING MONTH
716583SF	MAY. 1981

SECURITY INTEREST RATE	PRO RATA SHARE PERCENTAGE
12.5	2.22100577

This remittance advice covers the above security holder's proportional share of the distribution in the indicated pool of mortgages for the above reporting month. ☒ The check is enclosed. ☐ The check will be forwarded separately but no later than the 15th of the current month

A	CASH DISTRIBUTION DUE HOLDER FOR SCHEDULED PRINCIPAL AMORTIZATION	$	262.36
B.	CASH DISTRIBUTION DUE HOLDER FOR INTEREST		10,380.97
C.	CASH DISTRIBUTION OF ADDITIONAL PRINCIPAL COLLECTIONS		13.78
D	ADJUSTMENTS (+ or −) (Explain)		.14
E.	TOTAL CASH DISTRIBUTION DUE HOLDER	$	10,657.25
F.	OUTSTANDING BALANCE OF THIS CERTIFICATE AFTER CREDIT OF ABOVE DISTRIBUTION	$	996,296.92

EXPLANATION FOR ITEM D:
PAYOFF OR LIQUIDATION

I hereby certify that the information contained herein is true to the best of my knowledge and belief.

RUSSELL AND WICK COMPANY
(Issuer)

SECURITIES ACCOUNTING SECTION
P.O. Box 132
(Street)

R. W. Johnson
(Authorized Signature)

HOUSTON, TEXAS 77001
(City and State)

In the event of transfer of the security, the most recent Remittance Advice must accompany the certificate.

The one problem with purchasing GNMA securities is that investors need to be aware that these securities are like mortgages. Both principal and interest are paid and after maturity the security has no value.

Tennessee Valley Authority (TVA)

Tennessee Valley Authority obligations are authorized by Congress to promote economic development of the Tennessee River Valley and adjacent areas. TVA's debentures enjoy a senior claim upon the income derived from the power projects within its region built with proceeds of those offerings.

The interest paid on these obligations is subject to federal income taxes but is exempt from state and local income and property taxes.

Federal Financing Bank

The Federal Financing Bank was created by the Federal Financing Bank Act of 1973 to consolidate the market financing of other federal agencies. The bank is authorized to purchase any obligations issued, sold, or guaranteed by any federal agency, and to finance such purchases by issuing its own obligations in the market or to the Secretary of the Treasury.

The bank can issue discount bills (which have the same characteristics, and are auctioned in the same way as Treasury bills), notes, and bonds. Its obligations are direct obligations of the United States backed by its full faith and credit.

Interest paid on Federal Financing Bank obligations is subject to federal income taxes but is exempt from state and local income and property taxes.

Because of their high quality, availability, and marketability, short-term U.S. government and federal agency securities are excellent vehicles for investment of cash reserves and provide safe hedges for investment of capital while waiting for other opportunities to develop.

Mutual Funds

What Is a Mutual Fund?

A *mutual fund* is a type of investment by which many investors, with similar objectives and needs, pool their invested capital and employ experienced management to professionally buy and sell securities of many companies.

Mutual funds thus provide diversification, liquidity, and professional management to the investor who, individually, could not afford it.

Example: The importance of *diversification* can best be illustrated by examining the market decline of late 1972 and early 1973, during which the value of many mutual funds declined substantially. However, if the investor had owned any of the following common stocks, the decline of his or her assets would probably have been much greater.

	From	To	Percentage Decline
Equity Funding Corp.	46	0	100%
Levitz Furniture	60½	6	90%
Winnebago Industries	48½	5	90%
Mattel	34¾	4½	87%
Fleetwood Enterprises	49½	9	82%

And, because trading in Equity Funding shares was suspended for a period of time, the investor would not have been able to liquidate his or her shares at any price, but by owning a pro-rata interest in a mutual fund, the *liquidation privilege* would have continued.

The two years, 1973-1974, perhaps the worst period for stock prices since the 1929 crash, unfolded many problems for mutual funds. The aftermath witnessed mergers of mutual funds, net redemptions, unhappy investors, and more stringent regulations. Also, the mutual fund industry shifted emphasis and introduced many new products to meet investors' changing needs. The mid- to late 1970s saw the introduction of fixed-income funds, municipal bond funds, and money market funds.

As history is an indication of the future, the economy, stock prices, and mutual funds recovered. Mutual fund shares continue to be an advantageous and popular means of investing for many investors and investment situations.

Types of Investment Companies

Investors refer to three types of investment companies. They are:

1. *Open-end.* An investment company that continually offers new shares for sale to the public and whose shares are redeemable on any business day at "net asset value." *Net asset value* (or bid price) is the exact closing dollar value of each of the securities in its portfolio, plus all other assets such as cash and minus any liabilities. The net asset value per share is determined by dividing the total net assets by the number of shares outstanding at the time of evaluation. The pricing usually takes place after the close of the exchanges on any business day, and the total number of shares can vary each day depending on the number of purchases and redemptions.
2. *Closed-end.* An investment company with a fixed number of shares issued and outstanding, the shares being traded on a securities exchange or in the over-the-counter market, like the securities of many corporations.
3. *Unit investment trust.* An investment company that offers the investor pro-rata shares, known as "units," in a fixed portfolio of securities. The securities within this portfolio are self-liquidating and therefore need not be managed. An over-the-counter market often exists for the shares of a unit investment company.

In this section, the open-end investment company, or mutual

fund, and unit investment trust are discussed. Closed-end funds are examined in the next chapter.

Types of Mutual Funds

No single gun is suitable for all types of hunting, nor is one fishing rod suitable for all types of fishing. Similarly, no one mutual fund is suitable to the vast majority of investors' needs and objectives. Many different types of mutual funds are therefore offered. What does an investor want his or her money to do? How much risk is an investor willing to assume? These are questions that must be answered before a mutual fund is selected. A widow generally should not purchase an aggressive growth mutual fund. A businessperson whose objective is long-term growth of capital would probably not be interested in an income or blue-chip fund. However, there are exceptions to every investment situation; therefore, selecting the particular mutual fund to meet the needs and purposes of the individual investor is of extreme importance.

A general description of the types of mutual funds follows. Many funds actually fall into two or more categories, so the novice investor should consider discussing his or her personal objectives, needs, and means with a broker, who will be more familiar with the various types of funds.

Balanced Funds

These funds utilize the concept of balanced investment management—that is, investments among the various types of securities: stocks (common and preferred) and all types of bonds (government, municipal, or corporate). Because many balanced funds are restricted to a fixed percentage of each type of security in the portfolio, they do not always enjoy the full participation that the securities market may demand in any one area.

Bond Funds

A bond fund invests in either corporate or tax-exempt bonds and features relative safety of principal and current income. Bonds in the portfolio are usually managed, bought, and sold as in a stock portfolio. Many of the newer bond funds are of the closed-end type, which will be discussed later.

Dual Funds

These funds are a special type of closed-end investment company that offer two classes of shares—*income* and *capital*, usually in equal dollar amounts. The income shares are similar to preferred stock in that a minimum accumulative dividend must be paid. However, the income shares receive all of the income earned on the entire portfolio, and the capital shares receive the benefit of all capital appreciation.

In essence, the income shares offer the investor income from leveraging their investment—income on income and capital shares.

Example: If $10 is invested in an income share, and assuming an equal number of income and capital shares outstanding, the investor would receive income on $20.

At some stated time in the future all income shares will be retired. Each income shareholder will be paid par value (issue price), and the holders of the capital shares will receive the balance pro-rata to their ownership. This is a new concept offering double leverage.

Exchange Funds

These types of mutual funds are now being offered as limited partnerships because of the Internal Revenue rulings of 1967. The exchange fund offered to swap its shares for the investor's shares of individual securities, and no capital gains tax liability accrued to the investor. The fund assumes the investor's cost basis. Should the fund sell the shares, a capital gains liability will exist. Most of the exchange funds are heavy with shares of common stocks with large capital gains, and the funds therefore have a large built-in potential capital gains tax liability. When redeeming shares of an exchange fund, redemptions will usually be made in shares of an individual security rather than cash, so the investor will determine his or her tax liability rather than having it accrue to the fund.

It may be advantageous for some to use shares of exchange funds as gifts, allowing the charity to sell the shares. A charitable deduction is thereby established, and the investor need not worry about a capital gains tax liability.

Fully Managed Funds

These mutual funds can invest in any security they deem reasonable according to market conditions. Theoretically, the portfolio could be entirely in cash, completely in bonds, wholly in growth-oriented securities, or all in defensive issues. The balanced concept of investing is probably used most often by professional money managers.

Growth Funds

A growth fund offers the investor capital gains opportunities with appropriate risk. These funds generally pay very little in dividends because they invest in companies that reinvest most of their profits into research and development. The profit should come from capital appreciation. The danger in growth funds is overspeculation, as was seen in the late 1960s and early 1970s, which exposes the investor to an undue amount of risk. This type of fund should be thoroughly researched and the commensurate risk fully understood. The investor may choose between funds with a moderate growth objective or a high-risk *performance* fund.

Growth-Income Funds

Investors in these funds are seeking reasonable income from their investments, along with some opportunity for growth of income. The investor whose objectives pretty much follow the "middle of the road"—that is, one who does not want to take excessive risks, yet wants his or her money to compound at a reasonable rate—should consider this type of fund.

Income Funds

Income funds' primary objective is maximum yield. Most Income funds can invest in preferred and common stocks, as well as convertible bonds and high-yielding common stocks. However, the investor seeking high current yield will probably have to forego some capital gains opportunities.

Leveraged Funds

Leveraged funds can adopt policies that permit them to borrow money in addition to the invested capital. If the market goes up, a profit is made on the borrowed money as well as on the invested capital. However, if the market goes down, money is lost on the borrowed money as well as on the invested capital. The leverage aspect usually means the funds will have a much greater volatility than the market in general. This type of mutual fund should be considered only by very sophisticated investors who are willing to assume the additional risk.

Money Market Fund

These are usually no-load and invest in short-term debt securities, certificates of deposit, commercial paper, bankers' acceptances, and government securities. Because of their size (buying power) and contacts, the funds can usually obtain a higher yield on short-term investments than can individual investors.

Prices of some money market funds are constant at $1 per share—buy at $1, sell at $1—and only the rate of interest fluctuates. The price of some of the funds fluctuates as does the value of the underlying securities in the portfolio. Changes in value can increase or decrease the price, or increase or decrease the yield. These changes will be discussed later.

Interest, earned on a daily basis, is either paid to the shareholder or reinvested at the end of each month. The rate of interest paid fluctuates on a daily basis because a percentage of the short-term investments in the portfolio mature daily and must be reinvested. The new rate may be higher or lower than the rate on the maturing paper, depending on market conditions.

Money market funds provide a profitable short-term or temporary investment because the yields at times are larger than most investors can obtain elsewhere, and the funds can usually be redeemed on one day's notice.

Municipal Bond Funds

One of the newest types of mutual funds is the municipal tax-exempt bond fund. Mutual funds were first permitted to pass through their tax-exempt income to shareholders because of legislation passed in 1976. Up to 1976, the only tax-exempt funds that could pass through tax-exempt income to their shareholders were the *unit investment trusts.*

Municipal bond funds appealed to investors seeking tax-exempt income by investing in a broad range of tax-exempt securities issued by states, cities, and other local governments. The interest earned from the tax-exempt bonds is passed through to shareholders free of federal income tax. The shareholders of most municipal bond funds must include a large portion of the interest received as taxable income for state income tax purposes. Only the income derived from their state of residency is exempt from state income tax.

Option Income Funds

The investment objective of these funds is to seek a high current return by investing primarily in dividend paying stocks on which call options are traded on national exchanges. Current return generally consists of dividends, premiums from the expired call options, net short-term gains resulting from the sales of portfolio securities on the exercise of options, and profits from closing (buying) purchase transactions.

Unit Investment Trust

The unit investment trust is best exemplified by the tax-exempt bond fund. The *tax-exempt bond fund* is an investment company of the unit trust type comprising a diversified, professionally-selected portfolio of municipal bonds that offers the investor income exempt from all federal income taxes.

The sponsor, usually a brokerage house with municipal bond expertise, assembles a portfolio of tax-exempt bonds, then deposits them with the trustee, a large bank, and offers the public unit participation in the fund. The investor purchases a *unit* (a part of the existing portfolio), usually priced at about $100 plus accrued interest (see "Accrued Interest," pages 102–105), which entitles him or her to a proportionate share of the tax-free interest income.

Example: Typically, a portfolio consists of 30 separate issues of bonds with a total value of $30,000,000. Each unit has a value of about 1/300,000 of the portfolio, and a unitholder owns an undivided interest in the principal and interest income of that $30,000,000 portfolio.

Upon call, redemption, or maturity of a bond in the portfolio, the trustee must distribute the proceeds (capital) to the unitholders in proportion to their shares. As a unit investment trust, there can be no reinvestment of proceeds.

The trustee provides the following services to the investor:

1. clips interest coupons,

2. watches for calls in advance of maturity,

3. collects and distributes interest,

4. provides an audited annual report to unitholders,

5. collects and distributes proceeds from calls, redemptions, and maturities, and

6. safekeeps the bonds.

The tax-exempt bond fund has no *maturity* as such. The portfolio usually consists of long-term bonds of 20- to 30-year maturities that provide the investor with tax-free income for as long as possible, eliminating the need to continually make reinvestment decisions. At some time in the future, when most bonds in the portfolio have matured, the remaining bonds will be liquidated by the trustee and proceeds distributed, dissolving the fund.

When a bond in the portfolio is called, redeemed, or matures, the trustee distributes to the unitholder his or her portion of the proceeds, most of the distribution being a tax-free return of capital. Technically, under Section 676(a) of the Internal Revenue Code of 1954, each unitholder will have a taxable event (capital gain or loss) when a bond in the portfolio is disposed of. However, as a matter of practical application, most people do not declare a capital gain or loss until they sell the units or have recovered their investment cost from principal distributions. *An investor should consult a tax advisor for advice relating to his or her individual circumstance.*

The *sales charge* (or load), usually 3 to 4½%, is included

in the public offering price on new issues. There is no management or redemption fee; however, a nominal trustee and evaluation fee, usually less than $.25 per $1,000 unit, is charged annually.

Many firms are sponsoring bond funds. Some are: John Nuveen & Co., E.F. Hutton & Co.; Paine, Webber, Jackson & Curtis; and Merrill Lynch, Pierce, Fenner & Smith. John Nuveen & Co. (61 Broadway, New York), a pioneer in this product, has sold a series of these funds since 1961, and is the largest single sponsor of the tax-exempt funds with upwards of $1 billion outstanding.

Benefits

The tax-exempt bond fund offers:

1. *The Tax-Exempt Feature.* The investor must consider how much he or she would have to obtain in taxable income to equate to the fund's tax-free income.

Example: These funds generally were offering current returns of 8½% to 10¼% late in 1984 and early 1985. The after-tax yield to the investor is the attraction, when compared with taxable securities. One fund was offered in 1975 at an initial price of $103.15 per unit, paying $7.22 annually. An investment of $10,315 plus accrued interest would have brought the investor $722 annually, or 7.00%.

If, in that year the investor had a taxable income of $40,000 and files a joint return, he or she was in the 33% tax bracket and would have had to obtain a taxable return of approximately 11.94% to equal 8% offered by a tax-exempt fund. In effect, the investor could receive $8,000 income per year tax-free. All that was required was to invest $100,000 in the tax-exempt bond fund. (The 1986 Tax Reform Act has placed a maximum on income tax rates and therefore has reduced the appeal of the tax-exempt feature for some investors.)

Instate bonds are bonds issued by a municipality or state in which the owner is a resident. Puerto Rico's obligations are exempt from *all* state and local taxes. Interest from instate bonds in the portfolio is exempt from state and local taxes. Some tax-exempt bond funds are put together to include municipal issues from only one state so that the investor who is a resident of that state will receive regular income exempt from federal, state, and local taxes.

Example: E.F. Hutton & Company, Inc., through its New York Series Tax-Exempt Fund, provides New York residents income exempt from federal income taxes and New York income taxes.

2. *Diversification.* In a manner of speaking, a bond fund investor is buying a share in a "Millionaires' Portfolio." Because municipal bonds are issued in $5,000 denominations, a portfolio containing 30 issues would require an investment of $150,000 to get the same diversification available through a bond fund.

3. *Selection and Surveillance of Portfolio.* In selecting a tax-exempt bond fund, it is imperative that the sponsor have the municipal bond research capacity for continual surveillance of the portfolio.

4. *Liquidity.* The trustee is obligated to redeem the units, some on any business day, others once a week. Obviously, the funds that only redeem weekly could develop problems. Many sponsors provide a "secondary market" for the units, and they purchase them at net asset value plus accrued interest and reoffer them to other investors. By providing the secondary market, the sponsor eliminates the necessity for the trustees having to redeem bonds to meet redemptions and, in my opinion, this feature adds to the quality and longevity of the bond fund.

Normally, there is a liquidity problem for the odd-lot municipal bond investor. A round-lot of municipal bonds is generally considered to be 25 bonds ($25,000 face value) and most business is done in amounts of $100,000, $500,000, or $1,000,000. Therefore, a dealer repurchasing small lots must make enough profit to cover his or her "risk"—the problem in finding a buyer for a small amount of a particular bond. This can cost the seller several "points" (a *point* is $10 per thousand).

A bond fund should provide a secondary market, as well as *proven ability, experience,* and *willingness* to meet its implied obligations.

5. *Convenience.* Interest checks are mailed regularly; the investor need not worry about no safekeeping, recordkeeping, or coupon collection.

6. *Conservation of Capital.* Municipal bonds, as a group, are considered to offer the highest degree of safety next to United States government bonds.

Comments

Any money to be invested in a tax-exempt bond fund should be surplus, idle money. The investor's tax situation should be such that his or her after-tax income will be increased by receiving tax-exempt income.

Services Provided by Mutual Funds

The following are some of the services provided by a mutual fund:

Single Purchase. Shares in a mutual fund represent a diversified, professionally managed list of securities indicating fractional ownership in perhaps 50 to 100 or more companies. The convenience of a single certificate simplifies recordkeeping, accounting, and decision making. Dividends and capital gains can be paid directly to the investor unless otherwise directed as in a "reinvestment account."

Automatic Reinvestment. Most mutual funds offer shareholders automatic reinvestment privileges, thereby allowing reinvestment of income and capital gain distributions in additional shares. Capital gains distributions are usually reinvested at net asset value. Dividend income and net short-term profits are reinvested by most funds at the net asset value. Even if an investor automatically reinvests the income and capital gains distributions from a mutual fund, the amount of the distribution will have to be included as taxable income each year.

Income. The owner of mutual fund shares receives varying amounts of income from dividends and interest on the fund's portfolio securities, after operating expenses and management fees. He or she may also receive as income net short-term profits on securities held for less than six months.

Capital Gains Distribution. The shareholder also receives, on an annual basis, net long-term profits realized on the sale of portfolio securities held for longer than six months, when and if they occur. Regardless of the length of time a mutual fund is owned, the capital gains distribution is considered a long-term capital gain for tax purposes.

Accumulation Accounts. Most mutual funds offer the individual of modest means an opportunity to build capital assets with relatively small purchases, usually out of current income over a period of time. This is also known as "systematic investing," "periodic investment plan," or "pay-as-you-go investing."

Accumulation plans should be regarded as long-term investments and can be used in conjunction with pension, profit-sharing, thrift, and other investment programs.

Withdrawal Plans. Most mutual funds offer a service allowing shareholders to receive regular payments from their investments, calculated as fixed dollar amounts or on any of several other bases. The most important feature of a withdrawal plan is that the balance of the principal remains fully invested and always at work. Withdrawal plans, an important element of the total investment package, are covered in detail later in this chapter.

Exchange Privilege. This privilege allows a shareholder to exchange his or her holdings from one fund to another within the same group of funds. This transaction may be necessary as an investor's needs and objectives change. For instance, the investor may have originally invested in a.growth fund to accumulate capital. But upon retirement, the objective becomes one of stability and current income; therefore, the investor could exchange the shares for an income fund.

Many investors now use a *family* of funds, that is, several mutual funds with differing objectives under one management as a means of managing their money. When they feel stock prices will rise, they switch to a common stock growth fund. In uncertain times, they will want to transfer their account to a money market fund. If they feel interest rates will decline, they may want to own a bond fund.

There are many investment advisory services to assist investors with timing (conversion) decisions. Some mutual funds make a nominal charge for this service.

An exchange causes a taxable event on the sale of the original fund. When making an exchange, it is important that the cost basis of the shares being sold be determined: Dividend and capital gains distributions reinvested over the years are added to the cash originally invested to determine the taxable cost basis.

An investor may use the exchange privilege to advantage when a market decline results in a loss in one fund. By making an exchange, a loss for tax purposes may be taken. After a period of time (at least 31 days) a conversion back to the original fund can be made—a considerable tax advantage with very little, if any, out-of-pocket cost.

Example: Mr. Investor purchased 1000 shares of XYZ Growth Fund at the asked price of $10.87 ($10,870) in January of 1988. In June of 1988 his shares had a value of $7,000. At that time, the shares could be exchanged to XYZ Income Fund, creating a tax loss of approximately $3,870. After 31 days, the XYZ Income Fund shares could be exchanged back to XYZ Growth Fund, and, depending on market conditions, a short-term gain or loss may have been created on this latter transaction. The short-term loss on the original exchange can be used to offset other profits or carried forward to offset profits in future years.

Note: In making such an exchange, you must be aware of IRS regulations regarding *wash sales*—a loss on the same or similar securities is not allowed if repurchased thirty days before or after the closing transaction establishing the loss.

An investor in a high tax bracket may buy shares of one fund in a group and then, after a short time, convert these shares to the fund he or she wants to be in. The sales charge will then become a short-term tax loss.

Example: Buy 1,000 shares of XYZ Income Fund at the asked price of $10.87 per share ($10,870). In a short time sell these shares at $10.00 ($10,000) and exchange the proceeds to XYZ Growth Fund, thereby creating a short-term tax loss of $870.

Liquidity. Open-end investment companies stand ready to redeem their shares at any time, providing the investor with a ready cash market for his or her shares. A shareholder can sell part or all of his or her shares at any time and does not have to depend on a buyer. The fund itself will buy them back, usually at net asset value at the time of redemption, which may be lower or higher than the investor's cost, depending on market conditions.

Redemption procedures vary. Usually if the investor possesses issued certificates, they may be redeemed by telephone by most brokerage houses with delivery of properly guaranteed certificates to follow. The stock power must be guaranteed (signed) by a brokerage house who is a member of a national exchange or a national bank. If the shares are unissued and held by a transfer agent,* usually a redemption letter and a stock power with signatures guaranteed are required.

Rights of Accumulation. By this right, an investor is entitled to a reduction in the sales charge on new purchases based on existing holdings within the fund or family of funds. Most mutual fund organizations offer this privilege to all investors. The right exists when a new purchase, combined with the value of existing holdings, exceeds a *breakpoint* (a dollar value of mutual fund shares whereby the sales charge becomes lower).

Example: Mrs. Moderate Means owns $40,000 worth of XYZ Mutual Fund, in which the breakpoint is $50,000. She purchases $12,000 in shares, bringing her total ownership up to $52,000 and entitling her to the lower sales charge rate on the $12,000 purchase.

Letter of Intention. An investor who signs a letter, stating that he or she intends to invest an indicated amount within a period of 13 months, is entitled to an initial quantity discount. All investments made within this time period are made at the sales charge applicable to the total intended investment.

Example: Because he will be converting certificates of deposit over the next year or so, Mr. Getrich can reasonably invest $25,000 over 13 months, but only has $5,000 at the moment. He may sign a $25,000 letter of intent, thereby investing at that commission rate for the 13-month period.

If the investor fails to complete his or her letter of intention, the investor will be required to pay the difference in the sales

---

*The custodian, usually a bank, is under contract to the mutual fund to hold in custody and safekeeping the securities and other assets of the fund. The custodian often is the mutual fund's registrar, transfer agent, and dividend disbursing agent. It in no way participates in the management of the mutual fund.

charge, either in cash or by redeeming an appropriate number of shares held in escrow.

Information. Mutual funds are required to inform shareholders regularly on the operations of the fund and how the investor's money is being invested. These reports will list the names and amounts of securities held, and in most cases they will also show the major changes within the portfolios.

Mutual funds mail the shareholder a statement each time a transaction occurs in his or her account. On page 168 is a cumulative confirmation from Massachusetts Financial Services, which is similar to ones used by most mutual funds.

Most mutual funds report to the investor the distributions, investment income, and capital gains to be included in federal tax returns. The year-end tax statements are also mailed to each shareholder.

A most important consideration is a mutual fund's benefits and services. The only performance question is, "Does the mutual fund offer the investor the services needed and has that mutual fund consistently been able to accomplish its stated objectives?"

The Cost of Investing In Mutual Funds

Every investment has a cost. Cost per se should not be a determining factor in the investment of one's money, but an investigation should be made to ensure that the cost is not excessive if the investment has the potential for accomplishing the results desired. Investors who decide to select and purchase their securities (with a broker's assistance) should invest in financial publications such as *The Wall Street Journal, Business Week,* and *Barron's*, besides spending a considerable amount of time and paying commissions on each buy and sell transaction. Should they elect to have their money invested by an investment counselor, commissions on buy and sell transactions must be paid, and there will be a fee to the investment counselor, and often a custodial fee must be paid to the bank or trust department holding the securities. Also, a fee must be paid for the year-end tax work. If investors desire to have their money invested by the trust department of a bank, a fee must be paid to that trust department.

MFS FAMILY OF FUNDS

MASSACHUSETTS CAPITAL DEVELOPMENT FUND

Year-To-Date-Statement

YOUR ACCOUNT NUMBER	DISTRIB OPTION*	SOCIAL SECURITY OR TAX IDENTIFYING NO	ACCOUNT TYPE*	STATEMENT DATE	REPRESENTATIVE	DEALER NUMBER
16-5311-123-456	A	123-45-6789	1	12-31-82	Harper Richmond	5086454005

PLEASE REFER TO THIS NUMBER IN ALL CORRESPONDENCE

JOHN Q. INVESTOR
100 PARK AVENUE
RICHMOND, VA 23211

SHAREHOLDER

DEALER

DAVENPORT & CO. OF VA, INC.
P.O. BOX 1377
RICHMOND, VA 23211

YEAR-TO-DATE ACTIVITY IN YOUR ACCOUNT

DATE	TRANSACTION NUMBER	TYPE OF TRANSACTION	DOLLAR AMOUNT	PRICE PER SHARE	SHARES THIS TRANSACTION	TOTAL SHARES
01/04	N040378	SHARES PURCHASED	5000.00	8.98	556.793	556.793
01/29	N290796	SHARES PURCHASED	200.00	8.86	22.573	579.366
02/26	N260098	SHARES PURCHASED	200.00	8.49	23.557	602.923
03/31	N310924	SHARES PURCHASED	200.00	7.88	25.381	628.304
04/30	8000001	DIVIDEND REINVESTED @ .15	90.44	7.88	11.477	639.781
04/30	8000002	CAP GAIN REINVESTED @ .349	210.42	7.31	28.785	668.566
04/30	N300656	SHARES PURCHASED	200.00	8.32	24.038	692.604
05/28	N280529	SHARES PURCHASED	200.00	8.04	24.876	717.484
06/30	N300438	SHARES PURCHASED	200.00	8.11	24.661	742.141
07/30	N300833	SHARES PURCHASED	200.00	8.01	24.969	767.110
08/31	N310052	SHARES PURCHASED	200.00	8.97	22.297	789.407
09/30	N300345	SHARES PURCHASED	200.00	8.84	22.624	812.031
10/29	8000003	DIVIDEND REINVESTED @ .15	118.41	8.84	13.395	825.426
10/29	N290774	SHARES PURCHASED	200.00	10.21	19.589	845.015
11/30	N300321	SHARES PURCHASED	200.00	11.36	17.606	862.621

THIS IS A SUMMARY OF YOUR ACCOUNT

CURRENT YEAR'S ACTIVITY			YOUR FUND SHARE BALANCE		
INVESTMENTS	DIVIDENDS	CAPITAL GAINS	CERTIFICATE SHARES HELD BY YOU	+ ON DEPOSIT WITH AGENT	= TOTAL SHARES OWNED
7,408.85	208.85	210.42	200	662.621	862.621

FEDERAL TAX INFORMATION - FORM - 1099 - DIV

REFER TO ENCLOSED TAX INFORMATION NOTICE FOR ASSISTANCE IN FILING YOUR RETURN

BOX A	BOX B	BOX C	BOX D	BOX E
419.27	210.42	208.85	87.72	121.13

THIS TAX INFORMATION HAS BEEN FORWARDED TO THE INTERNAL REVENUE SERVICE

* SEE REVERSE SIDE   IF YOU HAVE ANY QUESTIONS REGARDING YOUR ACCOUNT PLEASE CONTACT MASSACHUSETTS FINANCIAL SERVICE CENTER, 50 MILK STREET - BOSTON, MA 02109

MFS FAMILY OF FUNDS

INVESTMENT/INSTRUCTIONS

USE THIS FORM TO FORWARD YOUR NEXT INVESTMENT OR TO GIVE INSTRUCTIONS FOR CHANGES IN YOUR ACCOUNT PLEASE MAIL TO
MASSACHUSETTS FINANCIAL SERVICE CENTER
50 MILK STREET - BOSTON, MA 02109

YOUR ACCOUNT NUMBER	DISTRIB OPTION*	SOCIAL SECURITY OR TAX IDENTIFYING NO

PLEASE REFER TO THIS NUMBER IN ALL CORRESPONDENCE

SHAREHOLDER

MAKE CHECK PAYABLE TO

PLEASE INVEST $_____
IN ADDITIONAL SHARES

PLEASE PRINT YOUR SOCIAL SECURITY NUMBER ABOVE IF NOT SHOWN ON THIS STATEMENT

CHANGE MY DISTRIBUTION OPTION TO:
(CHECK ONLY IF YOU WISH A CHANGE FROM YOUR PRESENT OPTION)

☐ A. DIVIDENDS REINVESTED CAPITAL GAINS IN ADDITIONAL SHARES

☐ B. DIVIDENDS IN CASH CAPITAL GAINS IN ADDITIONAL SHARES

☐ C. DIVIDENDS IN CASH, CAPITAL GAINS IN CASH

RIGHT OF ACCUMULATION

IN ORDER TO BENEFIT FROM RIGHT OF ACCUMULATION YOU MUST INFORM US OF OTHER ACCOUNTS WHICH MAY QUALIFY AS DESCRIBED IN THE FUND'S CURRENT PROSPECTUS PLEASE LIST THE REGISTRATIONS AND ACCOUNT NUMBERS ON REVERSE SIDE

Again, the fee should not be the determining factor. Rather, do the investments and services of the manager solve the needs and objectives of the investor? Most investors seem to be much more concerned about the quality of the investment service and the accomplishment of their objective than with the cost of the investment.

Types of Cost

Basically there are three types of costs associated with the ownership of mutual fund shares:

1. Sales or acquisition charge, also known as the offering price.

2. Management fee.

3. Administrative expenses.

Sales Charge. The *offering price* (or ask price), is the net asset value per share plus sales charge or commission, if any. This is the price at which the buyer purchases shares of the mutual fund. The offering price can be calculated as follows:

Offering price per share = Net asset value per share ÷ 100% − % Sales charge

Example: Assuming the net asset value is $10 per share and an 8% sales charge, the offering price is:

$$\$10 \div (1.00 - .08) = \$10 \div .92 = \$10.87$$

The sales charge or acquisition cost is often a deterrent for some individuals. But the sales charge is the only commission paid. It is a one-time commission. If the investor is willing to consider the purchase of a long-term, say 10- or 15-year commitment, he or she can divide that sales charge by the number of years the investor intends to hold the shares.

Example: If the investor plans to own the shares for 10 years and the sales commission is 8 percent, it will cost 0.8% per year to own the shares and obtain all the services.

The typical sales charge in the purchase of mutual fund shares is 8 1/2%, scaled down for quantity orders. The typical sales charges for quantity purchases are:

Less than $15,000	8½%
$15,000 to $25,000	8%
$25,000 to $50,000	6%
$50,000 to $100,000	4%
$100,000 to $250,000	3%
$250,000 and over	1½%

The usual dealer concession (the amount retained by the broker) is a percentage of the sales charge, and the percentage varies with different funds.

Whether investing a large sum of money, investing under a letter of intent, or investing with a right of accumulation, always consider the breakpoint and the reduced commission.

Example: If an investor has $22,000 in cash to invest and the sales charge is 8%, the purchase cost would be $1,760. However, if an additional $3,000 investment can be made, the sales charge would be $1,500 (6% of $25,000). The investor can have a $260 savings (less interest expense) if he or she borrows $3,000 to make the breakpoint, then liquidates enough shares to repay the loan.

$22,000 @ 8%	$1,760
$25,000 @ 6%	1,500
Savings	$ 260
Less: Interest on $3,000 for 60 days assuming 8%	40
Total savings	$ 220

Management Fee. The management fee is a contractual obligation between the mutual fund and the advisor to the portfolio. The *advisor* is the organization employed by the mutual fund to manage the portfolio and assets of the fund. The terms of the management fee, which are defined in the prospectus, usually average ½%, and may have provisions providing for a decrease in management fee as the total assets of the mutual fund increase. The management fee is deducted from dividend income of the portfolio before income distributions are made to the shareholders.

Administrative Expenses. These are the expenses for custodian fees to banks, auditing fees, printing charges, mailing expenses, and state and local taxes. The administrative expenses usually average ¼% to ½% of the average assets of the portfolio, and, like the management fee, are deducted from dividend income before distribution to the shareholders.

The management fee and administrative expenses of most mutual funds usually average less than 1%. Often there is a provision that if the sum of the management fee and administrative expenses exceeds a certain percentage of the portfolio (for instance, 1% to 1½% of the average assets), the mutual fund will be reimbursed by the advisor for the excess.

In dollar amounts, the management fee and administrative expenses should be less than $10 per $1,000 of average net assets per year. Few investment programs can offer the *total* management of an individual's money for less than $10 per $1,000 invested. Also for this expense, the shareholder will get a year-end tax statement giving a summary that must be reported on his or her individual 1040 tax return, if it is not included on Schedule D.

Load vs. No-Load. Most mutual fund shares are sold and distributed by underwriters (or distributors). These are usually wholesale organizations that handle mutual fund sales through investment dealers (stockbrokers). Some mutual fund organizations employ their own sales force, and others, having no sales force, rely on advertisements for sale. The latter are usually called "no-load funds" because no sales commission is charged.

Why should an investor pay a commission (or *load*) to buy a mutual fund when he can buy a *no-load* fund? The reason is because many investors do not have the expertise to select the proper mutual fund to meet their needs and objectives.

The investor must investigate the objectives, management, fee structure, and services. The investor must invest by mail, and when problems arise—and anyone who deals in securities knows they will from time to time—he or she must solve them by mail or telephone. The investor has no one representing him or her. It is possible to take two to three months for an investor to liquidate some mutual funds, because the owner often does not know the procedures or paper required.

William E. Donoghue, President of the Donoghue Organization, Inc., a publisher of newsletters on mutual funds and a registered investment advisor gives good advice. He says, "The first day you make any investment, you should learn how to sell and regain control of your money."

Most mutual funds are sold to satisfy a need. A broker is able to analyze the needs of the investor and to recommend the mutual fund best suited—whether it be monthly income with potential growth of capital (withdrawal plan), accumulation of wealth (open account-bank draft), exchange privileges for tax benefits, or one of the many services offered by management companies.

Investors who have the experience, knowledge, and where-withal to select their own fund may save the commission (or load) by doing so. For those with the qualifications, the savings may be well-warranted. For investors without the ability to handle their own affairs, the commission saved could become very expensive.

An investor selecting a no-load fund must be able to determine the fund that best meets his or her investment objectives. The investor must also be able to recognize when a fund is changing its scope or experiencing difficulties. When an investor's needs and/or objectives change, the investor should be able to recognize that a change to another fund in the same group may be advantageous.

Further, investors in no-load funds must be able to solve any problems that may arise. Problems may be as simple as changing registration or as complicated as attempting a redemption. (For additional information, contact the No-Load Mutual Fund Association, 11 Penn Plaza, New York, NY 10001 (212) 563-4540.)

Regulation

The Securities Act of 1933 requires registration of securities offerings, as well as the filing of full information with respect to the offering and the company fund and its advisor and distributor.

Investment Company Amendments Act of 1970 was the first significantly effective amendment to the Act of 1940. Brought about by the spectacular growth of the mutual fund industry in the late 1960s, the 1970 Act deals with management fees, sales charges, contractual plans, and many other areas of mutual fund operations to further protect the mutual fund investor.

These laws are administered by the Securities and Exchange Commission, which makes rules and regulations to carry out its purpose. In addition to the federal laws governing mutual funds, each state has its own laws and regulations that govern the offering and sale of securities within that state. These laws are referred to as *blue sky laws.*

The federal and state laws and regulations do not guarantee an investor a profit upon investing in a mutual fund. These laws are designed to protect the investor from fraud or misdealings and to ensure that the public is informed as to objectives and risk. Only the prospectus contains all the material facts relevant to a mutual fund's operations and policies.

The sales of mutual fund shares to the investing public are under the direction of the National Association of Securities Dealers (NASD), registered under the Maloney Act in 1938 as an amendment to the Securities Exchange Act of 1934. The NASD supervises the over-the-counter (OTC) securities market, administering the Rules of Fair Practice and Code of Procedure for handling practice complaints. The Investment Companies Department of the Executive Office is charged with the responsibility of reviewing investment companies' sales literature, and the department works closely with the Investment Companies Committee of the Board of Governors on the many problems concerning this phase of the securities business.

Neither Congress nor the Securities and Exchange Commission imposed the NASD on the investment banking and securities business. Rather, the privilege of self-regulation was actively sought, and the organization's success is attributable largely to the countless hours of work devoted to the association by many individuals in the securities business.

The *Investment Company Institute,* founded in 1941, is composed of mutual funds, their investment advisors, and their underwriters. Its purpose is to represent these members and shareholders in matters of legislation, regulation, taxation, public information, advertising, statistics, and economic and market research. The institute is a clearing house, to which interested persons may turn for information about the mutual fund industry. It also serves as a speaker and fact-finder in many areas affecting its members, their shareholders, and the investing public. Anyone may write to them for assistance at: Investment Company Institute, 1775 K Street, N.W., Washington, D.C. 20006 (202) 293-7700.

Why Invest in a Mutual Fund?

A mutual fund also offers investors an opportunity to do indirectly what they might do personally if they had adequate time, inclination, background, experience, and sufficient resources; that is, diversify and supervise their investments among many companies. Many investors—particularly the busy executive, the widow with no experience, or the young couple just getting started—do not have the advantages of knowledge, time, or experience; therefore, a good mutual fund can be most beneficial and welcome.

In a mutual fund, the investor participates in proportion to his or her shareholding in the net income from the securities owned by the fund. Costs of the operation are divided equally among all shareholders and are deducted from the earnings of the securities before distributions are made.

Ownership of mutual fund shares offers the investor three potential profit opportunities:

1. dividends from investment income,
2. capital gains distributions, and
3. an increase in net asset value.

Dividends from Investment Income

This represents the net dividends and interest received from the securities in the portfolio less expenses (management fees and administrative expenses). Short-term trading profits, net profits from securities held for less than six months, are considered dividend income. The securities pay dividends to the mutual fund, and the dividends are then paid to each shareholder in proportion to his or her percentage ownership of the entire portfolio.

Dividend income from a mutual fund is considered ordinary income for tax purposes and is entered under the dividend section of the 1040 return. It is subject to the $100 dividend exclusion ($200 for a married couple filing a joint return). Interest income and short-term profits are indicated as income *not* qualifying for the dividend exclusion. A mutual fund's 1099 will tell investors the amount of their dividend income that can be applied to the exclusion and the amount that cannot.

The dividend income from a mutual fund may be more predictable and stable, relative to the dividends from an individual corporation, because the fund's dividend income represents income from many different securities.

Capital Gains Distributions

As market conditions warrant, the mutual fund's portfolio manager will sell securities for a profit or loss. The *net realized long-term gain,* net profits from securities held for longer than 6 months is distributed annually to the shareholders in proportion to their shares in the entire portfolio. Regardless of the length of time an investor owns mutual fund shares, a capital gains distribution is always considered as long-term capital gain for income tax purposes.

Some mutual funds pay the capital gains tax on the net realized long-term gain, and the investor will receive a proportionate tax credit for his or her personal return.

Subchapter M of the Internal Revenue Code allows mutual funds to avoid being taxed by passing dividend and capital gains distributions directly to the investor, under what has come to be known as *the conduit theory.* Double taxation for the investor is thus avoided. To qualify, the mutual fund (among other things) must distribute to its shareholders at least 90% of the dividends and interest received. Usually, however, capital gains distributions are includable in the shareholder's taxable income at 40% of the amount distributed. The mutual fund will forward to the taxpayer each year the amount of capital gains distributions that are to be included in his or her 1040 return.

Even if dividend income and capital gains distributions are reinvested, the investor must still include those amounts on his 1040 tax return. And because the distributions are subject to taxation even if reinvested, the dollar amount of those reinvestments add to the investor's cost basis for tax purposes, as follows:

Cash invested	$25,000
Dividend income reinvested	5,000
Capital gains distributions reinvested	10,000
Cost basis for tax purposes	$40,000
Sales proceeds	50,000
Amount of capital gains	$10,000

For valuation of mutual fund shares in an estate, the bid price (net asset value per share) should be multiplied by the number of shares owned. The Internal Revenue required evaluation in an estate at the offering price, but this was reversed by the U.S. Supreme Court decision in the *Cartwright* case in May of 1973.

Increase in Net Asset Value

This advantage is reflected in the redemption or liquidity feature of mutual funds. The owner of open-end mutual fund shares may redeem them at net asset value on any business day.

If the shares are unissued and held by the transfer agent, a letter requesting redemption usually has to be written by the shareholder and a stock power attached to the letter. The client's signature on the stock power must be guaranteed by an officer of a national bank or by an officer of a securities firm that is a member of one of the exchanges. Blank stock powers can be obtained from most banks and brokers. (See page 177.) The shares are redeemed at the net asset value on the day after the mutual fund receives the redemption letter.

If an investor is attempting to redeem mutual fund shares without the assistance of a broker or advisor, it is advisable to mail the redemption request by registered mail with a receipt of delivery requested. You can determine the address with which to communicate on your latest confirmation statement. If you own issued certificates, they must be included in your redemption letter.

If the shareholder is holding issued certificates, they may often be redeemed, like any other security, by a broker placing an order to sell. The investor receives the net asset value of that afternoon. Even with issued shares, some mutual funds require a confirmation letter from the investor with the signature guaranteed. The specific requirements of a mutual fund should always be reviewed whenever a redemption is being undertaken.

The investor, upon redemption of his or her shares, may show a profit or a loss on the investment depending on the market value of the underlying securities held by the fund on the day of redemption.

STOCK/BOND POWER

ASSIGNMENT SEPARATE FROM CERTIFICATE

For Value Received,...

hereby sell, assign and transfer unto ....
....(   ) Par Amount
....(..................) Shares of ....

....

standing in.. name on the books of said ....

.... represented by Certificate No. ....herewith

and do hereby irrevocably constitute and appoint..

.... attorney to transfer the said stock/bond on the books of the within named
Company with full power of substitution in the premises.

    Dated...

                                 ....

IN PRESENCE OF

....

Performance

The true performance of a mutual fund can be measured only in relation to its particular objectives and the individual needs of the investor over an extended period of time.

Even comparing funds can be futile. A growth mutual fund such as Fidelity Capital cannot be compared with a growth-income fund such as Investment Company of America or with a tax-exempt bond fund, such as Federated Tax Free Income Fund. Each has different objectives, each is designed to solve a special need of the investor. Each portfolio contains different securities, offers varying degrees of risk, and utilizes entirely different management concepts.

Performance may be analyzed, actually, only in the context of general market conditions. Bear in mind, however, that comparing a mutual fund with the Dow-Jones Industrial Average or with the Standard & Poor's 500-Stock Index can also be misleading. The Dow-Jones Industrial Average includes 30 stocks, and a substantial move in certain of the securities can reflect a disproportionate move in the average. The Standard & Poor's 500-Stock Index can also be misguiding if the mutual fund does not include the same securities as in the averages.

Despite the impressive, long-term performance by mutual funds, it should be pointed out that the performance on such investments is *not guaranteed*. The current interest on savings accounts may be guaranteed; however, this interest rate can fluctuate and is not usually guaranteed for any extended period of time. There is a definite element of risk involved in any fixed-income security—inflation.

The risk in mutual fund ownership, however, generally has resulted in a better return over an extended period of time than most fixed-interest investments. An investor's objectives must be reviewed to determine the best and most suitable investment.

Example: Consider the effect of 5% inflation on $100 invested at 5% assuming a 30% tax rate. In spendable income, an investor's annual loss amounts to $1.75—1¾% ($5.25 less $3.50)—and over an extended period of time, this will definitely erode the purchasing power of the invested capital:

Income (interest on $100 investment at 5%)	$5.00
Federal income tax @ 30%	−1.50
Spendable income	$3.50
5% inflation on income (the $5 interest)	.25
5% inflation on capital (the $100 investment)	5.00
Total loss	$5.25
Less: Spendable income of	$3.50
Loss of	$1.75

An individual seeking a monthly income in a retirement program who invests in fixed-income investments has no opportunity for increasing his or her capital, or income flow. "Withdrawal plans" may offer investors a type of fixed-income with the potential of increasing the investor's capital and, perhaps more importantly, income. With inflation eroding the purchasing power of many investors living on fixed incomes, it is usually wise to invest some assets for potential growth of capital and income. The capital required to obtain certain monthly incomes at varying returns is as follows:

To Receive a Monthly Income of	5%	5½%	6%	7%
$ 400	$ 96,000	$ 87,300	$ 80,000	$ 68,600
$ 500	$120,000	$109,100	$100,000	$ 85,700
$ 750	$180,000	$163,600	$150,000	$128,600
$1,000	$240,000	$218,200	$200,000	$171,400

Mutual funds can be important and useful investments to achieve the objectives of many investors. Also, the broad services and many types offered can simplify an investor's decisions and readily be used to solve complicated financial programs.

Professional management offered by mutual funds is extremely important. Although shares have decreased in value during severe market declines, recovery to new highs has been a part of the American way. Mutual funds, that is, professional management and ease of ownership, offer the opportunity to participate in portfolios of securities that otherwise might not be available to many investors.

Problems Encountered With Mutual Funds

Following are examples of difficulties experienced by investors.

Example: An investor wrote a redemption letter to a mutual fund on January 18, 1980. The shares were redeemed on January 22, 1980, but the investor did not receive the redemption check until February 11, more than three weeks later.

When the fund was confronted with the circumstances, it said a redemption check was written on January 23, but was destroyed in the mail room. A second redemption check was not written until February 6, two weeks later. When asked about the delay and why the shareholder was not informed of the problems and paid interest on the money due, the answer was: "It is the policy of the transfer agent to make corrections only when requested by the shareholder." How many shareholders are able to recognize such a problem? Several weeks later, a check for the correction was received by the investor. The check amounted to 2½% of the original proceeds. That amount of loss would have been a high price for an investor to pay for not recognizing a problem or not knowing with whom to discuss the problem.

Example: Another investor wrote a redemption letter to a mutual fund on November 14, 1979. The sales proceeds were not received by the investor until December 26, 1979—almost six weeks later. After a great deal of useless correspondence and communication, it was finally learned that the mutual fund was no longer publicly offered. The custodian bank and transfer agent were the trustees for the fund, and all redemptions had to be handled by the bank.

It was pointed out that the investor was informed of this in literature, periodically mailed. That is a matter of conjecture, because the investor did not know whom to write or how to solve his problem.

Example: Another situation arose from a simple redemption of a few shares of a mutual fund for an estate. The redemption letter was mailed by the client and the letter contained all of the necessary and required papers. The fund redeemed only the portion of the account that was represented by certificates. The unissued shares held by the custodian were not redeemed. (Most mutual funds issue certificates that represent the number of shares owned by an investor. Also, a mutual fund's custodian may hold the shares in an account for the investor. These are usually referred to as unissued shares. Unissued shares facilitate withdrawal and reinvestment plans. Most mutual funds will show a shareholder's unissued shares to three decimal points, some to four decimal points!) A letter from the fund's shareholder service agent stated that another set of redemption papers would be needed to redeem the unissued shares.

The investor answered the letter with the necessary paper. It took over four months and several letters for the transfer agent to redeem the remaining shares.

These stories may or may not be typical of investors attempting to communicate with a particular fund and solve their problems, but many investors have difficulties. Investors often wonder who to write and how to get a reply. Perhaps the best answer is to write the fund itself, because they are legally responsible for the actions of their transfer agent or custodian. If no answer is obtained in a reasonable period, investors can bring their problem to the Investment Company Institute (ICI). The ICI has been able to help many investors obtain information on their mutual fund holdings.

Another answer to solving problems with mutual funds or any publicly traded investment is to write the Securities and Exchange Commission, Division of Investment Management, 500 North Capital Street, Washington, D.C. 20549.

Often investors have questions as to taxes, transfers, the use of shares as collateral for a loan, obtaining issued certificates, and many more. Assistance in answering questions is also a service provided for the original commission (or load).

Closed-End Funds

What Is a Closed-End Fund?

A *closed-end investment company* is a type of fund with a fixed number of shares outstanding and usually does not redeem its shares at net asset value. It is therefore *closed* in the sense that there is no continuous offering of new shares as in an open-end mutual fund. The directors of a closed-end fund, with certain restrictions, can authorize the issuance of additional shares, convertible issues, or rights.

The shares are usually traded on one of the exchanges or in the over-the-counter market, but the market price, determined by supply and demand, has no effect on funds available for investment, as in an open-end mutual fund, because of the fixed capitalization.

Closed-end funds differ from open-end funds in the following ways:

Closed	*Open*
Capitalization	
May issue different classes of stocks and bonds. Relatively fixed capitalization.	Issues common stock only. Continuous offering of additional shares—and redemptions—making for a constantly changing number of shares outstanding.

Redemption

Investor sells in the open
market at whatever price has
been established by supply and
demand.

Investor redeems directly with
the fund, usually at net asset
value (NAV).

Sales Charge

Traditional commission.

Zero for no-load funds, and
up to 9% for load funds.

Marginability

Most large funds are exchange
traded and may be purchased
on margin.

Not listed. Cannot be
purchased on margin. But fully
paid shares may be deposited
in a margin account for their
loan value.

Pricing

Most sell at a discount from
net asset value, but may sell
at parity or even at a premium.

Cannot sell at a discount.
Shares trade in a range from
net asset value (no-load
funds) up to a premium of
approximately 9½% (load funds).

With regard to the last point of comparison, the market price of closed-end investment company's shares is usually compared with their *asset value* to determine whether they are selling at a *premium* or a *discount*. To calculate net asset value, total the market value of all securities in its portfolio, plus all other assets such as cash, deduct all liabilities, then divide by the number of shares outstanding. When a share has a market price above its net asset value, it is said to be selling at a *premium*. When its price is below the net asset value, it is said to be selling at a *discount*.

Historically, the shares of most closed-end investment companies have sold at discounts, and many investors have pre-determined discounts at which they will buy shares.

How Shares Are Quoted

The net asset value, market price, and discount premium are published each Monday in *The Wall Street Journal.*

Objectives

Closed-end investment companies have investment objectives ranging from the highly speculative letter stock funds to more conservative bond funds, many formed in the 1970–73 period. Because of diversification, marketability, and availability of quotations, bond funds offer an alternative to bond ownership. However, the yield of a bond fund should always be compared with yields in the general bond markets and the premium or discount from net asset value.

Why Invest in Closed-End Funds?

Management

Each closed-end investment company has a Board of Directors responsible to the stockholders for the overall management of the fund. The Board of Directors usually employs a full-time, professional management team to supervise and manage the day-to-day operations of the fund and to make whatever changes may be needed.

Diversification

As in the open-end mutual fund, the assets of a closed-end investment company are invested in a broad range of securities, offering the investor a diversification of risk.

The investor has only one set of records to keep and one set of tax forms to file.

Dual Purpose Funds

Dual purpose funds are a special type of closed-end investment company, originally offered to the investing public in 1967, that offer two classes of stock: income and capital, usually in

Monday Listing of Closed-End Investment Companies.

PUBLICLY TRADED FUNDS

Friday, June 28, 1985

Following is a weekly listing of unaudited net asset values of publicly traded investment fund shares, reported by the companies as of Friday's close. Also shown is the closing listed market price or a dealer-to-dealer asked price of each fund's shares, with the percentage of difference.

	N.A. Value	Stk Price	% Diff
Diversified Common Stock Funds			
AdmExp	18.94	17½ −	7.6
BakerFen	43.97	37¼ −	15.3
GenAInv	18.47	17⅜ −	5.9
Lehman	15.28	14⅜ −	5.9
NiagaraSh	16.38	15¾ −	3.9
Overseas	5.78	5¾ −	0.5
Source	36.34	38⅞ +	7.0
Tri-Contl	26.70	26½ −	0.7
Specialized Equity and Convertible Funds			
AmCapCv	27.01	29¾ +	10.1
ASA	b47.21	49½ +	4.9
BancrftCv	26.81	24⅞ −	7.2
aCastle	31.02	31⅛ +	0.3
CentSec	13.81	13⅛ −	5.0

	N.A. Value	Stk Price	% Diff
Claremont	z	z	z
CLAS	z	z	z
CLAS Pfd	z	z	z
EmMedTch	13.17	12 −	8.9
Engex	13.74	10 −	27.2
EqStrat	b11.56	9¾ −	15.7
Japan	11.56	11⅛ −	3.8
Korea	11.49	14¾ +	28.4
Mexico	b z	z	z
Nautilus	z	z	z
NewAmFd	13.66	13½ −	1.2
Pete&Res	27.60	26¾ −	3.1
Z-Seven	16.08	14¾ −	8.3

a-Ex-dividend.   b-As of Thursday's close. z-Not available.

equal dollar amounts. The income shares, similar to preferred stock in that a minimum accumulative dividend must be paid, receive all income earned on the entire portfolio. The capital shares receive the entire capital appreciation.

Each class of stock leverages the other. Initial purchases had a two-to-one leverage: income shareholders receive income from an equal number of capital shares, and capital shareholders enjoyed the benefits of as many income shares at work.

Leverage on the capital shares does not remain constant. For instance, as the fund's assets increase, the leverage on the capital shares decreases. Also, the purchasing of capital shares at a discount from net asset value, or a decline in assets, increased the leverage in capital share ownership. Income shares may pick up additional dividend payouts through increased assets only by having more funds available for investment income-producing securities. This effect is referred to as income leveraging.

Dual-purpose funds do not distribute any long-term capital gains to the capital shareholders, paying instead the capital gains tax at the corporate rate of 30%. The capital shareholder, however, must include his or her share of the capital gain in taxable income, and take a credit against tax liability for the tax paid for owned shares. The shareholder then increases the cost basis of his or her shares by the amount of the 70% undistributed capital gain.

At some stated time in the future, all income shares of a dual purpose fund will be retired. At that time, each capital shareholder will receive the balance of the capital. As the redemption date approaches, the shares will have a built-in gain or loss depending upon whether the market price is at a premium or discount from redemption price. The income shares offer an investor a substantial yield with a predetermined redemption value at a set time in the future.

The Cost of Investing in Closed-End Funds

The cost of closed-end fund shares consist of management fees and commissions. Before income is distributed to the shareholder, a *management fee and a funds expense* are deducted and paid to the manager or advisor. The investor also pays a *regular* commission upon the purchase or sale of closed-end investment company shares. If the shares are traded over-the-counter, the investor pays a *spread* between bid and asked prices (received by the market maker for risking his or her capital). Shares are bought on the offering (asked) price and sold on the bid price.

Regulation

Like open-end mutual funds, closed-end investment companies are subject to regulation under the Securities Act of 1933, the Securities Exchange Act of 1934, and the Securities and Exchange Commission. Such regulation does not ensure that the company will be successfully operated or profitable to the investor, but it does ensure that the investor will be kept informed about its activities and developments.

Information

Information on closed-end investment companies may be obtained from the Standard and Poor's *Stock Record Sheets* and Moody's *Finance Manuals.* On pages 187–188, see the re-

---

Tri-Continental Corp. 2256

NYSE Symbol TY Options on Phila (Mar-Jun-Sep-Dec)

NAV	Price	% Difference	Dividend	Yield	S&P Ranking
Mar. 8'85	Mar. 8'85				
24.96	24¾	−0.8	²1.13	²4.6%	NR

Summary

Tri-Continental is the largest publicly traded (closed end) investment company. With the bulk of investments in common stocks, it offers participation in a high-grade portfolio under professional management. The common shares have recently sold only slightly below net asset value, in contrast to the sizable discount at which they sold several years ago.

Business Summary

Tri-Continental Corp., the largest diversified publicly traded investment company in the U.S., invests primarily for the longer term with the objective of producing future growth of both capital and income while providing reasonable current income. Funds are invested in established and better-known securities.

Net assets at December 31, 1984 and December 31, 1983 were distributed as follows:

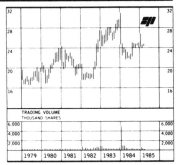

TRADING VOLUME
THOUSAND SHARES

	12/84	12/83
Common stock:		
Consumer goods & services	14.1%	3.2%
Communications	10.0%	6.9%
Finance & insurance	9.9%	3.5%
Computers & services	6.4%	4.8%
Aerospace & defense	6.1%	3.1%
Transportation	5.5%	8.2%
Industrial equipment	5.4%	2.5%
Energy	5.4%	---
Wholesale & retail trade	3.5%	9.1%
Chemical	3.5%	10.2%
Other	12.7%	9.5%
Total common stock	82.5%	79.4%
U.S. Gov't obligations	13.6%	12.5%
Net cash and other short-term holdings	3.9%	8.1%

The 10 largest investments at December 31, 1984 (representing 37% of common stock investments) were IBM, Coca-Cola, McDonald's, Boeing, Bristol-Myers, Ford Motor, Standard Oil of Indiana, New York Times (Class A), Rohm & Hass, and Chubb.

Management and administrative services are provided by J. & W. Seligman & Co. The management fee rate is 0.45% of the first $500 million of the fee base (as defined), ranging down to 0.20% on the fee base over $3.25 billion. The management fee in 1984 was $3,278,966, equivalent to an annual rate of 0.36% of net investment assets.

The company offers a dividend reinvestment plan whereby all or part of distributions may be reinvested in additional shares. TY reports audited statements of operations and changes in net investment income on a semi-annual basis only.

Important Developments

Jan. '85—Major additions and increases to the portfolio during the quarter ended December 31, 1984 included American International Group, Ameritech Corp., Bristol-Myers, Chubb Corp., Ford Motor, Honda Motor, R.J. Reynolds, and Southern California Edison. Eliminations and reductions included Advanced Micro-Devices, Associated Dry Goods Corp., Atlantic Richfield, Chevron, Hewlett-Packard, Motarola, U.S. Tobacco, and Kerr-McGee.

Next earnings report due in early May.

Per Share Data ($)

Yr. End Dec. 31	1984	1983	1982	1981	1980	1979	1978	1977	1976	1975
Net Asset Value¹	25.36	30.82	29.08	26.08	31.55	25.66	22.53	23.44	27.68	23.68
Yr-End Prices	24⅞	29⅜	26⅞	20¾	23⅝	19⅞	17⅝	20⅝	22	18½
% Difference	−2%	−5%	−8%	−20%	−25%	−23%	−22%	−12%	−21%	−22%
Dividends—										
Invest. Inc.	1.13	1.09	1.08	1.15	1.14	1.06	1.06	0.99	0.90	0.86
Capital Gains³	2.40	4.46	1.48	2.72	1.64	1.08	1.01	1.21	1.19	0.66
Portfolio Turned	72%	44%	40%	36%	41%	23%	26%	21%	17%	15%

Data as orig. reptd. 1. Bef. dilution from exercise of wts. 2. Paid in the past 12 mos. from invest. inc.; excl. 2.40 from capital gains in Jan. 1985. 3. Realized.

Standard NYSE Stock Reports
Vol. 52/No. 57/Sec. 22

March 22, 1985
Copyright © 1985 Standard & Poor's Corp. All Rights Reserved

Standard & Poor's Corp.
25 Broadway, NY, NY 10004

ports on Tri-Continental Corp., a fund whose objective is long-term growth, and Drexel Bond Debenture Trading Fund, which invests in debt securities (bonds). Information may also be obtained from the Investment Services of either organization. Each of the closed-end mutual funds will also make information available in response to a letter or call. Also, prices and net asset

2256 Tri-Continental Corporation

Income Data (Million $)

Year Ended Dec. 31	Total Invest. Inc.	Net Invest. Income Total	Net Invest. Income Per Sh.	Realized Cap. Gains Total	Realized Cap. Gains Per Sh.	[2]% Net Inv. Inc./Net Assets	% Expenses To [2]Net Assets	% Expenses To [2]Invest. Inc.	Price Range Com. Stk.
1984	**47.9**	**42.9**	**1.14**	**87**	**2.43**	**4.5%**	**0.6%**	**10.4%**	**31 -21⅝**
1983	41.7	36.4	1.08	142	4.46	3.6%	0.5%	12.9%	29¾-24⅜
1982	39.4	35.0	1.08	46	1.49	4.5%	0.6%	11.2%	27⅝-17⅝
1981	38.3	33.9	1.15	75	2.69	4.7%	0.5%	11.5%	24½-18½
1980	35.4	32.3	1.14	43	1.60	4.2%	0.4%	8.7%	24 -16⅞
1979	32.4	29.3	1.07	28	1.10	4.6%	0.5%	9.5%	20¼-16⅝
1978	29.3	26.5	0.99	24	0.96	4.5%	0.5%	9.6%	21 -17⅛
1977	27.8	25.2	0.98	29	1.24	4.1%	0.4%	9.5%	22⅝-18¾
1976	25.0	22.5	0.90	27	1.19	3.5%	0.4%	10.0%	22 -18½
1975	23.5	21.2	0.87	14	0.64	3.9%	0.4%	9.8%	22⅞-16½

Balance Sheet Data (Million $)

Dec. 31	Net Assets	% Change NAV	% Change [1]S&P 500	% Change Bonds AAA	Investments Cost	Investments Mkt.	% Net Asset Distribution Net Cash	ST Oblig.	Bonds & Notes	Com. Stk.	Other Invest.
1984	**949**	**-4.9**	**+1.4**	**+3.6**	**890**	**1,022**	**d7.8%**	**11.7%**	**13.6%**	**82.5%**	**Nil**
1983	1,019	+10.9	+17.3	-10.2.	769	1,013	0.6%	7.5%	12.5%	79.4%	Nil
1982	929	+21.1	+14.8	+34.0	694	974	d4.8%	9.1%	12.2%	83.5%	Nil
1981	767	-12.4	-9.7	-16.7	626	762	0.7%	8.9%	16.7%	73.7%	Nil
1980	876	+27.0	+25.8	-15.6	573	878	d0.2%	6.0%	2.0%	92.2%	Nil
1979	697	+18.2	+12.3	-13.8	552	710	d1.9%	8.9%	2.0%	91.0%	Nil
1978	595	+1.4	+1.1	-8.9	520	596	d0.2%	14.9%	0.7%	84.6%	Nil
1977	594	-11.2	-11.5	-6.4	523	610	d2.7%	12.4%	2.4%	87.9%	Nil
1976	670	+19.6	+19.1	+9.7	505	687	d2.6%	9.2%	2.7%	90.7%	Nil
1975	567	+30.7	+31.5	+0.6	477	579	d2.0%	8.1%	1.3%	92.6%	Nil

Data as orig. reptd. 1. Bef. reinvestment of dividends. 2. As reptd. by co. d-Deficit.

Net Asset Value Per Com. Sh. ($)

As of:	1984	1983	1982	1981
Mar. 31	23.75	30.14	21.47	29.48
Jun. 30	22.99	32.68	21.09	28.87
Sep. 30	24.97	31.53	24.17	25.06
Dec. 31	25.36	30.82	29.08	26.08

Net asset value per share (adjusted for the capital gains distribution) declined 2.0% in 1984. During the same period the Standard & Poor's 500 Price Index was up 1.4%.

Total investment income for 1984 rose 15%, year to year. Net investment income advanced 18%, to $1.19 on 13% more shares from $1.14. Net realized gains amounted to $87,371,974, versus $142,020,388. Change in unrealized appreciation decreased $111,834,401 and $35,968,717, respectively.

Net Invest. Inc. Per Com. Sh. ($)

Quarter:	1984	1983	1982	1981
Mar. 31	0.27	0.25	0.28	0.26
Jun. 30	0.31	0.26	0.26	0.25
Sep. 30	0.27	0.28	0.27	0.30
Dec. 31	0.29	0.29	0.26	0.34
	1.14	1.08	1.08	1.15

Dividend Data

Virtually all net investment income is paid out to shareholders. Realized capital gains are accumulated during the year and distributed the following March. Dividends have been paid since 1945. A dividend reinvestment plan is available.

Amt. of Divd. $	Date Decl.	Ex-divd. Date	Stock of Record	Payment Date
0.26	Jun. 12	Jun. 18	Jun. 22	Jul. 1'84
0.29	Sep. 11	Sep. 17	Sep. 21	Oct. 1'84
0.34	Dec. 11	Dec. 17	Dec. 21	Jan. 2'85
†2.40	Jan. 15	Jan. 30	Feb. 5	Mar. 4'85
0.24	Mar. 12	Mar. 18	Mar. 22	Apr. 1'85

†Long-term capital gains; in cash or stock.

Next dividend meeting: mid-Jun. '85.

Capitalization

Long Term Debt: None.

$2.50 Cum. Preferred Stock: 752,740 shs. ($50 par); red. at $55.

Common Stock: 35,919,888 shs. ($0.50 par). Institutions hold about 1%.

Warrants: 30,600, ea. to purchase 5.93 com. shs. at $3.79 a sh.

Office—One Bankers Trust Plaza, NYC 10006. **Tel**—(212) 432-4000. **Chrmn & CEO**—F. E. Brown. **Pres**—R. T. Schroeder. **Secy**—C. J. White. **Tres**—W. F. Kuhn. **Investor Contact**—Elizabeth Smith. **Dirs**—F. E. Brown, S. R. Currie, L. A. Lapham, W. B. Marshall, J. C. Pitney, W. M. Rees, H. J. Schmidt, R. T. Schroeder. **Transfer Agent**—Union Data Service Center, Inc., NYC. **Registrar**—Chase Manhattan Bank, NYC. **Incorporated** in Maryland in 1929.

Information has been obtained from sources believed to be reliable, but its accuracy and completeness are not guaranteed. P. A. Berman value of closed-end mutual funds will also make information available in response to a letter or call. Also, prices and net asset value of closed-end companies are published each Monday in *The Wall Street Journal*.

In 1973, closed-end investment companies began a new phase of development. With many closed-end mutual funds sel-

Drexel Bond-Deb. Trad'g Fund   775

NYSE Symbol DBF

NAV	Price	% Difference	Dividend	Yield	S&P Ranking
Oct. 12'84	Oct. 12'84				
16.70	16¾	+0.3	2.00	11.9%	NR

Summary

This publicly traded investment company invests at least 75% of its assets in investment grade bonds, with the remainder in bonds which may be of lower quality and may have equity features. Its objective is to generate a high rate of return, primarily from interest income and trading activity.

Business Summary

Drexel Bond-Debenture Trading Fund is a diversified management investment fund which seeks a high rate of return, primarily from interest income and trading activity. Recently, the company restructured its investment portfolio to increase current income.

At June 30, 1984 investments aggregated $37,960,719 (at market; 91% of total assets). Net assets at June 30, 1984 and March 31, 1984 were divided as follows:

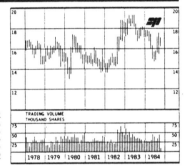

	6/84	3/84
U.S. Government	34%	39%
Electric utilities	22%	22%
Communications	18%	18%
Industrial and misc	13%	15%
Oil and gas	11%	9%
Total debt securities	98%	103%
Net cash and other	2%	-3%

Normally, the fund invests at least 75% of its assets in debt securities, rated investment grade (BBB or better) by Standard and Poor's Corp. or Moody's Investors Services; short-term securities of issuers that have any security rated investment grade; U.S. Governments and Agencies; and bank obligations. The remaining 25% may be invested in bonds or preferred shares that may have equity features.

The investment quality of the portfolio at June 30, 1984, based on Standard & Poor's ratings, was as follows: Government & Agencies 34.7%, AAA 5.5%, AA 27.9%, A 14.5%, BBB 9.7%, BB 2.8%, and B 4.9% (the last three categories were comprised entirely of electric utility bonds).

The investment adviser to the fund is Drexel Management Corp. It is paid at an annual rate of ⅝ of 1% on the first $40 million of the fund's month-end

net assets, and ½ of 1% on the excess. The fee is reduced by the amount by which brokerage commissions paid to Drexel Burnham Lambert Inc. exceed $10,000 in a given year. Investment advisory expenses amounted to $266,661 in fiscal 1983-4, compared with $253,118 in 1982-3.

Shareholders may have their dividends and distributions automatically reinvested in additional shares of the fund, issued at the lower of market price or net asset value.

The fund had a capital loss carryforward at March 31, 1984 of approximately $12,918,000 available to offset any future capital gains. The fund said that to the extent that these losses were offset by future capital gains, it was unlikely that the gains so offset would be distributed to shareholders, since any such distributions would be taxable to shareholders as ordinary income.

Next earnings report due in early November.

Per Share Data ($)

Yr. End Mar. 31¹	1983	1982	1981	1980	1979	1978	1977	1976	1975	1974
Net Asset Value	16.65	18.63	14.55	15.38	15.40	19.09	19.60	20.33	19.45	17.46
Yr-End Prices	17	18⅝	15	15⅛	13⅞	15¼	16⅞	17	17⅝	16⅛
% Difference	+2%	Nil	+3%	-0.2%	-10%	-20%	-14%	-16%	-9%	-8%
Dividends—										
Invest. Inc.	2.00	2.00	1.99	2.03	1.63	1.47	1.44	1.32	1.44	1.44
Capital Gains	Nil	Nil	Nil	Nil	Nil	Nil	Nil	Nil	Nil	Nil
Portfolio Turned	207%	264%	232%	251%	247%	237%	138%	151%	231%	166%

Data as orig. reptd. 1. Of foll. cal. yr.

ling at substantial discounts from net asset value, merger with open-end mutual funds became a greater and greater probability. The first such merger was Surveyor Fund with Eberstadt, an open-end growth mutual fund. Obviously, such a merger affords a capital gain to the holder of the closed-end fund selling at a

775

Drexel Bond-Debenture Trading Fund

Income Data (Million $)

Year Ended Mar. 31[1]	Total Invest. Inc.	Net Invest. Income Total	Net Invest. Income Per Sh.	Realized Cap. Gains Total	Realized Cap. Gains Per Sh.	[4]% Net Inv. Inc./ Net Assets	% Expenses To [4]Net Assets	% Expenses To Invest. Inc.	[2]Price Range Com. Stk.
1983	**5.59**	**4.91**	**1.98**	**d1.86**	**d0.75**	**11.3%**	**1.6%**	**12.1%**	**19⅜–16¾**
1982	5.46	4.95	2.01	6.49	2.64	12.1%	1.3%	9.4%	18⅞–13⅝
1981	5.29	4.73	1.94	d2.66	d1.09	13.7%	1.6%	10.5%	16¼–13⅝
1980	5.58	4.80	1.99	d1.34	d0.56	12.2%	2.0%	14.1%	17½–13
1979	4.89	4.31	1.79	d3.83	d1.59	10.1%	1.4%	11.8%	17¼–14¼
1978	4.37	3.79	1.57	d2.50	d1.04	8.2%	1.3%	13.3%	17 –14½
1977	4.03	3.45	1.44	d0.43	d0.18	7.1%	1.2%	14.2%	18¼–16
1976	3.99	3.39	1.41	d0.36	d0.15	7.1%	1.3%	15.1%	18⅝–16
1975	4.17	3.57	1.48	1.40	0.58	8.2%	1.4%	14.5%	18⅞–14⅝

Balance Sheet Data (Million $)

Mar. 31[1]	Net Assets	% Change NAV	% Change [3]S&P 500	% Change Bonds AAA	Investments Cost	Investments Mkt.	% Net Asset Distribution Net Cash	S T Oblig.	Bonds & Pfd.	Com. Stk.	Other Invest.
1983	**41.4**	**−10.6**	**+4.1**	**−11.9**	**45.9**	**42.5**	**d2.8%**	**Nil**	**102.8%**	**Nil**	**Nil**
1982	45.8	+28.0	+36.6	+31.5	45.8	45.5	0.6%	Nil	99.4%	Nil	Nil
1981	35.6	−5.4	−17.7	−10.0	41.2	37.4	d4.9%	1.0%	103.9%	Nil	Nil
1980	37.0	−0.1	+33.2	−2.8	41.1	36.4	1.6%	Nil	94.6%	3.8%	Nil
1979	37.1	−19.3	+0.5	−29.5	45.9	39.9	d7.7%	11.0%	94.5%	2.2%	Nil
1978	46.0	−2.6	+13.9	−7.4	54.2	53.6	d16.6%	32.1%	81.4%	3.3%	Nil
1977	47.2	−3.6	−9.4	−4.2	50.8	49.2	d4.3%	12.7%	81.5%	10.1%	Nil
1976	49.0	+4.5	−4.2	+2.1	47.9	47.7	2.6%	Nil	94.6%	2.8%	Nil
1975	46.8	+11.4	+23.3	+3.4	50.2	47.7	d1.8%	Nil	100.8%	1.0%	Nil

Data as orig. reptd. **1.** Of the foll. cal. yr. **2.** Cal. yr. **3.** Bef. reinvestment of dividends. **4.** As reptd. by co. d-Deficit.

Net Asset Value Per Share ($)

As of:	1984-5	1983-4	1982-3	1981-2
Jun. 30	15.37	18.33	14.63	14.80
Sep. 30	16.47	17.84	16.91	13.01
Dec. 31		17.33	18.19	14.50
Mar. 31		16.65	18.63	14.55

During the six months ended September 30, 1984 net asset value per share decreased 1.1%. For the same period, the Standard & Poor's index of high-grade industrial bonds was up 2.7%.

Total investment income (entirely interest) for the three months ended June 30, 1984 decreased 1.2%, year to year. Expenses rose 8.8% and absorbed 13% of income, versus 12%. Net investment income was off 2.6%, to $0.49 a share from $0.51. There was net realized and unrealized loss on investments of $1.27 a share, compared with $0.31.

Net Invest. Income Per Sh. ($)

Quarter:	1984-5	1983-4	1982-3	1981-2
Jun.	0.49	0.51	0.51	0.50
Sep.		0.49	0.51	0.48
Dec.		0.49	0.51	0.48
Mar.		0.49	0.48	0.48
		1.98	2.01	1.94

Dividend Data

Distributions were initiated in 1972 and placed on a quarterly basis in mid-1977. A dividend reinvestment plan is available.

Amt. of Divd. $	Date Decl.	Ex-divd. Date	Stock of Record	Payment Date
0.50	Dec. 6	Jan. 9	Jan. 13	Feb. 2'84
0.50	Apr. 5	Apr. 16	Apr. 23	May 3'84
0.50	Jun. 25	Jul. 13	Jul. 19	Aug. 7'84
0.50	Sep. 12	Oct. 1	Oct. 5	Nov. 2'84

Finances

During the fiscal year ended March 31, 1984 the fund borrowed money from a bank periodically. Maximum month-end borrowings during that period were $5,448,728 and average daily borrowings totaled $1,797,583 at a weighed average interest rate of 11.91%.

Capitalization

Bank Loan Payable: $2,237,383.

Common Stock: 2,493,820 shs. ($1 par). Institutions hold about 3,000 shs. Shareholders of record: 5,665.

Office—1500 Walnut Street, Philadelphia, Pa. 19102. **Tel**—(215) 545-4100. **Pres**—R. J. Vitale. **Secy**—V. Stanton, Jr. **VP-Treas**—O. P. Lewnowski. **Dirs**—J. Balog, J. G. Christy, W. P. Davis III, W. W. Hagerty, H. G. Lloyd III, J. L. Shane, R. J. Vitale. **Transfer Agent & Registrar**—Bank of New York, NYC. **Incorporated** in Delaware in 1971.

Information has been obtained from sources believed to be reliable, but its accuracy and completeness are not guaranteed. Daniel H. Rucki discount from its net asset value. In November of 1983, the Madison Fund converted from a closed-end investment company to an operating company with primary interest in U.S. oil and gas properties. The investor would be well-advised to follow the development of these mergers.

Closed-end investment companies offer opportunities to participate in diversified, managed portfolios of securities. Also, the premium or discount of prices can afford additional advantages. The closed-end bond funds are an excellent means for the investor to purchase a fixed-income portfolio.

Systematic Investing:
The Small Investor

Many potential investors have neither the income nor the capital to justify establishing an investment portfolio of any kind. Installment purchasing is not a new concept to most families. After a small down payment, the balance of the purchase price, plus interest, is paid in fixed installments, usually monthly. The use of credit cards is a form of installment purchasing.

The same principles of installment purchasing can be applied to investing. The primary investment objective of the small investor is not percentage gain, but the *accumulation of wealth.* The figures on pages 193–197 for the investments of $25, $50 and $100 per month show the actual results of three aggressive growth funds. In 10, 20 or 30 years, the small investor can become the big investor.

Dollar Cost Averaging

Dollar cost averaging is the long-term, *regular* investment of the same *amount of money* in a security that fluctuates in price. The investments may be monthly, quarterly, or annually, but each should be a fixed amount. The amount invested purchases more shares when the price of the security is low, and fewer shares when the price is high. The average cost per share is thereby lowered. Dollar cost averaging is usually successful because the long-term trend of stock prices has been upward.

Dollar cost averaging is a long-term concept that takes maximum advantage of short-term market cycles by reinvesting, and therefore compounding, earnings. Obviously, an investor cannot make money unless his capital is being invested. There are, then, basically two important requirements for successful dollar cost averaging investing:

$25/Month

Year Ended	Cumulative Investments	Dividends Reinvested	Dollar Values of Capital Gains In Shares	Total Value
1955	$ 300	$ 3	$ 16	$ 310
1956	600	10	29	665
1957	900	16	18	827
1958	1,200	23	13	1,591
1959	1,500	28	51	2,138
1960	1,800	40	30	2,622
1961	2,100	42	93	3,588
1962	2,400	51	43	3,240
1963	2,700	61	91	4,140
1964	3,000	73	53	4,842
1965	3,300	89	120	6,369
1966	3,600	103	216	6,750
1967	3,900	92	183	8,986
1968	4,200	128	143	9,434
1969	4,500	132	223	9,739
1970	4,800	173	316	9,428
1971	5,100	165	305	11,922
1972	5,400	154	676	14,759
1973	5,700	186	172	12,061
1974	6,000	215	0	8,051
1975	6,300	186	254	10,340
1976	6,600	165	309	11,535
1977	6,900	218	342	11,059
1978	7,200	310	397	12,835
1979	7,500	391	578	16,524
1980	7,800	468	1,760	23,468
1981	8,100	605	2,359	22,299
1982	8,400	845	2,371	28,874
1983	8,700	664	4,655	33,591
1984	9,000	916	2,440	32,418

Consistent Investing

The investor must have the ability and determination to invest at regular intervals, regardless of price fluctuations. Persistence is perhaps the most important feature of dollar-cost-averaging, and the bank draft is perhaps the least painful way of being

$50/Month.

Year Ended	Cumulative Investments	Dividends Reinvested	Dollar Values of Capital Gains in Shares	Total Value
1955	$600	$6	33	620
1956	1,200	20	57	1,331
1957	1,800	32	37	1,654
1958	2,400	46	26	3,182
1959	3,000	56	103	4,275
1960	3,600	80	61	5,244
1961	4,200	84	185	7,175
1962	4,800	101	86	6,481
1963	5,400	121	182	8,279
1964	6,000	147	106	9,685
1965	6,600	177	240	12,740
1966	7,200	206	432	13,505
1967	7,800	184	366	17,982
1968	8,400	257	287	18,878
1969	9,000	264	446	19,489
1970	9,600	347	632	18,869
1971	10,200	330	611	23,862
1972	10,800	309	1,353	29,546
1973	11,400	373	345	24,150
1974	12,000	430	0	16,123
1975	12,600	372	508	20,706
1976	13,200	331	618	23,099
1977	13,800	437	685	22,145
1978	14,400	621	795	25,707
1979	15,000	783	1,157	33,107
1980	15,600	938	3,527	47,033
1981	16,200	1,212	4,729	44,705
1982	16,800	1,694	4,754	57,912
1983	17,400	1,331	9,338	67,395
1984	18,000	1,838	4,896	65,072

persistent. Upon investor authorization, a mutual fund has money deducted from the investor's checking account, invests it and mails a statement to the investor. The important feature is that the investments are automatic—no procrastination. The plan can still be stopped or modified by instructions to the mutual fund, but the bank draft usually encourages more regularity and longevity.

If the investor needs money, he or she may use the shares as collateral for a loan. If the loan can be repaid from current income, the systematic investment may continue and offset the interest on the loan to some degree. If the loan must be repaid with money originally intended for systematic investment, then at least the total investment already committed remains intact and at work for the investor.

Investment with Growth Objectives

When dollar-cost-averaging in growth securities, the greater fluctuations allow better buying opportunities on market declines and greater potential profit on market rebounds. An investor utilizing dollar-cost-averaging is seeking future capital and his or her objective, therefore, is usually growth.

Example: The following demonstrates, in simplified fashion, how dollar-cost-averaging works.

Dollar-Cost-Averaging: $50 Invested Regularly

Regular Investment	Price per Share	Shares Acquired
$50	$10	5.00
50	12	4.17
50	14	3.57
50	13	3.85
50	12	4.17
50	10	5.00
50	8	6.25
50	7	7.14
50	8	6.25
50	12	4.17
50	10	5.00
50	11	4.55
$600	$10.58*	59.12

*Average one-time price per share.

Twelve regular investments of $50 each are made. Each investment buys a different amount of stock according to the varying prices per share. Over the course of 12 investments, the average cost per share works out to be $10.15 (600 total investment divided by 59.12 shares). If an investor had bought 59.12 shares at once during this same period, he or she may have paid $7 to $14 per share. If the investor bought the shares at the *average price* of $10.58, he or she would have paid a total of $625.49—and he would have to continually monitor the market for the right time to invest. Because the overall trend of the market is upward, however, the dollar-cost-averaging method has a cost advantage of $25.49 ($625.49 value—$600 total dollar-cost-averaging investment), or 4.25%.

The mutual fund concept lends itself to dollar-cost-averaging and compounding through the open account (dividends and capital gains distributions are automatically reinvested). The investor can mail his or her check (monthly, quarterly, or when he or she desires) to the mutual fund.

All dividends and capital gains distributions may be automatically reinvested. This is important in the initial stages of accumulation. The distributions will be small and not particularly meaningful if paid in cash, but by reinvestment—compounding— the value in the future could be significant.

Example: A lady in her seventies had bought stock, five or ten shares at a time, for over 40 years. At her death, her stock portfolio was worth over $250,000.

Investors may also want to consider consulting a broker and accumulate a few shares of a particular stock over a period of time. Many brokers may not want to handle five-or-ten share orders, but small accounts can become large accounts. Many brokers realize this and investors should seek out a broker who is willing to work with them.

Many investors have joined investment clubs (see Chapter 11) to take advantage of dollar cost averaging. Some investment club members have not only learned about investing, they have accumulated over $100,000 in their club.

Example: A young girl in northern Virginia started a dollar-cost-averaging investment program in the late 1960s. She accumulated almost $100,000, by regularly investing $50 to $100 a month.

In summary, small investors should make the best use of the one advantage available to them—time. Making small, but

$100/Month

Year Ended	Cumulative Investments	Dividends Reinvested	Dollar Values of Capital Gains in Shares	Total Value
1955	1,200	13	65	1,240
1956	2,400	39	115	2,662
1957	3,600	65	74	3,309
1958	4,800	91	53	6,364
1959	6,000	113	206	8,550
1960	7,200	160	121	10,490
1961	8,400	168	371	14,357
1962	9,600	203	172	12,970
1963	10,800	243	363	16,572
1964	12,000	294	211	19,388
1965	13,200	355	480	25,506
1966	14,400	413	865	27,049
1967	15,600	369	733	36,025
1968	16,800	515	575	37,832
1969	18,000	529	895	39,069
1970	19,200	695	1,267	37,838
1971	20,400	661	1,225	47,863
1972	21,600	620	2,714	59,284
1973	22,800	748	693	48,476
1974	24,000	863	0	32,373
1975	25,200	747	1,020	41,585
1976	26,400	665	1,241	46,401
1977	27,600	877	1,375	44,495
1978	28,800	1,248	1,597	51,674
1979	30,000	1,574	2,327	66,582
1980	31,200	1,886	7,096	94,635
1981	32,400	2,439	9,518	89,988
1982	33,600	3,410	9,574	116,630
1983	34,800	2,681	18,809	135,758
1984	36,000	3,703	9,865	131,120

regular, investments over the course of a working lifetime can lead to large payoffs in later years. Perhaps the number one reason for lack of success with a systematic investment program is that investors stop investing when the first reversal occurs. The systematic investor's philosophy must be one of confidence, despite temporary setback, in the long-term upward tendency of the market.

Withdrawal Plans

Withdrawal plan in a mutual fund enables an investor to receive a regular, level income from invested capital. The mechanics of the plan are quite simple: Mutual fund shares are purchased or deposited. The fund is instructed to mail monthly or quarterly checks in any reasonable amount to the investor or to any designed recipient. Most mutual funds suggest a withdrawal of 6%, though at times 7% or even 8% may be justified.

A typical initial requirement is a $10,000 investment for a monthly withdrawal or a $5,000 investment for quarterly withdrawal. Minimum withdrawals are usually $50.

Each withdrawal is obtained by liquidating enough full and fractional shares to realize the required amount. Since shares are redeemable at net asset value without sales charge, the amount received per share may be more or less than the cost. Withdrawal payments are therefore not dividends, yield, or income. The payments are essentially composed of dividends plus an orderly liquidation and distribution of the investment.

All dividend and capital gains distributions are automatically used by the mutual fund to purchase full and fractional shares, usually at net asset value (without cost), for the investor's account. Through this procedure, no cash balances are left idle in the account, and the capital is always fully invested. Some mutual funds do not reinvest the dividends, but use them first to make up the regular payments.

For a successful plan, the fund must be able to "put back in" at least as much as the investor "takes out." Obviously, the withdrawal amounts must be in proportion to the earning ability of the fund, so the automatic reinvestment of dividends and capital gains distributions plus growth will be able to replenish the shares liquidated to make the withdrawal.

This is not to say, however, that for each and every withdrawal period the reinvestment must offset the amount taken out. An investor's perspective should be long-term. Even after selecting a fund that consistently pays dividends (the only kind that will support a withdrawal plan), the amount reinvested may not equal the payments over the course of any given year. Over a long-term period, though, the shares withdrawn should be replenished by the reinvestment procedure. The key, in a word, is in *cash flow*. In the long run, in fact, the capital appreciation potential of most funds should permit the stepping up of withdrawals without depleting the principal.

Example: The table on page 200 shows the performance of a growth-income fund, with $100,000 invested and a 6% ($6,000) annual withdrawal (increased every 5 years) over a 20-year period.

In nine of those years, the annual withdrawal exceeded the dividends and capital gains reinvested. However, over the full 20 years, withdrawals amounted to $210,000 and the value of the remaining shares accumulated to $246,751—almost two and a half times the amount invested. Had $100,000 been invested at a straight 6% for 20 years, it would have earned only $120,000; and, of course, the principal itself would not have increased at all. Further, the annual income provided by the withdrawal plan enables the investor to utilize the money before inflation takes its toll.

Clearly, fixed-income investments, such as savings accounts or short-term bonds, do not provide the potential capital appreciation often realized by most mutual funds withdrawal plans. In a savings account or certificate of deposit, principal does not increase or decrease, and the rate of return is guaranteed only for a specific period. Further, rates earned will increase or decrease as the general level of interest rates rises and falls.

A withdrawal plan may be compared to an annuity (see the chapter on "Life Insurance"), but there are basic differences. An annuity may offer a uniform income guarantee for life, but the investor has no control over the invested capital, cannot make periodic redemptions when and if needed. At the death of the annuitant, or joint annuitants if the payments are based on two lives, the capital remaining in the contract is forfeited to the writer of the annuity (usually an insurance company). In a withdrawal plan, the investor has complete control, and he or she may decrease or increase payments—or stop them altogether—as circumstances warrant. The investor may also redeem at any time all or part of his or her holdings, and at death the remaining capital becomes part of the estate, distributable to the heirs as directed. Briefly stated, the withdrawal plan is much more flexible than the annuity.

Withdrawal Plan with $100,000 Investment Beginning January 1, 1965.

Year	Earnings		Annual Withdrawal	Monthly Withdrawal	Excess Earnings Reinvested	Ending Value
	Dividends	Capital Gains				
1965	2,206	7,066	6,000	500	3,272	115,784
1966	2,678	8,678	6,000	500	5,356	110,853
1967	3,016	6,536	6,000	500	3,552	136,425
1968	3,550	5,724	6,000	500	3,274	152,922
1969	3,809	9,172	6,000	500	6,981	130,848
1970	3,873	5,676	9,000	750	549	124,220
1971	3,768	2,471	9,000	750	−1,761	135,774
1972	3,695	4,385	9,000	750	920	147,603
1973	3,846	3,043	9,000	750	−2,111	114,206
1974	5,492	0	9,000	750	−3,508	85,450
1975	4,707	595	12,000	1,000	−6,698	102,957
1976	3,975	1,855	12,000	1,000	−6,170	120,401
1977	3,833	2,128	12,000	1,000	−6,039	104,991
1978	3,836	0	12,000	1,000	−8,164	107,765
1979	4,293	1,295	12,000	1,000	−6,412	115,355
1980	4,964	2,714	15,000	1,250	−7,322	122,906
1981	5,575	8,406	15,000	1,250	−1,019	109,112
1982	6,206	6,946	15,000	1,250	−1,848	127,309
1983	5,516	5,622	15,000	1,250	−3,862	137,174
1984	5,350	6,213	15,000	1,250	−3,437	130,069

Taxation of Withdrawal Amount

As in any mutual fund, all reinvested dividends and capital gains must be included in an investor's income before calculating income-tax liability.

As the mutual fund automatically liquidates shares to make the periodic payment, the investor is selling an asset. The sale results in a capital gain or capital loss and will be short- or long-term depending on whether or not the shares being sold have been owned for longer than six months.

Generally, investors use the *first-in/first-out* method to determine gain or loss. This usually means that the cost of the liquidated shares will be the cost of the "oldest" shares purchased. The gain or loss will be long- or short-term depending on how long the original shares were owned. Usually, the shares liquidated will be held for longer than six months so the gains will be taken as long-term: only 40% of the gain will be included in taxable income.

Investors may, however, use shares obtained in the reinvestment of dividends and capital gains as the shares sold, if the result will be a more advantageous tax situation.

Most mutual funds do not provide investors the tax information on the redemption of shares for their withdrawal plan. They do provide the amount of dividends and capital gains reinvested and the portion of the dividend that qualifies for the dividend exclusion. The investor then has some flexibility in determining the gain or loss according to which shares are used to determine cost.

It is extremely important for investors who have a withdrawal plan to keep the cumulative confirmation statements, which are the historical record of shares purchased, dividend and capital gain reinvestments, and shares redeemed.

In summary, the withdrawal plan produces:

1. level current income,

2. growth of income, and,

3. usually, appreciation of capital over the long run.

This is an extremely beneficial combination of features, which may be put to several uses. Income from such a plan may be used, for instance, to supplement regular income, to support relatives, to pay mortgages, to provide allowances for children away from home, and even to make alimony payments.

Case Examples

Many investors have found mutual fund withdrawal plans a convenient means of solving financial problems. Some people who have accumulated mutual fund shares use the shares to create a withdrawal plan. Others buy mutual fund shares for the express purpose of establishing a withdrawal plan.

Following are several examples of how mutual fund shares were used to solve financial payment requirements.

Example: Mr. and Mrs. Fisherman had been accumulating shares of a mutual fund for several years. They had been making monthly investments of at least $100. The value of their shares has risen to approximately $65,000.

The Fishermans decided to buy a summer cottage. The mortgage payments will be $325 per month. Rather than sell their growth-income mutual fund, and not have a mortgage, the Fishermans established a systematic withdrawal plan for $325 a month. They instructed the mutual fund to mail the monthly check directly to their mortgage company.

When the mortgage is paid, the Fishermans will have their cottage and their remaining mutual fund shares.

Example: Mrs. Support sends her elderly mother $300 a month. Because of her busy schedule in keeping house and raising three children, she often forgets to mail the check or it is mailed at various times during the month. She would like to find a means of relieving her mother of the worry as to when the check will arrive.

Mrs. Support decided to place $60,000 in a mutual fund and direct the fund to send her mother a check in the amount of $300 on the 5th of each month. Mrs. Support hopes the fund will grow through dividend and capital gains reinvestment by more than the amount of the payment.

It should be pointed out that Mrs. Support could have used a revisionary trust and possibly saved income taxes had she done so prior to March 1, 1986. She would have had to tie up her money for at least 10 years, or for the life of her mother.

However, had this arrangement been established after March, 1986, Mrs. Support would have had to pay income taxes had her mother died and the trust reverted back to her at the time of death.

Example: Mr. and Mrs. Jones have a daughter going to college in the fall. After considering the miscellaneous costs their daughter will incur, they decided she will need $150 a month.

The Jones' thought about redeeming some of their investments periodically to send her the money, or sending the money out of current income.

A third alternative seemed the best. The Jones' had been accumulating shares of a mutual fund for the last several years. They have made regular investments depending on the amount of discretionary income. They decided to instruct the mutual fund to mail a check to their daughter in the amount of $150 on the first of each month. The check would be mailed directly to their daughter at college. This decision relieved the Jones' from having to worry about mailing the check on a timely basis, or what to do if they did not have the money in the bank after paying their monthly bills.

Example: Mr. and Mrs. Traveller buy a new car every three years. For many years they had financed the car through their Friendly Bank.

Several years ago Mrs. Traveller's aunt passed away, and left her a modest inheritance. She invested the inheritance in a mutual fund.

One day while reviewing their investments with their broker, they were advised that rather than making car payments to Friendly Bank, they should establish a systematic withdrawal plan using their mutual fund shares to make the car payments. The mutual fund was instructed to make the car payments directly to Friendly Bank rather than to Mr. and Mrs. Traveller.

Another alternative considered by the Travellers, but discarded, was to sell a part of their accumulated mutual fund holdings. In this manner they would not have a car payment, but would lose the mutual fund shares.

The Travellers anticipated the value of their mutual fund holdings will increase more than the monthly payments of the car note.

Example: Mr. Separated, recently divorced, is to pay his exwife $500 a month in alimony payments. Rather than mail his exwife a check each month, Mr. Separated decided to place $100,000 in a mutual fund and direct the fund to make the required payment.

Because the payment will represent dividends, capital gains, and sale of shares, Mr. Separated feels he will experience a net income-tax savings by using the systematic withdrawal plan.

As can easily be seen, several of the foregoing examples demonstrate the benefits of accumulating money in the mutual fund shares and making use of a withdrawal plan. Mutual funds offer a great deal of flexibility *after* capital has been accumulated.

Annuities

What Are Annuities?

Annuities are contracts between a life insurance company and a buyer. This type of contract allows the buyer to make a single investment, or a series of investments, during the "accumulation period." The insurance company guarantees the buyer the right at any time to withdraw all, or any portion, of the contract values or to "annuitize" the contract by electing to take monthly income payments for the buyer's life or a designated period, beginning immediately or at some future date.

People bought, and still buy, annuities because of Section 72 of the Internal Revenue Service Code, which states that earnings on the contract accrue (compound) on a tax-deferred basis. There were, and are, tax benefits during annuitization (the payout period) that are discussed later.

The primary advantage of an annuity is quite simple. If the money were not invested in an annuity contract, the individual would have to pay current income tax on the earnings.

Evolution of Annuities

Annuities have gone through several evolutions. For years, annuities were sold by insurance companies as vehicles to guarantee a specific and fixed retirement income. Individuals paid to the insurance company a certain amount of money in return for a guaranteed fixed monthly retirement benefit. The promise was: you cannot outlive your income.

As all investors know, people living on a fixed income have had a very difficult time since the mid-1950s. The cost of everything they acquired, from housing to food to gasoline, increased. Level annuity payments did *not* keep pace with the cost of living.

Thus the birth of what is referred to as a "variable annuity." The accumulated values and payments were no longer committed to fixed rates. The underlying investments were in stocks, bonds, or real estate in an attempt to keep pace with inflation. The value of the annuity contract rose and fell based on the values of the stocks, bonds, or real estate underlying the contract.

The variable annuity took a different twist, and the annuity concept was modified in the 60s and early 70s by The First Investment Annuity Corporation of America. They developed and marketed an insurance/investment product known as the "investment annuity." The investment annuity was also known as a "wraparound" annuity because the insurance contract allowed the investor to select his or her own investments such as a mutual fund or a selected portfolio of stocks or bonds.

After several running battles with the Internal Revenue Service, the company's new marketing concept came to an end in 1977 when the IRS ruled that the investment earnings would no longer be sheltered from current income taxes. The IRS, however, grandfathered all then-current holders.

The mutual-fund industry learned the advantages of deferral quite quickly. Many mutual funds teamed up with insurance companies and wrapped their funds with annuities. The advantage was simple to understand. The investor owning the fund outright had to pay current income taxes on the fund's earnings and a capital gains tax on any realized capital gain. When wrapped with the annuity, taxes on all earnings were deferred.

The savings and loan industry, which was losing substantial assets during the 70s, found the wraparound annuity so enticing that it sought the insurance companies that would create annuity products into which the depositor could place savings. This meant that tax on the earnings would be deferred until the money was withdrawn from the contract. The annuities that wrapped savings deposits were referred to as "savers' annuities."

In October of 1980, the IRS ruled that depositors had almost total control of the savings accounts or certificates of deposit wrapped by the annuity. The IRS ruled that the policyholder, not the insurance company, would be considered the owner of the account for federal income tax purposes. Thus the end to a tax advantage for the S&L's.

The mutual funds breathed a sigh of relief because they were not included in the 1980 ruling. The relief, however, only lasted briefly. In September of 1981, the IRS acted again. The IRS said that all earnings of a mutual fund, even when wrapped by an annuity, would be taxable to the investor in the year earned. The reason was that the policy owner, the investor, had control of the investments, not the insurance company. This was the end of the era for wrapping investments with an insurance contract to obtain a tax deferral on earnings.

The IRS stated that variable annuities can be afforded tax deferral on earnings so long as the investment portion of the contract was managed by an insurance company, and only available to the annuity contract owners. As one executive said referring to the long-standing battles on the taxation of annuities, "Annuities will now be sold for what they are: long-term investments for retirement."

Types of Annuities

There are two types of annuities:

1. With a *fixed annuity,* the buyer's money earns a guaranteed rate of interest during the accumulation period. Both principal and interest are guaranteed against loss by the insurance company. When the buyer takes money from the contract and if he or she elects monthly income upon annuitization, the amount is based on the annuitant's age, sex, and payment option selected. The amount of the monthly check is guaranteed.

Example—the Traditional, or "Nest Egg" Approach (Fixed Income Annuity). The Smiths invest $30,000 in 1952 for two purposes: (1) to provide some current income and (2) to serve as a nest-egg at retirement. Although in 1952 the typical passbook savings account paid a mere 3% let's say that the couple were lucky enough to find a fixed annuity that yielded 12%. That percentage translates to $3,600 a year or $300 a month. In 1952, that would have been a great investment.

By 1981, however, the Smiths are still earning the same amount of money—no more and no less. Yet prices, as we all know, have gone up dramatically since the fifties. The original $30,000 and the interest payments of $300 a month buy only a fraction of what they did several decades ago.

The traditional, or "nest egg," approach simply does not protect the Smiths against the tremendous toll taken by inflation. Here is how their investment stacks up:

Original investment $ 30,000
Total interest received $108,000
Value of interest $ 30,000

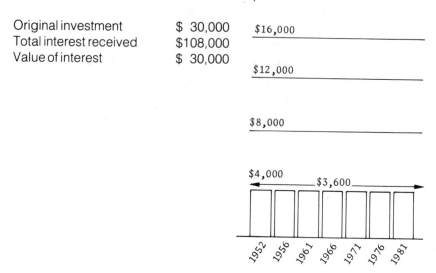

2. With a *variable annuity,* during the annuitization period the value of the annuitant's variable account fluctuates with the changing market values of the underlying securities held in the account. The buyer may make withdrawals from his or her annuity account. However if the buyer accepts a monthly income upon annuitization, the amount of the check is based on the annuitant's age, sex, and payment option selected as well as the investment results of the underlying portfolio. Subsequent monthly checks throughout the lifetime of the annuitant will vary in amount.

Example—the Purchasing Power Approach (Variable Annuity). The Joneses, unlike the Smiths, were not so concerned with locking in a fixed amount of income per year as they were with maintaining their purchasing power. The Joneses put their money—$30,000—into a variable annuity, whose yield kept pace with inflation. The investment was a fund whose earnings and dividends increased each year.

As a result, the Joneses not only enjoyed greater income as the years rolled by, but they also saw their principal grow from the original $30,000 to $292,658!

Original investment $30,000
Total dividends received $137,995
Value of investment $292,658

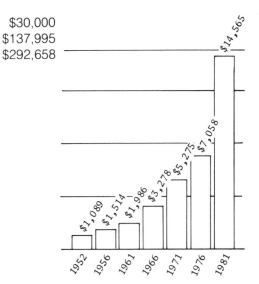

A comparison of this approach with the fixed annuity shows how the Smiths have failed to keep up with the Joneses.

The owner of a variable annuity is in much the same position as the purchaser of mutual fund shares who either makes a lump sum purchase or periodic payments over a number of years. At some time, the investor decides he or she wants capital back or income. The annuity differs from investment in a mutual fund in that:

1. If the investor owns a mutual fund, all earnings are taxable in the year paid. This includes realized capital gain.

2. During the accumulation period, the investor incurs no income tax liability for reinvested dividends, interest, or realized capital gains. The insurance company pays a 30% corporate capital gains tax on realized capital gains; a proportionate amount of that tax may be deducted from the benefits credited to the annuitant's account.

Accumulation and Payment Units

Participation in a variable annuity is measured in two types of units.

Accumulation Unit. This unit represents the annuitant's prop-ortionate share in the accumulation fund. When an annuitant makes a payment to the fund, commission costs and fees for expenses and mortality guarantees are deducted. (Expense and mortality fees as well as an annual policy fee, which can range from $25 to $50, are usually deducted from the account once a year or when the account is terminated.) The balance is then used to purchase units, usually calculated to three decimal places. The investor can select whether he or she wants the money invested in a fixed-income account, or money market account, a common stock account, or an account that only purch-ases bonds. In effect, the accumulation unit is calculated and purchased very much like mutual fund shares.

Payment Units. Once a contract is annuitized the number of units owned never changes. The payout per unit, however, may vary as it is based on the investment performance (less fees, or premium charges, for the guaranteed expenses and mortality). The first payment is calculated using the annuity pay-ment rate stated in the contract (the "guaranteed" rate). This actuarially computed rate is based on a nominal rate of return. Subsequent payments will fluctuate with the management results of the underlying investment portfolios. Some variable annuities allow exchanges of units after annuity payments begin (post-an-nuitization transfers). This provides investment flexibility and con-trol of payments during the payout (annuitization) period.

The amount of each subsequent payment is then determined by the performance of the fund from one valuation date to the next. If the performance is better than the assumed return, the value increases and the annuitant's payment increases. Con-versely, if the performance is less than the assumed return, the payment decreases.

The insurance company does not guarantee the amount of the payment; it only guarantees that a payment will be made in accordance with the contractual terms. It is therefore wise to select as low an assumed rate of return as circumstances permit, and allow for a periodic increase of income.

How Annuities Are Purchased

Annuities contracts may be purchased in one of three ways:

1. *Periodic payment:* Payments (investments) are made over a period of time with annuity payments to commence at some future date.

2. *Single payment, deferred contract:* The purchase price is paid in a lump sum with annuity payments to commence at some future time. This type is also known as a "single premium deferred annuity."

3. *Single payment, immediate contract:* The purchase price is paid in a lump sum with annuity payments to begin immediately.

When the annuity payments begin, part of each is taxable as income and part is not taxable. (This is called the "exclusion allowance calculation.") The portion of the payment that is not taxable is considered return of principal (invested capital). The nontaxable part is the annuitant's cost basis, and is amortized over the remainder of the investor's life expectancy. The specific amount is calculated as follows:

1. The annuitant's age at the time payments start is subtracted from his or her total life expectancy, as determined by Treasury Department actuary tables.

2. The total dollar investment of the annuitant is divided by the number of payments expected, according to the annuitant's remaining years.

3. This operation yields a dollar amount for each payment that represents the annuitant's nontaxable cost basis. The balance of the payment is taxed as income.

Parties to an Annuity Contract

Like an insurance contract, an annuity contract has four parties.

1. *Insurance Company.* This company collects deposits and guarantees (underwrites) the contract. Underwriting includes accumulation, payments, death benefits, and annuitization.

2. *Annuitant.* The annuitant is similar to the insured in a life insurance contract. It is the person on whose life the contract is based (written). Accumulation and payout benefits are based on the age and sex of the annuitant. The death of the annuitant causes the contract to mature and the value of the contract (amounts deposited plus accrued earnings), either in lump sum or installments, is paid by the insurance company to the beneficiary.

3. *Beneficiary.* The beneficiary is the person (persons) or organization that will receive the value of the contract either as a lump sum or in installments upon the death of the annuitant. The beneficiary can be the same person as the owner.

4. *Owner.* The owner is the person, persons, or entity entitled to the ownership rights stated in the contract, and in whose name or names the contract is issued. The owner has the right to change any contract designation, including the beneficiary. Some contracts allow the change of annuitant by the owner. The death of the owner (if he or she is not the annuitant) causes a change in ownership, not a maturity of the contract. If the owner dies, the values in the contract (amounts deposited plus accrued earnings) continue intact and earnings continue to accrue tax deferred.

The variable annuity can be used to defer taxes on income over as many as three generations.

If the annuitant should die before payments start, the contract matures; the beneficiary becomes the new owner and is subject to income tax on the contract value, which is the cash value of the contract at the time of death in excess of the cost basis.

Except for the varying amount of each payment, the modes of variable annuity payments if the contract is annuitized are similar to those in life insurance policies or fixed annuity contracts.

1. Payments for the life of the annuitant with no benefit after the annuitant's death. At the death of the annuitant, the insurance company keeps all remaining contract values.

2. Payments for life with a certain number of payments such as

120 (10 years) or 180 (15 years) being guaranteed to the named individual, individuals, or organizations. If the annuitant dies before the guaranteed number of payments is made, the remaining guaranteed payments are made to a named individual, individuals, or organizations. If the annuitant dies before the guaranteed number of payments is made, the remaining guaranteed payments are made to a named individual or individuals, or the estate of the annuitant.

3. Payments for the joint lives of the annuitant and a named survivor. This option can also include a certain number of guaranteed payments. Certain payment guarantees may be included as a survivor option. Obviously, however, payments are higher if no guarantees or survivors are included in the contract.

Example: Mr. and Mrs. Self-Sufficient bought an annuity contract several years ago. They are presently considering retirement. Mr. Self-Sufficient is 65 years old and Mrs. Self-Sufficient is 62 years old. They have contracted the insurance company and have been told their payment options are as follows.

Payment for life to Mr. Self-Sufficient.

Payment for life for Mr. Self-Sufficient's life, but with payments guaranteed for 5, 10, 15 or 20 years.

Payments for the joint lives of Mr. & Mrs. Self-Sufficient.

Payments may also be guaranteed for a fixed period of 5, 10, 15, or 20 years.

As discussed at the beginning of this chapter, the raging tax controversy of deferred annuities seems to be over. Highlights of current tax laws affecting variable and fixed annuities are as follows:

1. The annuity allows investors to defer taxation on all income until the value of the contract is withdrawn. The deferral includes earnings that can be classified as interest, dividends, and capital gains.
2. To qualify for the tax deferral, an annuity's investment ac-

counts must be available only to annuity buyers and the accounts must be managed by insurance companies. After February 28, 1986 contracts held by the corporations or partnerships will be taxed as ordinary income to the owner of the contract.

3. Withdrawals from annuity contracts are now treated for income tax purposes as last-in/first-out (LIFO). This means that any withdrawals would first apply to accrued income and be fully taxable. After all income is withdrawn, withdrawals would be nontaxable because of return of capital. These tax provisions do not refer to annuitization of the contract in which a portion of each payment is considered return of capital.

4. After February 28, 1986, a 10% tax penalty is charged on all withdrawals of accumulated earnings prior to age 59½ or within 10 years of the original contract date, whichever comes first. A word of warning should be sufficient; money should not be placed in a deferred annuity if the investor feels the money may be needed before age 59½ or within 10 years.

Why Buy Annuities?

Like any investment, the variable annuity has advantages and weaknesses. For example, the contract guarantees payments for life. At a time when developments in medicine are pushing the average life expectancy up and up, that guarantee is a valuable one. However, those payments may increase or decrease, so the guarantee is not an ironclad protection against future declines in market value. Also, once payments begin, the annuitant will never have to worry about investment decisions on the amount in the contract. Neither will he or she ever see that money again. After all guaranteed payments are made to the annuitant or to the annuitant's survivor, the insurance company keeps all assets remaining on the contract. Nothing is available for the heirs. Therefore, care should be exercised in the choice of annuity payment options.

Variable, and to some extent, fixed annuities are becoming important and popular investment alternatives. Generally, they are suited for investors who want to defer taxation on income while their capital accumulates. Withdrawal of cash before certain key dates may trigger penalties and income taxes. When investing in an annuity, make certain you understand *all* of the key terms and important dates.

In some instances, an investor may want to use an annuity for income and to gain some income tax advantages. Investors using an annuity to obtain income and favorable income tax treatment should realize that they are generally giving up control of their money.

A summary of the benefits of the modern variable annuity and investor flexibility through accruing an annuity is as follows:

1. Safety of principal.

2. Tax deferral of accumulation of income within the contract.

3. Guarantees of interest if a fixed annuity or fixed account in a variable annuity is selected.

4. Annuity contracts have flexibility and liquidity. The owner can change investment vehicles within what is provided by the insurance company at certain intervals. The owner can withdraw funds from the annuity when and if needed.

5. Guaranteed lifetime retirement income (if elected).

6. Special tax treatment of annuitized payments.

7. Avoidance of probate upon death of the annuitant.

8. Possible estate tax benefits.

Using Annuities for Income and Growth

The four flowcharts below demonstrate how an investment can be split between two types of annuities to accomplish a two-fold goal: (1) to provide current income and (2) to preserve principal.

In each chart, the investment is divided between a single payment, immediate contract and a single payment, deferred contract. The immediate contract starts paying monthly income right away. At the same time, the deferred contract allows the balance of the investment to grow, compounding over five years

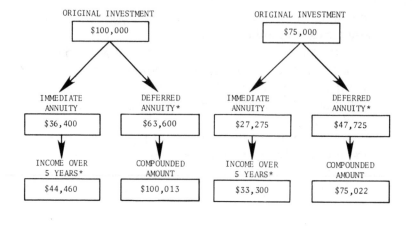

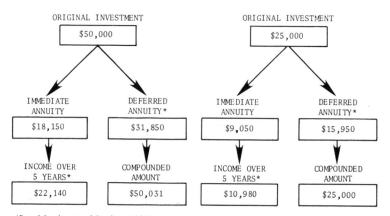

*Payable in monthly installments.
**Compounded at an assumed 9.5% rate.

at an assumed rate of 9.5%, to equal the amount of the original investment.

Annuities as Alternatives

The variable annuity can be considered as an alternative to a mutual fund or some deferred compensation plans. Edward L. Dunford, CLU, agent for Connecticut General Life Insurance Company, says, "If a man is trying to accumulate money for retirement, I will probably sell him a variable annuity. If he is trying to accumulate money to have a lump sum of capital for future purposes, such as the purchase of a summer cottage, trip for the family, education of the children, I am going to recommend a mutual fund."

As mentioned earlier, a deferred annuity can be used to defer income for as many as three generations.

Example: Suppose Grandfather buys a single premium deferred annuity contract and, upon purchase, names Grandson as annuitant and himself as beneficiary. His death would then cause the ownership of the contract to pass to his heirs (his wife or children or both), just like any other asset he owns. It would also be included in his gross taxable estate. However, the contract itself would continue accumulating interest, tax deferred, until such time as Grandson, the annuitant, dies.

Now assume that after Grandfather dies, son becomes owner. Son now controls the contract and changes the beneficiary to himself so that the proceeds flow to him in the event of the annuitant's (Grandson) premature death. Any person who was alive on the date of the original purchase may be a designee in the contract. Keep in mind that, while the owner and beneficiary designations can always be changed, only in certain contracts can the annuitant of the contract be changed.

Upon Son's subsequent death, the policy can still be continued and inherited by Grandson (the annuitant). The interest can also continue to compound tax deferred in this instance for three generations. Grandson is now both owner and annuitant and will probably change the beneficiary to his wife, trust or children.

Example: Mr. Self-Sufficient is 55 years old. Because the next 10 years will represent peak earnings and he will be in maximum tax brackets, he decides to deposit $50,000 into a single premium deferred annuity. This allows Mr. Self-Sufficient to defer income tax on the earnings of that $50,000. He also likes the fact that with a deferred annuity he can decide when taxes are to be paid. He can decide when income is to be withdrawn from the contract, which in essence means he is managing his income tax payments. After 4½ years, at age 59½, he can begin to withdraw as he sees fit. If he feels that he will not need the proceeds from this annuity because he is covered by a substantial employer retirement plan, and has substantial income-producing assets other than his deferred annuity, he can allow his account to accumulate, or even change the beneficiary as part of his estate-planning activities.

For instance, Mr. Self-Sufficient is the owner of the annuity contract. His life insurance trust is the beneficiary and his 30-year-old son is the annuitant. His reasons for these arrangements are that if he does not need the money from the contract, the full value and appropriate tax liability will pass to the life insurance trust. Unless his son dies prematurely, the deferral benefits could last for a substantial number of years.

Use of an Annuity for Deferred Compensation

Another example of the use of a variable annuity is for deferred compensation. Deferred compensation plans differ (such as those for school teachers and nonprofit organizations, state and municipal employees, and executives or highly compensated employees), but the principle is the same.

A portion of earned income is deferred until some later date. This reduces current income and taxes. Properly structured (in an annuity), such deferred income accumulates on a tax-deferred basis. In a variable annuity, these assets can be managed by the person making the deferral. Finally, while taxes are ultimately due on the entire amount (deferred amount, dividends, and capital gains), the owner may manage the payment of these taxes with his or her own situation in mind, without consideration of when the gain accrued in the account.

A key argument for highly compensated individuals is that of tax-free investments versus tax-deferred annuities. To compare:

Tax-Free	*Tax-Deferred*
Example: Municipal Bonds	Example: Variable Annuities
Simple interest	Compound interest
Prepaid taxes (lower yield due to structure has net effect of prepaying taxes)	Deferred taxes (tax dollars accumulate and the proportionate gain is to the owner)

An Annuity Investment in a Retirement Trust
"Why Fund a Tax Shelter with a Tax Shelter?"

Investment flexibility within a retirement program has taken on new importance, not only due to fluctuating economic and market conditions, but for clear-cut, legal reasons as well. Section 404 of the Employee Retirement Income Security Act (ERISA) of 1974 encourages investment flexibility in a separate account for each participant in a retirement program. In such an arrangement, an employer is relieved of fiduciary responsibility for the investment designations made by each employee.

An ideal range of investments for a separate account program is often provided by annuities. The question is often raised why offer both types of annuity contract units? Many annuities have additional costs—an annual administrative fee, an additional asset charge—so why provide the same investment management under the annuity as is available directly in the funds? It is to make available the following additional features and benefits. Some individuals may want the opportunity to participate in these additional benefits.

1. No initial sales charge.

2. Dividends reinvested at net asset value.

3. Guaranteed death benefit on life of designated annuitant.

4. Guarantee of annuity purchase rates.

5. Availability of fixed account with guarantee of principal and interest.

6. Guarantee that expenses under the contract will never be increased.

7. Guarantee that individual cannot outlive annuity payments.

8. Transfer of subaccounts without charge.

9. ERISA diversification—reasonable choice, separate account plans.

Options

What Is an Option?

An option is a *contract* giving the holder (a *long*) the right to either buy or sell a financial instrument at a specified price (*striking* or *exercise* price) *before* a specified time (*expiration date)*. Options in the securities industry once were almost exclusively confined to listed common stocks. Today, options may be traded on such diverse items as: U.S. Treasury Securities, Foreign Currencies, Futures Contracts, and Stock Market Indices.

A contract to *buy* a security is a *call* while an option to sell is a *put*. If the original purchaser is a long, as noted above, it follows that the original seller is a short. For somewhat obscure reasons, option sellers have long been referred to as *writers*. In return for granting the option, a writer receives from the buyer a *premium*—cash that belongs to the seller whether or not the long ever decides to *exercise* the option; that is, buy or sell the underlying security according to the contract terms.

Trading Options

Options are traded in both the over-the-counter (OTC) and exchange (*listed*) markets. Prior to 1973 trading was exclusively OTC. The introduction of exchange-traded options in that year has effectively closed down the older OTC market mechanism described in earlier editions of this book. Unless otherwise specified, it is usually understood that each (stock) option calls for the purchase or sale of 100 shares of the underlying security. This is true of both OTC and listed options.

Over-the-Counter (OTC)

Until the introduction of listed options, the market for OTC (*conventional*) options was dominated by about 30 small, highly specialized firms forming the "Put and Call Brokers and Dealers Association." With the exception of some inventoried "special options," each individual option was created specifically on demand. *Every* detail—the particular stock, striking price, expiration date, and premium—was individually negotiated. Each option was therefore unique, making for obvious trading difficulties and an illiquid secondary market. Furthermore, there was a dearth of easily accessible information and at least a suspicion that transaction costs involving the option dealers were exorbitant.

The introduction of listed options reduced the conventional options markets drastically, as these options possessed all of the advantages of OTC options, but few of the disadvantages. The older options firms either disbanded or adapted to the listed markets by combining with the established retail stock brokerage firms. Nevertheless a sizable conventional options business exists today, although generally not available to the smaller investor. Institutional broker/dealers often create options for their clientele when those options available in the listed markets have terms the institutions find unattractive, or when there is no comparable listed option available. This is particularly true of options on fixed-income securities like GNMAs or corporate bonds. The options departments of retail firms also accommodate customers with conventional options when an appropriate listed option cannot be found, for example, on certain OTC stocks. The typical investor, however, should confine options activities to the listed markets for ease of execution, lower transaction costs, and greater visibility. Options are tricky enough to deal in without adding complications.

Listed Options

The introduction of exchange-traded options by the Chicago Board Options Exchange (CBOE) in 1973 has been one of the great success stories in the history of modern finance. By standardizing the basic option terms (stock, expiration date, and striking price) the CBOE created interchangeable contracts that could easily be traded on an exchange. The only item left open to negotiation is the premium, which can be determined by the open outcry auction system very similar to that used by futures traders on the CBOE's parent, the Chicago Board of Trade.

The concept was immediately successful and quickly mimicked by the American Stock Exchange in early 1975 and somewhat later by both the Philadelphia and Pacific Stock Exchanges. The NYSE, itself the home of almost all the stocks underlying these options, did not enter the options arena until 1983 and then only for *index options.* Listed options trading provided two critically important characteristics almost totally lacking in the conventional market—visibility and liquidity.

Any registered representative may now call up last sale, bid, ask, and volume quotations on the electronic quotation equipment available in every brokerage office. Customers may receive complete records of the previous day's trading in the *Wall Street Journal, The New York Times* and most other major city newspapers.

Options Clearing Corporation. The liquidity of listed options stems from the "clearinghouse" concept borrowed from futures trading. The exchanges jointly own the Options Clearing Corporation (OCC), which is both issuer and guarantor of all listed options. Once the brokers on the floor agree to the premiums, the link between buyer and seller is broken.

On the day following the trade, premiums are paid to the OCC by the longs, and credited by the OCC to the sellers. From that point, either party's actions with that contract will involve only the OCC, which has become, in effect, the common long to all shorts and the common short to all longs. By becoming the "other side" of all trades, the OCC removes any concern about the failure of either party to perform according to the contract if an exercise occurs.

The very short-term nature of options trading (overwhelmingly 90 or fewer days) makes the issuance of certificates impractical. All customer positions are simply recorded as computer entries. While no physical evidence of the contract itself exists, an investor receives a confirmation of each transaction and a regular account statement just as for an account with regular stock or bond positions.

Expiration Dates and Striking Prices

Conventional (OTC) option striking prices are established through negotiation and are often set at the market price of the underlying security at that time. Similarly, expiration dates are subject to negotiation. About 90 days is the usual time span.

Listed options, on the other hand, have both standardized strike prices *and* expiration dates. The striking prices are ordinarily set at 2½, 5, or 10 point intervals, depending on the market price of the underlying stock. When a stock moves in price to touch the current highest or lowest interval, new striking prices are introduced two business days later (unless the option is very near expiration).

Example: If XYZ stock is currently at about $30 a share, there would usually be striking prices for XYZ options at 25, 30, and 35. Should XYZ stock rise to 35, trading in options with a 40 striking price would commence two business days later.

All listed options expire at 11:59 P.M. on the Saturday following the third Friday of the expiration month. Each underlying stock is assigned to one of three different trading cycles, each with expiration months 90 days apart—January, April, July, October; February, May, August, November; March, June, September, December. Only the nearest 3 months are offered at any one time.

Listed options are quoted by both striking price and expiration month.

Example: An "IBM January 120" call identifies the right to purchase 100 shares of IBM common stock at a price of $120 a share no later than the third week in January. Such a contract is separate and distinct from an IBM January 130 call or from an IBM April 120 call.

Listed options may be traded in either cash or margin accounts, although some strategies involve potentially unsecured risks and are restricted to margin accounts. Because the brokerage firm members of the OCC are required to settle with the

Clearing Corporation on the business day following the trade, most of them demand payment on or before that day.

Regulation T of the Federal Reserve System, however, does not distinguish between other securities and options for settlement purposes and thus does not require payment for seven business days following the trade date. Potential traders should be certain of their broker's policy *prior* to entering into any transactions.

It should also be noted that the purchase of an option must be *paid in full* whether in a cash or a margin account. Furthermore, even though fully paid, options are not credited with any loan value in a margin account so an investor cannot borrow from an options position, even a profitable one.

Other Important Terminology

Because trading options can be complex, a prospective investor should be careful to get a firm grounding in the basic terminology of the market. While a number of these expressions have already been outlined, there are a few other indispensable terms to know.

Opening transactions. Such trades create *new* options positions. *Opening sales* create or increase short positions. Opening sales are "writing" transactions.

Closing transactions. Such trades reduce or eliminate existing positions. *Closing purchases* cancel short positions whereas closing sales cancel long positions.

In the Money. A call is "in the money" when the market price of the underlying stock is higher than the striking price of the option.

Example: An XYZ October 60 call is in the money by 5 points when XYZ stock is at 65.

In a similar manner, a put is in the money when the stock is priced at *less* than the striking price. When an option is "in the money," the difference between the striking price and the stock price is said to be the option's "intrinsic value."

Out of the Money. A call is "out of the money" when the stock price is *less* than the striking price of a call. Such an option has *no* "intrinsic value." Puts are out of the money when the market price is *higher* than the option's exercise price. Because such options often have very small premiums, sometimes as little as 1/16 or $6.25, for an entire contract, speculators often buy them. For the most part, out-of-the-money options are poor bets as the chance of loss is very large, at least from the long's viewpoint. "You get what you pay for" is an expression as applicable to options trading as to life in general.

Net Premium. This confusing term is probably better rendered as "time value," that is, the portion of the total premium paid relating to the length of time remaining on the option. Option premiums are determined, as noted earlier, by an auction market. What makes a fair premium to both bidder and offerer is determined by three factors:

1. *Relation of the stock price to the striking price.* Except under unusual circumstance, and normally for very brief periods, an "in the money" option always sells for at least its "intrinsic" value.

Example: An XYZ June 45 put would have to sell for at least $500 if XYZ stock were at 40. There is no such relation with out-of-the-money options.

2. *Relative volatility.* Speculators are drawn to volatile stocks and are willing to pay more for the motion perceived inherent in such a stock than in a more placid issue.

3. *Time remaining.* All options are wasting assets. As the clock ticks, every option loses some of its "time value" (or net premium). Logically, a buyer in January should be willing to pay more for—and a seller demand more for—XYZ July 60 calls than for April 60 calls, which expire 90 days earlier. As an option approaches its expiration it loses its "time value" and approaches its intrinsic value (if any). If the option is far away from its striking price, it may cease trading altogether. It follows that the premium for an out-of-the-money option, having no intrinsic value, must consist *entirely* of time value. This is precisely what makes trading such options risky. The underlying stock must often make a substantial move just for the trader to break even.

Who Trades Options and Why

The advent of listed options has opened up a vast new market and many profit possibilities, both for brokers and their customers. Unfortunately the relatively "cheap" prices of options often induce the wrong type of speculation and draw the wrong investing crowd. It is *not* a game for the oddlot buyer or the casual investor who wants to "take a flyer."

Options are complex vehicles. Anyone unwilling or unable to spend a great deal of time in learning a complex subject is well advised to say "thanks—but no thanks" to a solicitation to participate. The arena is one where professionals frequently lose and where losses are the norm. It is no place for an amateur dabbler.

On the other hand, for those of sufficient means and abilities, these markets are "the fastest game in town." The dramatic growth of options trading in the past decade is ample proof that the appeal of these markets is both extensive and enduring.

In certainly oversimplified but essentially correct terms, one can say that option buyers tend to be speculators seeking a highly leveraged trading vehicle with limited risk. Option writers, on the other hand, are generally more interested in generating a cash flow and a return on investment hoped to be superior to that of simple ownership of the underlying securities themselves.

Why Investors Buy Call Options

A case can probably be made for the buying of call options with an ultimate goal of acquiring a stock for "investment" via exercise. To be frank, however, the great majority of options traders are outright speculators and where one draws the line between speculation and gambling isn't always entirely clear.

Once one accepts the speculation motive, the option often offers much that the underlying stock does not:

1. *Leverage*—the premium to control 100 shares of stock is usually much less than the purchase price of the stock itself, even if purchased on margin.

Example: In December IBM stock is @124. An IBM April 130 call option is@$575. Buying 100 IBM for cash costs $12,400 or $6,200 on margin. If IBM stock goes to 140, the margin investor makes $1,600 on a $6,200 investment. The option buyer makes $425 on a $575 investment (at 140, a 130 call is worth at least $1,000, less the $575 premium paid).

2. *Limited risk*—The very worst that can happen to the investor holding a call is its expiration, which would result in the loss of the premium.

Example: In theory, of course, the cash buyer of 100 IBM @124 *could* lose $12,400, although in practice the idea is silly. Nevertheless, had an investor purchased 200 IBM for about $15,000 in 1979 and sold it for less than $10,000 in the depressed market in 1981, a very real $5,000 would have been lost. The fact that IBM later recovered to $120 per share would have been scant consolation to the investor who lost $5,000 on a blue-chip investment.

The investor must always keep in mind that an "option" is precisely what its name implies—a *choice*. An option is not the underlying security; it does not pay dividends; it does not reward the patient long-term holder. There are blue-chip stocks, and there are options on blue-chip stocks. There are, however, no blue-chip options.

Why Investors Buy Put Options

Besides speculation on a price increase, the listed option—in this case a *put*—may be used to speculate on a price decline. The classic tactic for an anticipated price drop is the *short sale.* The short seller borrows shares and sells them at the current price hoping to repurchase them at a lower price later. If this is accomplished, the borrowed shares are returned to the lender and the speculator profits on the difference between the higher sale proceeds and the lower cost to "cover" the sale by buying the borrowed shares back.

The short sale, however, is very risky. Because borrowed shares have been sold, the *potential risk is unlimited.* Short sales *must* be done in margin accounts and the short seller must post cash or other collateral equal to 50% of the sale. The order must be executed on a "plus" or "zero plus" tick to satisfy the provisions of the '34 Act. All of these complications indicate why short selling is not frequently employed by the typical speculator, as indeed it should not. The short seller should possess a level of sophistication and risk-taking ability well beyond that of even the experienced margin buyer.

The put option addresses the most important of these concerns. As with a call, the put allows the holder to take action when and if he or she desires. Thus, the put buyer obtains the right to make a retroactive short sale should he or she choose to do so. The only money at risk is the purchase price (premium) of the put itself.

Example: A speculator, feeling XYZ shares are likely to fall from 70 to 60, purchases 1 XYZ June 70 put for $375. If the market does drop to 60, the put will be worth at least $1,000 and the investor may then: (a) exercise the option, creating a short position in XYZ stock, or (b) sell it for $1,000 (plus any remaining time value), nearly tripling the original investment. In either case the investor has made a substantial profit on the price deterioration of XYZ stock. Additionally, only $375 of capital was committed (vs. $3,500 for a short sale) and that number represents the maximum possible loss, even had the stock gone to $100 per share or more.

Using Options as "Insurance"

Even though the option vehicle itself is inherently speculative, when used in conjunction with a stock position it can be thought of as sort of an "insurance policy." A long put, for instance, may be used to limit losses (or lock in profits) on a long stock position. Likewise, a long call can be used for the same purposes versus a short stock position.

Example: A speculator likes the appreciation potential of XYZ Corp.; a volatile trading favorite. She feels it could rise by about 20 points from its current price of 45. On the other hand, if the market weakens, XYZ could easily drop back to 30. The speculator thus buys 100 XYZ @45 and also buys 1 XYZ October 40 put for $100. If the stock indeed rises to 65, the option will expire worthless for a total loss of $100. This reduces the $2,000 profit on the stock.

Suppose, however, the market *did* weaken, sending XYZ's price to 27. The speculator could then exercise the put and sell @40 what had been purchased @45. The loss is therefore limited to $600 (loss from 45 to 40 on the stock plus the put premium) no matter how low XYZ actually drops.

(See the section of the "Futures" chapter entitled "Futures and Options Compared.")

Why Investors Write Call Options

The option writer receives the premiums paid by the buyer and in return agrees to deliver the underlying stock (if exercised). The intended strategy is to earn a superior rate of return through the receipt and reinvestment of premiums.

The most widely practiced type of writing is selling *covered calls*. It is a relatively conservative and easily implemented strategy that may be effected in a cash account. It has considerable appeal for both individual and institutional investors.

When the investor buys the underlying stock and sells a call option on the stock, the investor immediately establishes the price at which he or she is willing to sell.

Example: The investor buys 100 XYZ @ 70 and simultaneously sells 1 XYZ October 70 call for $600 premium. In this case, if the market moves up (by any amount), the option will ultimately be exercised. The stock, which was purchased @ 70, will be sold @ 70, leaving the $600 premium as a profit. Thus, if XYZ rises by less than 6 points, the premium will have provided a superior return. If, however, XYZ rises by *more* than 6 points, it would have been better had the investor simply bought and held the stock. Should the market move to 80, the stock would show a $1,000 profit whereas the call premium of $600 will now appear inadequate compensation to the writer.

Unlike the buyer, then, the writer is less concerned with leverage and a big price move. The writer instead is concentrating on *probabilities* rather than on *possibilities*. He or she hopes that the premium received will be more than sufficient to protect against a dramatic price change. Reasoning that such moves are relatively rare, the investor is willing to play certain odds. After all, there are only three things that can happen to a security price—it can advance, decline, or remain unchanged. To the covered writer, two of these three will produce a profit and the third *might*, depending on how much the price declines.

Example: GO common is @ 47. An investor buys 100 GO @ 47 and sells 1 GO June 45 call for $500. If the market advances, remains unchanged, or drops by fewer than 2 points, the option will be exercised. As the call striking price is 45, the investor will sell for that price shares that cost 47, an apparent $200 loss. The premium of $500, however, is added to the $4,500 exercise price to produce sales proceeds of $5,000, a $300 profit on the entire transaction. If the stock falls by more than 2 but fewer than 5 points, the profit is something less than $300. If the price falls by more than 5 points, the loss on the stock will then exceed the expired option premium, causing an overall loss.

Any such examples should be qualified by considering commissions and tax consequences. In many instances, an appealing "paper trade" may turn out to be a net loser when the real world of transaction costs intrudes.

Why Investors Write Put Options

Selling put options is far less understood by investors than selling calls. Investors are familiar with owning stock and the concept of fixing a sale price through writing a call is relatively easy to understand. As shown previously, covered call writing works best in a neutral environment, or at least when the writer is not strongly bullish on the underlying stock.

Put writing, on the other hand, is a decidedly bullish strategy. In return for the premium, the writer agrees to *deliver cash* and accept stock in return. The writer's goal is to see the market rise far enough for the put to expire, or to see the market stay unchanged.

Example: An investor with no stock position sells 1 LIT September 60 put for $500 at a time when the market price of XYZ stock is 57. If the market rises above 60, the put will expire and the writer makes the $500 premium. If the market stays unchanged, the holder will exercise the put and sell 100 LIT to the writer for $6,000. Because the writer received $500 at the outset, the actual cost is only $5,500, 2 points under the current market level. Of course, if the market drops below 55, the put writer starts to lose money, having paid an effective price of $5,500 for the stock.

From this example it is clear that a bullish investor *not anticipating an immediate price rise* might be better off selling a put rather than buying a call or the actual stock. The premium may be immediately reinvested while the investor awaits a clearer market trend. Unless the market rises or falls much more sharply than anticipated, the investment results should be superior to an outright purchase.

Straddles and Combinations

If few traders are successful with these vehicles, the reason is easy to understand: the results rarely justify the cost. A *straddle* combines a put and a call on the same underlying stock. Each option has the same exercise price and expiration date. The buyer consequently has fixed a price *both to buy and sell* the security. In order for the buyer to profit, the market must swing up or down substantially. The trader thus will profit in the event of any substantial move, no matter in what direction, but will likely lose if the price change is not large.

Example: With DAL @ 33, a trader buys 1 DAL July 30 call for $500 and 1 DAL July 30 put for $150, a total premium outlay of $650. The market price of DAL must rise higher than striking price plus the combined premiums or drop below the striking price by the same amount. A price rise higher than 36½ or lower than 23½ is profitable, but anything short of these prices loses money.

A *combination* is similar to a straddle except that the trader varies either the expiration dates, or (as is more likely) the striking prices, for example, 1 DOW Oct 60 call and 1 DOW Oct 55 put. The concept is basically the same as a straddle and the break-even formula given previously. The combination may have one side in the money, two sides in the money, or two sides out of the money. For example, the combination cited above would have both "legs" out of the money with the stock priced between 55 and 60.

Obviously, an investor might *write* straddles or combinations with or without attendant stock positions. Here the goal is simply the reverse of the buyer's. The writer feels the stock is unlikely to move sharply enough through the option's lifespan to offset the premiums received. While in general this appears to be a good bet, the exposure of being exercised on *both* the put *and* the call creates a risk that none but a very aggressive trader should contemplate.

Spreads

The spread provides a method for the options trader to enhance profit and limit the risk inherent in outright long or short options positions. In a spread, the trader simultaneously buys one option on a stock and sells a different option on the same stock. Both may be calls, or both may be puts—differing in either prices, expiration months, or both. The difference in the premium paid for the long option and that received from the short option creates the *spread*. The trader's aim is to see this spread *widen* or *narrow*, depending on the spread's construction. As the market price of the underlying stock changes, the prices of the options change in *unequal* amounts, thus causing this spread to expand or contract from its original amount.

Example: In October, MTC stock is currently at 103. A spreader is moderately bullish on MTC, seeing the stock trading at 110 by late January. At this time MTC January 100 calls are trading at 7½ and January 110 calls are trading at 4. The spreader simultaneously *buys* one January 100 call for $750 and *sells* one January 110 call for $400. This produces an out-of-pocket cost (a *debit*) of $350.

If the market rises to 110 as anticipated, the January 100 call will be worth approximatey $1,000. The January 110 call, however, will have little or no value as it approaches expiration and will either expire or be liquidated for a nominal amount. The profit is thus $250 on the long option plus $400 on the short option, or $650—precisely the difference between the striking prices of the options, less the "debit" (cost) of the spread. In other words, the original spread of $350 ($750 − $400) had *widened* to $1,000 ($1,000 − 0).

Had the market moved higher than 110, no further profit would ensue because every point of profit on the January 100 call will be offset by a point of loss on the January 110 call.

When the spread widens to its maximum extent, you see the major drawback to spreads—limited profit potential should the market price exceed original expectations.

If the market had fallen and remained below 100, the spread would have *narrowed*. Ultimately both options would expire and the spreader would lose $350 (the $750 loss on the January 100 call is partially cushioned by the $400 premium of the expired January 110 call).

There are many different spread possibilities on any underlying stock. They can be structured to respond to bullish, bearish or neutral market conditions. In general, they are less risky than outright long or short options positions and similarly, offer less profit potential in the event of a significant price move. Trading spreads is clearly for neither the novice nor the casual investor. The positions must be carefully monitored. Early exercises of the short "legs" of option spreads can ruin the most carefully developed strategies. Because transaction costs are multiplied by the increased number of contracts employed, theoretical profits often evaporate on a net basis. Spreads must be transacted in margin accounts. From the foregoing it should be clear that only highly sophisticated speculators need apply.

Other Types of Options

Index Options

The most recent development in options is trading puts and calls on the *entire market,* not on an individual security. Many an investor has been chagrined to find that even though the "market" is going up, his or her own stocks are not. By purchasing an *index option* the investor eliminates the need to select individual securities and needs only to judge the overall trend of the market correctly. The question that naturally arises is—what is "the market"?

At first, the exchanges employed artificially created market indicators because of potential copyright problems with the formulators of the well-known measurements such as the "Standard and Poor's 500 Index" or the "Dow Jones Industrial Average." The Chicago Board Options Exchange developed an index originally named the "CBOE 100" and later renamed the "Standard and Poor's 100" when licensing questions were resolved. Its 100 component stocks are appealing to both traders and institutional investors. It has become the most actively traded of the index options and is ordinarily referred to by its symbol—OEX. The Amex countered with its "Major Market Index" and both it and the NYSE introduced options on their own composite indexes, the XAM and NYA respectively. Trading has even been ex-

panded to smaller subindices representing such industry group-
ings as Computer Technology, Oil and Gas, and Gold and Silver.

For a premium payment similar to that for an ordinary option,
for example, 4¾, the trader obtains a participation in a broad
market move. There is thus no concern about "firm-specific" or
"industry" (right on the market—wrong on the stock) risk. The
trader still must be correct on the market trend, however, meaning
he or she is still subject to the "systematic" risk that the market
in general might move counter to his or her position. Naturally,
writing such options could be used as partial hedges against
diversified stock portfolio declines.

Index options would be completely impractical if exercises
required delivery of the various stocks underlying the particular
index. Rather, exercises are completed through a *monetary* settlement similar to that which had been successfully used in the
settlement of stock index futures. In any event, well over 90% of
all outstanding contracts will be closed out prior to expiration
and/or exercise.

Interest Rate Options

The wide swings in interest rates prevalent in the 1970s and
early 1980s produced large fluctuations in the price of fixed-
income securities. The bond markets were quite unaccustomed
to this type of price volatility. There were neither practical opportunities to take advantage of anticipated price rises nor means
of hedging against price declines. The futures markets were the
first to develop such means and have been by far the most
successful. Options, however, have some distinct advantages
(as well as disadvantages) over futures; and interest-rate-related
options have been introduced by both the Amex and the CBOE.

There are currently four listed debt option contracts:

1. $1,000,000 principal amount, 13-week U.S. Treasury Bill
   (Amex).
2. $100,000 principal amount U.S. Treasury Note (Amex).
3. $100,000 principal amount U.S. Treasury Bond (CBOE).
4. $20,000 principal amount U.S. Treasury Bond (CBOE).

Several other contracts, such as GNMA and CD options, have been proposed, but introduction does not seem likely.

Because interest rates and bond prices move in *opposite* directions, the use of these options requires a sort of upside-down thinking for the trader familiar only with equity options.

Example: Suppose a trader expects long-term bond yields to *rise* from 11% to 12%. The equity-oriented options trader might think the appropriate strategy to profit from this expectation would be to buy calls (or write puts). *Rising interest rates,* however, *mean lower bond prices,* and the bond trader's strategy, in fact, would be exactly the reverse—*buy* puts (or write calls).

With the exception of the T-Bills, most government securities trade in percent and 32nds of one percent of par. Likewise, note and bond option premiums are so quoted.

Example: A premium of 1.24 is actually 1 and 24/32 percent of par value, or simply "1 3/4" to a bond trader. For the $100,000 CBOE Treasury Bond option this is a dollar value of $1,750 ($100,000 × .0175) and for the $20,000 "mini" contract $350 ($20,000 × .0175).

Option strategies are quite similar to those employed by equity options traders. Debt option investors may buy puts and calls, write naked or covered options, and even trade spreads, combinations, and straddles.

Example: With long-term U.S. Treasury bonds trading at 94, an investor buys $100,000 principal amount ($94,000) and simultaneously sells 1 U.S. Treasury Sept 94 call for 1.28 ($1,875). In other words, the investor has created a covered call. If the market advances by any amount, the option will be exercised and the investor will sell the bonds for a profit of $1,875. If the market remains unchanged, the option will expire, leaving the investor still in possession of both the bonds *and* the $1,875 premium. If the market drops by less than 1.28, that is, to no lower than 92⅛, the investor breaks even. Naturally, the bonds continue to accrue interest unless and until exercise occurs.

Options on Foreign Currencies

Floating currency exchange rates have produced volatility in currency exchange rates similar in nature (if at least partially different in cause) to the interest rate fluctuations in the recent past. Because volatility necessarily creates opportunity, it was only a question of time before the financial markets addressed the situation. Indeed, the very first "financial futures" were currency contracts on the International Monetary Market in Chicago.

Currency options are traded on the Philadelphia Stock Exchange. Each of several different currencies—the Canadian dollar, the pound sterling, the Deutsche mark, the Japanese yen, and the Swiss franc—are measured against the dollar. Premiums are quoted in cents per unit on all options except the yen, which is 1/100 of a cent per unit.

Example: The Deutsche mark call contract requires delivery of 62,500 marks if exercised. A premium quote for a March 36 contract might be 0.90, or $562.50 (62,500 × $.0090). If one DM was currently trading around 35¢ and rose to 38¢, an option to buy at 36 would become worth $1,250 (the 2¢ difference between 36 and 38 × 62,500). This would double the trader's original investment.

Because of their relatively small size, the Philadelphia currency options provide speculators and hedgers easier access to this market than the futures market affords. The intrabank "forward" market for currencies involves multiples of $1,000,000 and is all but closed to any except major banks and multinational corporations. Foreign currencies, however, remain difficult for most investors to understand and the currency *options* market adds another level of complexity, so much so that there has been relatively little individual participation thus far.

Futures

What Is a Futures Contract?

Until 1972 this market was linked exclusively with physical goods such as soybeans, cocoa, silver, or pork bellies. Hence, the term "commodities" fully described the futures market. Since that time the fastest growing part of this business has been that of futures contracts on financial instruments, such as Treasury bonds or stock indexes. While traditional commodities still trade actively, in some cases more actively than ever, the divergence between the two branches has become so great that few, if any, participants can trade both successfully.

A futures contract is a *standardized, exchange-traded contract* calling for the delivery of (1) a specified amount of, (2) a specified commodity in, (3) a specified month in, and (4) a specified number of locations. Unlike a securities transaction, no transfer of property is involved unless and until delivery actually occurs. In fact, probably fewer than 5% of all contracts actually result in a delivery of the actual commodity. Money does not change hands between the buyer and seller of a futures contract, although each is required to post an "earnest money" (margin) deposit to ensure responsibility for the *entire contract* in the delivery month. A futures contract is *not* an *option*. If held through the last trading day in the delivery month, the holder of the contract *must* accept delivery and the seller *must* deliver. Futures contracts, in other words, do not expire "unexercised." Also, they never result in a delivery prior to the appointed month, whereas an option on a security may normally be exercised (and delivery demanded) any time from the trade date to the expiration date.

Example: A typical Chicago Board of Trade (CBT) September corn contract may serve as an illustration. Unless offset, the contract requires the seller to deliver 5,000 bushels of #2 yellow corn during the month of September to a CBT approved elevator in Decatur, Illinois, or some other specifically approved location. Conversely, the buyer is required to pay the settlement price on that day and accept ownership. The seller normally may dictate the day and, within limits, the point of delivery. Deliveries occur through the transfer of evidences of ownership such as warehouse receipts, although the buyer indeed owns the actual warehoused commodity. The ever-popular story of the forgetful speculator arriving home to discover a defrosting mound of 38,000 pounds of frozen pork bellies in his front yard is pure fable.

Trading and Contract Specifications

The first-time commodities trader is confronted with a number of strangely named contracts, often denominated in what appear to be capriciously chosen amounts.

Example: Just what *are* "pork bellies" anyway, and why is the contract size 38,000 lbs., not 2,500 or perhaps 50,000 lbs.? And why are the trading variations in 1/100¢ increments on some contracts, 1/4¢ on others, and $1/32 on still other futures?

Actually there is a good reason for this variety. In most cases, the contract size for physical commodities—corn, oats, and the like—is determined by standard usage in the cash or "spot" markets. Particularly with agricultural commodities, the contract size often represents a standard railroad car load. Indeed, veteran traders still use the term "car lots" interchangeably with "contracts," as in "I'm long 5 car lots of wheat."

Beginning traders find it relatively easy to follow the market. As noted earlier, futures traders can trade successfully with a narrower focus than can stock traders. There is no "commodity market" per se with which to contend. Once the trader has learned the contract terms for his or her particular positions, there is little difficulty translating prices into dollars lost or gained.

Example: All the major grains on the CBT trade in 5,000 bushel contracts with quotations in dollars and cents per bushel. As soon as one realizes that each cent price move yields $50 profit or loss on the futures contract, a price change from $3.73 to $3.86 is quickly read as $650, whether one is following soybeans, wheat, oats, or corn.

The futures trader can use just about any type of order a stock trader might use—market, limit, stop, and so on. Orders are customarily entered for a particular number of contracts, such as *sell 2 June silver 935.3 STOP*. Orders for grain futures are written in numbers of bushels, in multiples of 5,000. Thus, a grain speculator enters an order to *buy 25 M December oats*, not 5 December oats.

In most commodities there is no way to deal in amounts smaller than the standard contract size. In stocks, of course, it is possible to trade odd lots of fewer than 100 shares, and many a sophisticated investor cuts his or her eye teeth trading 25 or 50 share lots. The Mid America Commodity Exchange, however, does offer "odd lots" (or "mini" contracts) in a number of different futures—1,000 bushel grain contracts and small gold and Treasury bond contracts, among others. Because the margin is proportionately lower on these contracts, beginning speculators might well investigate this market as an introduction to futures trading. It also serves the smaller farmer by offering a hedge vehicle for those whose production is less than the standard 5,000 bushels—a fairly formidable amount for the small farmer.

Commissions

Futures commissions are charged on a "round turn" basis, meaning that the total charge to buy and sell is deducted once. In general, commissions are modest considering the dollar value of the contracts, and may be reduced even further by dealing with a discount broker. It should be remembered that the inherently short-term nature of this market leads to numerous transactions and the total commission bill can very quickly add up to substantial amounts. Speculators frequently experience trades that on paper appear profitable but on a *net* basis are breakeven (or losers).

Margin

Futures *margin* is not margin in the securities sense at all. Rather, it represents good faith deposit or "earned money"— enough equity to demonstrate that the contract made by the customer will be honored *in full*, if and when delivery occurs. Futures positions are normally margined at something between 5% and 15% of the contract value, far lower than the 50% deposit currently required on stock purchases by Regulation T.

Commodity margin accounts are much simpler than security margin accounts because nothing is borrowed. Futures accounts have no loan or hypothecation procedures, no debit balances, and no interest charges. At the close of each day's trading, the clearing house establishes a "settlement price" (basically that day's closing transaction price) and all accounts are "marked to the market." Unrealized profits are credited to accounts that benefited from that day's price action and debited from those adversely affected.

Example: A speculator buys one August gold contract at $400 an ounce and deposits $4,000 margin (10% of the $40,000 value of the 100 ounce gold contract). The next day gold rises in price and "settles" at $408.50. The customer's account equity is increased to $4,850, the profit on an $8.50 price rise on the 100 ounce contract. Likewise, a trader who sold a contract short $400 and deposited $4,000 would now have an equity of only $3,150. Note that the percentage gain (or loss) on equity is substantial. The long trader deposited $4,000 and in one (not necessarily typical) day has reaped an $850 profit, or 21.25%. It is sometimes assumed that commodities prices are hypervolatile. As this illustration shows, it is the low margin that exaggerates profits or losses, not the actual price change of the commodity. In our example, gold moved from $400 to $408.50 about 2% and yet a 21% profit was produced.

Besides initial margin, a futures trader must maintain adequate "maintenance" margin. This level ranges anywhere from 20% to 50% below original margin and customarily represents about one day's "limit move" against the trader. Should this level be pierced, the customer will receive a maintenance (or "variation") call to restore the equity to the original margin level. Failure to meet the call promptly empowers the broker to liquidate the undermargined position.

Example: A trader buys one July corn contract at $3.35 a bushel and deposits the $1,250 initial margin. Because the contract calls for 5000 bushels of corn at delivery, the current contract value is $166,750 (5000 × $3.35) and the margin required thus about 7.5% of this value. Grain traders often look at margin on a per bushel basis, which in this case is 25¢ a bushel ($1,250 ÷ 5,000/bu.). Maintenance margin might be set at 20¢ a bushel, or $1,000. Therefore, the price could drop to $3.30 (down 5¢ from the original plurchase price) without causing margin problems.

However, a drop of greater magnitude would result in the issuance of a "variation call."

Example: If the market dropped, for instance, to $3.28, the trader would lose $350 (7¢/bu. × 5,000) and his equity would drop to $900, $100 below the maintenance level. The trader would now be required to deposit sufficient cash (or equivalent) to replenish his or her equity to the *original $1,250.* Should the trader fail to do so, the broker will close out the position.

Futures Exchanges

There are nine major futures exchanges in the United States, several in London, and one in Canada. Trading is done by open outcry in "pits" or "rings"; the former term is used largely in Chicago, which is by far the world's leading futures market. While trading futures bears a number of similarities to stock trading, there are notable differences. Futures exchanges do not make use of the specialist system typical of U.S. securities exchanges, nor are there "market makers" such as seen in the OTC markets. Another major difference is the practice of limiting maximum daily price changes on futures exchanges, whereas stock exchanges do not do so.

Example: The exchange may set a 10¢ limit on trading of soybean futures. This means that the price may not vary by more than that amount *above or below* the previous day's close. If yesterday's November soybeans closed at $7.53 a bushel, today's price may not be higher than $7.63 or lower than $7.43. Trading is not permitted at prices higher or lower than those levels, although in theory trades could take place at prices *between* $7.43 and $7.63 inclusive. *In practice,* trading usually stops when the limit has been reached because those in an advantageous position usually remove their bids or offers from the market. Thus, if soybeans began trading "limit up" at $7.63, it's likely that prospective sellers will cancel offers to sell at that price in anticipation of still higher prices tomorrow. Even though buyers may be willing to pay the maximum $7.63, there are no offers to sell, and trading effectively ceases.

Futures exchanges permit the same type of order that stock exhanges do, such as market, limit, stop and so on. Because of the volatile nature of futures trading, however, market participants make much more frequent use of limit and stop orders than do stock traders. With their very short-term horizon, many futures deposit of about 5%. Nevertheless it is a most significant sum and indicates the size, depth, and liquidity of the futures markets.

The dollar value of such contracts is roughly $12 billion, more than twice that of an average NYSE trading day. Of course, this is something of an "apples vs. oranges" comparison as NYSE trades represent the full exchange of dollars between buyer and seller, whereas futures traders post only a margin deposit of about 5%. Nevertheless it is a most significant sum and indicates the size, depth, and liquidity of the futures markets.

The exchanges and their principal contracts are:

1. The Chicago Board of Trade—grains and financial futures.

2. The Chicago Mercantile Exchange (and its International Monetary Market subsidiary)—livestock and financial futures.

3. The Commodity Exchange, Inc. (NYC)—metals.

4. The New York Mercantile Exchange—petroleum, potatoes, metals.

5. The New York Cotton Exchange—cotton, orange juice.

6. The New York Coffee, Sugar, and Cocoa Exchange—those commodites.

7. The Kansas City Board of Trades—grains and stock indexes.

8. The Mid America Commodity Exchange—"mini" contracts in grains, gold, financial futures.

9. The Minneapolis Grain Exchange—grains.

10. The New York Futures Exchange—financial futures.

The Chicago exchanges, particularly the CBT, dominate futures trading in the U.S. This dominance results not only from its original agricultural preeminence but also from its stunning innovations, particularly in the financial futures area. While markets in other cities, even London, have copied the Chicago-born concepts, none have been nearly so successful.

It should be noted that not all innovations succeed and that once popular contracts often fall out of favor and atrophy. For example, an ambitious attempt by the NYSE to create a Treasury security and currency futures market alternative to Chicago failed dismally and the New York Futures Exchange survives only through trading of the NYSE Composite Index contract. Likewise, an attempt to establish a market in New Orleans concentrating on rice failed. Chicago itself has had its share of failures, among them commercial paper futures and an attempt to cash in on the success of the New York Mercantile Exchange's petroleum futures. Indeed, it takes a real commodities veteran to recall active trading in the likes of "iced broilers," "wool tops," or "shell eggs."

Clearinghouses

Finally, affiliated with each exchange, is a "clearinghouse," a facility jointly owned by the exchange's members. The clearing house acts as an intermediary between buyer and seller. By interposing itself between buyer and seller, the clearing house guarantees the liquidity and performance of each contract. Thus, the original buyer and seller need have no concern about the other's financial ability to perform on the contract as the clearing house is, in effect, the other party to all trades. Each exchange member contributes to a clearing fund and is normally liable for additional emergency assessments. No customer has ever lost money because of the failure of an American clearing house to honor its obligations.

Who Trades Futures and Why

In many ways futures trading is simpler than securities trading. For one thing, there are only about 40 actively traded American commodities compared with many thousands of different common stocks. Margins, short sales, and tax considerations are far less complicated than in securities trading. Accordingly, a futures trader chooses investment opportunities from a very small sample and trades are effected with generally simpler mechanics than those associated with securities. It is also considerably easier to follow news and market developments that might have an impact upon, for example, wheat prices than it is to follow the myriad of details that surround any individual stock—dividends, earnings, the competition, interest rates, the overall market, and so on.

One should, however, note the emphasis on the word "trading." With the exception of some commercial interests, the futures trader's horizon is *very* short term. As with options, with which they have many similarities, futures are *totally* inappropriate for the typical "buy 'em and forget 'em" investor. Without the ability (or choice) to follow the market closely and make rapid decisions, no "investor" should try to turn "trader."

The apparent simplicity of futures trading is deceptive. Numerous skilled securities traders have learned to their chagrin that, despite the similarities, these are different markets indeed. Nevertheless, the excitement generated by volatile price savings and the huge profit potential generated by low-margin leverage continues to exert a powerful pull on the performance-minded speculator.

Long Positions

As with stocks, holders of long positions expect a price rise (or are attempting to protect against such a rise).

Example: In May a trader expects the soybean crop to be disappointingly small. A reduced supply can usually be expected to push prices higher and thus profit the person who controls the right to buy 5,000 bushels of the beans in September. The trader buys one September soybean contract when the price is $7.30 a bushel. The forecast proves accurate and in August it is apparent that a drought-reduced crop will be in very short supply. Prices have risen to $8.00 a bushel in anticipation, and the trader sells the contract for a 70¢ bushel profit ($8.00 − $7.30). Because there are 5,000 bushels in each contract this price rise would result in a $3,500 profit. Assuming a typical margin deposit of $2,000 (or even lower), the return on invested capital is very handsome indeed.

Almost all longs will likewise liquidate their contracts but in September some long positions will remain open. Every open long contract will result in the holder receiving delivery of soybeans. These holders are invariably commercial interests with a need for the commodity itself, in this case soybean "crushers" (processors) or exporters. Because of the delivery and storage costs, speculative traders should *never* put themselves at risk of accepting delivery. Simply put, this means liquidating all positions *prior* to the first trading day of the delivery month.

Short Positions

Short sales in the commodities' markets are the *norm*, not the exception. The sale of a borrowed stock or bond at one price and an attempt to repurchase it at a lower price is relatively uncommon when compared to the customary trading of long positions. In futures, on the other hand, *all opening sell transactions are short sales by definition.* The seller is creating an obligation to deliver the commodity specified in the contract unless he or she offsets it with a purchase later.

Futures short sales are more easily affected than short sales in securities. Nothing need be borrowed or delivered at the outset; margin deposits are small—the same as for long positions; sales may be made at at any time—there are no "plus ticks" to contend with.

As with long positions, shorts must be offset or a delivery will result. In this case, the seller ("short") will have to deliver the appropriate amount and grade of the contract item to an acceptable location. Once again, those speculators who lack this ability should be very wary of trading in the final month of a contract's life. The typical speculator, of course, should have realized his or her profit (or mistake) well prior to this time.

Example: A trader expects gold to fall from its current level of $400 an ounce to about $375, and sells short two gold contracts of 100 troy ounces each. The market declines to $378 where the trader covers the short sales by making a purchase at that price. The trader's profit is $4,400 ($22/oz. × 100 oz. per contract

× 2 contracts). Had the market gone up instead, the risk exposure to the trader is limited *only* by the level at which he or she could purchase 200 troy ounces of .999 fine gold. Had gold, for instance, gone to $450 an ounce, the trader would have lost $10,000 ($50/oz. × 100 oz. per contract × 2 contracts).

Hedging

Despite their reputation for being highly risky, futures would not in fact exist were it not for their use as vehicles designed to *reduce* risk, not to create it. If traders were simply placing bets on subsequent prices of commodities, the futures markets would have little more socially redeeming value than racetracks or casinos.

Both producers and users of the commodity can protect themselves against adverse price fluctuations by *hedging* their actual ("cash" or "spot") market position with an opposite position in the futures market. In this way, a loss of one position may be largely offset by the profit on the other.

Example: In May, a wheat farmer estimates his fall harvest at about 10,000 bushels. The current cash price for wheat is $3.25 a bushel, but the price for September futures is $3.40 a bushel, a level that would assure the farmer a reasonable profit. He sells short two September wheat contracts of 5,000 bushels each, creating a hedge. Should the wheat market decline in price, his inventories (the growing wheat) will be worthless, but his short futures contracts will show a profit. On the other hand, if wheat prices rise, the inventories would increase in value while the futures would show a loss.

Suppose by September the cash wheat price had fallen to $3.23. By selling his crop at that price the farmer would almost certainly sustain a loss. His short sale, however, could probably be covered at a substantial profit. Because cash and futures become virtually identical in the delivery month through arbitrage trading, the September futures would have to have fallen to nearly $3.23. A covering purchase at that level would produce a 17¢ bushel profit (sold short $3.40 and covered $3.23); the farmer effectively sold his grain at the hopper for $3.40; that is, $3.23 from the actual grain sale plus $0.17 from the futures profit.

Of course, hedges are almost never as perfect as this example, but they greatly reduce the risk exposure of the participants in the actual cash markets. This reduced risk has many beneficial effects to the economy, including lower prices to the ultimate user, often the consumer.

Hedgers attempting to protect against price declines are those who already have the commodity in store or are producing it (farmers, grain elevator operators, lumber dealers, cattle raisers, etc). They hedged by *selling short* in the futures market as in the example above. Those who use the commodity are concerned with a price rise, and thus would be *long* hedgers. Such hedgers include exporters, manufacturers, and processors.

The markets need both speculators and hedgers to succeed. Without the activity of the speculators, the markets lack liquidity because the hedgers tend to be largely concentrated on one side of the market or the other. Without the hedgers there is little economic justification for the existence of the market in the first place.

Spreads

A popular way to trade futures without assuming the risk of an outright long or short position is the "spread," the simultaneous creation of both a long *and* a short position in two different futures contracts. The spread may be between different delivery months in the same commodity (the most popular variety), the same commodity traded on different exchanges, a basic commodity and its products, or even between two entirely different commodities that have related price movements.

The spread trader assumes that historical or other price patterns occasionally diverge from normal ranges. Expecting the patterns to change back into their normal ranges, the spreader buys one contract and simultaneously sells another. When prices of the commodity involved change, the change will not be reflected equally in both contracts. Either the long position will advance more rapidly than the short or vice versa. This action will either widen or narrow the spread—the price differential between the two contracts.

Example: (Live hogs futures contracts is 30,000 lbs. Price quotations are in cents and hundredths of a cent per pound.)

In March, June hogs are priced $49.82 and October hogs are $55.45, a spread of 5.63¢. A trader thinks this spread is too wide and expects it to be narrower within two months. The trader thus buys one June contract and sells one October at the given prices. By May 15 the June contract has advanced to 51.85 and the October to 55.62. With each cent price move worth $300 (30,0000 lbs. × $.01), the long "leg" has produced a $609 profit (2.03 × $300) while the short side has a $51 loss (0.17 × $300). In fact, the trader's prediction that the spread would narrow has been vindicated. The 5.63 spread at the outset has been reduced to 3.77, a narrowing of 1.86¢. Of course, this 1.86 price differential when multiplied by $300 yields a profit of $558, precisely the same as the net profit on the long versus short legs illustrated ($609 − $51 = $558).

Spreads are often represented as "limited risk" methods of futures trading but one should be careful not to be misled. It is true that spreads are *often* less risky than outright long or short positions because any loss on the unprofitable leg is at least partly offset by profits on the other. Still, there have been situations where *both* legs of the spread went against the trader at once. In general, however, most spreads are less volatile than speculative long or short positions and qualify for a reduced margin, often about 50% of the speculative requirement. In addition, spread commissions are usually lower when the spread is traded as a "package" as opposed to its independent parts.

Spread trading is still speculative, no matter how it is otherwise evaluated. There are large risks involved. The complicated nature of analyzing the trade and proper order entry are facets best left to experienced traders.

Financial Futures Contracts

The application of the futures trading concept to the financial markets has been an enormous success. From a rather slow start with currency futures on the International Monetary Market (CME) in 1972, trading has mushroomed to the point where a financial contract, the CBT U.S. Treasury Bond, is the most active of all futures. Other financial contracts rival such long-established favorites as wheat and live hogs.

Today's investors are much more aware of the interrelationships linking financial markets than were their predecessors. They are aware that changes in interest or exchange rates may have a dramatic impact on their stock or bond investments. By utilizing financial futures these investors may hedge against the damaging effects of such changes, or alternately, seek to profit by correctly forecasting their direction. There are three primary categories of financial futures—currency exchange rate contracts, interest rate contracts, and stock market index contracts.

Foreign Currency Futures

These contracts are offered on eight foreign currencies and are quoted in terms of U.S. dollars. Essentially a long position will be profitable if that particular currency appreciates against the U.S. dollar. The most active contracts are those most associated with international trade—the British pound, the Deutsche mark, the Japanese yen, and the Swiss franc. Sporadically active dealing occurs in the French franc, Dutch guilder, Canadian dollar, and Mexican peso.

Example: A speculator notes that the U.S. inflation rate is higher than Japan's. Also observing an unfavorable trade balance with Japan, the trader buys one Japanese yen contract at .4542. The yen contract calls for delivery of Y12,500,000 and is quoted in points, each equal to $.000001. Thus, each point = $12.50 (the first two zeros are dropped in the quotation). If the contract rises in value to .4888, the trader gains 346 points for a profit of $4,325 ($12.50 × 346).

Interest Rate Futures

There are several financial futures contracts on fixed-income investments. Long-term investments include contracts on U.S. Treasury Bonds and GNMAs. In addition there are intermediate-term 10-year Treasury Note futures as well as several very short-term vehicles—90-day Treasury Bills, Euro-dollar deposits, and CDs. Each fills a specific need and each allows for hedging and speculative opportunities in the event of a wide swing in interest rates.

The speculator anticipating a sharp *rise* in long-term rates could profit through a *short sale* of U.S. Treasury bond futures. Traders not familiar with the way the bond markets operate must always bear in mind the *inverse* relationship of futures (and bond) prices and interest rates; that is, as rates go *up*, prices go *down*.

On the other hand, a dealer in short-term money market

instruments could hedge the value of his or her inventory through the use of Treasury Bill futures. If short-term rates rise rapidly, the value of his or her inventory will drop and cause substantial losses. If, however, the dealer had sold short Treasury Bill futures, they would have fallen in price also. Thus, the profits on the futures short sale would offset most, if not all, of the inventory losses on the dealer's position. Naturally, someone anticipating a rate decline would profit by taking a long position in futures. This action effectively "locks in" the current favorable rate.

Example: A speculator feels that longer-term rates have peaked at 12% and are poised for a substantial decline. He buys a September U.S. Treasury bond contract at 66-24. The Treasury bond contract is quoted similarly to the actual Treasury bonds— in percents (and 32nds of a percent) of par value. Each contract calls for the delivery of $100,000 U.S. Treasury bonds, so each 1% of par ("point") = $1,000 and each 32nd (a "tick") = $31.25.

Rates in fact decline to about 10.8% and bond prices rise to about 71-00 where the trader sells his contract. The profit of 4-8 points equals $4,312.50 (138 "ticks" × $31.25). With a typical margin of $3,500, or so, the speculator would have more than *doubled* his money on a 10% change in price had his forecast been correct—and lost it all, and *then some*, if wrong.

Stock Index Futures

These contracts allow the investor to speculate on (or hedge against) the direction of the *entire stock market*. This is accomplished through futures whose prices are based on three of the most widely followed measures of the "market"—the Standard and Poor's 500 Stock Composite Index, the New York Stock Exchange Composite Index, and the Value Line 1500 Stock Average. While no index can possibly measure something as huge and diverse as the "stock market," each of these indicators gives a good, if slightly different, picture of what is happening to most of the stocks that investors are interested in.

The trader with a definite opinion about the direction of the market can, in effect, speculate by "buying the market," or selling it for that matter. In other words, he or she eliminates the risk of choosing the wrong stock—the one that goes exactly counter to the trader's otherwise correct prediction of the market's direction. While it may be difficult to forecast the direction of the market—and indeed it clearly is—it is ordinarily a good deal less difficult than picking a stock or stocks within the market grouping *and* the correct market directions simultaneously.

Similarly, a portfolio manager can use these futures to hedge an existing portfolio. A well-diversified portfolio has little "stock specific" risk; that is, the risk of error when selecting only a few stocks from the market universe. Diversification, however, provides little defense against a general market decline. To counter this "systematic risk," a short hedge with index futures may offset some or all of the loss in value on the portfolio. As with the commercial agricultural hedger, the portfolio manager can use futures profits to counter-balance "cash" market losses.

Unlike standard futures contracts, stock index (and a few of the newer) futures are based on a *cash* settlement. The utter impracticality of delivering 500 or 1500 different stock issues against a short position is self-explanatory. With a stock index future, ultimate "delivery" simply means a final mark-to-the-market where the actual index value will be compared to the closing trade. Long positions are credited with the amount by which the closing trade exceeds the index, and short positions are debited the same amount. Naturally, if the closing trade is lower, this is reversed.

Example: A speculator has become very pessimistic about the stock market on a short-term basis. Feeling blue-chip stocks to be the most vulnerable, he sells short the contract most nearly "blue chip" in price action, the S&P 500. The contract value is $500 times the current index. If the contract is sold at 161.50, its total value is $80,750 and every full point price change is thus worth $500. The market *does* drop by about 5% and the S&P futures price declines to 154.00. By correctly forecasting this 7.50 point drop the speculator makes a profit of $3,750 ($500 × 7.50).

Futures and Options Compared

Both vehicles offer exciting speculative prospects—low margins, big profits, plenty of thrills. Unfortunately, *losing* lots of money is also "exciting," in a perverse sort of way, and is at least as likely an outcome as profits. Despite their speculative appeal, futures and options can be used conservatively to hedge positions or, in the case of covered calls, to generate additional

income. Both are clearly more complex concepts than the underlying securities or cash markets.

Each of these products operates within a relatively short
time horizon. Successful trading in either one demands careful,
time-consuming attention to the market and quick, decisive
action when required. Most investors possess neither the free
time nor the requisite decisiveness to be good traders of *anything*, let alone options and futures.

The similarities, however, should not be overemphasized.
There are two distinctly different "investment" formats. The basic
difference of concern is that futures don't expire. Every futures
contract left open in the delivery month will ultimately receive a
delivery, be it pork bellies, gold or cash. Another major distinction
is that options may be either traded or exercised any time after
purchase until expiration. No delivery can be made or demanded
on a futures contract until the "spot" month arrives. Finally, there
is the matter of the *premium*. The option buyer pays, and the
writer receives, a one-time amount called the premium, an
amount determined in the open exchange auction. This premium
effectively determines the points at which the buyer and the
writer break even. Any priced movement beyond those points
results in profits or losses. The futures contract, on the other
hand, establishes a specific *price*. While both long and short
traders deposit margin, neither pays nor receives a nonrefund-
able premium. Ultimately, therefore, options provide a *range of
profitability* whereas futures provide a *price level* only.

To a certain extent the premium provides the option trader
with a safety net unavailable to the futures trader. That is, the
option buyer knows at once what the loss potential is—precisely
the premium paid; never one penny more. To the futures trader
there is no guarantee that the original margin for either a long
or short position defines the maximum extent of the loss.

A recent development has combined these two devices, so
that one can now trade *options on futures*. The idea is to combine
the limited risk of the long option (or the premium for the short
option) with the leverage and other appeals of the futures contract. The exercise of a call option, for example, results in the
exercising holder assuming a long futures contract while the
exercised writer assumes a short position. Active trading has so
far occurred in options on the following futures—Treasury
bonds, gold, and Deutsche marks, and more are on the way.

If all this sounds terribly confusing, it is. There are largely professional-dominated markets where the casual investor is ill-advised to tread. Indeed, the federal government, through the CFTC, *requires* that *every new futures customer* receive a copy of the following :

Example: RISK DISCLOSURE STATEMENT

This statement is furnished to you because Rule 1.55 of the Commodity Futures Trading Commission requires it.

The risk of loss in trading commodity future contracts can be substantial. You should therefore carefully consider whether such trading is suitable for you in light of your financial condition. In considering whether to trade, you should be aware of the following:

(1) You may sustain a loss of the initial margin funds and any additional funds that you deposit with your broker to establish or maintain a position. You may be called upon by your broker to deposit a substantial amount of additional margin funds, on short notice, in order to maintain your position. If you do not provide the required funds within the prescribed time, your position may be liquidated at a loss, and you will be liable for any resulting deficit in your account.

(2) Under certain market conditions, you may find it difficult or impossible to liquidate a position. This can occur, for example, when the market makes a "limit move."

(3) Placing contingent orders such as a "stop-loss" or "stop-limit" order, will not necessarily limit your losses to the intended amounts since market conditions may make it impossible to execute such orders.

(4) A "spread" position may not be less risky than a simple "long" or "short" position.

(5) The high degree of leverage that is often obtainable in futures trading because of the small margin requirements can work against you as well as for you. The use of leverage can lead to large losses as well as gains.

This brief statement cannot, of course, disclose all the risks and other significant aspects of the commodity markets. You should therefore carefully study futures trading before you trade.

If this is not warning enough, the risk disclosure document for future *options* is even more cautionary. The message is clear—if you don't understand, stay out. If you do understand, think at least twice before committing your money.

Life Insurance

The Insurance Policy

Types of Insurance Companies

Basically, there are two types of insurance companies:

1. participating, or "mutual," and

2. nonparticipating, or "stock."

1. Individuals insured by *mutual* companies become members, that is, owners, of the company, each paying a specified premium into a common fund out of which policies are paid off. The premium is usually overpaid, and the overpayment is returned to the insured in the form of dividends, after expenses are deducted. The "dividends" of a mutual company, because they are a return of overpayment, are not considered taxable income. The policyholders, therefore, "participate" in the mutual company in the sense that the premiums and insurance costs may rise and fall with the company's profits and losses.

Such "dividends" are *not* afforded the same tax treatments as cash dividends on securities.

2. A *stock* company, on the other hand, guarantees its premiums and insurance costs, because its capital is divided into shares held by individuals or institutions (investors) other than the policyholders. The projected net cost of this type of life insurance policy is therefore much easier to calculate.

3. Simply stated, mutual companies are owned by the policyholders, and stock companies are owned by shareholders. Examining the advantages and disadvantages of each would require a book of its own.

Generally, premiums initially will be higher for participating policies because the participating policies return part of the premium in the form of dividends.

In certain types of situations such as business insurance, where loans to carry policies are anticipated and future lower premiums will be required (or helpful), participating policies are the best alternatives. Where the most permanent insurance for the minimum dollar is needed, nonparticipating is advisable.

Example: The following table compares participating and nonparticipating whole life policies:

$25,000 *whole life insurance* 35-*year-old-male*

Gross Annual Premium:

Participating	$ 557.24
Nonparticipating	458.50
Difference	$ 98.74

Actual Premium Outlay:

Note the use of dividends on the participating policy to reduce the premium.

Policy	Nonparticipating	Participating
1	$ 458.50	$ 532.24
2	458.50	511.74
3	458.50	483.49
4	458.50	471.74
5	458.50	456.24
...	...	...
10	458.50	378.24
...	...	...
20	458.50	99.99

Comparative Cost Summary: 20 *Years*

Total gross premiums	$9,170.00	$11,144.80
Total dividends	—	4,147.25
Net payments	$9,170.00	$ 6,997.55
Average annual payment	$ 458.50	$ 349.88
Guaranteed cash value	$8,375.00	$ 8,825.00

For a male age 35, it is easy to see that the participating policy costs more in premium dollars at inception. In the nonparticipating policy, the same premium dollars could purchase $5,384 more death protection. The argument in favor of participating policies is that dividends will offset the additional premium in the long run and the policies have more flexibility because of increased cash in the policy (cash value plus dividends).

The other side of the coin is that the $98.75 diffference could be invested each year. If the owner could net a 5% after-tax yield, the difference would accumulate to $3,428.50 in 20 years or $6,888.80 in 30 years. This goes a long way toward offsetting the additional cost.

The argument is like the hen and egg story. Which came first? The type of company, participating or nonparticipating, must depend on personal circumstances. No one type is best for everybody or every situation.

Parties to the Insurance Contract

Every insurance contract has four parties:

1. *Insurer*—The company that guarantees to pay certain sums of money in the event of an untimely death of the insured. The insured may also guarantee living benefits in certain types of policies such as: paid up insurance, policy loans, cash value, or extended term insurance. These features are covered later in this chapter.

2. *Insured*—The person on whose life the policy is carried. The death proceeds will be paid upon the death of the insured.

3. *Beneficiary* (Beneficiaries)—The person (persons) or organization that will receive death proceeds upon the death of the insured. The policy may name several people, trusts, or businesses, depending upon the purpose for which the policy was purchased.

4. *Owner*—The owner is the person, organization, or trust that owns the policy and has all rights to change beneficiaries, type of policy, and so forth. The owner may be other than the insured or beneficiary. Remember, death proceeds are in-

cludable in the estate of the owner; therefore, if the owner and the insured are the same, large amounts of insurance inflate the size of the estate and unnecessarily increase the amount of estate taxes.

To reduce the size of taxable estates, husbands and wives will often give existing policies to each other or to their children. A word of caution when giving a policy: a reportable gift tax situation may result. Be certain to consult professional tax advisors *before* changing ownership.

Also, remember, once a policy is given, it cannot be taken back. Transferring or determining ownership of life insurance policies is often an excellent medium of estate planning, but enter the transaction with caution.

Types of Policies

Allthough insurance companies offer a variety of policies, many are designed specifically for selling and marketing purposes. Most policies fall into the following general types:

1. term,

2. ordinary or whole life,

3. debit (industrial),

4. endowment,

5. annuity, and

6. universal life.

1. Term Insurance. Perhaps the simplest and cheapest, this is pure protection. It is comparable to home or automobile insurance. The insured pays a stipulated rate (the premium) for a certain number of years (the term) for a specified death benefit (the face amount) to be paid to a designated person (the beneficiary). If the insured lives, he or she is entitled to nothing. There is no remaining value to the policy. The insurance company keeps the premium, having earned it by assuming the risk.

Term insurance policies may take many forms. The term of

the policy may be 1 to 20 years, perhaps longer in some cases. Both the premium and the death benefit value may be either level (that is, fixed) or decreasing over the term. Some policies may be renewed at regular intervals for higher premiums until the insured reaches a certain age, usually 70. Many policies may be converted into other forms of insurance, thus guaranteeing that the insured may purchase permanent insurance regardless of change in his or her physical condition.

Term insurance is suitable for anyone in need of a great deal of protection for a minimal cash outlay and for people who only have protection needs for a certain period of time.

Many groups and associations provide term insurance. The securities industry makes group term insurance available at extremely attractive rates through the National Association of Securities Dealers and the Securities Industry Association. Many medical, dental, and legal associations, labor unions, college alumni associations, and civic organizations sponsor such plans for their memberships. The policies provide cheap protection.

Example: Young married couples often buy a 20-year, decreasing term policy with a level premium, thus providing the largest amount of protection while the need is greatest. As the couple accumulates other assets, they are better able to augment the decrease in insurance protection in the event of premature death.

Credit life insurance, a form of term insurance, is purchased to equal the amount of a loan; if the borrower dies prematurely, the insurance proceeds pay off the loan.

2. *Ordinary or Whole Life.* Sometimes called straight life insurance, this type of policy combines protection with savings. The insured pays a fixed premium for life, in return for the insurance company's guarantee to pay a specified sum upon the death of the insured.

Compared with term insurance, the premium is greater. The net or total premiums are usually higher in the earlier years than in the later years. The initial premiums are larger than mortality statistics require partially because they include the insurance company's cost of acquiring the policy (salesman's commission, underwriting charges, medical examinations, and so forth). The primary reason for the higher premium, however, is that the insurance company invests those extra premium dollars to produce earnings. In turn, the earnings are credited to the insured's account in the form of a cash value.

Obviously, as earnings increase and cash values earn interest, the insurance company's risk of loss in the event of payout diminishes, and a smaller part of the premium is at risk for the insurance company each year. This makes it possible for insurance companies to charge a level premium. (Most ordinary life insurance policies do not begin accumulating cash value until the policy is in force for one to three years.)

Insurance companies offer many variations of the ordinary life policy. One is a limited-payment life policy, which limits the number of years premiums are payable. An example is a "20-pay life"—premiums are payable for 20 years; or "life paid-up at 65"—premiums are payable until the insured reaches age 65. Obviously, in a limited pay life, the premiums would be higher than those in a standard ordinary life policy, and cash values will generally be higher.

Considered on a net-cost basis, ordinary insurance is viewed by some people as an investment because of the accumulation of cash value. The net cost is the difference between the total amount paid in premiums over the years and the cash value at a certain age, usually 65. Generally, the net cost of the ordinary policy is much smaller than that of a term policy in the long run because the insured gets back part of his or her premium dollars.

A word of caution: When reviewing net cost or the cash value at age 65, please appreciate that the amounts only apply if you live. If you die, your beneficiary does not receive the death benefit plus the cash value, only the death benefit. If a mutual policy is owned, the beneficiary would receive the death benefit plus the accumulated dividends (not the cash value).

Ordinary life insurance policies generally allow the insured to use the cash values in different ways:

- The cash value may be used to purchase paid-up ordinary insurance for a reduced face amount.

- Up to 92% of it may be borrowed by the insured at a fairly standard interest rate stipulated in the policy; recently this rate was raised to 8%. Some of the older policies carry a 5% loan provision.

- The policyholder can cash in his or her policy for the cash surrender value, which is also specified in the policy.

- The cash value may be used to purchase term insurance, for the same face amount as the ordinary life policy, but for a certain number of years. The amount of term insurance available is stated in the policy.

3. *Debit (Industrial).* This type of insurance is a type of ordinary insurance in which premiums are collected by an agent in person, usually weekly or monthly. Generally, debit insurance is a high-cost and low death benefit type of policy. The salesperson making periodic calls to collect premiums must be paid for his or her time. The same premium dollars could usually be better used to purchase larger benefits by using other types of policies.

4. *Endowment.* This is a policy that provides a certain face value (cash) either at a stipulated age or after a certain number of premium payments. Generally, an endowment contract guarantees that the face amount will be paid to a beneficiary if the insured dies before all payments are made. So that the insurance company can have the additional money to fund the investment medium, the premiums are usually much higher than those of an ordinary policy with the same face value.

Thus, endowment policies are usually purchased to insure the availability of funds to meet specific future goals such as children's education, planned retirement, or a trip around the world. A possible alternative to an endowment plan is the purchase of decreasing term insurance and the investment of the difference. This approach, of course, requires a much more active effort and regimentation on the part of the premium payer than is called for in an endowment.

5. *Annuity.* This policy guarantees a lifetime income to the insured, or annuitant, in return for either a periodic or a lump-sum payment to an insurance company. If the annuitant cannot make a single lump-sum premium payment, he or she may pay a certain amount periodically until at some stipulated time in the future the policy reverts to a payout basis. Annuity policies may be purchased in one of the same three ways that variable annuities are purchased.

With an annuity, the insurance company is betting that the insured will not outlive his or her capital, whereas with term, ordinary or endowment policies, the company is betting on the long life of the insured.

The most important feature of an annuity is the guarantee of a specific, lifelong income. Other investments may produce a higher current yield but do not have such a guarantee; and if adverse conditions occur, an individual's income could be reduced. The disadvantage of an annuity is that it does not provide the investor an opportunity to increase income as personal needs increase or as inflation reduces the purchasing power of the income. Perhaps the most significant blessing of an annuity is the peace of mind that it provides.

Annuities are discussed in the detail they require in the next chapter.

6. *Universal Life*. This type of policy represents a dramatic change in the design and emphasis of the traditional life insurance policy. In response to the economic climate created by high rates of inflation, the public turned to such investments as money market funds and Treasury bills to shield their dwindling assets and income—and they began to search out top value for their insurance dollar.

The concept of universal life is comparatively simple. In effect, the cash value portion of the traditional whole life policy has been separated (or "unbundled") from the pure term insurance protection and clearly identified as a cash account. The earnings credited to the cash account are generally tied to an identifiable rate of return on invested funds, such as a specific bond index, 90-day T bills, or the insurance company's own rate of return on its investment portfolio. Upon taking out the policy, the applicant decides on an appropriate amount of insurance; the applicant's age and sex determine the "target" premium for the policy, as in the traditional policy.

As each premium is paid, a fixed expense charge is deducted (for commissions, administration costs, etc.) and the balance is added to the cash account. Each month, interest at current rates is credited to the account and the cost of pure term life insurance protection is deducted. There is a guaranteed minimum rate of interest for the life of the contract (4% to 4½%) but no maximum. In mid-1985, for example, insurance companies were crediting interest at rates of 10% to 12%.

Two death benefit options are generally available. Option A pays the initial face amount, which includes the cash value—as in the traditional whole life or endowment policy. Under Option B, the death benefit is the face amount *plus* the cash value.

What makes universal life unique is its flexibility. It can be tailored to the insured's current needs and then altered, whenever necessary, without having to issue new policies. For example, premium deposits may be increased, decreased, or even discontinued for a time. The policyholder can increase or decrease the death benefit, accelerate the cash growth with additional unplanned premium deposits, make nontaxable cash withdrawals, or borrow money from the contract. Cash withdrawals or suspension of premium payments need not affect the death benefit, as long as there is enough of a cash balance in the account to pay the current monthly cost of the pure protection in effect.

Standard Life Insurance Policy Provisions

The following provisions (policyholder rights) are in most insurance contracts.

Grace Period. Most insurance policies provide the insured with a grace period of 31 days after the due date of a premium to make the payment without forfeiting the insurance. Often, even after an insurance policy has defaulted, the insured may reinstate the policy for a limited period, usually five years, upon providing evidence of insurability (proof that he or she is still in good health) and paying the back premiums.

Owner. Usually the owner of the policy may change the beneficiary designation at any time.

Incontestable. Most policies are incontestable after the policy has been in effect for two years (for some companies, one year). The incontestable clause prohibits the insurance company, after the incontestable period, from contesting claims based on information included in the application. The only exception to the clause is when a policy contains a misstatement as to the age of the insured. In that case, the face amount of the policy is adjusted to reflect the amount the premiums would have purchased at the insured's age at the time the policy was issued. After a policy becomes incontestable, the face amount of the policy will be paid even if the insured commits suicide.

Automatic Premium Loan. The usually optional automatic premium loan provision enables the insurance company to take an automatic loan from the cash surrender value to pay an unpaid premium. (As previously discussed, policy provisions usually permit the cash value of a policy to be used by the insured in a number of ways.)

Policy Riders

Riders that provide additional benefits may be attached to most policies for additional premiums:

Accidental Death. Accidental death, sometimes referred to as double indemnity, provides that should the insured's death occur within 90 to 180 days (depending on specific policy provisions) of the date of an accident, the insurance company will pay additional proceeds above the face amount of the policy. Double indemnity means the beneficiary will be paid twice the policy's face amount in the event of accidental death. Triple indemnity calls for payment of three times the face value.

Waiver of Premium. Waiver of premium provides that should the insured become disabled for a continuous period, usually six months, all future premiums will be waived. The policy will remain in force, and cash values will continue to accumulate. The waiver of premium is generally so inexpensive, yet so valuable, that it is considered a must.

Policy Purchase Option. The policy purchase option permits the insured to purchase additional insurance, equal to the original policy, every three or five years (depending on policy provisions) between the ages of 25 and 40 for a premium corresponding to the age at which the option is exercised. There is no contractual obligation to purchase additional insurance. This rider is an option usually added to policies for younger people to enable them to purchase up to six times the original face amount without their having to provide evidence of insurability.

Family Protection Rider. Family protection riders provide a certain amount of insurance on the spouse of the insured and a smaller amount on each child, thus furnishing minimal amounts of insurance for family members.

Family Income Riders. The family income rider, a form of decreasing term insurance, supplies a certain amount of income per month for a certain number of years in the event of the policyholder's death. The beneficiary may still take the benefits in cash at a computed present value of future payments rather than the monthly income.

There are also a number of decreasing term and level riders available for most policies, providing additional insurance at a low net cost.

Beneficiary Designation

The four general types of beneficiary designations are:

1. The *named individual* designates an individual or group of individuals such as the spouse or children of the insured, to whom the death proceeds are to be paid directly. Contingent beneficiaries should be named in case the insured survives the primary beneficiary.

2. *Estate of the insured.* If the named beneficiary does not survive the insured and no contingent beneficiaries are designated, most insurance policies provide that the proceeds are to be paid to the insured's estate. The practice of many individuals of simply naming their estate as beneficiary is generally not advisable because the proceeds are then subject to the expenses of probate and sometimes to state inheritance taxes.

3. The more and more popular *inter vivos* (*life insurance*), *trust*, sometimes called a "life insurance trust," allows the death proceeds to be paid into a trust established by the insured during his or her lifetime. This is another estate planning method that can reduce probate cost and ease estate settlement costs.

4. The *testamentary trust*, effective upon the death of the insured, is part of the decedent's will, and passes the insurance proceeds into the hands of a named trustee for proper management and payments as spelled out in the trust agreement.

There are some generally accepted misconceptions regarding the inclusion of death proceeds in an estate. First and foremost, insurance proceeds, upon the death of an insured, are includable in his or her estate for federal estate tax purposes if the insured owns the policy. However, if the proceeds are payable to a named beneficiary—and usually the inter vivos or testamentary trust is considered a named beneficiary—the death proceeds are not subject to probate, probate costs, or inheritance taxes in most states. The proceeds are paid directly to the named beneficiary, and no executor's fees are charged. In extremely large estates the avoidance of probate processing can result in substantial savings in time and money.

To avoid life insurance proceeds (the death benefit) from being included in the estate of the insured, it is often advisable to allow the wife (spouse) or children to own the policy.

Example: Bill Jamerson owns the majority of a closely held corporation. After completing an estate analysis, he determines that his estate is valued in excess of $1 million, mostly the value of the closely held business, and he needs an additional $500,000 life insurance. He does not want to be the owner of the policy because the proceeds would be included in his estate and the majority of the death benefit would be paid in estate taxes.

Bill decides to let his wife be the owner and beneficiary of the policy. This means that, upon his death, the proceeds would not be includable in his estate nor would they be taxable income to his wife. The key is that his wife must pay the premiums. Since Mrs. Jamerson has some independent income she is thus able to pay the premiums.

Note: If the insured pays the premiums, even though the owner is another individual, the Internal Revenue may rule that for estate tax purposes the proceeds are taxable. A possible solution to the problem would be for the insured to make a gift (within the gift tax limits) to the owner so that the premiums can be paid.

If the death proceeds are paid to a named beneficiary other than the estate of the insured, they are also free from the claims of the insured's creditors. And if the named beneficiary receives the proceeds in installments, those installments will be free from the claims of creditors of the beneficiary. A creditor who has a legal claim against the assets of a named beneficiary cannot attach life insurance payments to that beneficiary. If the death proceeds are payable to the estate of the insured, all creditors of the insured have a claim against those proceeds.

Methods of Payment of Death Proceeds

The death proceeds of an insurance policy may be paid in a number of ways in accordance with the wishes of the beneficiary. With a limit of twelve months, most insurance companies pay interest on the death proceeds from the date of death until the beneficiary makes a decision on the final method of payment. The alternative methods of payment are usually outlined in the policy and may include some or all of the following:

1. *A lump-sum payment* is the payment of the face amount (minus any indebtedness, plus the accrued interest) to the beneficiary, who then must make the decisions as to where and how the money will be invested. If the beneficiary is the insured's estate or an insurance trust, lump sum is the only practical settlement option.

2. *Installments in a fixed amount for a fixed period* may be monthly or on any regular basis mutually agreeable to the insurance company and the insured. This settlement option is usually set up to furnish income to a survivor who is awaiting the start of other income, such as Social Security Retirement Benefits.

3. *Life income for the beneficiary* supplies a fixed amount of income to the beneficiary during his or her lifetime. Usually a fixed number of payments is guaranteed to someone other than the beneficiary, or to the estate of the beneficiary, should the beneficiary die before the guaranteed payments are made.

4. *Interest on the proceeds* may be drawn by the beneficiary should the proceeds be left with the insurance company. Of course, the beneficiary retains the right to withdraw all or part of the principal at any time.

Reasons for Taking Out Life Insurance

Life insurance should be an integral part of every investor's financial and estate planning.

Life insurance is usually purchased to provide for an individual's heirs should he or she die before being able to accumulate an estate. It is, in effect, an "instant estate" that allows a person's spouse, children, or other dependents to continue in the same lifestyle that would have been provided had the insured lived. Life insurance may also be used to provide liquidity in the insured's estate: the proceeds of a policy would (1) enable the heirs to avoid liquidating other assets at undesirable times or prices and (2) pay estate taxes and other settlement costs.

For some, life insurance is a type of forced savings. The accumulated cash value in a policy is money available for emergencies, children's education, retirement, among many such needs.

Life insurance is often used to fund business agreements such as stock redemption plans, buy-sell agreements, and deferred compensation plans. (Business insurance is highly technical and is not relevant to the purposes of this book.)

How much life insurance an individual needs is a "guess-timate" at best. A rough estimate may be arrived at by coordinating present assets and liabilities (such as real and personal property, securities, savings accounts, and the like) with funds that would become available upon the death of the insured (such as the proceeds from a deferred compensation plan, Social Security, and so on). Other considerations would be the survivor's ability to work, income-producing assets, assets available once debts are retired, and the financial status of the insured's family. Often an in-depth study is required to determine the exact amount needed; however, an individual should avoid becoming "insurance poor"—inadvertently depriving the family while he or she is alive so they may live extravagantly after his or her death.

The following examples illustrate the extremes of life insurance.

Example: Jane and Ted Smith, both in their mid-twenties, have been married for four years. They have two children, a son aged one and a daughter aged three. Ted is a trainee in a bank and has a good future. Neither have any family wealth to fall back on in case of emergencies. They have to depend on Ted's income for present and future needs. Jane does not work because taking care of the children is a full-time job. It takes all of their income to make ends meet; therefore there is little left over for savings or extras.

Ted is concerned about Jane and the children should he

die prematurely. If he should die, he wants his family to be able to continue living in their house, to provide for the children's college education, and adequate income for Jane so she will not be forced back to work while the children are young.

An insurance advisor has shown them whole-life policies to provide the needed protection and to help with their savings program. He has also shown them term insurance, which would provide the maximum protection for minimum dollars.

In reviewing their insurance program, Ted realized that the bank carries a $100,000 term insurance policy on his life, and he is able to purchase cheap term insurance from his college alumni association. He is also aware that Social Security would provide some income for his family while the children are young.

Because of their present circumstances, Jane and Ted have decided that protection is more important than savings. They will use the dollars allocated to insurance to purchase the maximum amount of term insurance. They will make sure the policies are convertible into a form of permanent insurance in case Ted's health should fail at a later date. They also plan to work with the insurance agent and periodically convert a part of the term insurance to permanent policies so as to have adequate permanent coverage for long-term needs.

Example: Ben Johnson, an engineering consultant, is 55 years old. He and his wife, Betty, aged 52, have three grown children. The children have their own families and are doing well.

Recently, when we asked about his life insurance program and estate plans, Ben responded, "The children are grown, I have no responsibilities, we have no mortgage on our home and we do not have enough assets to worry about."

When Ben listed his assets at the insistence of his advisors, he was surprised to discover their value was much greater than he had originally thought. When he included the value of his company retirement plans, real estate equity (including their home), stock and bond holdings, life insurance he owned, a few business interests, he discovered his estate would be approximately $800,000. This did not take into account the fact that these assets should increase in value over the next few years, and as their value increased so would the estate taxes and settlement costs.

At the present value, it was estimated that it would cost almost $100,000 to settle Ben's estate. This includes estate and state inheritance taxes, legal and accounting fees, probate costs, and so forth. The $100,000 is money or assets Ben and Betty had planned to be used to provide Betty an income in the event of Ben's untimely death.

Ben realized he had to make a decision. He could either purchase additional life insurance, or allow his estate to shrink by the amount of estate settlement costs. He had worked long and hard to accumulate these assets, and for a few dollars a year (insurance premiums) he decided to purchase the additional life insurance.

Ben and Betty decided that she would be the owner of the insurance policy so that upon Ben's death his estate would not be inflated by another $100,000. Betty would pay the premiums from income she received from stocks in her name or Ben would make a gift to her each year in an amount sufficient for her to pay the premiums.

Jane and Ted had to purchase life insurance to create an estate; that is, to provide assets in the event of Ted's untimely death. Ben and Betty, on the other hand, purchased life insurance to conserve assets already accumulated.

An estate plan, as well as the amount of life insurance to own, is a personal decision, and should be made after reviewing all facts. Of equal importance to the "fact facts," which are a list of assets and liabilities, are the "people facts." What does the family want to provide? Are there moral obligations that need to be taken care of? What standard of living should the survivors maintain in the event of an untimely death of a provider? All of this must be reviewed with a competent insurance advisor.

Life Insurance Loans

During periods of high interest rates, such as the 1970s and early 1980s, owners of insurance policies should review their contracts as to the amount of accumulated cash value and dividends. Most insurance contracts issued before 1976 provide that the owner can make a loan against the cash value in the policy at 5% interest. Most policies issued after 1976 carry a loan interest rate of 8%.

The insurance company is obviously using the owner's money (cash value and accumulated dividends, if any, in a participating policy) to make investments. If the owner makes a policy loan, and certain provisions are met, the 5% paid to the insurance company would be tax deductible. If these proceeds could be invested in money market funds, short-term Treasury Bills, or certificates of deposit, earning 10% to 12% or higher, a nice piece of change could be earned at the stroke of a pen.

For the interest on the life insurance loan to be tax deductible, insurance premiums must have been paid in four out of the first seven years. The IRS code says that for interest on debt incurred "to purchase or continue life insurance" to be deductible, at least four of the first seven yearly premiums must be paid.

Example: Mike Johnson has been paying on a $100,000 insurance policy for over 20 years. The policy has $20,000 of cash value and loan provisions that call for a 5% interest rate on any loans.

Mike decides to borrow the $20,000 cash value at 5%. Since he has paid 4 out of 7 annual premiums, the $1,000 interest cost is tax deductible.

Mike invests the $20,000 of loan proceeds at 10%, thus netting him $2,000 in income. Since Mike is in a 50% tax bracket, the net cost of the interest is $500 and the net spendable income is $1,000. Therefore, at the stroke of a pen, Mike has made $1,000.

Since Mike does not want to reduce his death benefits, he invests the loan proceeds only in Treasury Bills and money funds. If he should die while the loan is outstanding, the insurance company will pay $80,000 less any accrued interest ($100,000 less $20,000 loan).

The person considering a loan against an insurance policy's cash value should keep in mind that if the insured dies before the loan is repaid, the insurance company would pay the beneficiary the face amount of the policy less the amount borrowed and interest to the date of death.

Also, if the borrower owns municipal bonds, or uses the proceeds to buy municipal bonds, he or she may not be able to deduct the interest paid on the loan. Anyone in such a situation should consult a professional tax advisor.

Another potential problem in borrowing cash value from a life insurance contract is the possibility of creating taxable income. If the owner borrows more than has been paid in net premiums, the difference could possibly be taxable income.

Life Insurance Traps

The owner of permanent insurance can surrender the policy for cash or make loans against the policy. Also, endowment contracts mature and are payable at a certain time.

Any of these events could result in potential income tax liability.

Example: If Mr. Insurance Believer had used his annual dividend to reduce premiums, $9,718 in premiums over the 20-year period would have been reduced by $3,300 (the amount of the dividends). Upon maturity he would have received the face amount of the endowment, $10,000, but his cost would have been $6,418, the amount of the premiums less the dividends. The difference, $3,582, would be taxable as ordinary income.

The same type of taxable situations may result on policy loans. If the owner of an insurance contract borrows more than was paid (or in the case of a participating policy, if the loan plus the withdrawal of accumulated dividends are in excess of total premiums), the difference could be taxable as ordinary income.

Any owner of an insurance contract considering substantial loans against the policies or the surrender of a policy, should write to the insurance company to obtain all data as to: (1) total amount of premiums paid, and (2) exact value of accumulated cash value, and (3) any dividends that have accumulated. With this information, professional tax advice should be sought before entering the transaction.

One insurance executive said, "Insurance companies will notify the Internal Revenue when a policy is surrendered that pays out more in proceeds than the cost of the policy." A little time and effort can often save tax dollars.

Trusts and Other Means of Shifting Income

To many people, the thought of a trust is frightening. The perception is that you cannot get to the cash for unusual needs or that impersonal trustees come to believe they own the money (rather than the beneficiaries). To some, the word "trust" is synonymous with lawyers, accountants, banks, and big fees.

There is also a misconception that to create a trust one must have immense wealth or be expecting an unusually large inheritance. A trust can often be a very valuable instrument to assist in the supervision or management of assets, or to save income and/or estate taxes.

The perception of trusts has changed dramatically over the last few years. An understanding of the basic concepts of trusts as well as an overview of how they work, should alleviate unwarranted fears.

What is a Trust?

Parties to a Trust

Following are the basic terms necessary to understand the language of a trust:

1. *The trust:* This is the written document that includes the terms, conditions, and instructions of the trust. The document names the trustees and beneficiaries.

2. *Trustee:* This is the person, persons, or institution such as a bank or law firm named in the trust instrument as being responsible for the management of the trust's assets. This

agent is also responsible for carrying out the instructions of the trust for the sole benefit of the beneficiary or beneficiaries.

3. *Beneficiaries:* These are the individuals or organizations that are to receive benefits from the trust. Benefits may be in the form of income or distribution of principal as per the written instructions in the trust document.

4. *The creator:* This is the person or persons who have a trust prepared and deposit assets (cash, stocks, real estate, and so forth) in the hands of the trustee for the benefit of the beneficiary. The beneficiary of the trust can also be the creator. A trust creator is often called a settlor, grantor, or donor.

5. *Funding of the trust:* A trust may have (or make provisions for depositing into it) money or property (assets) so it can create income and/or growth for the benefit of the beneficiaries. Providing for the depositing of the assets in the trust is called "funding the trust."

A trust, whether created during an individual's lifetime, or by his or her will, is the document—instructions—by which the creator's wishes are carried out. The trustee, whether an individual or bank, must follow the instructions of the creator.

Here is a simple example:

Example: John Reliable awakens early one Saturday morning. As he sits at the kitchen table, having his coffee before heading to the office for his usual half-a-day Saturday's work, he writes his son, Mike, a note. With the note he leaves $50. The note says, "Get the grass cut. Take care of the dog. Clean the car. Get your sister a birthday present. Return any unused money to me."

John Reliable has created a trust in his written note to his son. Mike Reliable is the trustee and is given the funding ($50) to carry out the provisions of the trust. In this example, Mike as trustee, is given latitude as to how to carry out the instructions. He may cut the grass himself or get someone to cut it. He may use his own judgment in taking care of the dog and he may wash the car himself. He is given discretion on what type of birthday present to get his sister.

The trust could have been more specific as to the creator's instructions to the trustee if the trustee had said:

Example: You cut the grass. Take the dog to the vet and get the dog's shots. Take the car to the car wash. Get your sister a blouse for a birthday present. Return all unused money to me.

Obviously, the second set of instructions restricts the trustee a great deal more.

If John Reliable had written in the instructions, "After you finish these chores, you may use $5 or $10 to go to the movies or to go to McDonald's for lunch," the creator is then paying the trustee a fee for carrying out his duties.

Types of Trusts

There are basically two types of trust:

1. A *testamentary trust* is created by provisions written into a will. The provisions of the testamentary trust do not come into being until the death of the creator.

2. An *inter vivos trust* is created and actually starts functioning while an individual is alive. It is also called a *living trust.*

There are two types of living trust:

I. A *revocable living trust* is one that can be terminated and/or in which the trustee or investment manager can be changed at any time the creator so desires. Generally, the beneficiaries also can be changed.

In such a trust, all income produced by the property and deposited into the trust is taxable to the creator. The principal of the trust is also includable in the creator's estate for estate tax purposes. Further, since the creator retains full control over the assets of the trust, there is no gift (for gift tax purposes) at the time the trust is created.

2. An *irrevocable trust* is often used to save income and estate taxes. To gain the tax savings, the creator must give up certain rights to the properties deposited in the trust. No strings may be attached to the provisions of the trust. Generally, the creator

may not receive any of the income earned by the assets of the trust nor can he or she invade the property, change the beneficiary, or alter the rights of the beneficiaries.

Anyone contemplating an irrevocable trust should give a lot of thought to the purpose of the trust and its provisions. The establishment of an irrevocable living trust constitutes an outright gift and the assets deposited into the trust may be subject to gift taxation in the year of creation. The amount of the tax depends on the value of the gift.

Why Open a Trust?

Advantages of Trusts

The advantages of establishing a trust and reasons for establishing a trust are many and varied. Clearly, a trust can be invaluable in conserving and managing assets, as well as reducing both income and estate tax liability.

Individuals creating a trust must make certain that the written document accomplishes their objectives. Remember: The trustee is the financial partner of the trust beneficiaries, but can only carry out the creator's instructions. Each trust should be individualized as much as possible to protect the creator as well as the beneficiaries. Many trusts are established simply to manage the assets of individuals who are not capable of managing their own money.

However, as will be described throughout this section, there are many other reasons for establishing trusts. Some of them are:

1. to save income taxes.

2. to protect the interest of beneficiaries.

3. to direct the distribution and disposition of capital and income in various ways.

4. to provide for special problems of children, disabled individuals, or spendthrifts.

5. peace of mind.

Problems with Trusts

Perhaps one of the most important and most misunderstood partners in a trust is the trustee. As previously explained, the trustee is responsible for the management of the assets deposited into the trust and for the distribution of income and principal to income beneficiaries as designated in the trust agreement.

John T. McGrann, President of the Bank of Virginia Trust Company, said, "The trustee is to be the financial partner of the trust's beneficiary, not an adversary. As much as possible, the trustee should put himself in the shoes of the creator."

The creator of a trust may name more than one trustee. He or she may have co-trustees (one, two, or three).

Example: Consider the example of Mr. Reliable who wants to establish a trust in his will. He feels Mrs. Reliable is quite capable of managing the income that his estate would provide, but is concerned about the possibility that she may die prematurely and that she may not be able to manage the principal. Mr. Reliable may decide to name Mrs. Reliable and a bank as co-trustees of the assets. Alternatively, Mr. Reliable may decide to name Mrs. Reliable co-trustee with his lawyer, stockbroker, or accountant. It is not necessary to name a bank in the creation of a trust.

In the past, many trusts were so restrictive that the trustee had little, if any, discretion or latitude in the management of the assets or disposition of the income or principal. Often the creator, in the design of the trust document, restricted the trustee so that the best interests of the beneficiaries could not be met.

Perhaps, when the trust was written, $400 a month was enough for Mrs. Beneficiary to live comfortably. Perhaps then, Jr. could have paid college expenses with money to spare on $1,200 a year. When the trust was written the creator did not foresee that his mother would become totally disabled.

Consider the trust that says, "The assets must be invested in XYZ stock regardless of changing circumstances" or the trust that stated that the family home or other real estate could never be sold. According to McGrann, "Circumstances such as these must be followed in the management of the trust assets and distribution of income. We must follow the instructions of the trust documents."

Today, most lawyers and financial advisors are aware of the problems of overly restrictive trust agreements, inflation, and changing family needs. Trusts are now written so as to provide more discretion and latitude to the trustees. In addition, a great deal of effort is now being devoted to ensuring that all people involved in a trust understand the document. It is extremely advisable that all beneficiaries, whenever possible, read and understand a trust document while the creator is alive and able to explain his or her intentions.

A word of caution: Many trust problems stem from either a lack of understanding of the trust document or the beneficiary's inability to communicate with the trustees. It is often suggested that the creator of a trust include a provision allowing for substitute trustees. This should be discussed with legal counsel but, in essence, the provision would state something to the effect, "If the beneficiaries desire, they may substitute a trustee for another trustee." This means that one bank trust department could be substituted for another or, if an individual is named trustee, a like individual with similar qualifications could be substituted as trustee.

Sprinkled Provisions

Many trust creators may want to consider what are called *sprinkled provisions* in the trust document. The sprinkled (sometimes called *sprayed*) provisions allow the trustee to distribute income and/or capital disproportionally to the income beneficiaries as the trustee sees fit. Often a sprinkle provision allows for the trustee to withhold income within the trust if it is in the best interest of the beneficiaries.

Let us consider some circumstances where the sprinkle provisions may be advantageous:

Example: Mr. Reliable has established a trust fund for his wife and the ultimate beneficiaries are his three children. The trust provides first and foremost for the well-being of his wife and certain portions of the income are to be reinvested for the benefit of the children. The trust throws off income of $100,000 per year. Mrs. Reliable does not need that amount of money to maintain her standard of living. One son is still in college. If Mrs. Reliable receives the income, she must then pay taxes on it before paying college tuition. If the trust makes distribution to the son, who then pays his college tuition, the overall tax consequences to the family unit will be lower as the son is in a substantially lower tax bracket.

If all income is not needed, the trust could retain a portion of the income and pay tax on that income. In essence, another taxpayer is provided for and this reduces the overall tax liability to the family.

Consider another set of circumstances:

Example: Mr. Reliable, in creating the trust, wanted to provide for his parents if it became necessary. When the trust was created, Mr. Reliable's parents were self-sufficient. After several years, Mr. Reliable's father passed away and Mrs. Reliable was having a difficult time meeting expenses. Since Mr. Reliable's wife and children were self-sufficient, the trust could be written so as to provide that a portion of the income from the trust, at the discretion of the trustee, could be paid to his mother.

Taxwise it would be advantageous to use the sprinkle provision rather than the income paid to Mrs. Reliable and/or the children who would then pay tax on the income before making any gifts to Mr. Reliable's mother.

Reversionary Trusts

The *reversionary trust,* sometimes referred to as a *short-term,* or *Clifford trust* is usually established either for a period of at least 10 years and a day or for the life of the income beneficiary, whichever occurs first. The creator deposits in the trust sufficient corpus (stocks, bonds, real estate, and so forth) to yield the required income. Income may be paid monthly, quarterly, or annually to the beneficiary, who then will be subject to income tax liability on the income distributed.

By using a reversionary trust, an investor diverts income to a beneficiary, who is usually in a lower tax bracket, while retaining ultimate ownership of the income-producing asset. Many investors use such a trust to make regular payments to parents, children, or relatives with *pretax* dollars.

After March 1, 1986, if the grantor has reversionary interest that is in excess of 5%, the benefits of most short-term trusts have been eliminated to prevent income splitting. In addition, trusts and estates will be required to make estimated tax payments.

To dilute the transfer tax benefits by generation skipping, a generation skipping tax (GST) will be imposed on any person more than one generation below the transferer.

These changes completely repeal retroactively the throwback rules modified by the 1976 Tax Reform Act.

At the designated date of termination, as set forth in the trust agreement, or at the death of the income beneficiary, the assets of the trust revert to the creator.

Establishing a Reversionary Trust

There are two basic questions to be resolved when establishing a reversionary trust:

1. *Who shall act as trustee?* The creator, spouse, or any named individual may act as trustee. A bank or a lawyer may also act as trustee, but expenses and management fees may be charged. Basically, the trustee is charged with the management of the trust's assets: Buy and sell recommendations may be required of him or her, or the creator may deposit mutual fund shares whereby professional management and reinvestment and withdrawal plans are provided. The trustee may also retain an investment manager.

2. *How shall it be funded?* Once a reversionary trust is established, the trust property may not in any way revert to the donor before the death of the income beneficiary or before termination of the trust as specified in the trust agreement. The assets may not be used as collateral, nor can the trust agreement be amended or revoked during its term.

A reversionary trust can be funded with high-yield mutual fund shares, bond funds, bonds, or high-yield stocks. Because the trust is generally considered an income vehicle, low-yield and volatile securities could present future tax and management problems.

Tax Consequences

Income Taxes. The income beneficiary currently is taxed on any income or capital gains distributed by the trust. If the trust agreement specifies that realized gains are to be distributed to the beneficiary, then their amount and character (short-term or long-term) are taxable to the beneficiary. Generally, if capital gains are retained in the trust, the amount and character of the gain will be taxable to the creator either in the year the gain is realized or upon the termination of the trust. The creator is taxed on any income not paid to the income beneficiary, and on any realized capital gains in the year they are realized.

Estate tax savings are insignificant because the reversionary interest is included in the creator's estate at his or her death. A term life insurance policy may be purchased to provide the creator's immediate beneficiaries a usable asset, as well as funds to pay estate taxes on the value of the reversionary interest. It is also possible to provide that the trust will terminate on the death of the creator, so long as his or her life expectancy is greater than 10 years when the trust is created. In this case, the principal would revert to the creator's estate at his or her death.

A reversionary trust can be used as an accumulation trust for a minor child. The trust can accumulate the reinvest income. Since a trust is treated as a taxpayer, it is allowed an exemption of $300. If the trust is being used for a minor child, income tax consequences to the child should be negligible, however, the creator should keep in mind that gift taxes may apply.

The creator of a reversionary trust with the accumulation of income for the beneficiary should be aware that upon dissolvement of the trust in 10 years and a day, the income beneficiary will be liable for income taxes on the accumulated income distributed to him or her. In addition, the IRS has a formula for determining what taxes the creator will pay, giving full credit for tax already paid by the trust.

Gift Taxes. A gift tax liability on assets in excess of exemptions is based on the present value of the expected income payments for the life of the trust.

Example: The present value of the right to income for 10 years is slightly in excess of 44% of the value of the income-producing property (thus, a gift tax would apply to $44,160.50 for the trust entity of $100,000 if held for 10 years or more). If a gift tax results, it must be paid by the creator.

Each taxpayer has a $10,000 per year tax-free gift privilege to as many individuals as he may desire. A couple can jointly give $20,000 per year, per individual, gift-tax free.

Capital Gains Taxes. Upon termination of the trust, the assets revert to the creator who assumes the cost basis of the assets in the trust. It is usually advisable to deposit property, rather than cash, into a reversionary trust. If cash is invested by the trust and the property acquired with the cash appreciates in value, the creator would be subject to a capital gains tax upon termination. But if the creator purchases property and deposits it with the trust, no capital gains liability results.

Who Establishes a Reversionary Trust?

Establishing a reversionary trust for a child may prove advantageous to some investors. The income paid by the trust to the child can be used to pay expenses that the parent is not legally obliged to provide. However, a child over the age of 14 is taxed at the parent's rate on unearned income. Beginning in 1987, the child can no longer apply his or her personal exemptions ($1,000 and the $100 dividend exclusion) while still a dependent, for income purposes. Upon termination of the trust, the assets revert to the parent.

For simplicity, it is advisable for all income to be paid in cash or securities. If securities are distributed to a minor beneficiary, the securities should be registered as "Custodian under the Uniform Gift to Minors Act," which will be discussed later.

An individual who is presently in a high-earning bracket, but who may need the assets at a later time, may find a reversionary trust beneficial. The income from the deposited assets is shifted to an individual in a lower tax bracket; and when the creator needs the assets, the trust terminates.

For example, an investor supporting an elderly relative may avoid some taxes, and thus have more spendable income, with a reversionary trust because the relative is probably in a lower tax bracket.

Example: Nedda supports her Uncle Antonio. In the 28% tax

bracket, she makes payments of $2,880 per year to her uncle. This amount represents a 10% return on $40,000 ($4,000 − 28% taxes = $2,880). If $28,800 of the securities yielding 10% were deposited in a reversionary trust, Antonio would receive $2,880 income and Nedda would free $28,800 for other investments. Uncle Antonio would be required to include the $2,880 payment in his taxable income.

As with other complicated estate planning vehicles, an individual should not attempt to be a lawyer or tax expert. The establishment of a reversionary trust could result in tricky tax situations involving possible gift tax liability and tax throwback provisions for reinvested funds, as the following section explains. Therefore, professional tax and legal advice should be obtained *before* entering into such an arrangement.

Charitable Remainder Trusts

A *charitable remainder trust* allows the use of appreciated assets to increase current income and at the same time receive substantial current income and estate tax savings. Such a trust is created by an individual who reserves a specified income from the trust's assets for him- or herself or for other named income beneficiaries. Upon the death of all income beneficiaries, the assets remaining in the trust pass to recognized charities as named in the trust document. The trust therefore enjoys a tax-exempt status and may invest without direct tax consequences, because it is established for the ultimate benefit of the recognized charities named as the trust *remaindermen.*

To establish a qualified charitable remainder trust, the named charities must qualify under section 170(c) of the Internal Revenue Code. Most large charities are recognized in this section of the Code.

The trust's creator receives an immediate income tax deduction for the *remainder interest* which is the amount assumed to be the assets remaining upon the death of the creator. This remainder is computed using actuarial tables published by the Internal Revenue Service and is a legitimate current tax deduction. Also, whenever contributions of appreciated assets are made to the trust, the trust can sell the assets without creating a tax liability. The donor's allowable annual charitable deduction for any year in which appreciated assets fund a charitable remainder trust is limited to 30% of his or her adjusted gross income. Any unused deductions may be carried forward for the next five taxable years. The creator is also eligible for an estate tax deduction for the value of the remaining trust assets at the time of his death. Such trusts may offer the creator many excellent tax benefits.

In the past, legal requirements regarding charitable remainder trusts were broad enough to allow latitude in payment schedules, secondary beneficiaries, and possible self-dealings between the trust and creator. The 1960 Tax Reform Act established new rules and tightened requirements for the charitable remainder trust. All existing trusts were required to conform to the new regulations.

Creation of a charitable remainder trust requires no advance IRS approval. The creator establishes his or her own trust, names the trustee, and stipulates a level of income to be paid. Then the creator claims the allowable charitable deduction and furnishes the necessary information together with his or her tax returns. To qualify for the income and estate tax deductions, contributions must be made on the forms specified by federal income tax regulations; therefore, it is imperative that an attorney draft the papers and review the proceedings to ensure compliance with all regulations.

Forms of Charitable Remainder Trusts

The two forms of the charitable remainder trust established by the 1969 Tax Reform Act are:

1. the *unitrust,* and,

2. the *annuity trust.*

Unitrust. Upon establishing the charitable remainder unitrust under IRS guidelines, the creator (1) transfers assets to a trust, which becomes the owner, (2) reserves a specified income for him- or herself and possibly other designated income beneficiaries, and (3) designates a recognized charity or charities as the recipient of all remaining assets at the death of all income beneficiaries. The designated charity neither receives nor controls any trust property until the death of all income beneficiaries, unless the charity is designated as a trustee.

The term of the unitrust may be for the lives of any number of individuals or for a definite number of years not to exceed 20.

The trust is tax-exempt and can therefore invest without direct tax consequences to the trust. In other words, it can liquidate property (securities) transferred to it without incurring any capital gains tax liability to the donor, and reinvest the proceeds to provide the desired income, diversification, and management. Additional contributions to a unitrust are allowable if the trust agreement includes such provisions.

The *unitrust agreement* must require that the beneficiary or beneficiaries receive *annual payments based upon a fixed percentage* (which cannot be less than 5%) of the net market value of the trust assets, determined each year on a stated valuation date or dates. Should the value of the assets in the trust increase, the beneficiaries' income increases. If the assets decrease, the amount of payments decreases.

Should the donor desire to protect the trust principal, the agreement may provide that the trustee be allowed to pay income beneficiaries only the actual income on the principal, if it is lower than the stipulated percentage. Deficiencies in distribution can be made up during years in which the trust income exceeds the stipulated payments (this is an optional provision in a charitable unitrust).

Example: Mr. Jones, age 64, donates assets with a current market value of $100,000 and a cost basis of $10,000 to a charitable remainder unitrust. The trust agreement provides that he is to receive an annual payment of 6% of the trust's assets, as valued at the beginning of each year for the rest of his life.

The following Internal Revenue table shows that the present value of the remainder interest factor for a charitable remainder unitrust with a payout of 6% for a male age 64 is .48626.

Percentage of Assets Required As Income

Male Age	5%	6%	7%	8%	9%
60	.48833	.43117	.38298	.34214	.30736
61	.50170	.44489	.39675	.35574	.32064
62	.51505	.45865	.41059	.36945	.33407
63	.52837	.47243	.42452	.38330	.34768
64	**.54168**	**.48626**	**.43855**	**.39730**	**.36149**

65	.55499	.50015	.45269	.41146	.37550
66	.56828	.51408	.46693	.42577	.38971
67	.58156	.52806	.48128	.44025	.40413
68	.59483	.54208	.49573	.45488	.41876
69	.60813	.55619	.51933	.46972	.43365

The .48626 factor is multiplied by the market value of the trust assets ($100,000) to determine the value of the charitable remainder. The resultant $48,626 represents the assets the IRS assumes will be left in the trust upon the death of Mr. Jones. If Mr. Jones wished to include others as income beneficiaries, obviously this figure would be less. It is a current income tax deduction for Mr. Jones in the year of transfer to the trust. Because the assets consist of appreciated property, his deduction for that year is limited to 30% of adjusted gross income with a 5-year carry-forward provision.

Should the trust liquidate the assets for greater income or for greater diversification, the tax-exempt trust incurs no tax liability on realized capital gains.

At Mr. Jones' death, the value of the trust's assets, less the present value of payments to other income beneficiaries, qualifies for an estate tax deduction, even though an income tax deduction was received by the grantor for the remainder interest. The remaining asset value is included as an asset in Mr. Jones' gross estate and may be taken as a charitable deduction. If Mrs. Jones is the remainder income beneficiary, no estate taxes will be due because a spouse may will or give assets to a spouse at the time of his death, the only tax benefit is the estate tax deduction.

Obviously, the more income beneficiaries named in the trust agreement means a smaller allowable charitable contributions deduction, because the value of the remainder interest decreases. Theoretically, the more payments (or lives) provided for by a unitrust, the smaller the amount available to the designated charity at the death of the last income beneficiary.

Annuity Trust. The IRS requirements for the charitable remainder annuity trust are the same as those for the unitrust except that the trust agreement must specify a *fixed dollar amount* (instead of a fixed percentage) as the annual payout.

The payout from the charitable remainder annuity trust remains constant for the term of the trust or for the life of the income beneficiary(s). The payout must be at least 5% of the market value of the property (or assets) transferred to the trust. Additional contributions may not be made to a charitable remainder annuity trust. However, an individual may establish more than one annuity trust.

Again, the trust itself is a tax-exempt entity and has no tax consequences. This feature affords the investor an opportunity to convert highly appreciated, low-income assets into an income-producing asset with positive tax consequences.

Example: Mr. Beefer, age 64, donates assets with a current market value of $100,000 (and a cost basis of $10,000) to a charitable remainder annuity trust, the terms of which provide that he is to receive $6,000 a year from the trust for the rest of his life.

The following table shows the present value of life interest and remainder for a male on 6% return. The annuity factor for a male age 64 is 8.2642:

Male Age	Annuity	Life Estate	Remainder
60	9.1753	.55052	.44948
61	8.9478	.53687	.46313
62	8.7202	.52321	.47679
63	8.4924	.50954	.49046
64	**8.2642**	**.49585**	**.50415**
65	8.0353	.48212	.51788
66	7.8060	.46836	.53164
67	7.5763	.45458	.54542
68	7.3462	.44077	.55923
69	7.1149	.42689	.57311

Estate and Gift Tax Regulation Section 20.2031-10.

The annuity factor is multiplied by the annual payout to determine the value of Mr. Beefer's life interest: 8.2642 × $6,000 = $49,585. To determine the remainder interest for immediate federal income tax deduction as a charitable contribution, Mr. Beefer's life interest is subtracted from the original market value of the gift: $100,000 − $49,585 = $50,415. The donor may deduct the

$50,415 as a charitable deduction on his current income tax return for the year of the transaction (up to 30% of his gross income), and any unused portion may be carried forward for up to 5 years.

Tax Consequences

The donor receives a current tax deduction for the present value of the remainder interest as a charitable contribution. There are also tax benefits at the death of the donor: The remaining value, less the present value of payments to other income beneficiaries, is a deduction for estate tax purposes.

Example: The value of Mr. Brown's charitable remainder trust at the time of his death is $200,000. If there were no second beneficiaries, the $200,000 would be included in his gross estate and taken as a charitable deduction from his estate.

However, Mr. Brown has named his son, Roscoe, as a second beneficiary. Roscoe is 50 years old and is supposed to receive an annual payment of 6% of the trust's assets. His annuity factor is 11.3329 as shown in the following table:

Male Age	Annuity	Life Estate	Remainder
35	13.8758	.83255	.16745
40	13.1538	.78923	.21077
45	12.3013	.73808	.26192
50	**11.3329**	**.67997**	**.32003**
51	11.1308	.66785	.32215
52	10.9267	.65560	.34440
53	10.7200	.64320	.35680
54	10.5100	.63060	.36940

This must be multiplied by $12,000 (6% of $200,000) to determine the total amount of anticipated payments due Roscoe. That amount ($135,995) must be deducted from the total value of the trust to determine Mr. Brown's estate tax deduction: $64,005. Roscoe, when his time comes, will receive no estate tax deductions.

Each payment from a charitable remainder unitrust or a charitable remainder annuity trust to either the donor or other designated beneficiaries is broken down into the following parts for tax purposes:

1. *As ordinary income.* Whatever earnings, dividends, and interest the trust made on the assets for the current taxable year and paid to the income beneficiary, plus whatever accumulated undistributed earnings it made in prior years but paid in the current year, are considered ordinary income and taxed as such.

2. *As long-term capital gain.* Whatever gains the trust realized and paid for the current year and whatever accumulated but undistributed net realized gains it made in previous years, but paid in the current year, are considered and taxed as long-term capital gains.

3. As *other income.* Whatever tax-exempt income the trust made for the year and paid to the income beneficiary, plus whatever undistributed tax-exempt income it made for the beneficiary in prior years but paid in the current year, is considered tax free to the income beneficiary. Tax-exempt income generally will not be taxable to the income beneficiary.

4. If none of the above apply to the current payout distribution, the payment will be considered a *tax-free distribution of the principal.*

Who Establishes a Charitable Remainder Trust?

One word of caution to individuals considering a charitable remainder trust. At the death of all income beneficiaries, generally the creator or the creator and his spouse if jointly held, all assets of the trust belong to the charity. No assets remain in the creator's or his spouse's estate.

In general, a charitable remainder trust should only be considered if the creator has no children, or if the children are financially self-sufficient enough so as not to have need for additional assets. A charitable remainder trust also may be suitable if the property being considered as a funding vehicle is only a very minor part of the estate of the creator.

Unitrust or Annuity Trust?

Which is more desirable? The answer to this question is a series of other questions: What are the current and future needs of the income beneficiaries? What does the creator wish to accomplish? Answer those questions, and the decision becomes clearcut.

Keep in mind a major difference between the types of charitable trusts:

1. The *unitrust* pays income that will rise and fall based on the value of the assets in the trust.

2. The *annuity trust* pays a fixed, level income.

If an individual anticipates, for example, that the need for current income will be continually increasing or would like to provide for that contingency, obviously the unitrust is more suitable. However, if the value of the trust's assets decline, so will the payout.

The annuity trust ensures a fixed dollar payout that will not be increased, even if the assets of the trust have a substantial appreciation. That appreciation, however, has a greater value for estate tax purposes than in the unitrust; it also provides a larger increase in the marital deduction in the donor's estate should the donor be survived by the spouse.

The key factor is suitability to the investor's total financial picture. Individuals, for instance, who have accumulated substantial wealth in highly appreciated assets would probably like to unlock the assets without incurring a capital gains liability. Someone searching for a way to increase spendable income, someone with a strong interest in a recognized charity, someone seeking potential estate tax savings, someone wanting to provide after his or her death an income to a specific individual, or someone with no heirs—any of these are possible candidates for one or the other charitable remainder trust.

Many mutual funds provide computer printouts indicating tax savings, present value of remainder interest, anticipated income, and a 20- to 30-year record of results. Mutual fund withdrawal plans (see "Mutual Funds") are excellent investment mediums to fund charitable remainder trusts because of accounting, reinvestment privileges, and professional management. Inquiries may be made directly to the mutual fund of the investor's choice.

Remember that charitable remainder trusts should not be entered into by an investor without first consulting tax and legal advisors.

Pooled Income Trust

A deviation from the charitable remainder trust is the *pooled income trust.* A pooled income trust is managed by a charity or an investment advisor retained by the charity. The fund is composed of donations of many individuals presumably who do not wish to create their own charitable trust. The donor rceives his or her prorated share of the income earned. The income may be payable over the life of the donor or the joint lives of the donor or his or her spouse. Some charities limit the number of beneficiaries to two, while others permit any number of beneficiaries.

A charitable trust deduction for cash or unappreciated assets may be equal to 50% of income tax liability. For appreciated assets the deduction is limited to 30% of current income tax liability. An individual may carry forward unused deductions for five years.

The pooled income fund differs as to taxation of distributions to the income beneficiaries. In a charitable remainder trust, the income may be taxed as ordinary income, capital gains, or return of capital depending on the source of the income within the trust. In a pooled income trust, all distributions to income beneficiaries are taxed as ordinary income.

Example: Mrs. Frugile's husband passed away a few years ago. She is now 67 years old and enjoys a taxable income of approximately $60,000 a year.

Mrs. Frugile's husband had purchased her James River common stock through the years. Her shares had substantially appreciated and were worth approximately $25,000. Her current yield, however, was only a little over 1%.

Mrs. Frugile had intentions of leaving a portion of her estate to her church and her husband's university, the University of Virginia. In fact, she had almost decided to leave $12,500 to each institution in her will.

She had read several articles about the charitable remainder trust whereby she could deposit her shares of James River into a trust and by doing so, increase her current income substantially. She would also receive a charitable deduction to reduce her current income tax liability.

Her lawyer advised her that the cost of establishing a trust for $25,000 may not be advantageous in light of the fact that her church and the University of Virginia had pooled trusts.

She contacted both institutions and learned that both had such accounts. She deposited half of her shares in the University of Virginia pooled account and the other half in her church's pooled account.

She now receives an approximate income of 8% on the $25,000 or $2,000 a year. In addition, she will get a charitable deduction for a portion of the value of the shares deposited.

When considering making charitable contributions, do not overlook the fact that there are alternatives other than those that first come to mind. Do not hesitate to ask your lawyer, accountant or investment advisor for various alternatives. In addition, the charities to which you may be inclined may have specific suggestions for making tax-advantaged gifts.

Installment Sale

From time to time, an investor would like to sell an asset, generally stock or real estate, purchased years before, but does not think he or she can afford the tax liability because the asset has appreciated so much. Or, although a stock has done well for an investor, the investor does not think he or she can afford to sell because of the tax liability. Such investors are often referred to as being "capital rich and income poor." The solution to such a situation may be an installment sale, in which the seller transfers the asset in return for periodic payments from the buyer over time. The payments in such a sale, at various interest rates, are shown on the next page.

A word of caution: under current law, if a family member makes an installment sale and a related buyer resells the property within two years, the resale of the property (or stock) by the "related purchaser" would trigger recognition of the gain by the initial seller to the extent that the amount realized from the resale

Approximate Monthly Payments on a $10,000 Installment Note

Maturity	4% Interest Rate		5% Interest Rate		6% Interest Rate		7% Interest Rate		8% Interest Rate	
10 YRS.	$101	(12.1%)	$106	(12.7%)	$111	(13.3%)	$116	(13.9%)	$121	(14.6%)
15 YRS.	$ 74	(8.9%)	$ 79	(9.5%)	$ 84	(10.1%)	$ 90	(10.8%)	$ 96	(11.5%)
20 YRS.	$ 61	(7.3%)	$ 66	(7.9%)	$ 72	(8.6%)	$ 78	(9.3%)	$ 84	(10.0%)
25 YRS.	$ 53	(6.3%)	$ 58	(7.0%)	$ 64	(7.7%)	$ 71	(8.5%)	$ 77	(9.3%)
30 YRS.	$ 48	(5.7%)	$ 54	(6.4%)	$ 60	(7.2%)	$ 67	(8.0%)	$ 73	(8.8%)
35 YRS.	$ 44	(5.3%)	$ 50	(6.0%)	$ 57	(6.8%)	$ 64	(7.7%)	$ 71	(8.5%)
40 YRS.	$ 42	(5.0%)	$ 48	(5.8%)	$ 55	(6.6%)	$ 62	(7.5%)	$ 70	(8.4%)

The figures are approximate—for planning purposes only. The monthly payments shown are for principal amount of $10,000. If, for example, a $50,000 note is contemplated, the payment should be multiplied by five. Figure in parentheses represents annual withdrawal rate necessary to provide monthly payout shown.

292

exceeded the payments received under the initial installment sale. If considering an installment sale between family members, one should consult an attorney.

Tax Requirements

Because the tax on long-term capital gains has now been reduced to a maximum of 28%, many tax advisors feel that the sale of a greatly appreciated asset and paying tax at a maximum of 28% is perhaps one of the greatest tax shelters around. The advent of the alternative minimum tax may change the circumstances surrounding a long-term capital gain. Again, however, the alternative minimum tax is only 21%.

The *installment sale* provisions of the Internal Revenue Code, section 453, deal with the problem of an individual wishing to dispose of a greatly appreciated capital asset, thereby converting it to additional income, and spreading the tax consequence of the sale proceeds over a number of years.

Because of the features of an installment sale, the seller may also reduce his or her estate as each payment is received and spent. The buyer, on the other end of the transaction, can usually resell the asset without significant capital gains consequences because his or her cost is likely to be near the present market value. Generally, the buyer uses the proceeds of the resale property to buy mutual fund shares, whose earnings may be used to make the installment payments.

The IRS requires that simple interest of at least 6% be applied to the installment obligation, otherwise the IRS will apply its rule of 7%.

The sale must be a bona fide arm's length transaction with substance. The IRS disallowed certain installment sales because the seller made all arrangements for the liquidation of the property before the person issuing the note (the buyer) came into the picture (Revenue Ruling 73-157). The IRS ruled it was a straight sale of an appreciated asset with all gains realized and all taxes due and payable in the year of the sale.

An installment sale may not be created with a minor, because a minor generally may not enter into contracts. However, a trust, with the minor as beneficiary, may be the buyer in an installment sale arrangement. The trust should be in existence and separately funded with a reasonable amount of assets prior to the installment sale.

Transfer at Death

At the seller's death, the unpaid portion of the installment note becomes includable in his or her estate for federal estate tax purposes. The unpaid amount is also includable for purposes of determining the marital deduction.

Further, if the remaining payments of the installment note are left to someone, the recipient reports the payments in the same way as the seller: The appropriate portion of each payment is reported as capital gains on his or her tax return, and the interest portion as ordinary income. However, the beneficiary of the note is entitled to a tax offset for any federal estate taxes paid by the holder's estate with respect to the installment note.

Should the installment note be forgiven at the death of the holder, the amount forgiven would probably be taxed as ordinary income to the buyer. Possibly, the buyer and estate could agree to a lump-sum settlement at the reduced "present value" of the remaining payments, resulting in a much reduced capital gains tax for the seller's estate.

Should the individual responsible for the payments die before the note has been paid in full, the unpaid balance is an obligation and liability of his or her estate. A term life insurance policy with reducing face value may be purchased to provide for the contingency of premature death.

An installment note may be secured if the seller obtains a lien on the assets of the obligor. The pledged assets may be those purchased on the installment basis or others owned by the buyer. The assets securing the note are included in the buyer's estate and are subject to federal estate and state inheritance taxes.

Benefits and Drawbacks

Benefits to the Seller. An installment sale:

1. unlocks assets that are frozen due to capital gains tax liability;

2. provides additional income with minimum income tax liability;

3. allows the receipt of realized capital gains and the commensurate tax liability to be pro-rated over the period payments are received;

4. reduces the effect of the capital gains tax significantly by spreading the receipt of the profits over an extended period of time;

5. reduces risk by diversification (avoiding a concentration of assets in a single holding);

6. decreases the seller's estate as each payment of the install-ment note is received and spent; and

7. furnishes the seller with a means to transfer assets to other family members with no gift tax liability.

Benefits to the Buyer. The installment sale enables the buyer to:

1. gain title to an asset with limited immediate cash outlay;

2. sell the greatly appreciated asset without payment of substan-tial income taxes (the buyer has purchased the asset at cur-rent market value and therefore, upon liquidation, any capital gain or loss would most likely be insignificant);

3. receive a tax deduction for the interest portion of each pay-ment on the installment note (the interest expense deduction may be applied against the buyer's dividend income and capital gains, as well as against other ordinary income); and

4. enjoy all future growth of the asset.

Disadvantages

The disadvantages of an installment sale are as follows:

1. The transactions are fairly complex and difficult to fully under-stand.

2. The seller faces substantial interest income which is taxable as ordinary income.

3. The present value of the remaining payments is included in the seller's estate.

4. A capital gains tax is assured, whereas if the asset is transferred at the seller's death, the capital gains pass onto the other parties and only an estate tax is paid.

IRS Ruling 73-536 has put a cloud over installment sales. Briefly, speaking to the intention of the parties involved, the ruling states that if an installment sale lacks reality and substance, it will not be allowed. Any transaction with the obvious intention of immediately reselling the asset to purchase mutual funds or other investments will likely cause close scrutiny by the IRS and, possibly, disallowance. Partial sale of the appreciated assets or a prolonged waiting period before a total resale may disperse some of "the cloud."

Many IRS rulings that disallow installment sale reporting will certainly be tested in the courts, and the final chapter is yet to be written. At the conclusion of these court cases and IRS rulings, a better understanding of the installment sale in financial planning will exist.

If an installment sale appears appropriate to your situation, competent legal advice should be obtained.

Example: Dudley Alright worked for a corporation for 35 years. During his tenure with the company he had purchased stock, had exercised stock options, and received performance shares. As he approached retirement , the market value of the company stock was $667,170. Mr. Alright had a cost basis in the stock of $166,656.

The company paid very little in dividends and after Mr. Alright's retirement a new management team took over.

Mr. Alright has an adult daughter who would inherit at least $600,000 of his estate if he should die now.

Mr. Alright wants to diversify his assets by selling his stock because he desires more income than the stock pays in dividends and he is concerned about the future management of the company. In addition, he would like to transfer all appreciation to his daughter, if possible.

Mr. Alright does not want to incur a large, lump-sum capital gains tax in order to accomplish his objective.

Example: Another set of circumstances that may require a similar solution would be Joe Tycoon, who in 1960 purchased a parcel of unimproved real estate for $50,000. He has since added $116,656 worth of improvements on the land, giving him a cost basis of $166,656. The real estate, even with the improvements (primarily fences and replanting of trees), provides no income. In fact, his taxes and insurance have been increasing each year thereby creating a negative cash flow.

Mr. Alright does have one possible solution: selling a portion of his stock each year, thereby spreading out the capital gains tax. Mr. Tycoon, generally speaking, would not have that option.

Solution: After consulting with their brokers, accountants and attorneys, both gentlemen decided to sell their assets to a child. Neither gentleman accepted a down payment, but each did receive a promissory note payable monthly for 20 years at 6% interest. The capital gains tax will now be spread over a 20-year period.

The children cannot immediately sell the stock (or real estate) and receive a check for the proceeds. They must wait two years.

Private Annuity

The _private annuity_ is a contract by which an individual (the _annuitant_) transfers his or her assets to another individual (called the _obligor_), usually a family member, for an _unsecured_ promise to pay an annuity for life.

A private annuity is similar to the commercial annuity purchased from an insurance company: Upon the death of the annuitant, the insurance company retains all assets transferred to a commercial annuity; in a private annuity, the obligor retains all assets. Upon the death of the annuitant, the contract has no value; and it is therefore not subject to estate taxes, assuming the annuitant lives more than three years from the date the contract is entered into. (If the annuitant dies within three years, the IRS can claim the contract was entered into with the contemplation of death.)

The purpose of a private annuity is to transfer assets from one generation to another, still deriving income from them but reducing lump-sum tax liabilities.

How Does a Private Annuity Work?

A simple example, perhaps, is the best way to demonstrate the workings of a private annuity.

Example: Mr. Investor, age 65, owns securities with a fair market value of $100,000, and a cost basis of $20,000. He sells these assets to his son under a private annuity contract for monthly lifelong payments.

First, the amount of annual payment (which *may* be monthly, quarterly, or annually) must be determined:

Market value at time of contract:	$100,000
Divided by the annuity factor for a 65-year-old male	÷ 8.0353
Annual payment	= $12,445.09

Now, the private annuity, like the installment sale, in effect spreads the capital gains liability over the annuitant's life expectancy, usually resulting in a tax savings. Each annuity payment, therefore, is broken down for tax purposes into three parts:

1. the tax-free exclusion part,

2. the part representing long-term capital gains, and

3. the part reflecting the actual annuity income.

1. A portion of each payment is considered for tax purposes as a return of principal (or cost basis) and it is therefore a *tax-free exclusion* for the duration of the private annuity contract. The exclusion portion of each payment is calculated thus:

Annual payment		$ 12,445.09
Times the life expectancy factor (from a factor table)*	×	15.00
Expected return		$186,676.35
Divided into the cost basis		20,000.00
Exclusion ratio		10.7%
Multiplied by the annual payment	×	$ 12,445.09
Amount of each annual payment excluded from taxable income		1,331.62
Divided by 12 for the excludable portion of each monthly payment	÷	12
		110.97

*These factors are determined by the U.S. Treasury Department for estate and gift tax regulation under Section 20.2031-10 of the IRS regulations.

2. After determining the excluded portion, the portion of each payment attributable to *capital gains* must be determined as indicated below:

Value of the securities received		$100,000.00
Less the cost basis	−	20,000.00
Gain		$ 80,000.00
Divided by the life expectancy factor	÷	15.00
Annual capital gain amortization		$ 5,333.33
Divided by 12 for the monthly capital gain amortization	÷	12
	$	444.44

3. Of a total payment of $1,037.09, some is excludable income ($110.97), some must be taxed as capital gains ($444.44), and the balance ($481.68) is fully *taxable annuity income*. The $444.44 capital gains portion continues until a total capital gain of $80,000 has been received. The subsequent monthly payments are to be reported as ordinary income after deducting the excluded portion.

Tax Consequences

As in any other financial planning tool, the private annuity has many federal tax, state tax, and legal consequences. Therefore an attorney and/or tax advisor should be consulted.

The Annuitant. Since these securities are conveyed for a contract to receive payment for life, the annuitant is not subject to a gift tax. (Providing the "fair market value" at the time of the contract equals the "present value of future payments.") A gift tax liability could result, however, if the securities sold are in one individual's name and the private annuity provides for joint annuitants with one of the annuitants having a greater life expectancy. If a husband, for instance, owns the securities and his wife is expected to survive him and to receive payments after his death, the difference between the actuarial expected incomes is considered a gift. However, if the husband and wife own the securities jointly, usually no gift tax results.

The Obligor. As soon as the obligor receives the assets of a private annuity (at the current market value), the holding period for tax purposes begins. The obligor must include in his or her taxable income all dividends and capital gains realized from the assets once they are transferred under the private annuity contract. The obligor also benefits from any growth of those assets, less, of course, the annuity payments.

Should the annuitant or joint annuitants die before the market value of the assets at the time of transfer are paid out, the obligor may have a tax liability. The difference between the value of the asset at the time of transfer and total annuity payments up to the time of the annuitant's death is considered a capital gain.

Example: If Mr. Investor died in five years after annuity payments totaling $62,225.45 were paid, the obligor incurs $37,774.55 ($100,000.00 − $62,225.45) as a capital gain. If the annuitant is insurable, a decreasing term life insurance policy may be purchased on his other life to offset any possible capital gains tax liability.

If the obligor dies prematurely, the annuity payments become an obligation and liability of his or her estate. A term insurance policy may be purchased on the obligor's life to protect against premature death and free the assets for heirs.

One point should be emphasized regarding private annuity contracts: the relationship between the annuitant and obligor must be close. The assets conveyed for the contract cannot be escrowed or secured in any way. *The annuity payments must be an unsecured obligation.* Further, in the planning of a private annuity contract, the annuitant's estate and tax bracket, as well as the obligor's income level, must be considered.

Pour-Over Trust

A *pour-over trust,* often called a life insurance trust, is created in conjunction with an individual's will. The trust is usually unfunded; no assets are placed in it until the creator dies. Then his or her insurance and/or corporate fringe benefit proceeds are usually made payable to the trust and received by it. Under normal circumstances, at the creator's death, the trust swells in value.

As life insurance proceeds or corporate fringe benefits become a larger and larger part of estates, the life insurance trust becomes a more important estate planning tool. The pour-over trust can be created so as to receive other assets such as stocks, bonds, or real estate owned by the creator at his or her death. The assets poured into the trust are usually passed by the creator's will.

The pour-over trust traditionally is set up so the trust can buy assets, usually nonliquid, from the estate of the creator. Consider the advantages to the owner of a small business. The owner provides liquidity to his or her estate and sets up the continued management of the business during his or her lifetime. Life insurance proceeds, which are payable to the trust, are normally used to buy the nonliquid assets.

Tax Consequences

If the pour-over trust is irrevocable, the creator may save estate taxes. For a trust to be irrevocable, the creator relinquishes all rights to change the trust and all control over the assets of the trust. The trust would become the owner as well as beneficiary of the insurance policies placed in it.

The creation of an irrevocable insurance trust may result in some gift tax liabilities. Also, the creator must determine how the premiums will be paid. Income producing assets may be deposited into the trust when it is created to pay insurance premiums, but this will have income tax consequences.

Advantages of a Pour-Over Trust

The advantages of establishing a pour-over trust are:

1. The creator is able to select his or her trustee and investment advisor during his or her lifetime.

2. The trust is not subject to continuing court and security costs as is a trust created under a will.

3. A pour-over trust is often more practical and flexible than a trust created by a will.

4. In the settlement of an estate, expenses and time are often reduced. Generally, the appointment of guardians and the filing of court records when minor children inherit assets are not required.

Individuals do not have to be wealthy to be afforded the advantages of a pour-over trust.

Example: Mr. Smith, age 50, has most of his assets tied up in a closely held business, fringe benefits, and insurance policies.

He creates a pour-over trust in connection with his will and names a close business associate, his lawyer, and his wife as co-trustees. The insurance policies and fringe benefits payable to the trust would be used to purchase his business interest to add liquidity to the business. In addition, the trust's liquid assets would be used to purchase a farm that he owns and dispose of the farm as he directs in the trust. Again the trust could include all of the provisions of a normal trust as outlined in previous sections of this book.

Anyone wishing to consider the advantages of a pour-over trust (or establishing one) should consult a financial planner and attorney to determine the precise advantages.

Other Means of Shifting Income

Interest-Free Loan

Many wealthy individuals, and some not so wealthy, are looking for ways to shift income to a family member in a lower income tax bracket.

Example: An individual in a 28% income tax bracket pays 28¢ of each dollar earned in taxes. Perhaps his son is in a 14% income tax bracket. The individual would like to shift income to his son in order to lower the effective tax rate on the income received.

As previously discussed, one strategy is to create a short-term reversionary trust. Another possible solution is the interest-free loan. The basis of the interest-free loan is a tax court case involving the Crown family.

The facts of the Crown case are:

- The Crown family partnership made an interest-free demand loan to a trust for the benefit of their children who were in a lower income tax bracket than the trust creator. The trust invested the money with all income being paid to the children.

- The IRS attacked the validity of the trust on the grounds that the transaction constituted a gift, for two reasons. First, the partnership granted the trust the right to use its money without charge, and that right is considered property under the gift tax law. Second, the exchange of cash for a promise to repay upon demand was an unequal exchange.

In essence, the tax court and Court of Appeals did not agree with the IRS and the Crowns effectively shifted the taxation on the income from taxpayers in higher brackets to those in lower brackets.

Since the Crown case, the IRS has released Revenue Ruling 73-61. Under it, an interest-free term loan is valued by actuarially determining the value of the use of the money for the entire term of the loan. According to one expert, if an interest rate is not specific in the term agreement, the IRS will assume a 7% rate. If a loan is for a definite period of time, a 7% annual rate will be assumed. "Interest-free" is considered a stated rate.

Under the Tax Reform Act of 1986, exceptions regarding interest-free loans have been established. In the case of gifts and loans between individuals that do not exceed $100,000, the amount transferred at the end of the year from borrower to lender will have interest attributed to the lender, but only to the extent of the borrower's net investment income. When the income is less than $1,000 there will be no interest transferred to the lender.

Example: John Shark, a lawyer, is in the 28% income tax bracket. He has approximately $100,000 of cash, which he has been investing in Treasury bills. Upon receiving approximately $10,000 per year in interest, he pays $2,800 in taxes.

Mr. Shark has two young children for whom he would like to accumulate money for their education. He creates a trust having a law partner serve as trustee. He lends $50,000 interest-free to the trust for the benefit of each child. The children are in a minimal tax bracket and when the $10,000 is earned by the trust, it is almost income tax free.

In essence, Mr. Shark is accumulating $2,800 a year for each child ($10,000) with little or no tax consequences. If the

$10,000 was accumulated in his name, it would be subject to a 28% tax.

Uniform Gifts to Minors

Many families find that their children earn money or are given cash at various times in their lives. Most people, conscious of the value of money, would like to invest this money.

A simple means of investing the money so that income and capital gains will not be taxable to the parents is to register the securities in the name of the child under the Uniform Gifts to Minors Act, with an adult serving as custodian. The custodianship is much like a trust. No agreement or other document is used, you simply register the securities as "Victor L. Harper, custodian for Victor L. Harper, Jr.," a minor under the Uniform Gifts to Minors Act of Virginia. No reporting or accounting is required, but the gift is irrevocable. Once the securities or assets are registered in the name of the child, they cannot be reverted to the custodian or any other third party.

The custodianship can be used to shift or to transfer assets to a child and to also shift income tax liability. However, bear in mind that children under 14 are taxed at the parent's rate on unearned income.

Example: John Shark bought 100 shares of Get Rich Quick at $10 a share. In four months the stock has appreciated to $50 a share and he wants to sell. He does not want the $4,000 gain in his own tax situation because he would pay $1,120 in taxes. Mr. Shark gives the 100 shares to his children (who are all over 14) under the Uniform Gifts to Minors Act and when it is sold it is a tax liability of the children.

When establishing a gift to minors registration, the children must obtain social security numbers and you must calculate their taxable income and, in some cases, as assets build, your children may have a tax liability. So long as you continue to provide the majority of their support, you will not lose them as a deduction.

It is a parent's obligation to pay for the support of a child; however, it is generally considered safe to use the cash in a custodian account to pay for things such as college or unusual trips.

Another word of caution when using a custodianship. If you

are the donor of assets, you should not list yourself as custodian. If you die before the custodianship ends, the assets are includable in your estate.

Keep in mind when establishing a custodian account for your children that when they reach the age of majority, which may be age 18 to 21 depending on state law, the property must be turned over to him or her. It is their property and the custodian loses control.

Example: Dudley Alright started using the Uniform Gifts to Minors Act when his children were born. Each time the grandparents, aunts, or uncles would give cash to his children, he would place it under the Uniform Gifts to Minors Act. Each year he would give a couple of thousand dollars to each child and would immediately buy stock with the cash. Alright would name his brother as custodian so as not to have an estate problem.

The results were amazing. As his children reached college age, they had several thousand dollars in securities. The dividends were used to pay for a trip to Europe, and several extended ski trips. When the children entered college, Mr. Alright was careful not to sign any obligations with the school or accept bills indicating that he was personally liable. The children assumed that liability and it was paid for from the custodianship.

In other words, Dudley Alright used his children's lower tax bracket to accumulate assets to be used for their benefit at a later date.

Recently, a son graduated from college and, after paying all college expenses and a few trips, he realized he still had $10,000 in securities. What a nice way to start adult life!

Investment Clubs

What Is an Investment Club?

An *investment club* is a group of congenial individuals who meet regularly, usually once a month, and pool their money, time, knowledge, and efforts to discuss and invest in securities. The investment club is a method whereby individuals are able to gain experience and acquire knowledge about stocks, financial statements, and securities markets. It is a proven means of learning and profiting—by doing with others what an individual cannot accomplish alone.

Setting Up the Club

The National Association of Investment Clubs (NAIC)

Investment clubs serve a vital national function in that they create many new investors, trained in successful investment techniques, and in so doing, provide a substantial and regular flow of capital for the needs of growing industries.

The purpose of the National Association of Investment Clubs (NAIC), a division of the National Association of Investors Corporation, a nonprofit organization owned by its membership, is to encourage the creation of investment clubs and assist clubs in becoming successful operations. The association's address is 1515 East Eleven Mile Road, Royal Oak, Michigan 48067.

According to New York Stock Exchange figures, there are almost 20,000 investment clubs in the U.S. Over 5,000 clubs and 90,000 of their members belong to NAIC. Some 10,000 individuals belong to the association.

An investment club pays only $30 a year plus $6 per member

for membership in NAIC. Members receive *Better Investing,* a magazine published by NAIC. By joining the National Association of Investment Clubs, every member of the club is covered with a $25,000 Fidelity Bond, which protects up to $25,000 of the club's property, providing the club meets prescribed requirements. Additional bonding is available through NAIC, and rates will be quoted upon request. Personal training service is available from NAIC's local councils in 35 cities. The association maintains a continuous lobbying service that results in many benefits to its members.

The *Investment Club Manual,* published by the National Association of Investment Clubs (1515 East Eleven Mile Road, Royal Oak, Michigan 48067—$12.00 per copy), explains in great detail how to organize a club. It contains a sample partnership agreement, tax information, record-keeping procedures, and security analysis techniques—a time-tested guide for investment clubs and individual investors.

An organizational meeting should be held, attended by all interested parties and, of course, an investment expert (broker). Generally, club members deposit all monthly payments into a common checking account, and one check is mailed to the broker handling the account. One club member is appointed to be the club's liaison with the broker. This member handles any requests for information or material, and usually contacts the broker before meetings for information about stocks the club already owns and new stocks the club might find worthwhile. The club should discuss and study in detail at least two securities each month. The securities should be good quality companies that meet the investment club's goal of being able to double in five years.

Securities may be registered in the club's name and mailed to the address of one of the members, or the certificates themselves may be held in safekeeping by the club's brokerage house. The Stock Transfer Agents Association's Rule 13-03 provides that club securities may be transferred directly into and out of the club's name on the signature of one member and without the need for supporting papers:

> *Investment Clubs.* Recommended form of registration for stock owned by an investment club which is a partnership is ' _____ Investment Club, a Partnership.' When so registered, the stock may be transferred on an assignment

by _____ Investment Club, a Partnership, by
_____ a General Partner', without submission
of the partnership agreement or any other papers, *provided*
the signature is guaranteed in the usual manner.

By this procedure, all dividends and corporate literature go
directly to the club, and the brokerage firm is not involved in
handling these items.

Types of Organization

An investment club by its nature, may take only two forms
of organization: It must be either a partnership or a corporation.
All other forms are variations of these. There are three considerations for club members when deciding upon the type of organization.

1. *Taxes:* The question is, in which form of organization will
the members pay the lower taxes on money earned? The advantage is definitely with a partnership, since in the corporate form
double taxes are involved: first the corporation pays taxes on
profits; then the individual pays taxes on income from the corporation. The Commerce Clearing House Service's publication entitled *The Tax Impact on an Investment Club as a Corporation*
demonstrates this point well: It follows the path of a dollar of
income coming into an investment club first as a partnership,
then as a corporation showing, in each tax bracket, how much
of that dollar winds up in an individual club member's pocket in
either case. The illustrations in this booklet clearly show that from
a tax standpoint, the partnership is the most favorable form of
organization for an investment club.

2. *Clerical work:* The club must consider the amount of
organizational, clerical, and record-keeping work required. The
partnership form, again, has a definite advantage since a simple
agreement is all that is required. The corporation, on the other
hand, must have by-laws registered with the state in which it is
incorporated, not to mention many other forms and reports that
must be filed periodically with government agencies.

3. *Personal liability:* Many investment clubs make the type
of entity decision mainly on the basis of personal liability.

CLUB BROKER AGREEMENT

Name of Broker here: _____

Gentlemen:

The undersigned hereby authorize you to open an account for them to be known as the _____ and _____ Agent Account (or _____ Partnership Account). The undersigned hereby authorize _____ and _____ (whose signatures appear below) as their agent and attorney-in-fact to buy, sell (including short sales) and trade in stocks, bonds and any other securities and/or commodities and/or contracts relating to the same on margin or otherwise in accordance with your terms and conditions for the undersigned's account and risk and in the undersigned's name, or number on your books. The undersigned hereby agree to indemnify and hold you harmless from and to pay you promptly on demand any and all losses arising therefrom or debit balance due thereon.

You are authorized to follow the instruction of _____ and _____ in every respect concerning the undersigned's account with you, and make deliveries of securities and payment of moneys to him or as he may order and direct. In all matters and things aforementioned, as well as in all other things necessary or incidental to the furtherance or conduct of the account of the undersigned, the aforesaid agent and attorney-in-fact is authorized to act for the undersigned and in the undersigned's behalf in the same manner and with the same force and effect as the undersigned might or could do.

The undersigned hereby ratify and confirm any and all transactions with you heretofore or hereafter made by the aforesaid agent or for the undersigned's account. This authorization and indemnity is in addition to (and in no way limits or restricts) any rights which you may have under any other agreement or agreements between the undersigned and your firm.

(Continued)

This authorization and indemnity is binding on the undersigned and their estates and is also a continuing one and shall remain in full force and effect until revoked by the undersigned by a written notice addressed to you and delivered to your office at _____ (city), _____ (state), and shall continue after death or insanity of any of the undersigned until receipt by you of notice thereof but such revocation shall not affect any liability in any way resulting from transactions initiated prior to such revocation. This authorization and indemnity shall enure to the benefit of your present firm and of any successor firm or firms irrespective of any change or changes at any time in the personnel thereof for any cause whatsoever, and of its assigns of your present firm or any successor firm.

Dated _____

City _____   State _____

(Each member of club signs below)

_____

_____

_____

                                        Signature of Authorized Agents

(Witness) _____

(Witness) _____

PARTNERSHIP AGREEMENT
of the
MUTUAL INVESTMENT CLUB of SANDLERVILLE

THIS AGREEMENT OF PARTNERSHIP, made as of February 1, 1984, by and between the undersigned

(Names of all partners)

WITNESSETH:

1.   Formation of Partnership: The undersigned hereby form a General Partnership, in, and in accordance with the laws of, the State of Michigan.

2.   Name of Partnership: The name of the partnership shall be The Mutual Investment Club of Sandlerville.

3.   Term: The partnership shall begin on February 1, 1984 and continue until December 31, 1984, and thereafter from year to year unless earlier terminated as hereinafter provided.

4.   Purpose: The purpose of the partnership is to invest the assets of the partnership solely in stocks, bonds and securities, for the education and benefit of the partners.

5.   Meetings: Periodic meetings shall be held as determined by the partnership.

6.   Contributions: The partners may make contributions to the partnership on the date of each periodic meeting, in such amounts as the partnership shall determine, provided, however, that no partner's capital account (as hereinafter defined) shall exceed twenty (20%) per cent of the capital accounts of all partners.

7.   Valuation: The current value of the assets and property of the partnership, less the current value of the debts and liabilities of the partnership, (hereinafter referred to as "value of the partnership") shall be determined as of 10 business days preceding the date of each periodic meeting. The aforementioned date of valuation shall hereinafter be referred to as "valuation date."

(Continued)

8. Capital Accounts: There shall be maintained in the name of each partner, a capital account. Any increase or decrease in the value of the partnership on any valuation date shall be credited or debited, respectively, to each partner's capital account in proportion to the value of each partner's capital account on said date. Any other method of valuating each partner's capital account may be substituted for this method provided that said substituted method results in exactly the same valuation as previously provided herein. Each partner's contribution to, or withdrawals from, the partnership shall be credited, or debited, respectively, to that partner's capital account.

9. Management: Each partner shall participate in the management and conduct of the affairs of the partnership in proportion to his capital account. Except as otherwise provided herein, all decisions shall be made by the partners whose capital accounts total a majority in the amount of the capital accounts of all the partners.

10. Sharing of Profits and Losses: Net profits and losses of the partnership shall inure to, and be borne by, the partners in proportion to the credit balances in their capital accounts.

11. Books of Account: Books of account of the transactions of the partnership shall be kept and at all times be available and open to inspection and examination by any partner.

12. Annual Accounting: Each calendar year, a full and complete account of the condition of the partnership shall be made to the partners.

13. Bank Account: The partnership shall select a bank for the purpose of opening a partnership bank account. Funds deposited in said partnership bank account shall be withdrawn by checks signed by either of two (2) partners designated by the partnership.

14. Broker Account: None of the partners of this partnership shall be a broker; however, the partnership may select a broker and enter into such agreements with the broker as required, for the purchase or sale of stocks, bonds and securities. Stocks, bonds and securities owned by the partnership shall be registered in the partnership name unless another name shall be designated by the partnership.

Any corporation or Transfer Agent called upon to transfer any stocks, bonds and securities to or from the name of the partnership shall be entitled to rely on instructions or assignments signed or purporting to be signed by any partner without inquiry as to the authority of the person signing for the partnership.

At the time of transfer, the corporation or transfer agent is entitled to assume (1) that the partnership is still in existence and (2) that this agreement is in full force and effect and has not been amended unless the corporation has received written notice to the contrary.

15. No Compensation: No partner shall be compensated for services rendered to the partnership, except reimbursement for expenses.

16. Additional Partners: Additional partners may be admitted at any time, upon the unanimous consent of all the partners in writing or at a meeting so long as the number of partners does not exceed fifteen.

17. Voluntary Termination: The partnership may be dissolved by agreement of the partners whose capital accounts total a majority in amount of the capital accounts of all the partners. Notice of said decision to dissolve the partnership shall be given to all the partners. The partnership shall thereupon be terminated by the payment of all the debts and liabilities of the partnership and the distribution of the remaining assets either in cash or in kind to the partners or their personal representatives in proportion to their capital accounts.

18. Withdrawal of a Partner: Any partner may withdraw a part or all of his interest. He shall give notice in writing to the recording partner. His notice shall be deemed to be received as of the first meeting of the club at which it is presented. If notice is received between meetings it will be treated as received at the first following meeting. In making payment, the valuation statement prepared for the first meeting following the meeting at which notice is received will be used to determine the value of the partner's account. Between receipt of notice and the withdrawal valuation date, the other partners shall have and are given the option during said period to purchase, in proportion to their capital accounts in the partnership, the capital account of the withdrawing partner. If the other partners exercise

(Continued)

their option to purchase, the partnership business shall not terminate. If the other partners do not exercise their option to purchase, the partnership shall be terminated and liquidated in accordance with the terms of paragraph 17 of this partnership agreement.

19.   Death or Incapacity of a Partner: In the event of the death or incapacity of a partner, receipt of such notice shall be treated as a notice of withdrawal. Liquidation and payment of the partner's account shall proceed in accordance with paragraphs 18 and 20.

20.   Purchase Price: Upon the death, incapacity or withdrawal of a partner, and the exercise of the option to purchase by the other partners, said other partners shall pay the withdrawing partner or his estate, as the case may be, a purchase price, when payment is made in cash, equal to ninety-seven percent of his capital account or his capital account less the actual cost of selling sufficient securities to obtain the cash to meet the withdrawal, whichever is the lesser amount. Said purchase price shall be paid within two weeks after the valuation date used in determining the purchase price. Payment may be made in cash or securities at the option of the remaining partners of the club. Where payment is made in securities, the full purchase price of the account will be paid the partner for that part of the account purchased with securities. If the partner desires an advance payment, the club at its earliest convenience may pay him 80% of the estimated value of his account and settle the balance of the account in accordance with the valuation date set in paragraph 18. Where payment is made in securities, the club's broker shall be advised that the ownership of the securities has been changed at least by the valuation date used for the withdrawal.

21.   Forbidden Acts: No partner shall:
    (a)   Have the right or authority to bind or obligate the partnership to any extent whatsoever with regard to any matter outside the scope of the partnership business.
    (b)   Without the unanimous consent of all the other partners, assign, transfer, pledge, mortgage or sell all or part of his interest in the partnership to any other partner or other person whomsoever, or enter into any agreement as the

result of which any person or persons not a partner shall become interested with him in the partnership.

(c) Purchase an investment for the partnership where less than the full purchase price is paid for same.

(d) Use the partnership name, credit or property for other than partnership purposes.

(e) Do any act detrimental to the interests of the partnership or which would make it impossible to carry on the business or affairs of the partnership.

This Agreement of Partnership is hereby declared and shall be binding upon the respective heirs, executors, administrators and personal representatives of the parties.

IN WITNESS WHEREOF, the parties have set their hands and seals the year and day first above written.

Partners:

(Signatures of Partners)

In a partnership, the individual partners are personally liable for all acts of the partnership. They are not, however, liable for the personal acts of the individual members of the partnership or for their personal businesses and activities. Since the only business activity of an investment club is the purchase and sale of securities—and that is conducted through the club's broker—the possibility of any extensive liability seems unlikely, so long as the club does not engage in margin buying or short selling.

In the corporate form of organization, the individual's personal liability is obviously limited to the amount of money that he or she has invested in the club.

Record Keeping

After forming an investment club, it is necessary to establish a system of record keeping. Accounting procedures for the investment club consist of two functions:

1. *Determining each member's interest:* Often, a member's proportionate interest in the club varies, resulting in unequal interest among members. Such a situation may arise from the introduction of new members, a member's withdrawal of money for financial needs, or an older member's withdrawal for, say, retirement purposes.

For these reasons, "valuation units" are normally used to determine the value of each member's interest in the club. A unit is originally set at a fixed amount.

Example: $10 for one unit; $20, two units; $25, 2.5 units; and so on.

Each subsequent monthly contribution is divided by the value of the valuation unit to determine the number of units to be credited:

Example: If the unit is valued at $15, a deposit of $10 would add .667 ($10 ÷ $15) units to the member's account. A depositor of $30 would add two ($30 ÷ $15) units to the members' account, etc.

To determine a member's total value:

● divide the club's net worth by the total number of units in the club to determine the value per unit,

● then multiply the value per unit by the number of units in the individual's account.

2. *Recording cash transactions:* A ledger should be kept for each security showing (a) date purchased, (b) number of shares, (c) cost per share, (d) selling price, (e) cash received, and (f) net profit (long- or short-term).

Investment clubs should also obtain the National Association of Investment Clubs' Accounting Manual ($7). The accounting kit, which is the manual and all forms necessary to handle record keeping, is $13. The manual's suggested procedures have proved successful for many investment clubs. The NAIC also maintains an inventory of forms that clubs may order as needed.

Note: It may be well to check with the National Association of Investment Clubs, 1515 East Eleven Mile Road, Royal Oak,

Michigan 48067 for possible recent regulatory or tax changes affecting investment club operation.

NAIC offers a number of record-keeping tools at moderate prices:

1. *NAIC Accounting Kit.* Accurate and complete club records are vital for tax reporting purposes, to permit members to make deposits and withdrawals from the club as desired, and to preserve equity among the members' accounts. NAIC's Accounting Kit provides complete instructions plus enough blank forms to keep the average club's records for about two years. Complete kit is $13.00.

2. *NAIC Receipt Pads* enable your treasurer to give members a convenient monthly receipt for their deposits plus a statement of their total interest in the club. Each pad contains 50 sets (original and duplicate). 2 for $1.75.

3. *Dividend & Security Record Sheets.* For your own personally owned securities, you need complete purchase, dividend, and sale records. This NAIC form will serve an individual as well as a club. 20 blanks cost $2.50.

4. *NAIC $25,000.00 Fidelity Bond.* NAIC membership provides a $25,000.00 Fidelity Bond covering every eligible member. It has saved the funds of many clubs that have suffered fidelity type losses. Larger clubs can obtain coverage up to $1,000,000.

5. *PERT (Portfolio Evaluation Review Technique).* These forms are a handy way of following, every month, the progress of each stock in your portfolio—an essential record of how your securities are performing. 25 forms cost $2.00. Also, PERT Worksheets make it easier for you to record important data for transfer to the PERT form. 25 Worksheets cost $2.00.

6. *NAIC Stock Study Course.* A 12-lesson course you can take at home at your own speed. Developed by NAIC's Investment Education Institute, it incorporates all the NAIC principles. Complete course, $50 per individual; $40 for NAIC members. Or $40 for teacher and $6.00 per individual ($3.00 if individual already has *The Investors Manual*).

Taxation

An investment club has to file tax returns like any other business entity.

Partnership. Club members sometimes think that because they do not draw money out of the club, they have no taxable income. This is incorrect. Dividends and realized capital gains are taxable even though members leave the money in the club for many years. Though a club partnership itself does not pay taxes, all its taxable income is allocated to the individual members each year, and they must report their share of the club's income and capital gains or losses on their personal tax returns.

A Tax Identification Number must be obtained. A partnership may write or call the nearest U.S. Treasury Office and ask for Form SS-4, the application form for a partnership (see page 319). The partnership club also files the partnership information return form, Form 1065. Usually all that is necessary is: (1) the club's name and address; (2) the income and expense statement; (3) the balance sheet; (4) the distribution-of-earnings statement with each member's address and social security number added; (5) a list of companies from which dividends have been received and the amount for each; and (6) a list of securities sold, showing the name of the security, date bought, date sold, cost, selling price, and net profit (this list should be divided into short- and long-term sections). The Treasury Department provides procedures for investment club partnerships to request exemption from filing Form 1065. NAIC recommends requesting this exemption, but cautions that this does not relieve individual members of the club from reporting their share of club income in their personal tax returns.

Corporation. An Internal Revenue office can supply the necessary forms. The corporation pays taxes on earnings with no tax liability accruing to the members until a distribution is made.

State and Local Taxation. An investment club may be required to file state income tax returns, city income tax returns, and intangible property tax returns. Therefore, each club should review the requirements of its local authorities.

• U S GOVERNMENT PRINTING OFFICE 1982 343 193

For clear copy on both parts, please type or print with ball point pen and press firmly

(See Instructions on pages 2 and 4)

Form **SS-4** (Rev. 11-81)
Department of the Treasury
Internal Revenue Service

Application for Employer Identification Number
(For use by employers and others as explained in the Instructions)

OMB No. 1545-0003
Expires 12-31-83

1 Name (True name as distinguished from trade name. If partnership, see instructions on page 4.)

2 Trade name, if any (Name under which business is operated, if different from item 1.)

3 Social security number, if sole proprietor

4 Address of principal place of business (Number and street)

5 Ending month of accounting year

6 City and State

7 ZIP code

8 County of business location

9 Type of organization
☐ Individual ☐ Trust
☐ Governmental (See instructions on page 4)
☐ Nonprofit organization (See instructions on page 4)
☐ Partnership
☐ Corporation
☐ Other (specify)

10 Date you acquired or started this business (Mo., day, year)

11 Reason for applying
☐ Started new business
☐ Purchased going business
☐ Other (specify)

12 First date you paid or will pay wages for this business (Mo., day, year)

13 Nature of business (See Instructions on page 4)

14 Do you operate more than one place of business? ☐ Yes ☐ No

15 Peak number of employees expected in next 12 months (If none, enter "0") ▶
☐ Nonagricultural
☐ Agricultural
☐ Household

16 If nature of business is manufacturing, state principal product and raw material used.

17 To whom do you sell most of your products or services?
☐ Business establishments
☐ General public
☐ Other (specify)

18 Have you ever applied for an identification number for this or any other business? ☐ Yes ☐ No

If "Yes," enter name and trade name. Also enter approx. date, city, and State where you applied and previous number if known. ▶

Date

Signature and title

Telephone number

Please leave blank ▶	Geo.	Ind.	Class	Size	Reas. for appl.

Part I

For Paperwork Reduction Act Notice, see page 2.

Investment Principles

The *Investors Manual* itemizes four primary principles that have proven to be successful for investment clubs. They are:

1. *Invest regularly:* Investments should be made regularly without regard to the level of the stock market. Though it is impossible to forecast short-term movements of the stock market, historically, stock prices have moved upward over the long term according substantial profits to the investor who utilizes the dollar-cost-averaging approach (see "Systematic Investing").

2. *Compound income:* Reinvesting the club's earnings and capital gains (the sales proceeds applies the principle of compounding).

Example: As stated in the manual, a fifteen-member club investing $20 a month should reach $20,000 in five years. Compounding has time and the rate of income (and growth) working for the club as follows:

$10,000 Invested at Compound Income*

Rate of Income (and growth)	10 Years	20 Years	30 Years
3%	$13,440	$18,060	$ 24,270
5%	16,290	26,530	43,220
8%	21,590	46,610	100,630
10%	25,940	67,280	174,490

*The Investors Manual.

3. *Investing in growth:* Buying securities of companies whose sales and earnings are growing faster than the general economy and faster than their competitors usually produces higher stock prices.

Example: Compare IBM with U.S. Steel. Investors have always been willing to pay a premium for growth, which is why a company with a 15% growth rate probably has a price-earnings ratio higher than a company growing at 6%. Again, compare IBM, Xerox, and Eastman Kodak with U.S. Steel, EXXON, or Continental Can.

4. *Diversification:* All securities do not move in the same direction at the same time. Even when all the fundamentals are correct, it often takes time for the price to reflect them; therefore, by owning more companies, the fundamentals may be reflected in the prices of different companies at different times, according better long-term results.

NAIC Investment Tools and Services

1. *The NAIC Stock Check List.* A guide to the new investor, this form helps the investor form an opinion of the current value of a stock. It serves as an introduction to NAIC's Stock Selection Guide. 25 forms for $2.

2. *The NAIC Stock Selection Guide and Report.* Designed to help you review the record of a particular stock and make an informed judgment of its investment potential. Widely recognized as a sound stock study procedure. 13 forms for $2.

3. *The NAIC Stock Selection Guide.* An abbreviated edition of the *Guide and Report,* for use by the investor who has become thoroughly familiar with the form.

4. *The Giant Stock Selection Guide.* This form in large size is an ideal way to present a company study to a group. It helps teach new groups how to use the Guide. Stimulates discussion in older groups. Paper copies are 7 for $5. Plastic coated for reuse are $8 each.

5. NAIC publishes a monthly magazine, *Better Investing,* to provide a steady flow of new investment ideas, stock study techniques, and the latest investment club news. It's one of the nation's most widely read financial publications. Individual subscriptions are $12 annually. The cost is included in the dues for NAIC members.

6. To make an intelligent comparison of several stocks you have studied and to guide you in the selection of the best, NAIC's *Stock Comparison Guide* is a valuable tool. 25 blanks cost $2.

7. *Giant Stock Comparison Guide.* Same as above but in giant size for use at club meetings. All members can see the comparisons at the same time. The Giant Guide helps in developing better group discussions and decisions. 7 blanks cost $5.

8. In addition to helping you start your investment club, *The Investors Manual* describes NAIC's complete stock study program. It gives detailed instructions for the use of each of NAIC's tools, how to record the information on the forms, and how to interpret it. The complete manual is $12 ($4.50 to NAIC Club Members).

9. *Portfolio Management Guide.* Once you have bought a stock, follow its earnings record with this convenient form. It reminds clubs to consider buy and/or sell decisions. 25 copies cost $2.

10. NAIC's *Ratio Calculator* helps you read price-earnings ratios and pretax profit margins directly from the data you've plotted on NAIC's *Stock Selection Guide.* Included with *The Investors Manual* or separately for 50 cents each. A giant size is included with the plastic-coated *Giant Stock Selection Guide.*

Why Investors Form Clubs

Many individuals would like to invest in the market, but "don't know anything about it." There are many young people with good futures who do not presently have a great deal of money but who would like to start learning about and investing in the securities markets. There is no ideal person to join an investment club. Anyone willing to spend the time to keep up the regular investment schedule, and to gain experience in the industry is a candidate.

Further, even though most investment clubs provide new investors with a medium to learn about stocks and investing, they may be equally helpful to experienced investors, offering a source of information for personal account-research ideas, suggestions, and contacts with the other members. Many clubs through the years have been composed of such investors.

Investors form clubs for three primary reasons:

1. *Education of the members:* Each member should learn to work with the tools, statements, and materials ncessary to analyze industries and particular companies. By accomplishing these techniques in a group, each individual member should become more competent in managing his or her personal investments.

2. *Profit on money invested:* To quote Thomas O'Hara, Chairman, Board of Trustees, National Association of Investment Clubs, "Success does not come overnight. It is necessary for the club to gradually accumulate funds as it is accumulating experience. Most clubs will find that quite often in about the first three years of their operation their assets will be less than the members have deposited in the club."

   An investment club can offer long-term profits to the individual members by virtue of regular investing and the principles of dollar-cost-averaging. If $25 is invested monthly by each member for 20 years ($6,000) with an average compound growth of 10%, the investor will accumulate $18,985.

3. *Social interaction for greater productivity:* It is important that members be compatible and enjoy each other's company because they are starting a long-term venture, and generally people who enjoy each other's company are usually more productive as a unit. Further, a variety of interests and backgrounds can bring to the club different points of view, and this need not be an obstacle if each member is willing to contribute his or her share of the effort in investigating and analyzing securities.

Practical Examples

Example: In 1940, a group of 16 Detroit businesspeople formed an investment club and began investing $10 to $50 a month each. Over a period of 43 years, the total cash invested by the members was approximately $146,000. In early 1983, the club was worth almost $1,300,000.

   This does not tell the whole story. About $315,000 had been withdrawn by members. One member of the club used a portion of his assets to open a sporting goods store. Today he owns three such stores. Another member of the Detroit group has assets of $150,000 in the club after withdrawals of $68,000. Her total cash investment is approximately $8,600.

Example: Fifteen business professionals from a rural southside Virginia community have accumulated almost $45,000 over the last 11 years. This has been accomplished with monthly investments of $15 to $20 per member. Over the period, the members have invested only about $30,000. A member of the southside Virginia club said, "The club gave me an insight into things I would never approach on my own. The decisions often lead to different ways of investing than an individual may do by himself."

Example: In six years, a group of young investors in Richmond, Virginia have accumulated over $55,000 by investing $25 to $50 per month per member. A member of this group described the benefits of membership as, "I formed a new circle of friends, learned about and developed a philosophy of investments, learned of different investments, and gained technical knowledge about securities and investments. Plus I made money."

Example: Another investment club saw investments of approximately $170,000 increase in value to almost $493,000 from June of 1956 to February of 1980. A member of this club said, "For the most part the money would not have been accumulated had Bill, Inc., not been formed. The investment club is not exclusively for small investors, it is also for those wanting to create their own mutual fund with personal involvement."

Individuals wishing to learn more about investments, investment philosophy and the techniques of investing should seek friends and associates to begin an investment club. It is not an easy road, but new friendships, and the accumulation of capital and knowledge are well worth the effort.

Retirement Plans

This section on retirement (or deferred compensation) plans is not intended to be all-encompassing; neither does it deal with all possibilities. Like a first-aid course, it is designed to present investors with enough information to recognize a need, to deal with simple situations, and to know when to consult an expert. This section should assist corporate employees to more fully understand and appreciate the benefits and opportunities of employer-sponsored retirement plans.

The investor or advisor who understands the basics of deferred compensation is better able to understand and handle other financial matters. The investor who receives a cash payout (vested portions) from a qualified retirement plan should be familiar with the rollover provisions of the Individual Retirement Account (IRA). These provisions allow the employee to defer taxation on the payout; and the interest, dividends, and capital gains on the money continue to accrue on a tax-deferred basis.

What Is a Retirement Plan?

Deferred compensation includes a variety of programs, all based on deferring or delaying the receipt of current compensation by an individual until sometime in the future—usually to the retirement years when the individual's normal working income source has terminated. The primary purpose of any deferred compensation plan is to provide a future benefit by deferring present compensation to employees.

There are two types of plans:

1. *nonqualified deferred compensation,* and,

2. *qualified deferred compensation,* the more widely used.

Nonqualified Plans

While most of this section is devoted to qualified plans, it is important to understand the concepts of nonqualified plans, since these latter arrangements will probably meet with greater use in the future as the result of new benefit limitations on qualified plans imposed by the Employee Retirement Income Security Act of 1974 (ERISA) and the Tax Equity and Fiscal Responsibility Act of 1982 (TEFRA).

A nonqualified plan usually involves a simple contract between the employer and employee that enables the employee to defer receipt of a portion of his or her current compensation until some later time. The deferred compensation remains a part of the general assets of the employer, and the employer is therefore not allowed any tax deductions until the compensation is actually paid. In addition, the employee generally has no tax liability for the deferred amount until he or she receives the benefits.

When a company is considering a deferred compensation plan for an employee, it should be careful that the deposits do not fall under the "constructive receipt doctrine." Constructive receipt is income not actually in a taxpayer's possession, but is considered taxable to him or her in the year during which it is credited to the employee's account, or set apart. If the employee has an immediate right to or control over the payments, the employee may be required to pay taxes currently, although receipt of the payments will be in later years.

Types of Nonqualified Plans

Nonqualified deferred compensation plans can be (1) funded or (2) unfunded.

An unfunded nonqualified deferred compensation plan is the company's unsecured promise to pay an employeee certain amounts at future dates. A reserve can be established to cover the liability and be placed in an insurance contract or a revocable trust. However, ownership of the reserve must rest with the employer.

A funded plan will use an irrevocable trust or an annuity with the employee having a beneficial interest. In the funded plan, monies are set aside each year into a trust fund or annuity payment to secure the promise to pay at a future date. In a funded plan, the employee is required to report the deferred compensation as income at the time all rights become transferable or are no longer subject to the risk of forfeiture.

The purpose of nonqualified compensation plans is to defer tax or income until such time as an employee is in a lower tax bracket. For example, a professional athlete's playing life is limited and his or her income will usually be lower after the playing years. Nonqualified deferred compensation is a way to level earnings and the resulting income taxes over a longer period of time.

In reviewing nonqualified deferred compensation, many people argue that an employee is much better off to take the income currently and pay taxes on it. The accumulated income derived from the money over a number of years may outweigh the tax benefits from deferral. Also, in periods of high rates of inflation, many people say a dollar earned today is worth substantially more than a dollar paid later.

Phantom Stock Plans. Many companies whose stock is publicly traded will use "phantom stock" as a type of nonqualified deferred compensation. In a phantom stock program, the company sets up an account for an employee and ties deposits to the price of the stock. The amount of dividends paid on the phantom stock is credited to the employee's account. At the time the account matures and is paid to the employee, all amounts accrued in the phantom stock account, which reflects the rise and fall of the stock price plus accumulated dividends, are paid immediately or over a period of time. The phantom stock program is definitely an incentive program for many employees and is a means to determine the amount of money an individual will receive as deferred compensation.

Anytime a company and an employee consider a nonqualified deferred compensation plan, the tax benefits both to the company and the employee should be reviewed carefully. If the employee is going to continue to be in a very high tax bracket after retirement, perhaps the nonqualified plan will not be to his or her advantage. Again, this is a situation that should be reviewed and studied on a case-by-case basis.

Qualified Plans

Qualified deferred compensation plans are those in which a business makes current tax-deductible contributions to a *fiduciary account* to be held for the future benefit of employees. Provisions of the Internal Revenue Code allow the assets in a qualified plan to accumulate on a tax deferred basis.

Generally, contributions are tax deductible to the employer and are not taxable to the employee until he or she receives the benefits. Benefits are usually payable to the employee and/or his or her family upon retirement, disability, or death. In some instances, vested benefits may be paid to the employee before retirement, such as when an employee terminates employment. The tax treatment of the payout in such cases, however, is often less favorable than at retirement. For more favorable treatment of preretirement distributions, review the section entitled "Individual Retirement Account Rollover," or taxation of retirement distributions on the ten-year forward averaging basis.

In summary, qualified deferred compensation has been described as pretaxed employer money that goes in as a deductible contribution, that accumulates tax free, that compounds by forfeiture in a profit-sharing plan (or reduces employer contribution in a defined benefit, or pension, plan), and that comes out as capital gains or as low-taxed retirement income.

Deferred compensation laws are a type of social legislation. If there were no private retirement plans in existence today, the entire burden of retirement benefits would come to rest on the federal government or with the individual and/or his family. By allowing tax deductions to assist taxpayers in providing for their own retirement income, the government is relieving itself of much of this burden. The creation of the Individual Retirement Account (IRA) is a tax benefit to encourage individuals to save for retirement.

Benefits

The major benefits of a qualified plan, listed below, are obviously general, but they can be helpful in mapping out an overall investment program.

Contributions are Tax Deductible to the Employer. A large part of the plan's cost is paid by dollars that would otherwise go for taxes. The corporate income tax rate for 1986 is 15% on the first $25,000, 18% on income over $25,000 to $50,000; 30% over $50,000 to $75,000; 40% over $75,000 to $100,000; 46% over $100,000 to $1,000,000; 46% plus 5% on excess of over $1,000,000.

Contribution and Accumulation Are Tax-Free to Employee Until Benefits Are Distributed. There is no tax payable on the earnings during the accumulation period while the assets are held in trust (a fiduciary account). When the money is eventually paid out, normally at retirement, it receives favorable tax treatment—possibly as low-taxed retirement income, capital gains, or some form of income averaging.

Employee Morale Improves. Through the installation of a qualified deferred compensation plan, a company demonstrates interest in its employees. This concern usually tends to ally the employees to the company, reduces turnover, and assists in recruiting new employees. The qualified plan helps employees and owners accumulate capital for the future so an enlightened program of employee retirements can be maintained for the good of the employer as well as the employee.

Security. Everyone feels more secure knowing that a nest egg is set aside for future years or that some provision exists in case of disability or death.

A Legal Method of Passing Tax-Deferred Dollars to Owners. Qualified deferred compensation plans can often be designed to be more beneficial to Mr. Highly Paid Majority Stockholder than to other employees. By this means, an owner-employer is allowed to set aside tax deductible dollars for his or her own future benefit.

Social Security

The federal Social Security program is a form of deferred compensation. Contributions are made by the employer and employee during the employee's working years, and benefits are payable upon the employee's retirement, disability, or death (survivor benefits). The amount of the payments varies in relation to the amount of contributions as set forth in a predetermined formula. Employers' contributions are tax deductible only as a business expense. Employees' contributions are made with after-tax dollars. The self-employment social security tax is not deductible, either as a tax or as a business expense.

If an employee works for two or more employers, each must deduct and pay Social Security taxes. If the employee has had more than the maximum deducted from his or her pay, the excess will be a credit against income tax payable.

Social Security is greatly misunderstood. It is not only a retirement plan but it also provides disability payments should a worker become disabled, survivor benefits to a worker's survivors in the event of untimely death and Medicare payments. Medicare is a hospitalization and medical insurance plan for people 65 and older.

Another misconception about Social Security concerns program funding. As the benefits have increased, so have the required contributions. Social Security is a "pay-as-you-go" system. Current contributions are supposed to pay current benefits. This is not like most retirement plans or insurance policies where monies are invested to pay for future benefits.

An employer and employee are required to pay into the system a percentage of earnings, up to a limit, each year. The limit is referred to as "the wage base." In order to fund the higher payments, the wage base and percentage have been substantially increased over the years. When Social Security was first introduced in 1937 the wage base was $3,000 with a 1% contribution. Recent wage base schedules and percentage contributions are listed below:

1983	$35,700	6.7%
1984	$37,800	6.7%
1985	$39,600	7.05%

Individuals can find how much has been paid into their Social Security by requesting a statement of earnings card from any Society Security office. This card is mailed to the Social Security administration, and a summary of their contributions as well as employer contributions will be mailed to them.

Request for Statement of Earnings.

```
┌──────────────────────────────────────────────────────────────────┐
│  (seal)   REQUEST FOR    SOCIAL                                     │
│           STATEMENT      SECURITY ➤  ┌──────┬──────┬──────┐         │
│                          NUMBER      │      │      │      │         │
│           OF EARNINGS    DATE OF     ┌──────┬──────┬──────┐         │
│                          BIRTH ➤     │MONTH │ DAY  │YEAR  │         │
│                                                                    │
│  Please send a statement of my social security earnings to:        │
│                                                                    │
│  NAME _____  } Print │
│                                                              Name   │
│                                                              and    │
│  STREET & NUMBER _____    Address│
│                                                              In Ink │
│                                                              Or Use │
│  CITY & STATE _____ ZIP CODE _____         Type-  │
│                                                              writer │
│  SIGN YOUR NAME HERE                                                │
│  (DO NOT PRINT) _____       │
│  Sign your own name only. Under the law, information in your social │
│  security record is confidential and anyone who signs another      │
│  person's name can be prosecuted.                                  │
│  If you have changed your name from that shown on your social       │
│  security card, please copy your name below exactly as it appears   │
│  on your card.                                                     │
│  ☆ U.S. Government Printing Office: 1978—270-383                    │
└──────────────────────────────────────────────────────────────────┘
```

Types of Business Entities

The selection of the most appropriate qualified deferred compensation plan depends not only on one's financial objectives, but also on the structure of the employer's business. Both practical and legal considerations dictate the suitability of the plan to be recommended. This section outlines various kinds of business entities; the deferred compensation plans appropriate to each are discussed in subsequent sections.

Unincorporated Business

1. A *sole proprietorship* is a business entity owned by a single individual. Even if the owner is the only employee, he or she may establish a qualified retirement plan, but the plan must provide for the coverage of other employees although there are presently none and the owner may not ever expect to employ any.

2. A *partnership* is a business entity owned by more than

one individual and is subject to a partnership agreement. A partnership dissolves upon the death or withdrawal of any partner. The partnership may establish a qualified retirement plan that must provide for coverage of all employees even if there are none at the time the plan is adopted and the partnership never expects to employ any.

3. A *joint venture* is a business entity in which a group of individuals associate in an endeavor for a profit. Though similar to a partnership, it has no partnership agreement. A joint venture may establish a qualified retirement plan, and it is treated as a partnership.

Incorporated Business

The incorporated business entity is a group authorized by law to act as a single individual; it may be composed of one person or a group of individuals. The corporation has continuity beyond the death of its shareholders; and, in most cases, its owners enjoy limited liability (that is, the liability of the corporation for its actions is limited to its own assets and does not extend to assets of the individual owners).

S Corporations. Subchapter S of the Internal Revenue Code allows small business corporations with not more than 35 stockholders, and that meet other IRS requirements, to elect to be taxed basically as a partnership. The owners of an *S corporation* enjoy such advantages of incorporation as continuity, deductibility of some benefits for shareholder-employees (employees who own more than 5% of the outstanding stock) and employees, limited liability in most instances, and the opportunity to establish qualified deferred compensation plans.

Professional Corporations and Associations. Another type of corporation is the *professional corporation* (P.C.) or *professional association* (P.A.). These became popular in 1969 when the IRS allowed professionals—doctors, lawyers, accountants, among others—to incorporate and to be taxed as other corporations under the Internal Revenue Code. All states in the U.S. now have laws permitting the incorporation of professional businesses with various differences from normal corporations, such as the partial or total absence of the limited-liability provisions.

Important advantages to the professional corporation used to lie in qualified deferred compensation plans, and the deductibility of many expenses not otherwise afforded sole proprietors and partners, such as hospitalization and group life insurance. The passage of the Tax Equity and Fiscal Responsibility Act of 1982 eliminated many of the qualified deferred compensation benefits. One major purpose of the legislation was to place all retirement plans on parity with corporation plans.

How to Select the Right Plan

Investors or business owners may decide that they need a retirement plan to save current income taxes, defer taxes on income until later years, and provide for retirement benefits. First, they are often convinced they want or need additional life insurance, annuities, stocks, bonds, mutual fund shares, or real estate. After deciding where to place the money, they have a retirement plan designed to make the investment.

Several years after establishing the plan, these investors find they have the wrong type of plan. They do not have the flexibility needed to meet changing conditions or perhaps the investments do not suit their changing desires or needs.

Many retirement plan experts strongly advise people and businesses considering the establishment of or changing of a retirement plan to first decide upon the type of plan needed, then have the plan designed so as to satisfy current needs as well as provide flexibility for changing circumstances and needs. Finally, decide upon the investments for the plan.

Remember, the person or organization advising usually has a motive to sell a particular product. Many life insurance agents design a retirement plan for life insurance. Many brokers more often than not suggest designing a plan in which primarily stocks and bonds can be placed. Banks will design a plan so their trust department or their savings accounts will participate. This is not always the case, but it is a possibility that individuals and business owners should be aware of.

Remember, first design the plan, then select the investments!

Qualified Deferred Compensation Plans

Before the passage of the Tax Equity and Fiscal Responsibility Act of 1982 (TEFRA), sole proprietorships, partnerships, and joint ventures could establish what was known as a Self-Employed Retirement Plan (also known as HR-10, or Keogh). (For the most part, parity has been achieved between self-employed individuals and employees of corporations. However, you should be aware that there are still some special rules that may apply to self-employed individuals. The specialized rules are beyond the scope of this book.) Corporations, which included professional corporations and professional associations, established pension or profit-sharing plans that were more liberal as to contributions, benefits, and inclusion of employees.

TEFRA basically gave parity to all retirement plans. "Keogh," or "HR-10," will no longer exist in our retirement plan vocabulary. There will only be one form of "unified" retirement plan for all business entities whether a proprietorship, partnership, joint venture, or corporation.

All working individuals will still be able to establish an IRA and contribute $2,000. The maximum amount will be phased out where adjusted gross income is over $2,000 on a joint return and $25,000 for an unmarried person. The deduction will be eliminated when the adjusted gross income reaches $50,000 for joint returns and $35,000 for an unmarried person. Where one spouse earns no income, the IRA contribution is $2,250 for a joint return. These provisions are in effect since December 31, 1986.

Because of TEFRA all qualified retirement plans will have to be amended to conform to the Act. Old Keogh plans established by sole proprietorships or partnerships do *not* necessarily have to be amended, although most of them in existence are more restrictive than would be required by TEFRA. Most employers who have Keogh plans will probably want to amend their plans.

TEFRA provides that all retirement plans must include certain provisions. The balance of this section discusses these provisions.

Overall Limits on Contributions and Benefits

The TEFRA stipulated that the maximum dollar limit for annual additions to defined contribution plans had to be reduced. *Annual additions* means the total of employer contributions to a participant's account, certain employee contributions, and all forfeitures. Prior to the TEFRA, defined contribution plans could provide for a maximum of $45,475 in contributions. The limit is now the lesser of 25% of compensation or $30,000. The maximum dollar limit for annual benefits payable under defined benefit plans must be reduced to the lesser of 100% of the highest three years preretirement compensation or to $90,000.

If a retirement plan was in existence on July 1, 1982, the limits of $30,000 and $90,000 will apply for calendar years 1983 through 1987. These limits will be changed annually beginning in 1988 to reflect cost-of-living-adjustments as measured by the Social Security Benefit Payment Index. Any plan established after July 1, 1982 will have to conform to the $30,000 and $90,000 limits immediately.

If retirement benefits from a defined benefit plan begin before age 62 (increases from age 55), the $90,000 limit must be reduced so that it is the actual equivalent of an annual benefit of $90,000 at age 62. The maximum reduction cannot be below $75,000.

The employer must have a plan that covers at least 70% of all nonhighly compensated employees. The employer must develop a plan that covers at least 50 employees; if less than 50, then 40% of those employed.

415 Limitation

The 415 limitation places an upside limit on the contributions/benefits attributable to an employee's qualified retirement plan account. There are two limits; the contribution to a defined benefit plan for an employee cannot exceed the lessor of $30,000 or 25% of compensation. Anticipated benefits under a defined benefit plan cannot exceed the lesser of $90,000 or 100% of the highest three year preretirement compensation.

The limits apply to each employer. Therefore, an individual working for two or more employers may have more than one "415 limitation" unless the employee is a substantial owner of the employers. If you feel you may qualify for more than one 415 limitation, you should seek assistance for the answer to your particular situation. No more than $2,000 can be placed in either account; contributions can be allocated to either spouse.

If the 415 limitation is exceeded, the corporation will be required to reallocate all contributions, which, in essence, is a complicated process of backing out the excess contributions that will not be tax deductible. A severe violation of the 415 limitation could lead to plan disqualification and the contributions will be fully taxable to the employer. In a defined benefit plan, excess 415 contributions would become nondeductible contributions to the plan.

Top-Heavy

TEFRA imposes additional restrictions on plans that primarily benefit "key employees." A key employee is, generally, any participant who during the plan year or for the four preceding plan years is: an officer earning more than $45,000 a year; one of the ten employees owning the largest interest in the employer; an owner of more than 5% interest; an owner of more than 1% interest with annual compensation of $150,000 or more. If a plan is structured so as primarily to benefit key employees, it is called "top-heavy."

A defined benefit plan is top-heavy in any year that the present value of the accumulated accrued benefits for participants or key employees exceed 60% of the present value of the accumulated benefits for all employees under the plan. A defined contribution plan is top-heavy in any year in which the sum of the account balances of participants who are key employees exceeds 60% of the sum of account balances for all employees under the plan. In essence, a qualified retirement plan is top-heavy if more than 60% of its accumulated benefits accrue to key employees.

Loan Limitations

Generally, a loan to a participant from a qualified retirement plan is treated as a taxable distribution to the extent it exceeds certain limits. If the loan is repayable within five years, it does not have to be treated as a distribution if it is less than: 1) $10,000, or 2) half of the present value of the employee's vested benefit in the plan, but not more than $50,000. The five-year repayment rule does not apply to any loan where the proceeds are used to acquire, construct, or substantially rehabilitate a principal residence of the participant or a member of his or her family.

The loan provisions apply to any loans, assignments, or pledges made after August 13, 1982. If any loan is renegotiated, extended, renewed, or revised after August 1982, it will be treated as an amount received on the date that it is modified.

Plan Contributions for Disabled Employees

Once an employee is disabled, an employer may elect to continue making deductible contributions to a qualified defined contribution retirement plan on his or her behalf. If the disabled employee is not an officer, owner, or highly compensated participant, he or she is immediately 100% vested in the contributions.

Withholding on Benefit Payments

TEFRA requires payors to withhold tax on all distributions made from qualified retirement plans, stock bonuses, or annuity plans or any other deferred compensation plans where the payments are not otherwise considered wages. This includes an IRA. A recipient may ask that the withholding be waived if the election is made in writing.

Why Establish and Participate in a Retirement Plan?

Retirement plans are an extremely beneficial and effective means of accumulating wealth.

Example: Consider Mr. Ingalls who is in a 42% federal income tax bracket. If we assume he remains in the 42% tax bracket until he retires, and if he places $10,000 a year into a retirement plan, he would be financially better off than if he took the $10,000 after tax each year and invested it on his own at 10%.

The $10,000 into the plan is tax deductible, therefore the full $10,000 is invested for his benefit. Also, Mr. Ingalls will not have to pay tax on the 10% earned on the contributions.

At the end of 20 years Mr. Ingalls will have accumulated $630,000.

If he does not invest in a profit-sharing plan, his $10,000 annual investment will be reduced by the amount of federal and state income tax. The federal tax will be $4,200, therefore he will only have $5,800 to invest. In addition, the 10% earnings on the annual contributions will be taxable at the 42% rate.

At the end of 20 years, Mr. Ingalls will have accumulated $221,000. The total value of tax deductibility and tax deferral of all earnings in this situation is $409,000. Obviously, the money will be taxable when withdrawn from the plan.

Individual Retirement Account (IRA)

The *individual retirement account* (IRA), created by the Employee Retirement Income Security Act of 1974 (ERISA), could be the most important development in deferred compensation in years. ERISA allowed any individual not covered under a qualified deferred compensation or governmental plan to establish such an account. An individual could contribute to an IRA the lesser of either $1,500 or 15% of his or her annual income, and then deduct the contributions from gross income in calculating tax liability.

Example: If a husband and wife both worked, and neither were participants in tax-deferred or government retirement plans, both could have established individual retirement accounts within the individual $1,500 or 15% limitations. Therefore, the family deduction could have been as much as $3,000 per year.

The Tax Reform Act of 1976 allowed an individual who qualified for an IRA to set aside a benefit for a spouse who didn't work outside the home. The limit was $1,750, with subaccounts of $875 for the individual and $875 for the spouse. The spouse's contribution was placed in a separate account.

How IRAs Are Taxed

The Tax Reform Act of 1981 now allows all working individuals to make a tax-deductible contribution of $2,000 or 100% of earnings, whichever is less, to an individual retirement account.

If both husband and wife are working, each may establish his or her own individual retirement account, thereby creating a $4,000 family deduction.

Example: A married worker with a nonworking spouse may contribute and deduct $2,250 ($2,000 for the worker and $250 for the nonworking spouse).

Example: Mr. Jones, a wealthy individual, establishes an IRA and a spousal IRA for his wife. Since Mrs. Jones has very few assets in her own name, Mr. Jones decides to place $2,000 in her IRA account and $250 in his.

If an individual is ineligible to make deductible contributions, nondeductible contributions to an IRA will be allowed to separate accounts of up to $2,000 of earned income or up to $2,250 for a spousal account. This went into effect as of December 31, 1986.

Obviously, the contributions are tax-deductible on IRS Form 1040. Earnings on the contributed amounts accrue tax-free until withdrawn, usually at retirement. Withdrawals cannot begin until age 59½ without the penalty, but must begin by age 70½. Early withdrawal for reasons other than death or disability become subject to ordinary income tax rates with an additional 10% penalty:

If you deposit $2,000 a year for:	Here's what the IRA would be worth:	Here's what the taxable investment would be worth, after taxes:
1 Year	$ 2,160	$ 1,296
5 Years	$ 12,672	$ 7,133
10 Years	$ 31,292	$ 16,150
15 Years	$ 58,648	$ 27,549
20 Years	$ 98,845	$ 41,959
25 Years	$157,908	$ 60,176
30 Years	$244,908	$ 83,205
35 Years	$372,201	$112,319
40 Years	$559,557	$149,125

Federated Securities Corporation, "IRAs—The Tax-Deferred Route to Retirement."

The following table shows the results of a $2,000/year IRA investment.

Years to Invest

Interest Rate	5	10	20	30	40
8%	$12,672	31,291	98,846	244,692	599,562
10%	$13,431	35,062	126,005	361,887	973,704
12%	$14,230	39,309	161,397	540,585	1,718,285

Funding

Contributions may be invested in any manner that is acceptable for qualified retirement plans, including mutual funds. Life insurance contracts are not permissible investments, but annuities or endowment contracts are. If an annuity or endowment contract is used to fund an IRA, the insurance cost is not deductible from gross income.

Many individuals select a bank or savings and loan certificate of deposit or savings account for their IRA investment. If a certificate is selected, and the individual wishes to move the money to another funding vehicle or selects early withdrawal, the funds withdrawn or transferred may be subject to the bank's or savings and loan's early withdrawal penalty as well as the early withdrawal penalty of 10%.

Many banks and savings and loans have established a *Time Deposit Open Account (TDOA)*. This is usually a three-year certificate of deposit, and the maximum rate that can be paid in 1984 is 8%. Compounded annually, this is 8.45%. The TDOA has a three-year maturity and each deposit usually extends the maturity for another three years. Always investigate the term, maturities, or possible penalties of a bank or a savings and loan association IRA deposit.

Federal Reserve regulations allow an individual over 59½ to move money from a certificate without a bank or savings and loan penalty. The federal regulations are minimum requirements, and savings institutions may still impose a penalty.

Example: In late 1982, Mr. Jones, age 63, wanted to transfer his IRA assets from Solid Rock Bank to an income mutual fund.

Even though the Federal Reserve regulations would allow the transfer without penalty, the bank would not.

The law also requires that each individual establishing an IRA be given the cost of the plan and all important information seven days before signing the contract. If the information is not given before signing, the individual has seven days to rescind the contract.

How to Handle Benefit Payments

Withdrawals from an IRA cannot be made until age 59½, but must begin in the year in which an individual attains age 70½. At least a partial withdrawal must be made during the year in which the individual becomes 70½. If the individual becomes disabled, withdrawals may be made at ordinary income tax rates without penalty.

Death benefits are distributed to named beneficiaries or to the estate of the individual. The value of the IRA is includable in the decedent's estate for calculating federal estate taxes, but probate and state administration costs can be avoided if properly assigned to a named beneficiary. Unlimited marital deductions allow all of an estate to pass to a surviving spouse estate-tax free. Death benefits are taxable income to a participant's beneficiary or estate.

A surviving spouse, who is a beneficiary under an IRA, may elect to treat the deceased spouse's IRA as his or her own and to defer payment from the IRA (or IRA rollover) until attainment of the surviving spouse's age 70½. The inherited IRA will continue to be treated as if it belonged to the surviving spouse for all purposes such as receipt of deductible contributions or the tax penalty for premature distributions prior to age 59½.

Withdrawals after age 59½ may be taken in the following ways:

Lump-Sum. The entire IRA may be withdrawn after age 59½. Such individuals will be able to choose a one time 5-year forwarding averaging of the lump-sum. As of January 1, 1986 the 10-year forwarding averaging and lump-sum distribution provisions are repealed as it applies to individuals who are over age 59½.

Installments Over a Fixed Term. The term must be either the individual's life expectancy, or the joint and last survivor life expectancy of the individual and spouse, or for a period of years not to exceed either of their life expectancies. Withdrawals are taxed at ordinary income rates, but earnings on the assets remaining in the IRA continue to accrue tax-free until distribution is made.

Purchase of a Commercial Annuity. The assets in the IRA may be used to purchase a commercial annuity with fixed or variable payments, which are taxed as ordinary income.

Things to Remember About Payments

Stories of the confusion created by the broad array of products being offered to fund an IRA are to be expected. The legislation is new and many of the products being offered to fund IRAs are also new. Many investors flocked to the high yielding fixed income accounts in the early 70s but were shocked to find they could not easily transfer their money to equity investments without being subject to substantial penalties. Others bought insurance products from their IRA and later found they did not suit their needs.

Listed below are a few thoughts about the new individual retirement account regulations and how the regulations may affect you:

- You have until the date your tax return is due to make your contribution and claim a deduction. Tax returns are due on April 15th unless it falls on a Saturday or Sunday; due date is the following Monday. The latest date is when most individuals file their tax return for the preceding year. You don't have to rush into an IRA plan. The advantage of early contributions is that the earnings on the contribution are sheltered for the entire year; however, that advantage will not offset a wrong or improper decision.

- You do not have to make the full $2,000, $2,250 or $4,000 contribution at one time. In most savings or investment programs, you may make periodic contributions. If you are going to make periodic contributions, make sure there are no additional costs or penalties for those contributions. Also designate, with each check, the tax year for which the contribution applies.

- Always investigate the cost of any plan. What is the *net* amount of money going into the savings or investment account?

- Always investigate the penalties for early withdrawal or changing investments. A high rate may sound good, but you may be giving up flexibility to get the high rate.

The most-asked question is, "What is the perfect IRA investment?" The answer is that there is no single perfect investment. Each individual must select the saving or investment program that is best suited for his or her needs. The most important point is to take advantage of the tax deductibility and tax-deferral of earnings provided by the new IRA regulations.

A divorced spouse is permitted to continue a spousal IRA that had been established at least five years before the divorce. The regulation applies if the taxpayer's former spouse had contributed to the IRA under the spousal IRA rules for at least three of the five years preceding the divorce. The limit on the divorced spouse's IRA is not less than the lesser of $1,125, or the sum of the divorced spouse's compensation and alimony includable in gross income.

Excess Contributions

If an individual contributes more than is allowable by the law to his or her IRA, he or she will be subject to a cumulative 6% excise tax. The tax can be avoided if the individual withdraws the excess contributions on or before the due date of the tax return.

Excess Accumulation

If an individual does not start drawing his or her IRA in the taxable year during which he or she reaches 70½, or if the minimum required amount is not distributed, the difference is considered excess accumulation. A 50% tax will be imposed on the amount by which the minimum required distribution exceeded the distributions actually received by the individual.

The tax may be waived by the IRS if the excess amount in

the IRA resulted from a reasonable error that the participant is taking reasonable steps to correct.

IRA Rollover

Many employees receive early distributions from retirement plans because of change of jobs, early retirement, or because their employer terminates the retirement plan. The IRA rollover allows the employee to establish a custodian account to hold the distributed assets and direct how the assets are to be invested. If the distributed assets are reinvested in the proper manner, they do not become taxable income to the employee, and all earnings continue to accumulate tax-deferred until withdrawal. Without the IRA rollover privilege, any preretirement distribution from qualified retirement plans such as pension or profit sharing, would be taxable income to the employee.

An employee receiving the premature distribution must roll the assets into an IRA rollover account by the sixtieth (60th) day after the lump-sum distribution is actually received. The employee may receive the distribution directly from the qualified retirement plan before transferring it to the rollover account.

The Revenue Act of 1978 provided several significant changes in the rollover provisions. An employee no longer has to invest the full amount of premature distributions. The employee may hold back a portion of the distribution for personal use and rollover whatever amount he or she desires. The amounts held back must be included as ordinary income for tax purposes, but the 10% tax penalty for premature distribution before age 59½ will not be changed.

The 1986 Tax Reform Act extends this penalty to early withdrawals and to withdrawals in tax-sheltered annuities. This tax will be waived in situations where distributions are part of a scheduled series of payments.

The total proceeds (but not necessarily the exact property) can be rolled.

Example: The employee receives 300 shares of XYZ Corp., at $30 a share, as part of the premature distribution. Within 30 days the shares are selling at $40. The employee may sell the shares and place the entire amount in the rollover account. Should the value of the shares decline, cash could be added to the proceeds so that the total value could be rolled.

The amount of employee voluntary contributions to qualified retirement plans cannot be rolled into an IRA rollover account. Interest on earnings on the voluntary contributions can be placed in a rollover account. An employee can designate the property distributed that will apply to voluntary contributions. This means that if the stock is distributed, the employee can use the amount of his or her voluntary contribution to apply to the stock rather than the cash if so desired.

Example: The employee has contributed $5,000 to a retirement plan and receives a $25,000 premature distribution. The employee can designate to what property the $5,000 applies. If no designation is made, a pro rata treatment is required by law.

The 1978 Revenue Act provides that the spouse of a deceased employee can now roll lump-sum death distributions into his or her own IRA rollover account. If distribution was not placed in a rollover account, it would be taxable income to the surviving spouse and includable in the gross estate of the deceased employee for estate tax purposes.

Withdrawals from an IRA Rollover Account. As in an IRA, any withdrawals from an IRA rollover account before an individual reaches age 59½ are treated as ordinary income for tax purposes. In addition, a 10% penalty is charged.

Example: Mr. Investor withdraws $5,000 from his rollover account before age 59½. The $5,000 is added to his other taxable income in calculating federal income taxes and an additional $500 penalty is charged.

The rollover provisions state that withdrawals can be made from a rollover account without penalty when an individual reaches 59½ (but must begin in the tax year in which the individual reaches 70½). This provision can add greatly to flexibility in retirement planning. The individual may withdraw, without penalty, as little or as much as he or she desires between the ages of 59½ and 70½. By the end of the tax year in which the individual reaches age 70½, a planned withdrawal must begin. The withdrawal period can be no longer than the life expectancy of the individual or the life expectancy of the individual and spouse. The time period for the systematic withdrawals must be determined in the year the taxpayer becomes 70½. Under the Tax Reform Act of 1984, an individual can now recalculate life expectancy each year. In theory, each year, as an individual gets older and as life expectancy extends, the payout can be extended over a much longer period.

Individuals who do not begin withdrawals as required by law will be subject to a penalty of 50% of the amount that should have been withdrawn.

Example: If $1,000 a year should have been withdrawn from the plan but only $500 was paid out, the penalty would be $250.

Many planners suggest individuals draw on taxable assets between the ages of 59½ and 70½, and continue to allow the tax-sheltered assets in a rollover account to accumulate tax free. This may reduce overall taxable income.

The Internal Revenue Service has provided the prototype forms for individual retirement accounts. Most mutual funds, insurance companies, and other financial institutions make the government forms or prototype forms available to anyone interested.

Simplified Employee Pension Plans

Because of the expense and time involved in administering retirement plans under the Employee Retirement Income Security Act of 1974 (ERISA), many plans have been terminated and the introduction of new plans has been retarded.

For this reason, the Revenue Act of 1978 created a new hybrid retirement plan arrangement. The new arrangement is called the simplified employee pension (SEP) and is a hybrid between an IRA and a corporate qualified plan.

A simplified employee pension is a regular individual retirement account (IRA) or annuity established and maintained solely by an employee, to which an employer contributes. In other words, the plan must be established by the employee, but the 1978 Act allows employers to contribute. The limits on the employer contributions were raised to $30,000 or 15% of annual compensation. A participant in a SEP plan, even an owner-employee, may also establish an IRA.

A maximum of $200,000 of an employee's compensation may be taken into consideration for determining the contribution to a SEP. The employer is required to have a written allocation formula and follow simple disclosure and administrative duties. The allocation formula must describe (1) eligibility requirements for participation, and (2) procedures for contributions by the employer.

Why Start a SEP?

One of the primary advantages to employers is the minimum reporting requirements. The use of the IRS Form 305-SEP is all that is required.

The following list highlights the provisions of the Revenue Act of 1978 as applied to SEP:

1. Any employee who is 21 years of age or older, and has been employed during at least three of the immediately preceding five years, must be a participant in the plan.

2. Contributions may not discriminate in favor of any employee who is an officer. Employers must make the same percentage of income contribution for all employees. This does not apply to integration with Social Security, which is discussed later.

3. If the employer's contributions are less than the lesser of $2,000 or 15% of annual compensation, the employee may contribute up to that limit.

4. Employer must make contributions directly to the plans' custodian, bank, or insurance company.

5. The amounts contributed to the SEP are in the full control of the employee and are fully vested and nonforfeitable.

The employer receives a tax deduction for contributions that must be made by April 15th of the following calendar. The full amount of the employer contributions must be included in the employee's W-2 form showing total annual compensation. The employee then takes a tax deduction for the employer and employee contributions to the plan. It is not necessary for the employer to withhold federal withholding tax or FICA tax on SEP contributions.

One of the primary advantages to employers is the minimum

reporting requirements required. The use of the IRS Form 305-SEP is all that is required.

The employee may take a deduction for amounts contributed by his or her employer even if the employee is an active participant in another qualified retirement plan, government plan, or tax-sheltered annuity.

Integration with Social Security may be very advantageous to many employers. An employer can reduce the amount of employee contributions by amounts paid for Social Security taxes (this does not include amounts paid by the employee).

Small employers, as of December 31, 1986, can establish 401(K) (page 362) simplified employee pension plans. Under this plan employees can defer up to $7,000 annually.

Employer Retirement Plans

An *employer retirement plan* is a qualified deferred compensation plan where in each year the employer deposits money into a fiduciary account for the *exclusive* benefit of the employees. Its primary purpose is to provide retirement benefits for employees. The contribution is tax deductible to the company, and the participants have no tax liability until benefits are actually received.

As previously discussed, before Congress passed the Tax Equity and Fiscal Responsibility Act of 1982 (TEFRA), corporations established profit-sharing or pension plans and self-employed entities established Keogh plans, also known as HR-10 plans. Corporate plans were more liberal, especially in contribution and vesting. As discussed earlier, TEFRA provided parity to most qualified plans. The qualified plans of some self-employed entities still have some limitations.

Who Is Eligible?

Under the Employee Retirement Income Security Act of 1974 (ERISA), any employee who has completed one year of service and attained the age of 25 must become a participant in an existing qualified profit-sharing plan. (A *year of service* is defined as a 12-month period during which the employee has at least 1,000 hours of service. This is usually based on the 12-month period following the employee's employment date, but it may be the plan year under certain circumstances.) However, a plan may require up to three years of service from employees to make them eligible for participation. All amounts contributed thereafter belong completely to the employee (are fully vested) and cannot be forfeited after completing the three-year requirement.

Younger employees may have to wait longer because of the provision that coverage does not have to begin until age 25, but credit must be given for service performed after attaining age 18 to satisfy the "year-of-service" requirement in a delayed vesting schedule. Management may reduce this minimum age requirement if it so desires.

Types of Plans

Basically, there are two types of employer-sponsored retirement plans. They are

1. Defined *contribution* plans, and

2. Defined *benefit* plans.

Defined Contribution Plans. In a defined contribution plan, the amount of benefits is based on the money paid into the plan and the investment performance of the plan's assets as allocated to each employee's account. The most common defined contribution plan is a *profit-sharing plan.* An employer's requirement to make contributions to a profit-sharing plan is usually contingent upon the earnings of the employer. Contributions are generally made from earnings or past accumulated earnings.

The Board of Directors, or the owners, meet annually to determine what percentage of profits (within limits that are discussed later) will be contributed to the plan. A company that is not earning money, or that can foresee future problems probably will make very little, if any, contribution to a plan.

The formula for determining the percentage or portion of profits to be contributed in any year can be quite flexible. The maximum allowed, however, is 15% of *covered compensation—* that is, 15% of the total compensation received by all employees who are eligible to be *covered* by the plan for the current year.

Example: If Mr. Major Stockholder has 50% or more of the covered compensation, he may have 50% of the annual contribution credited to his profit-sharing account, if the plan allocates pro rata on the basis of the respective compensation of all participants:

Covered compensation (total compensation for those employees eligible to participate in the profit-sharing plan)	$200,000
Corporate profits	$ 75,000
Total allowable contributions (15% of $200,000)	$ 30,000
Compensation of Mr. Major Stockholder	$100,000
Allowable contribution of Mr. Major Stockholder (50% of $30,000 contribution)	$ 15,000

Mr. Major Stockholder receives 50% of the total covered compensation; therefore, he will have $15,000 (50% of $30,000 contribution) credited to his profit-sharing account.

Defined Benefit Plans. Defined benefit plans (which in the past were usually referred to as pension, or annuity, plans) provide for definite, predetermined benefits. Briefly, an employer must first calculate the benefit to be received, and then determine contributions with the assumed performance of the contributions.

Pension plans and annuities are alike in that they provide for systematic payments at retirement. However, a pension plan must operate through a trust agreement, while an annuity plan, which may contain life insurance contracts, does not.

Defined benefit pension plans must be covered by the "Pension Benefit Guaranty Corporation" (PBGC). This federal agency was created by the Employees Retirement Income Security Act of 1974. The agency was established to guarantee retirement income to workers covered under defined benefit plans.

Before the creation of PBGC, when many workers reached retirement years, they found the pension plans under which they were covered did not have the assets to meet the guaranteed payments. The workers had no claim against the trustees or the employer.

The employer must pay an annual premium of $2.60 per participant to the PBGC. In 1984, the PBGC guaranteed over $1,600 of retirement income for each worker. The amount of retirement income guaranteed will be adjusted for increases in the cost of living. Also, if a plan does not have the assets to meet its retirement commitments, the PBGC will have a claim against 30% of an employer's net assets.

In order to avoid the legal obligation of having to make contributions, some employers will adopt a *target benefit plan.* This is a hybrid type of qualified plan, which combines some of the features of a defined contribution plan and a defined benefit plan. Generally, the desired benefits to be received by participants are established and the contribution levels are set to meet the targeted benefit. However, the actual retirement or disability benefit depends on the amount that has been contributed to the employee's account and the performance of the assets in the plan.

Integration with Social Security

The employer, of course, already has one retirement plan, Social Security, to which both the employer and employees contribute. If the employer desires to increase the percentage contributed only for higher-paid employees, the employer may exclude from initial participation all of the covered compensation of the eligible employees up to either the Social Security limit, or any lesser limit, such as $10,000 or $8,000.

An integrated plan may provide up to 5.7% of each participant's compensation in excess of the integration level (the Social Security limit, for example) first allocated to the participant out of the total plan contributions. After that allocation, the remainder of the contribution is allocated to all participants in the proportion that their compensation bears to the total covered compensation of all employees.

Integration with Social Security is a very complex subject. It may be an attractive idea to some employers, because it offers the opportunity to provide larger contributions for highly paid employees.

It is a good idea to consult an expert when considering a specific proposal and remember that all plans *must be approved* by the IRS.

Contributions and Benefits

The annual additions to a defined contribution plan (including those of self-employed businesses) cannot exceed the lesser of $30,000, or 25% of compensation for the plan year. Unlike the defined contribution plan, contributions to a defined benefit plan are made regardless of whether profits are made.

Benefits from a defined benefit plan cannot exceed the lesser of $90,000, or the average compensation received during the three consecutive highest paid years.

In a defined benefit plan, if an employee does not have ten years of service before retirement, his or her maximum payable benefit is reduced by 10% for every year he or she falls short of the years of service.

Example: Joe Faithful has worked for Solid Rock Corporation for seven years. His average compensation for the three consecutive highest paid years is $20,000.

During 1985 he reaches age 65 and retires. Since Faithful has only been participating in the plan for seven years, his maximum annual benefit is limited to .7 (or 70%). His maximum retirement benefit could therefore be $14,000.

The limits on both contributions and benefits were originally established by the Employee Retirement Income and Security Act of 1974. The act also provided for annual inflation adjustment to the limits. The Tax Equity and Fiscal Responsibility Act of 1982, TEFRA, defines the dollar limit in terms of contributions at $30,000 and the maximum limitation at $120,000.

A further limitation on profit-sharing plans is that the total allowable *annual addition* (contributions and forfeitures) to an individual's account is limited to the lesser of 25% of the individual's compensation, or $30,000 for each plan year. The dollar limitation is subject to cost-of-living adjustments beginning in 1988. The IRS will publish the new limit each year. In applying this limitation, all reallocated forfeitures, employer contributions (current and make up, if any), and a *portion* of employee contributions, both mandatory and voluntary, must be included.

Voluntary Contributions. An employee, if he or she chooses, may make voluntary contributions every year on his or her own behalf in amounts up to 10% of annual compensation. These contributions are not tax deductible, but the earnings accrue tax-free in the retirement trust until paid out in later years.

Vesting

Vesting refers to the portion of a participant's account that belongs to him or her should employment be terminated. The IRS must approve vesting schedules; however, the Employee Retirement Income Security Act of 1974 established three generally acceptable *minimum* vesting schedules. They are:

1. The participant becomes 20% vested after three years of service. Rising in equal increments, the individual will be fully vested after seven years.

2. 100% vesting upon the completion of five years of service.

3. *Rule of 45:* When the employee's age and years of service equal 45, or when a participant completes ten years of service, he or she becomes 50% vested. In qualifying under this rule of 45, the employee must have five or more years of service. After becoming 50% vested, the participant will accrue an additional 10% per year for the following five years.

If a plan is deemed to be top-heavy, there are only two allowable vesting schedules. They are:

1. Zero vesting for the first year, then 20% a year for each of the next five years. This would result in 100% vesting after six years. Or,

2. 100% investing after three years.

A consultant with Mercer-Meidinger pointed out that beginning in the early 1980s, even if a qualified plan was not deemed to be top-heavy, the IRS would only allow the three primary vesting schedules provided in ERISA if the employer could demonstrate that they are not discriminatory.

4/40 Vesting Schedule. The method to prove that the vesting schedules are not discriminatory is a complicated formula, but the bottom line is that turnover must be less than 6% a year. There are very few employers that have less than a 6% turnover in employment.

The IRS allows a "safe harbor" vesting schedule which is referred to as "4/40." The 4/40 vesting schedule provides for 40% vesting after the fourth year, 5% for each of the next two years, and 10% for the sixth through the tenth year. Therefore, full vesting is achieved after eleven years of participation.

Many plans established prior to the early 1980s were allowed to maintain their existing vesting schedules. However, most plans established in the last few years will use 4/40 vesting.

The plan document should provide for what happens to the employee's vested portion if he or she terminates employment. Such provisions may include (1) a lump-sum payment either at termination or at any predetermined time after termination, (2) purchasing a deferred annuity to commence at retirement, or (3) leaving the money in the plan until retirement.

Should the corporation become bankrupt or dissolve, the plan automatically terminates, and each employee is fully vested. The assets of the plan are not assets of the corporation; therefore, they cannot be prejudiced by the bankruptcy.

Reallocation of Forfeitures

In a profit-sharing plan, if an employee terminates, the non-vested portion of his or her assets in the plan are usually reallocated among the remaining participants in proportion to the annual contributions made to the plan. In a defined-benefit plan, forfeitures are usually used to reduce future contributions. In a company with a large turnover of employees, forfeitures to remaining participants can greatly compound the accounts of the remaining employees:

Example: Reallocation of Forfeiture According to Percentage of Contribution:

Participants	Assets in the Plan	Percentage of Assets	Reallocation of $3,600 Forfeiture
Mr. Major Stockholder	$15,000	50.0%	$1,800.00
Mrs. Smith	3,750	12.5	450.00
Mr. Dolittle	2,250	7.5	270.00
Ms. Ambitious	7,500	25.0	900.00
Miss Featherduster	1,500	5.0	180.00
Totals	$30,000	100.0%	$3,600.00

Funding

The employer establishes a trust, or insurance policies if insurance is used in the plan. The profit-sharing contributions are made to a trust. The trust must have trustees, which can be individuals or a corporate trustee, such as a bank. The trustee (or trustees) is legally responsible to see that the assets are invested in a prudent manner for the benefit of the plan's participants.

Every plan must have a fidelity bond to cover fiduciaries. The fidelity bond will repay the trust for stolen or misappropriated assets of the plan. A fidelity insurance policy may be purchased by the plan to cover wrongful acts or errors of omission.

The trust assets may be invested in common stocks, real estate, mutual fund shares, or any prudent investment. The plan must provide for diversification and liquidity.

The funding requirements of a profit-sharing plan can become very complicated. It is advised that trustees receive professional advice on appropriate investments for their particular plan.

Split-Funding. Split-funding of a plan means that part of the contributions are invested in assets, such as stocks, bonds, or real estate and part in life insurance. If the amount contributed is used in part to buy life insurance, each participant is provided a pre-retirement death benefit that may be larger than the value of his or her account balance in the plan. Some plans are designed to provide the utmost flexibility to participants. A participant in many retirement plans may designate part of his or her contribution, up to 50%, for the purchase of ordinary life insurance.

How Benefits Are Paid

Death Benefits. Retirement plans usually provide for pre-retirement death and disability benefits. The death benefits are payable to the named beneficiary or estate of the participant. Death benefits from a plan distributed to a named beneficiary avoid probate administration and expenses if taken in the form of an annuity.

However, the beneficiaries must include the amounts received as income for income tax purposes, just as the participant would have to do had he or she lived and taken distribution at retirement. The first $5,000 of the death benefit from retirement plans is received tax-free, and the $5,000 income tax exclusion is divided equally among beneficiaries if more than one is named by the employee. Tax liabilities on death distributions may be reduced by capital gains and special income averaging provisions, as well as by spreading the distributions over a number of years, which is described in greater detail in this section.

The reserve or cash value of life insurance proceeds is includable with other amounts distributed as taxable income to the beneficiary. However, life insurance proceeds from a split-funded profit-sharing plan in excess of the policy reserve or cash value are not includable as income to named beneficiaries. This can provide instant liquidity to an employee's estate.

Retirement Benefits. Retirement benefits can be taken in any combination of the three following methods:

1. *Lump sum.* As part of the 1986 Tax Reform Act, the ten-year forwarding averaging and the capital gains provisions for lump sum distributions have been repealed. Individuals will now be able to make a one-time choice of having five-year forwarding averaging for their lump sum distribution after age 59½.

Voluntary contributions are received tax-free because they were made with after-tax dollars.

2. *Installment payments.* Basically, equal installment payments are specified either for ten years, for the participant's life expectancy, for the joint and last survivor life expectancy of the participant and his or her spouse, or for over a term of years not to exceed either of these life expectancies. Each payment usually is taxed as ordinary income, except that the portion of each payment relative to voluntary contributions is tax-free. A tax expert should make the calculations for you.

Example: Mr. Jones retires at age 65. Assets in his company's profit-sharing plan equal $224,000. Ten percent of that, or $22,400, is voluntary contributions. He chooses an installment plan that pays him $1,866 a month, or $22,400 a year, for ten years. Since 10% of his total contribution was voluntary, 10% of each monthly installment, or $186.60, is tax-free. The balance is taxed as income.

3. *Purchase of commercial annuity (monthly payments).* Annuity payments may be for life, or for life with a certain number of payments guaranteed. The monthly benefits are taxed as ordinary income; and if a portion of the assets resulted from the employee's voluntary contribution, that percentage in relation to total value is received tax-free.

Example: Mrs. Smith retires with assets in her company's profit-sharing plan of $224,000. Her voluntary contributions were $24,000. Instead of monthly installment payments, however, she chooses to purchase a commercial annuity contract providing monthly payments of $1,500 ($18,000 per year), guaranteed for life.

Her voluntary contributions represent 10% of the assets; therefore, 10% of each payment ($150 per month of $1,800 per year) is received tax-free. She must pay ordinary income tax rates on 90%, or $1,350 per month ($16,200 per year).

Each employee should consult his or her own tax advisor about specific plans. Upon retirement, benefit options and tax consequences should be worked out with the advisor. If the assets remain in the plan and the employee elects to receive a monthly payment option, the undistributed portion will continue to accumulate income on a tax-deferred basis and the income tax liability will be spread over a number of years. However, it may be more advantageous for the investor to take a lump-sum distribution, and pay the taxes, thus maximizing the use of the funds.

Tax-Sheltered Annuity, or a 403(b) Plan

A tax-sheltered annuity, often referred to as a 403(b) plan, is not a qualified retirement plan. It is a program where employees working for schools and certain tax-exempt organizations are allowed to make contributions that do not exceed $9,500.

The amount of the salary reduction is not subject to current federal income tax, but employees must have FICA (Social Security) withheld on the amount of the salary reduction. Any withdrawals, even at retirement, are taxable as ordinary income.

Example: Beth is a school teacher and makes $20,000 per year.

Her husband is an engineer and because of their two incomes they are in the 40% federal income tax bracket. Beth elects to join the school's tax-sheltered annuity program and signs a contract to have her salary reduced by $3,000 per year. The $3,000 salary reduction saves Beth and her husband $1,200 in taxes per year ($3,000 × 40% = $1,200). All earnings on the income from the investments within the plan accrue tax deferred until the assets are distributed.

Who Can Establish a Tax-Sheltered Annuity?

Selected employees of certain tax-exempt organizations may establish a tax-sheltered annuity (TSA). In a TSA, the employer, if a qualified nonprofit organization under the IRS Code, agrees that its employees can establish the plan. The employee then signs a salary reduction agreement to place the amount of the salary reduction into an approved investment.

The contributions are fully vested and nonforfeitable. Unlike an individual retirement account, employees can withdraw their account balances at any time. Withdrawals are not subject to any tax penalty, but are taxable as income.

Because tax-sheltered annuities are not qualified retirement plans, an eligible organization can make contributions for any employee it elects to do so for. Discrimination rules do not apply. No FICA (Social Security tax) needs to be withheld on employer contributions to a tax-sheltered annuity plan. An employee can be a participant in other qualified retirement plans of the employer and still have a TSA. In addition, employees can have their own IRAs.

Qualified Investments

Tax-sheltered annuity contributions can be placed in any one of several specially designed fixed income or variable annuity contracts, or a face amount certificate from an insurance company. Also, the salary reductions can be placed in a custodian account of an open-end mutual fund or a closed-end investment company.

Generally, the employer must approve the investment into which the salary reduction can be placed. The primary reason for this is because if each employee decided upon a different investment, the record-keeping and sheer paperwork of most employers would make the plan cost-prohibitive. Most TSA plans have enough investment options approved by the employer so that the employee can make an investment selection that meets his or her objectives and needs.

Tax-sheltered annuities are generally considered a low-cost retirement plan or fringe benefit. Because there are very few filing requirements and the insurance company and/or mutual fund organization does most of the work in establishing the plan, as well as much of the ongoing service duties, costs are kept to a minimum.

Contribution Limits

Probably the most confusing part of a tax-sheltered annuity is the salary reduction (contribution) limits. The amount of the salary reduction excluded from taxable income and invested in the plan cannot exceed limits known as the "exclusion allowance." It is impossible to adequately discuss and describe the exclusion allowance in a book such as this. However, most employees will not contribute up to the limit.

The exclusion allowance for each taxable year is 20% of the employee's compensation, multiplied by the total number of years with the employer, which is then reduced by all 403(b) contributions made to the employer's plan in prior years. Generally, most experts say the practical limit for an annual salary reduction is 17% of W-2 compensation. Salary reductions to a TSA cannot exceed $30,000 per year.

Any employee of a nonprofit organization attempting to determine the exact amount of his or her exclusion allowance should seek the advice of the employer, who will usually ask one of the sponsoring investment organizations (insurance company or mutual fund) to do the calculation.

Catch-up Provision

TSA provisions allow those employees of a tax-exempt organization who over the years have not taken full advantage of the salary reduction programs to be able to make larger tax-deferred contributions. While the special catch-up provisions allow contributions that may exceed the standard formula limit, it is a one-time investment that can only be made in the year the employee terminates his or her employment. Catch-up provisions are very complex and anyone seeking to take advantage of them should seek the counsel of a professional tax advisor.

Taxation

As previously stated, the amount of an employee's salary reduction placed in a tax-sheltered annuity program is not subject to current federal income tax. An employee's salary reductions are subject to FICA (Social Security withholding tax). Employer contributions for the benefit of certain employees are not subject to FICA withholding.

All distributions or withdrawals from a TSA are subject to income tax as ordinary income. Because the tax-sheltered annuity is not a qualified retirement plan, lump-sum distributions are not eligible for the ten-year special averaging provisions. Distributions may qualify for regular income averaging procedures if a participant's taxable income, including the TSA distribution, meets the test.

The entire value of a tax sheltered annuity is includable in a decedent's taxable estate for federal estate tax purposes. The TSA's plan assets are subject to income tax when distributed to a participant's estate and/or beneficiary.

A senior consultant with Mercer-Meidinger, a national employee benefits firm based in Louisville, Kentucky, suggests that if an employee could have only a tax-sheltered annuity (TSA) or an IRA because of limited financial resources, he would suggest a TSA. His reason is simple. Under a TSA, withdrawals can be made at any time without a tax penalty. In an IRA, early withdrawals or withdrawals before age 59½ are subject to a 10% tax penalty in addition to being includable as taxable income.

Exchange or Rollover

Generally, a participant can exchange his or her investment in a TSA for another TSA. Exchanges are not subject to federal income tax if the participant signs a new agreement before the exchange is made. The participant must enter into a binding agreement to execute the exchange. The agreement is made between the employer and the custodian or insurance company that sponsors the TSA plan.

According to one expert, an exchange from an insurance

company contract to a custodian account in a mutual fund is permitted. To the date of this publication, the IRS has not commented on exchanges from a custodian account to an insurance company contract.

A participant in a TSA plan is permitted to exchange an insurance contract or a custodian account lump-sum distribution for an IRA rollover rather than another 403(b) or some other tax-sheltered annuity plan. A rollover into an IRA must be made within 60 days of the participant's receipt of the lump-sum distribution. In order to make the exchange for a rollover, the lump-sum distribution must equal at least 50% of the participant's plan account and meet one of four conditions:

1. attainment of age 59½,

2. termination of the plan or employment with the employer that maintains the TSA plan,

3. disability, or

4. death.

If a participant leaves the employment of a nonprofit organization, he or she can leave the assets in the plan and all earnings will continue to accumulate tax-deferred. For most investors, the best advice would probably be to leave the assets in the TSA plan because IRA rollovers have a 10% income tax penalty for early withdrawals and a TSA does not.

Tax-sheltered annuities are perhaps one of the most underused retirement plans in existence. The reasons for the underuse of tax-sheltered annuities by employees of nonprofit organizations are:

1. The availability of such plans has not been communicated effectively to employees of qualified nonprofit organizations.

2. Many people in eligible organizations receive such low salaries that they are unable to give up any income to support the plan.

3. Many of the employees feel that because they are covered under other retirement plans, they will not need additional supplemental retirement income.

Schools and other nonprofit organizations that qualify to provide their employees tax-sheltered annuities should take advantage of the programs as well as advertise the benefits of the plans and their availability to their employees.

If you work for a nonprofit organization that does not have a tax-sheltered annuity, you should encourage your employer to establish one.

401(K) Profit-Sharing or Stock Bonus Plans

The 401(K) retirement plan is a type of qualified plan that is increasing in popularity. It must be part of a qualified profit-sharing or stock bonus retirement plan or stock bonus plan. The 401(K) is unique in that it allows participants a choice. Each year a participant can take cash and pay taxes, or defer tax and place the amount of salary reduction into a qualified retirement plan. The 401(K) plan is often referred to as a salary reduction "pretax plan" because each participant has a choice of taking cash or placing a portion of this compensation into a qualified plan.

The 401(K) plan is not new. The roots go back to the 1950s and 1960s for tax-exempt organizations. Deferring taxes by salary reduction plans was actually sanctioned by Congress in the Tax Act of 1978. The 1978 Act put "for profit" organizations on the same level with nonprofit organizations, but with different rules. In essence, the new modifications and rules are a continuation of the federal government's philosophy of encouraging savings. The contribution limit is set at $7,000.

The essence of a 401(K) plan is that it permits a participant to reduce his or her compensation, monthly income or bonus, in order to have it contributed into a qualified plan. The contribution is not subject to current income tax and all earnings accrue tax-deferred.

Example: Jake Jefferson gets $10,000 in bonus. His wife works and he does not need the cash for current living expenses. Jake enters into an agreement with his employer to have the $10,000 placed in a qualified retirement plan. The $10,000 bonus, because it is not considered current compensation, is not shown on his W-2 form.

Example: Mike Jacobs gets a $10,000 bonus, but needs the

cash now. His wife does not work and he has three children. He takes the bonus in cash and it is taxable income to him in the year received. The $10,000 bonus will be included in his W-2 form as taxable income with his other compensation.

In order for the 401(K) plan to qualify for tax-deferrable benefits, several special provisions must be met. Some of them are:

1. The participant has the right to elect whether to receive a part of the contribution or all of it as cash, or have it deferred and contributed by the employer to the plan.

2. All contributions the employee elects to have contributed to the plan must be fully vested immediately. This also pertains to all earnings on the contributions.

3. The plan must restrict the distribution of contributions and their earnings to the following events: death, disability, attainment of age 59½, termination of employment, or hardship. Generally, hardship is considered to be major uninsured medical expenses, college expenses, or the purchase of a principal residence. In considering hardship, the trustees must consider an employee's other financial resources and conditions for withdrawal must be granted under a uniform and nondiscriminatory standard.

Also, a 401(K) plan must be nondiscriminatory. That is, it cannot favor highly paid executives. In order to prove that a 401(K) plan is nondiscriminatory it must meet one of two tests.

1. The average deferral percentage allocated to the top one-third of all eligible employees must not exceed 125% of the average deferral percentage of the lower two-thirds of all eligible employees.

2. If the average deferral percentage for the top one-third of all eligible employees over the average deferral percentage for the lower two-thirds of all eligible employees does not exceed 2%, and the actual deferral percentage for the top one-third does not exceed 200% of the actual deferral percentage of the lower two-thirds, the test is met.

The computation of these antidiscrimination tests is extremely complex and confusing. It is advisable to have an actuary or employee benefits consultant involved in designing and administering a 401(K) plan, if the employer is going to establish such a plan.

The antidiscrimination provisions must be met each year and, if they are not adhered to, the annual contributions will be taxable to participants as ordinary income.

If you are a participant in a 401(K) plan, you should do a family income analysis to see what portion of your income up to contribution limits you can afford to set aside. Remember, the part you take in cash is taxable as ordinary income and the amount placed in the plan is not subject to current income tax.

Review the previous examples. Jake Jefferson was fortunate enough to be able to defer current income tax on his entire bonus. Mike Jacobs, on the other hand, needed his cash now to cover family expenses. An employee may take cash for part of the distribution and defer a portion.

Taxation

As previously discussed, a 401(K) plan allows participants to decide whether to take compensation in cash and pay taxes now, or defer tax on a portion of their compensation and have the deferred portion placed in a qualified retirement plan. The part placed in a qualified retirement plan is not currently taxable and all earnings accrue tax-deferred until withdrawal.

Since a 401(K) plan is part of a qualified retirement plan, lump-sum distributions may qualify for the special ten-year income averaging tax treatment covered on page 362. Distributions made prior to age 59½ are not subject to a 10% tax penalty as in an IRA. In fact, "in service" distributions are not allowed except in cases of termination of employment, death, disability, or hardship, which was discussed previously.

Lump-sum distributions may be transferred to similar qualified retirement plans of another employer if the plan so permits, or may be placed in an IRA rollover account in order to continue tax deferral.

If distributions are taken as an annuity or paid over a period of years, the amounts received by a participant are taxable as ordinary income in the year received. The income tax treatment is the same as applicable for all qualified retirement plans.

401(K) vs. IRA

Since individuals can participate in both a 401(K) plan and an IRA, some may not be able to afford to participate in both plans because of limited financial resources.

If you can afford to participate in both a 401(K) and an IRA to the limit, you probably should because it is generally better to defer tax on income. Bear in mind that the maximum deduction will be phased out when adjusted gross income is above $40,000 for joint accounts and $25,000 for an unmarried person. In addition, the 401(K) plan will have a deferred limit of $7,000 annually. Under the 1986 tax laws, taxpayers will no longer be able to use income averaging to calculate their tax liability. Individuals 59½ and older will be allowed a one-time choice to have 5-year forward averaging if they take a lump-sum distribution of their retirement benefits.

The development and continuing popularity of the 401(K) plan is another effort by the federal government to address continual Social Security problems. Individuals who, on an on-going basis, set aside money for retirement, will be more financially secure in their retirement years. The federal government continues to be concerned as to who will take care of America's elderly. Therefore, as with the IRA, the 401(K) plan is another means of providing retirement security to more Americans.

Employee's Stock Ownership Plan (ESOP)

Employee Stock Ownership Plans (ESOP) were created by the Employees Retirement Income Security Act of 1974 (ERISA). An ESOP is a type of defined contribution plan that can be structured as a profit-sharing plan or a money purchase pension plan. The purpose for which Congress created an ESOP was to allow a corporation's employees to invest qualified retirement plan contributions in the employer's common stock.

The ESOP is a means by which employees can acquire an equity interest in their employer. The plan also gives the employer an additional financing method, as well as establishing a quotation standard for the common stock of many privately held corporations.

An ESOP plan is allowed to purchase an employer's stock annually, either directly from the employer or through a loan agreement with a commercial lender for the purpose of acquiring employer's common stock. Generally, the loans are secured by the common stock of the employer who, in some instances, will guarantee the loans. If a loan to buy the stock is secured, the loan is repaid from annual contributions to the plan.

As of December 31, 1986, individuals will be able to diversify up to 25% of their ESOP account when reaching age 55, with ten years of service, in order to minimize the investment risk. This will increase to 50% when individuals reach age 60, with 10 years of service.

As of December 31, 1986, individuals will be able to diversify up to 25% of their ESOP account when reaching age 55, with ten years of service, in order to minimize the investment risk. This will increase to 50% when individuals reach age 60, with 10 years of service.

ESOP plans were made more attractive because of provisions of the Tax Reform Act of 1975. The act allowed employers that established and maintained certain types of ESOP plans an "investment tax credit" for establishing and contributing to them. The Tax Reform Act of 1976 created a special type of ESOP known as a TRANSOP (Tax Reform Act—Employee Stock Ownership Plan). TRANSOPs are now referred to as PAYSOP. Even though there is no exact translation to the letters, PAYSOP refers to a payroll-based employee stock ownership plan.

PAYSOP Qualifications

A PAYSOP must meet more stringent qualifications in order for the employer to receive a special tax credit. Some of these requirements are:

1. Allocation of the employer's stock to plan participants must be in proportion to their compensation, which may not exceed $200,000.

2. Each participant must be fully vested at all times.

3. The plan must give the participants the right to vote the employer's stock allocated to their account if not publicly traded.

4. Distributions from a PAYSOP must be in the form of employer

stock or, if the stock is not readily marketable, the plan may call for purchases at a fair evaluation formula.

5. The Economic Recovery Act of 1981 (ERTA) provided for the continuation of the investment tax credit to employers who establish a PAYSOP.

Thrift Plans

Thrift plans are a special version of qualified retirement plans, but they serve different purposes. Among other effects, such plans encourage employees to save, because the employee must contribute after-tax dollars before the employer is required to contribute.

A *thrift plan* is a tax-qualified contributory retirement savings plan, usually established on a payroll-deduction basis. The employee authorizes the employer to deduct a percentage of compensation for each pay period, and the employer matches the employee's contribution in a predetermined percentage. The total amount may be invested at either the employer's or the individual employee's direction in investments authorized by the plan agreement, depending on the plan agreement.

The employer's contribution is tax-deductible as a business expense, and it is not charged as income to employees. The earnings accrue tax-free, with no tax liability until benefits are actually received.

Contributions

The thrift plan is a form of defined contribution plan. It is governed by the same applicable contribution and deduction limitations (see "Employer Retirement Plans" on pages 348–357).

Employee contributions to be matched by the employer are determined in advance. The employer contributes a predetermined percentage of the employee's contribution, usually ranging from 25% to 200%.

Example: Do-Anything Corporation has a qualified thrift plan that allows the employees to invest up to 6% of their monthly compensation, and the corporation puts up 25% of the employees' contributions.

The schedule of employee's allowable payroll deductions, matching funds, and total deposits is:

	Monthly Compensation	Allowable Payroll Deduction	Matching Contribution	Total Deposit
Mr. Owner	$4,000	$240	$60.00	$300.00
Mr. Do Nothing	400	24	6.00	30.00
Mr. Ambitious	2,000	120	30.00	150.00
Mr. Smith	1,000	60	15.00	75.00
Ms. Jones	500	30	7.50	37.50
Miss Featherduster	600	36	9.00	45.50
Mr. Fixit	800	48	12.00	60.00

Any employee may decide not to participate in the plan, and, naturally, no employer contribution is then made on his or her behalf. However, a specified minimum participation must be maintained for the plan to remain qualified.

This plan requires a minimum voluntary contribution of 3% and a maximum of 6%. An employee who contributes 5% (2% over the mandatory amount in order to participate) is allowed only a 16% matching contribution.

Voluntary Employee Contributions.

Example: Each employee in the Do-Anything Corporation who participates in the plan is allowed to make voluntary contributions to bring the *total* contribution to 10% of his or her monthly compensation.

	Allowable Voluntary Contributions
Mr. Owner	$160
Mr. Do-Nothing	16
Mr. Ambitious	80
Mr. Smith	40
Ms. Jones	20
Miss Featherduster	24
Mr. Fixit	32

Eligibility

When establishing the plan, the employer sets eligibility re-quirements for the employees as to length of continuous service and/or a certain attained age. The employer may not discriminate among employees. A plan may call for a matching contribution of a varying percentage dependent upon the length of continuous service with the company. For example, an employer may put up a 25% matching contribution for up to five years of service, 50% for ten years, and 75% for more than ten years.

Vesting

Employee contributions to thrift plans are fully vested at all times. Employer contributions are vested either (1) as set forth in the plan document, with minimum requirements the same as under profit-sharing plans (refer to "Profit-Sharing Plans," pages 362–365), or (2) at death, disability, or attainment of normal retirement age.

Example: The thrift plan of Do-Anything Corporation provides that employer contributions are vested at 10% per year of service, with full vesting at the completion of ten years (the requirements of this plan are shorter than the minimum requirements under the 1974 act).

Mr. Ambitious participated in the plan for seven years before terminating his employment. His payroll deduction contributions were $10,080, and his employer's contributions were $2,520, for a total contribution of $12,600. The present value of his account is $20,000. Of this sum, 80% of the present value resulted from his contributions; thus, $16,000 resulted from Mr. Ambitious' con-tributions and $4,000 from employer contributions.

Do-Anything's contributions are 70% vested (10% for each year of participation); therefore, Mr. Ambitious' vested interest is the present value of the original contribution ($16,000) plus 70% of the present value of the employer's contribution, $4,000 ($2,800), for a total of $18,800.

Forfeitures

Forfeitures resulting from nonvested funds can be divided among plan participants in the same proportion to their account balance or used to reduce future contributions.

Benefits

Most thrift plans provide that voluntary contributions, but not the matched employer contributions, may be withdrawn at any time without penalty. Often, many plans also allow the withdrawal of the appreciation attributable to voluntary contributions for specific purposes, such as illness, buying a home, and college expenses.

Death Benefits. Death benefits up to the $100,000 limit for all qualified plans distributed to a named beneficiary are exempt from federal estate taxation and avoid probate administration and expense. However, the beneficiaries must include the amounts received as income for income tax purposes just as the participant would have to do had he or she lived and taken distribution at retirement.

Tax liabilities on death distributions may be reduced by capital gains and special income-averaging provisions, as well as by spreading the distributions over a number of years.

Proceeds from life insurance policies, when part of a plan, in excess of the policy reserve or cash value are not includable as income to the named beneficiaries.

Retirement Benefits. See pages 351–352.

Who Implements Thrift Plans?

Thrift plans are usually implemented by corporations in addition to, or as a supplement to, profit-sharing or pension plans. They may also be ideal solutions for small companies that want a qualified plan but are not able to establish a profit-sharing or pension plan based solely on employer contributions.

Perhaps the most important feature of the thrift plan is that *if the employee does not contribute, the employer does not have to contribute.* Very often corporations find that, for one reason or another, a certain number of employees do not contribute, thereby effecting a reduction in the cost of the plan to the business. At the same time, a thrift plan can assist Mr. Owner-Employee in getting tax-free dollars from his business.

Most mutual funds and insurance companies have prototype forms to make it easy to establish thrift plans.

Payroll Deduction Savings Programs

In a *payroll deduction savings program,* the employer provides a payroll deduction privilege to those employees who wish to participate. The money must be invested in segregated participant accounts after the employee chooses from various approved investments, such as mutual funds, government bonds, savings accounts, or the corporation's own stock. This type of plan gives employees an opportunity to save and to invest their money, which they otherwise may not be able to do.

There are no tax advantages to the employer or to the employee. The employee invests after-tax dollars and must pay taxes on any accumulations, capital gains, or dividends, as in any other investment.

According to the Institute for Business Planning's *Mutual Fund Investment Planning.* "A payroll deduction investment program is not only an *employee* benefit, it is also a no-cost employer benefit." The only cost to the employer is that of bookkeeping for the payroll deduction.

Most mutual funds have prototype forms to assist in establishing payroll deduction savings plans.

Contributions

There are no limitations on the amount of contribution. However, the employer may and should establish rules concerning stopping and starting the plan—as long as all such rules are not discriminatory. For example, if an employee stops contributing, he or she might be prohibited from reentering the program for one year.

Eligibility

The employer may establish eligibility requirements for participation; however, most employers require only one year of continuous service.

Vesting

All contributions are fully vested at all times and are redeemable and payable at the employee's demand. Furthermore, the employee may use his or her account as collateral for a loan.

Payment of Benefits

The employee may demand lump-sum or partial payments at any time, because his or her account is fully vested. The employee's tax liability is that of any other personal investment in a similar investment vehicle.

As an alternative to or in addition to a payroll deduction savings plan, an employer may differentiate among employees and establish individual retirement accounts (refer to page 338) for his key employees. The IRA may not be used if the employer has established a qualified plan.

Thrift Plans and Payroll Savings Programs

Practical Examples.

Example: Build Fast Contractors, Inc. had many employees who would not or could not save money for future needs. Several years ago the company started an integrated profit-sharing plan. Because the plan was integrated at the Social Security wage base level ($39,600 in 1985) little or no money was invested for those who could not or would not save.

John Timms, the owner of Build Fast Contractors, Inc., felt he did not want to invest any more money in a retirement plan for his employees unless the employees would invest for themselves.

After a great deal of thought, planning, and consulting with retirement plan experts, John Timms decided to institute a thrift plan. His thought was that if an employee would invest for his or her own future, he would match those investments by 25%.

The plan would encourage his employees to invest and would help to protect their financial futures. His feelings were that ultimately his company would benefit because the employees would become better workers if they were financially secure.

Example: Stan Manos recently started a construction company. He was not able to afford to establish a qualified retirement plan because he needed to reinvest all of his profits in the business.

Stan Manos realized that his employees needed some form of savings plan to meet future needs. He felt that a mandatory plan or a plan that would generate peer pressure from other employees would encourage all employees to join and save.

He created a payroll deduction savings plan for his employees. Over a period of years, Stan Manos' employees were surprised at how much capital they had accumulated in such a short period of time.

Stan Manos is now a successful builder and is considering establishing a profit-sharing plan, but will keep his payroll deduction savings plan.

Mr. Manos also established an IRA for himself and his wife, who had to work during the start-up years. Now that Mrs. Manos is a homemaker, Mr. Manos will place $250 per year in her account. Contributions, however, can be made in either spouse's account up to $2,000.

Index